THE NEW INTERNATIONAL

WEBSTER'S POCKET SPELLING DICTIONARY

OF THE ENGLISH LANGUAGE

■ ◆◆◆ ■

This edition exclusive to

IDF

(949) 587-9207

Published by
Trident Press International

Cover Design Copyright © Trident Press International
Text Copyright © 1997 J. Radcliffe

ISBN 1-55280-276-0

Printed in Peru

IMPORTED BY/IMPORTE PAR
DS-MAX CANADA
RICHMOND HILL, ONTARIO
L4B 1H7

ENGLAND
WENTWALK LTD.
278A ABBEYDALE ROAD, WEMBLEY
MIDDLESEX, HA0 1NT

MALAYSIA
PRO ENTERPRISE SDN BHD
LOT 605, SS13/1K, OFF JLN.
KEWAJIPAN, 47500 SUBANG JAYA
SELANGOR D.E., MALAYSIA

DS-MAX
FOOTHILL RANCH, CA 92610-2619
IMPORTER: #16-1241510
949-587-9207

A

aard´vark
aard´wolf
a·back´
ab´a·cus
a·bac·te´ri·al
a·baft´
ab-a-lo´ne
a·ban´don
a·ban´don-a·ble
a·ban´doned
a·ban´don·er
a·ban´don-ment
a·base´
a·based´
a·bas´ed·ly
a·base´ment
a·bas´er
a·bash´
a·bash´ed·ly
a·bash´ment
a·bas´ing
a·bat´a·ble
a·bate´
a·bate´ment
a·bat´er
a·bat´ing
ab-ax´i·al
ab´ba·cy
ab-bé´
ab´bess
ab´bey

ab´bot
ab´bot·cy
ab-bre´vi-ate
ab-bre´vi-at·ed
ab-bre´vi-at-ing
ab-bre-vi-a´tion
ab-bre´vi-a-tor
ab-bre´vi-a-to·ry
ab´di-ca·ble
ab´di-cate
ab´di-cat-ing
ab-di-ca´tion
ab´di-ca-tive
ab´di-ca-tor
ab´do-men
ab-dom´i-nal
ab-dom´i-nal·ly
ab-du´cent
ab-duct´
ab-duc´tion
ab-duc´tor
a·beam´
a·be-ce-dar´i·an
a·bed´
ab-er´rance
ab-er´ran·cy
ab-er´rant
ab-er´rant·ly
ab-er-ra´tion
ab-er-ra´tion·al
a·bet´
a·bet´ment
a·bet´tal

a·bet´ted
a·bet´ting
a·bet´tor
a·bey´ance
a·bey´ant
ab-hor´
ab-horred´
ab-hor´rence
ab-hor´rent
ab-hor´rent·ly
ab-hor´ring
a·bid´ance
a·bide´
a·bid´ing
a·bid´ing·ly
a·bid´ing-ness
a·bil´i-ties
a·bil´i·ty
a·bi-o-gen´e-sis
a·bi-o-ge-net´ic
a·bi-o-gen´ic
a·bi-og´e-nist
a·bi-ot´ic
ab-ject´, ab´ject
ab-jec´tion
ab-ject´ly
ab-ject´ness
ab-ju-ra´tion
ab-jur´a-to·ry
ab-jure´
ab-jur´er
ab-jur´ing
ab-late´

1

ab·la´tion	a·bom´i·na·ble	a·brad´ing
ab´la·tive	a·bom´i·na·ble-ness	a·bran´chi·an
ab´laut	a·bom´i·na·bly	a·bran´chi-ate
a·blaze´	a·bom´i-nate	a·bra-si-om´e-ter
a´ble	a·bom´i-nat·ed	a·bra´sion
able–bodied	a·bom-i-na´tion	a·bra´sive
a´bler	ab-o-rig´i-nal	a·bra´sive·ly
a´blest	ab-o-rig-i-nal´i-ty	a·bra´sive-ness
a·bloom´	ab-o-rig´i-nal·ly	ab-re-act´
ab´lu-ent	ab-o-rig´i·ne	ab-re-ac´tion
ab-lu´tion	a·bort´	ab-re-ac´tive
ab-lu´tion-ar·y	a·bor´ti-cide	a·breast´
a´bly	a·bor´ti-fa´cient	a·bridge´
ab´ne-gate	a·bor´tion	a·bridge´a·ble
ab-ne-ga´tion	a·bor´tion-ist	a·bridg´er
ab´ne-ga-tive	a·bort´ive	a·bridg´ing
ab´ne-ga-tor	a·bor´tive·ly	a·bridg´ment
ab-nor´mal	a·bor´tive-ness	a·bris´tle
ab-nor-mal´i-ties	a·bound´	a·broach´
ab-nor-mal´i-ty	a·bound´ing	a·broad´
ab-nor´mal·ly	a·bound´ing·ly	ab´ro-ga·ble
ab-nor´mal-ness	a·bout´	ab´ro-gate
ab-nor´mi·ty	about–face	ab´ro-gat´ed
a·board´	a·bove´	ab´ro-gat-ing
a·bode´	a·bove´board	ab-ro-ga´tion
a·boil´	a·bove´ground	ab´ro-ga-tive
a·bol´ish	a·bove´men-tioned	ab´ro-ga-tor
a·bol´ish-a·ble	ab-ra-ca-dab´ra	ab-rupt´
a·bol´ish·er	a-brad´a·ble	ab-rup´tion
a·bol´ish-ment	a·brad´ant	ab-rupt´ly
ab-o-li´tion	a·brade´	ab-rupt´ness
ab-o-li´tion-ism	a·brad´ed	ab´scess
ab-o-li´tion-ist	a·brad´er	ab´scessed

2

ab-scise´
ab-scis´sa
ab-scis´sion
ab-scond´
ab-scond´ed
ab-scond´ence
ab-scond´er
ab´sence
ab´sent *(adj.)*
ab-sent´ *(v.)*
ab-sen-ta´tion
ab-sen-tee´
ab-sen-tee´ism
ab´sent·ly
ab´sent-mind·ed
ab´sent-ness
ab´sinthe
ab-sin´thi·an
ab´so-lute
ab´so-lute´ly
ab-so-lute´ness
ab-so-lu´tion
ab´so-lut-ism
ab´so-lut-ist
ab-so-lu-tis´tic
ab´so-lu-tive
ab´so-lut-ize
ab-sol´u-to·ry
ab-solv´a·ble
ab-solve´
ab-solved´
ab-sol´vent
ab-solv´er

ab-solv´ing
ab-sorb´
ab-sorb´a·ble
ab-sorb-a-bil´i·ty
ab-sorb´ance
ab-sorbed´
ab-sorb´ed·ly
ab-sorb´ed-ness
ab-sor-be-fa´cient
ab-sorb´en·cy
ab-sorb´ent
ab-sorb´er
ab-sorb´ing
ab-sorb´ing·ly
ab-sorp´tance
ab-sorp´tion
ab-sorp´tive
ab-stain´
ab-stained´
ab-stain´er
ab-ste´mi-ous
ab-ste´mi-ous·ly
ab-sten´tion
ab-sten´tious
ab-ster´gent
ab-ster´sion
ab´sti-nence
ab´sti-nent
ab´sti-nent·ly
ab´stract *(n., adj.)*
ab-stract´ *(v.)*
ab-stract´ed
ab-stract´ed·ly

ab-stract´ed-ness
ab-stract´er
ab-strac´tion
ab-strac´tion·al
ab-strac´tion-ism
ab-strac´tive
ab-strac´tive·ly
ab´stract·ly
ab´stract-ness
ab-stric´tion
ab-struse´
ab-struse´ly
ab-struse´ness
ab-surd´
ab-surd´ism
ab-surd´i·ty
ab-surd´ly
ab-surd´ness
a·bub´ble
a·bu´li·a
a·bu´lic
a·bun´dance
a·bun´dant
a·bun´dant·ly
a·bus´a·ble
a·buse´
a·bused´
a·bus´er
a·bus´ing
a·bu´sive
a·bu´sive·ly
a·bu´sive-ness
a·but´

a·but′ment
a·but′tal
a·but′ted
a·but′ter
a·but′ting
a·buzz′
a·bysm′
a·bys′mal
a·bys′mal·ly
a·byss′
a·byss′al
a·ca′cia
ac′a-deme
ac-a-de′mi·a
ac-a-dem′ic
ac-a-dem′i-cal
ac-a-dem′i-cal·ly
ac-a-de-mi′cian
ac-a-dem′ics
a·cad′e·my
a·cap-pel′la
a·cau′dal
a·cau′date
a·cau-les′cent
a·cau′line
a·caus′al
a·cau-sal′i·ty
ac-cede′
ac-ced′ence
ac-ce-le-ran′do
ac-cel′er-ant
ac-cel′er-ate
ac-cel-er-a′tion

ac-cel′er-a-tive
ac-cel′er-a-tor
ac-cel′er-a-to·ry
ac′cent *(n., v.)*
ac-cent′ *(v.)*
ac-cen′tu-ate
ac-cen-tu-a′tion
ac-cept′
ac-cept-a-bil′i·ty
ac-cept′a·ble
ac-cept′a·bly
ac-cept′ance
ac-cept′ant
ac-cep-ta′tion
ac-cept′ed
ac-cept′er
ac-cep′tor
ac′cess
ac-ces′sa·ry
ac-ces-si-bil′i·ty
ac-ces′si·ble
ac-ces′si·bly
ac-ces′sion
ac-ces-so′ri·al
ac-ces′so-ri·ly
ac-ces′so-rize
ac-ces′so·ry
ac′ci-dence
ac′ci-dent
ac-ci-den′tal
ac-ci-den′tal·ly
ac-cip′i-tral
ac-claim′

ac-claim′ing
ac-cla-ma′tion
ac-clam′a-to·ry
ac-cli′mat-a·ble
ac-cli′mate
ac-cli′mat·ed
ac-cli-ma′tion
ac-cli-ma-ti-za′tion
ac-cli′ma-tize
ac-cliv′i·ty
ac-cli′vous
ac-co-lade′
ac′co-lade
ac-com′mo-date
ac-com′mo-dat-ing
ac-com-mo-da′tion
ac-com-mo-da′-
   tion·al
ac-com′mo-da-tive
ac-com′pa-nied
ac-com′pa-nies
ac-com′pa-ni-ment
ac-com′pa-nist
ac-com′pa·ny
ac-com′plice
ac-com′plish
ac-com′plished
ac-com′plish-ment
ac-compt′
ac-cord′
ac-cord′a·ble
ac-cord′ance
ac-cord′ant

ac-cord´ed
ac-cord´ing
ac-cord´ing·ly
ac-cor´di·on
ac-cor´di·on-ist
ac-cost´
ac-couche-ment´
ac-cou-cheur´
ac-count´
ac-count-a·bil´i·ty
ac-count´a·ble
ac-count´a·bly
ac-count´an·cy
ac-count´ant
ac-count´ing
ac-cou´ter
ac-cou´ter-ment
ac-cred´it
ac-cres´cence
ac-crete´
ac-cre´tion
ac-cre´tive
ac-cru´al
ac-crue´
ac-crue´ment
ac-cru´ing
ac-cul-tur-a´tion
ac-cum´ben·cy
ac-cum´bent
ac-cu´mu-late
ac-cu´mu-lat-ing
ac-cu´mu-la´tion
ac-cu´mu-la-tive

ac-cu´mu-la-tor
ac´cu-ra·cy
ac´cu-rate
ac´cu-rate·ly
ac´cu-rate-ness
ac-curs´ed
ac-curs´ed·ly
ac-cus´al
ac-cu-sa´tion
ac-cu´sa-tive
ac-cu´sa-tive·ly
ac-cus´a-to·ry
ac-cuse´
ac-cused´
ac-cus´er
ac-cus´ing
ac-cus´ing·ly
ac-cus´tom
ac-cus´tomed
ace
ac´er-bate
a·cer´bic
a·cer´bi·ty
ac´er-ose
ache
ached
a·che´ni·al
a·chiev´a·ble
a·chieve´
a·chieved´
a·chieve´ment
a·chiev´ing
ach´i·ness

ach´ing·ly
ach-ro-mat´ic
ach-ro-mat´i-cal·ly
a·chro´ma-tism
a·chro´ma-tize
a·chro´ma-tous
ach´y
ac´id
a·cid´ic
a-cid´i-fi-a·ble
a-cid-i-fi-ca´tion
a·cid´i-fied
a·cid´i·fy
a·cid´i·ty
ac-i-doph´i-lus
a·cid´u-late
a·cid-u-la´tion
a·cid´u-lous
acid–washed
ac-knowl´edge
ac-knowl´edge-
   a·ble
ac-knowl´edged
ac-knowl´edg-ing
ac-knowl´edg-ment
a·clin´ic
ac´me
ac´ne
ac´o-lyte
a´corn
a·cous´tic
a·cous´ti-cal
a·cous´ti-cal·ly

ac-ous-ti´cian
ac-quaint´
ac-quaint´ance
ac-quaint´ance-
  ship
ac-quaint´ed
ac-qui-esce´
ac-qui-es´cence
ac-qui-es´cent
ac-qui-es´cent·ly
ac-qui-esc´ing
ac-qui-esc´ing·ly
ac-quir-a-bil´i·ty
ac-quir´a·ble
ac-quire´
ac-quire´ment
ac-quir´er
ac-quir´ing
ac-qui-si´tion
ac-qui-si´tion·al
ac-quis´i-tive
ac-quis´i-tor
ac-quit´
ac-quit´tal
ac-quit´ted
ac-quit´ting
a´cre
a´cre-age
ac´rid
a·crid´i·ty
ac´rid·ly
ac´rid-ness
ac-ri-mo´ni-ous

ac´ri-mo·ny
ac´ro-bat
ac-ro-bat´ic
ac´ro-nym
ac-ro-pho´bi·a
ac-ro-pho´bic
a·cross´
a·cryl´ic
act
act´able
act´ing
ac´tion
ac´tion-a·ble
ac´tion-less
ac´ti-vate
ac-ti-va´tion
ac´ti-va-tor
ac´tive
ac´tive·ly
ac´tive-ness
ac´tiv-ism
ac´tiv-ist
ac-tiv´i-ties
ac-tiv´i·ty
ac´tor
ac´tress
ac´tu·al
ac-tu-al´i·ty
ac-tu-al-i-za´tion
ac´tu-al-ize
ac´tu-al·ly
ac´tu-al-ness
ac-tu-ar´i·al

ac´tu-ar-ies
ac´tu-ar·y
ac´tu-ate
ac´tu-at-ing
ac-tu-a´tion
ac´tu-a-tor
ac´u-ate
a·cu´i·ty
a·cu´men
ac´u-pres-sure
ac´u-punc-ture
ac´u-punc-tur-ist
a·cute´
a·cute´ly
a·cute´ness
ad´age
ad´a-man·cy
ad´a-mant
ad-a-man´tine
ad´a-mant·ly
a·dapt´
a·dapt-a-bil´i·ty
a·dapt´a·ble
ad-ap-ta´tion
ad-ap-ta´tion-al
ad-ap-ta´tion-al·ly
a·dapt´er
a·dapt´ive
a·dap´tive·ly
a·dap´tive-ness
ad-ap-tiv´i·ty
a·dap´tor
ad-ax´i·al

add´a·ble
add´ed
ad´dend
ad-den´da
ad-den´dum
ad´dict *(n.)*
ad-dict´ *(v.)*
ad-dict´ed
ad-dic´tion
ad-dic´tive
ad-di´tion
ad-di´tion·al
ad-di´tion-al·ly
ad´di-tive
ad´dle
ad´dled
add–on
ad-dress´
ad-dress´a·ble
ad-dress-ee´
ad-dress´er
ad-dress´ing
ad-dres´sor
ad-duce´
ad-du´cent
ad-duc´i·ble
ad-duc´ing
ad-duct´ *(v.)*
ad´duct *(n.)*
ad-duc´tion
ad-duc´tor
a·dept´ *(adj.)*
ad´ept *(n.)*

a·dept´ly
a·dept´ness
ad´e-qua·cy
ad´e-quate
ad´e-quate·ly
ad´e-quate-ness
ad-here´
ad-her´ence
ad-her´ent
ad-her´ent·ly
ad-her´ing
ad-he´sion
ad-he´sive
ad hoc
a·dieu´
ad in-fi-ni´tum
ad in´ter·im
a·dios´
ad-ja´cen·cy
ad-ja´cent
ad-ja´cent·ly
ad-jec-ti´val
ad´jec-tive
ad-join´
ad-joined´
ad-join´ing
ad-journ´
ad-journed´
ad-journ´ment
ad-judge´
ad-judg´ing
ad-ju´di-cate
ad-ju´di-cat-ing

ad-ju-di-ca´tion
ad-ju´di-ca-tive
ad-ju´di-ca-tor
ad-ju´di-ca-to·ry
ad´junct
ad-junc´tion
ad-junc´tive
ad-junct´ly
ad-ju-ra´tion
ad-jur´a-to·ry
ad-jure´
ad-ju´ror
ad-just´
ad-just-a-bil´i·ty
ad-just´a·ble
ad-just´er
ad-just´ment
ad-jus´tor
ad´ju-tant
ad´ju-vant
ad–lib *(v., adj.)*
ad lib´i-tum
ad-min´is-ter
ad-min´is-trate
ad-min´is-tra´tion
ad-min´is-tra-tive
ad-min´is-tra-
   tive·ly
ad-min´is-tra-tor
ad´mi-ra·ble
ad´mi-ra·bly
ad´mi-ral
ad´mi-ral·ty

7

ad-mi-ra´tion
ad-mire´
ad-mired´
ad-mir´er
ad-mir´ing
ad-mir´ing·ly
ad-mis-si-bil´i·ty
ad-mis´si·ble
ad-mis´sion
ad-mis´sive
ad-mit´
ad-mit´tance
/ ad-mit´ted
ad-mit´ted·ly
ad-mit´ting
ad-mix´
ad-mix´ture
ad-mon´ish
ad-mon´ish-ing·ly
ad-mon´ish-ment
ad-mo-ni´tion
ad-mon´i-to·ry
a·do´
a·do´be
ad-o-les´cence
ad-o-les´cent
ad-o-les´cent·ly
a·dopt´
a·dopt´a·ble
a·dopt´er
a·dop´tion
a·dop´tive
a·dop´tive·ly

a·dor´a·ble
a·dor´a·bly
ad-o-ra´tion
a·dore´
a·dored´
a·dor´er
a·dor´ing
a·dor´ing·ly
a·dorn´
a·dorned´
a·dorn´ing
a·dorn´ment
a·down´
ad-ren´a-lin
a·drift´
a·droit´
a·droit´ly
a·droit´ness
ad-sorb´
ad-sorb´ent
ad-sorp´tion
ad-sorp´tive
ad´u-late
ad-u-la´tion
ad´u-la-to·ry
a·dult´
a·dul´ter-ant
a·dul´ter-ate
a·dul-ter-a´tion
a·dul´ter-a-tor
a·dul´ter-er
a·dul´ter-ess
a·dul´ter-ous

a·dul´ter·y
a·dult´hood
ad va-lo´rem
ad-vance´
ad-vanced´
ad-vance´ment
ad-vanc´ing
ad-van´tage
ad-van´taged
ad-van-ta´geous
ad-van-ta´geous·ly
ad-van-ta´geous-
    ness
ad´vent
ad-ven-ti´tious
ad-ven-ti´tious·ly
ad-ven´ture
ad-ven´tur·er
ad-ven´ture-some
ad-ven´tur-ous
ad´verb
ad-verb´i·al
ad´ver-sar-ies
ad´ver-sar·y
ad´verse
ad´verse·ly
ad-verse´ness
ad-ver´si·ty
ad-vert´
ad-vert´ence
ad-vert´en·cy
ad-vert´ent
ad-vert´ent·ly

8

ad´ver-tise
ad-ver-tise´ment
ad´ver-tis·er
ad´ver-tis-ing
ad-vice´
ad-vis-a-bil´i·ty
ad-vis´a·ble
ad-vis´a·ble-ness
ad-vis´a·bly
ad-vise´
ad-vised´
ad-vis´ed·ly
ad-vise´ment
ad-vis´er
ad-vis´ing
ad-vi´sor
ad-vis´o·ry
ad´vo-ca·cy
ad´vo-cate
ad-vo-ca´tion
ad´vo-ca-tor
ad-voc´a-to·ry
adz, adze
aer´ate
aer-a´tion
aer´a-tor
aer´i·al
aer´i-al-ist
ae´rie
aer-o-bat´ics
aer-o´bic
aer-o-dy-nam´ic
aer´o-naut

aer-o-nau´ti-cal
aer-o-nau´ti-cal·ly
aer-o-pho´bi·a
aer´o-plane
aer´o-sol
aer´o-space
a´er·y
aes´thete
aes-thet´ic
aes-thet´i-cal
aes-thet´i-cal·ly
aes-thet´ics
ae´ther
a·far´
af-fa-bil´i·ty
af´fa-ble
af´fa-bly
af-fair´
af-fect´
af-fec-ta´tion
af-fect´ed
af-fect´ing
af-fect´ing·ly
af-fec´tion
af-fec´tion·al
af-fec´tion-ate
af-fec´tion-ate·ly
af´fer-ent
af-fi´ance
af-fi´anced
af-fil´i-ate
af-fil´i-at·ed
af-fil-i-a´tion

af-fin´i-ties
af-fin´i-tive
af-fin´i·ty
af-firm´
af-firm´a·ble
af-firm´a·bly
af-fir-ma´tion
af-firm´a-tive
af-firm´a-tive·ly
af-firm´ing·ly
affix´ (v.)
af´fix (n.)
af-flict´
af-flic´tion
af-flict´ive
af´flu-ence
af´flu-en·cy
af´flu-ent
af´flu-ent·ly
af-ford´
af-ford-a-bil´i·ty
af-ford´a·ble
af-ford´a·bly
af-fray´
af-fright´
af-front´
af-front´ive
a·fi-cio-na´do
a·field´
a·fire´
a·flame´
a·float´
a·flut´ter

9

a·foot´
a·fore´men-tioned
a·fore´said
a·fore´thought
a-fore´time
a·foul´
a·fraid´
A´–frame
a·fresh´
af´ter
af´ter-birth
af´ter-burn·er
af´ter-care
af´ter-deck
af´ter-ef-fect
af´ter-glow
after–hours
af´ter-im-age
af´ter-life
af´ter-math
af-ter-noon´
af´ter-shave
af´ter-shock
af´ter-taste
af´ter-thought
af´ter-ward
af´ter-wards
a·gain´
a·gainst´
a·gape´ *(ajar)*
a·ga´pe *(love feast)*
a-gaze´
age

aged, ag´ed
age´less
a´gen-cies
a´gen·cy
a·gen´da
a·gen´dum
a´gent
ag-glom´er-ate
ag-glom-er-a´tion
ag-grade
ag-gran´dize
ag-gran´dize-ment
ag´gra-vate
ag´gra-vat·ed
ag´gra-vat-ing
ag´gra-va´tion
ag´gra-va-tor
ag´gre-gate
ag´gre-gate·ly
ag´gre-gat-ing
ag-gre-ga´tion
ag´gre-ga-tive
ag´gre-ga-to·ry
ag-gress´
ag-gres´sion
ag-gres´sive
ag-gres´sive·ly
ag-gres´sive-ness
ag-gres´sor
ag-griev´ance
ag-grieve´
ag-grieved´
ag-grieve´ment

a·ghast´
ag´ile
ag´ile·ly
ag´ile-ness
a·gil´i·ty
ag´ing
ag´i-tate
ag´i-tated
ag´i-tat-ed·ly
ag´i-tat-ing
ag-i-ta´tion
ag´i-ta-tive
ag´i-ta-tor
a·gleam´
a·glow´
ag-nos´tic
ag-nos´ti-cal
ag-nos´ti-cism
a·go´
a·gog´
ag´o-nist
ag-o-nis´tic
ag´o-nize
ag´o-niz-ing
ag´o·ny
ag-o-ra-pho´bi·a
a·grar´i·an
a·gree´
a·gree-a-bil´i·ty
a·gree´a·ble
a·gree´a·bly
a·greed´
a·gree´ing

a·gree´ment
ag´ri-bus·i-ness
ag-ri-cul´tur·al
ag´ri-cul-ture
ag-ri-cul´tur-ist
a·gron´o-mist
a·gron´o·my
a·ground´
a´gue
a´gue-weed
a´gu-ish
a·head´
a·hoy´
aide–de–camp
ail´ment
aim´less
aim´less·ly
aim´less-ness
air´brush
air´craft
air´field
air´flow
air´foil
air force
air´freight
air´i·ly
air´i-ness
air´ing
air´less
air´lin·er
air´ lock
air´mail
air´man

air´ mat-tress
air´plane
air pock´et
air´port
air pres´sure
air´show
air´sickness
air´speed
air´stream
air´strip
air´tight
air´ traf-fic
air´waves
air´way
air´wor·thy
air´y
aisle
a·jar´
a·kim´bo
a·kin´
al´a-bas-ter
à la carte
a·lac´ri·ty
à la king
à la mode
a·larm´
a·larm´ing
a·larm´ing·ly
a· larm´ist
a·las´
al´ba-tross
al-bi´no
al´bum

al-bu´men *(egg white)*
al-bu´min *(protein)*
al´che-mist
al´che·my
al´co-hol
al-co-hol´ic
al-co-hol-ic´i·ty
al´co-hol-ism
al´cove
al-co-vi-nom´e-ter
al den´te
al´der
al´der-man
al-der-man´ic
ale
ale´house
a·lert´
a·lert´ly
a·lert´ness
al-fres´co
al´ga, al´gae
al´ge-bra
al-ge-bra´ic
al-ge-bra´i-cal
al-ge-bra´i-cal·ly
al´go-rithm
a´li·as
al´i·bi
al´i-bi-ing
al´ien
al´ien-a·ble
al´ien-ate

al´ien-at-ing

al´ien-a´tion

al´ien-ist

a·light´

a·lign´

a·lign´ment

a·like´

al´i-ment

al-i-men´ta·ry

al-i-men-ta´tion

al´i-mo·ny

a·line´

a·line´ment

a·live´

al´ka·li

al´ka-line

al-ka-lin´i·ty

al´ka-loid

all–American

all–around

al-lay´

al-lay´ing

all clear

all–day

al-le-ga´tion

al-lege´

al-lege´a·ble

al-leged´

al-leg´ed·ly

al-le´giance

al-leg´ing

al-le-gor´ic

al-le-gor´i-cal

al-le-gor´i-cal·ly

al´le-go-ries

al´le-go-rist

al´le-go-rize

al´le·go·ry

al´ler-gen

al-ler-gen´ic

al-ler´gic

al´ler-gist

al´ler·gy

al-le´vi-ate

al-le´vi-at-ing

al-le-vi-a´tion

al-le´vi-a-tive

al´ley

al´leys

al´ley-way

al-li´ance

al-lied´

al-lies´

al´li-ga-tor

all–important

al-lit´er-ate

al-lit-er-a´tion

al-lit´er-a-tive

all–night

al´lo-cate

al´lo-cat-ing

al-lo-ca´tion

al-lot´

al-lot´ment

al-lot´ted

al-lot´ting

all–out

all–over

al-low´

al-low´a·ble

al-low´ance

al-lowed´

al´loy

all–powerful

all–purpose

all right

all–round

all-spice

all–star

al-lude´

al-lure

al-lured´

al-lure´ment

al-lur´ing

al-lu´sion

al-lu´sive

al-lu´sive·ly

al-lu´sive-ness

al´ly *(n.)*

al·ly´ *(v.)*

al-ly´ing

al´ma-nac

al-might´y

al´mond

al´mo-ner

al´most

a·loft´

a·lone´

a·long´

a·long-side´
a·loof´
a·loof´ness
a·loud´
al´pha
al´pha-bet
al-pha-bet´ic
al-pha-bet´i-cal
al´pha-bet-ize
al-read´y
al-right´
al´tar
al´tar-piece
al´ter
al-ter-a-bil´i·ty
al´ter-a-ble
al-ter-a´tion
al´ter-cate
al-ter-ca´tion
al´ter-nate
al´ter-nat·ed
al´ter-nate·ly
al´ter-nat-ing
al-ter-na´tion
al-ter´na-tive
al´ter-na-tor
al-though´
al´ti-tude
al´to
al´to-geth·er
al´tru-ism
al´tru-ist
al-tru-is´ti-cal·ly

al-u-min´i·um
a·lum´ni
a·lum´nus
al´ways
a·mal´ga-mate
a·mal-ga-ma´tion
a·mal´ga-ma-tor
a·man-u-en´sis
am-a-ret´to
a·mass´
a·mass´a·ble
a·mass´ment
am´a-teur
am´a-teur-ish
am´a-teur-ism
am´a-to·ry
a·maze´
a·mazed´
a·maz´ed·ly ✓
a·maze´ment
a·maz´ing
a·maz´ing·ly
am-bas´sa-dor
am-bas-sa-do´ri·al
am´bi-ance
am-bi-dex´trous
am´bi-ence
am´bi-ent
am-bi-gu´i·ty
am-big´u-ous
am-bi´tion
am-bi´tious
am-biv´a-lence

am-biv´a-lent
am´ble
am´bled
am´bling
am´bling·ly
am-bro´si·a
am´bu-lance
am´bu-la-to·ry
am´bush
am´bushed
am´bush·er
a·me´lio-rate
a·me-lio-ra´tion
a·me´lio-ra-tive
a·me´lio-ra-tor
a´men´
a·me-na-bil´i·ty
a·me´na·ble
a·mend´
a·mend´a·ble
a·mend´a-to·ry
a·mend´ed
a·mend´ment
a·mends´
a·men´i-ties
a·men´i·ty
a·mi-a-bil´i·ty
a´mi-a·ble
a´mi-a·bly
am-i-ca-bil´i·ty
am´i-ca·ble
am´i-ca·bly
a·mid´

13

a·midst´
a·miss´
am´i·ty
am-ne´sia
am-ne´si·ac
am´nes·ty
a·moe´ba
a·mong´
a·mongst´
a·mor´al
a·mo-ral´i·ty
a·mor´al·ly
am-o-ret´to
am´o-rous
a·mor´phous
am´or-tize
am´or-tiz-ing
a·mount´
am´per-age
am´pere
am´per-sand
am-phet´a-mine
am-phib´i·an
am-phib´i-ous
am-phib´i-ous·ly
am´phi-the-a-ter
am´ple
am´ple-ness
am-pli-fi-ca´tion
am´pli-fied
am´pli-fi·er
am´pli·fy
am´pli-fy-ing

am´pli-tude
am´ply
am´pu-tate
am´pu-tat-ing
am-pu-ta´tion
am´pu-tee´
a·muck´
am´u-let
a·muse´
a·muse´ment
a·mus´ing
a·nach´ro-nism
a·nach-ro-nis´tic
a·nae´mi·a (Br.)
an-al-ge´sic
an´a-log
a·nal´o-gies
a·nal´o-gize
a·nal´o-gous
a·nal´o-gous·ly
an´a-logue
a·nal´o·gy
an´a-lyse (Br.)
a·nal´y-ses
a·nal´y-sis
an´a-lyst
an-a-lyt´ic
an-a-lyt´i-cal
an-a-lyt´i-cal·ly
an´a-lyze
an´a-lyz-ing
an´ar-chism
an´ar-chist

an-ar-chis´tic
an´ar-chy
a·nath´e·ma
an-a-tom´i-cal
a·nat´o-mist
a·nat´o-mize
a·nat´o·my
an´ces-tor
an-ces´tral
an´ces-try
an´chor
an´chor-age
an´cho-ret
an´cho-vies, an-
    cho´vies
an´cho-vy
an-cho´vy
an´cient
an´cil-lar·y
and´i-ron
an´droid
an´ec-dot·al
an´ec-dote
a·ne´mi·a
a·ne´mic
an-es-the´sia
an-es-the-si-ol´o-
    gist
an-es-thet´ic
a·nes´the-tist
a·nes´the-tize
an´eu-rysm
a·new´

an´gel
an´gel-fish
an-gel´ic
an´ger
an-gi´na
an-gi´na pec´to-ris
an-gi-os´to·my
an´gle
an´gler
an´gle-worm
an´gling
an´gri·ly
an´gri-ness
an´gry
an´guish
an´guished
an´gu-lar
an-gu-lar´i·ty
an´i-mal
an´i-mal-ism
an´i-mate
an´i-mat·ed
an´i-mat-ed·ly
an´i-mat-ing
an-i-ma´tion
an-i-ma-tor
an-i-mos´i·ty
an´i-mus
an´ise
an´i-seed
an-i-sette´
an´kle
an´klet

an´nal
an-neal´
an-nealed´
an-nex´ (v.)
an´nex (n.)
an-nex-a´tion
an-ni´hi-late
an-ni-hi-la´tion
an-ni´hi-la-tor
an-ni-ver´sa-ries
an-ni-ver´sa·ry
an´no-tate
an-no-ta´tion
an´no-ta-tor
an-nounce´
an-nounce´ment
an-nounc´er
an-nounc´ing
an-noy´
an-noy´ance
an-noyed´
an-noy´ing
an´nu·al
an´nu-al-ize
an´nu-al·ly
an-nu´i·ty
an-nul´
an-nulled´
an-nul´ling
an-nul´ment
an´num
an-nun´ci-ate
an-nun-ci-a´tion

an-nun´ci-a-tor
a·noint´
a·noint´ed
a·noint´er
a·noint´ment
a·nom-a-lis´tic
a·nom´a-lous
a·nom´a-lous·ly
a·nom´a·ly
an-o-nym´i·ty
a·non´y-mous
a·non´y-mous·ly
an-o-rex´i·a
an-o-rex´ic
an-oth´er
an´swer
an´swer-a·ble
an´swered
an´swer-ing
an-tag´o-nism
an-tag´o-nist
an-tag-o-nis´tic
an-tag´o-nize
an´te
an´te-bel´lum
an-te-cede´
an-te-ced´ence
an-te-ced´ent
an´te-cham-ber
an´te-date
an-ten´na
an-te´ri·or
an´te-room

15

an´them
an-thol´o·gy
an´thro-poid
an-thro-po-log´i-
 cal
an-thro-pol´o-gist
an-thro-pol´o·gy
an-thro-po-
 morph´ic
an-thro-po-mor´-
 phize
an´ti
an-ti-bi-ot´ic
an´ti-bod-ies
an´ti-bod·y
an´tic
an-tic´i-pate
an-tic´i-pat·ed
an-tic´i-pat-ing
an-tic-i-pa´tion
an-tic´i-pa-tive
an-tic´i-pa-to·ry
an-ti-cli´max
an´ti-dote
an´ti-freeze
an-ti-grav´i·ty
an-ti-his´ta-mine
an´ti-mat-ter
an-ti-pas´to
an-tip´a-thy
an´ti-quate
an´ti-quat·ed
an´ti-quat-ing

an-tique´
an-tiq´ui·ty
an-ti-sep´tic
an-ti-so´cial
an-tith´e-sis
an-ti-thet´ic
an-ti-thet´i-cal
an-ti-thet´i-cal·ly
an-ti-trust´
an´to-nym
an´vil
anx-i´e·ty
anx´ious
anx´ious·ly
an´y
an´y-bod·y
an´y-how
an-y-more´
an´y-one
an´y-place
an´y-thing
an´y-time
any-way
an´y-where
a·part´
a·part´heid
a·part´ment
ap-a-thet´ic
ap-a-thet´i-cal·ly
ap´a-thy
a ·pér-i-tif´
ap´er-ture
a´pex

aph´o-rism
aph-o-ris´tic
a´pi-ar·y
a·piece´
a·poc´a-lypse
a·poc-a-lyp´tic
a·poc´ry-phal
a-po-lit´i-cal
a·pol-o-get´ic
a·pol-o-get´i-cal
a·pol-o-get´i-cal·ly
ap-o-lo´gi·a
a·pol´o-gies
a·pol´o-gise (Br.)
a·pol´o-gist
a·pol´o-gize
a·pol´o-giz-ing
a·pol´o·gy
ap-os-tol´ic
ap-os-tol´i-cal
a·pos´tro-phe
a·poth´e-car·y
ap-pal´ (Br.)
ap-pall´
ap-pall´ing
ap-pall´ing·ly
ap-pa-rat´us
ap-par´el
ap-par´ent
ap-par´ent·ly
ap-pa-ri´tion
ap-peal´
ap-pealed´

ap-peal´er	ap´pli-cant	ap-pre´ci-at-ing
ap-peal´ing	ap-pli-ca´tion	ap-pre-ci-a´tion
ap-peal´ing·ly	ap´pli-ca-tive	ap-pre´cia-tive
ap-pear´	ap´pli-ca-tor	ap-pre´cia-tive·ly
ap-pear´ance	ap´pli-ca-to·ry	ap-pre´cia-to·ry
ap-peared´	ap-plied´	ap-pre-hend´
ap-pear´ing	ap-pli´er	ap-pre-hend´ed
ap-pease´	ap-pli-que´	ap-pre-hend´ing
ap-pease´ment	ap-ply´	ap-pre-hen´si·ble
ap-peas´er	ap-ply´ing	ap-pre-hen´sion
ap-peas´ing	ap-point´	ap-pre-hen´sive
ap-peas´ing·ly	ap-point´ed	ap-pre-hen´sive·ly
ap-pel´lant	ap-poin-tee´	ap-pren´tice
ap-pel´late	ap-point´er	ap-pren´ticed
ap-pel-la´tion	ap-point´ing	ap-pren´tice-ship
ap-pend´	ap-point´ment	ap-prise´
ap-pend´age	ap-por´tion	ap-prised´
ap-pend´aged	ap-por´tioned	ap-pris´ing
ap-pend´ed	ap-por´tion·er	ap-prize´
ap´pe-tite	ap-por´tion-ment	ap-proach´
ap´pe-tiz·er	ap-pos´a·ble	ap-proach-a-bil´i·ty
ap´pe-tiz-ing	ap-pose´	ap-proach´a·ble
ap-plaud´	ap´po-site	ap-proached´
ap-plaud´er	ap-po-si´tion	ap-proach´ing
ap-plaud´ing	ap-pos´i-tive	ap-pro-ba´tion
ap-plause´	ap-prais´al	ap-pro´pri-ate
ap´ple	ap-praise´	ap-pro´pri-at-ed
ap´ple-jack	ap-praised´	ap-pro´pri-at·ly
ap´ple-sauce	ap-prais´er	ap-pro´pri-ate-ness
ap-pli´ance	ap-prais´ing	ap-pro´pri-at-ing
ap-pli-ca-bil´i·ty	ap-pre´cia·ble	ap-pro-pri-a´tion
ap´pli-ca·ble	ap-pre´ci-ate	ap-prov´al
ap´pli-ca·bly	ap-pre´ci-at·ed	ap-prove´

ap-proved
ap-prov´ing
ap-prov´ing·ly
ap-prox´i-mate
ap-prox´i-mat·ed
ap-prox´i-mate·ly
ap-prox´i-mat´ing
ap-prox-i-ma´tion
ap-pur´te-nance
ap-pur´te-nant
a´pron
ap´ro-pos
apse
ap´ti-tude
apt´ly
apt´ness
aq´ua
aq´ua-cade
aq´ua-cul-ture
aq´ua-lung
aq-ua-ma-rine´
aq´ua-plane
a·quar´i·um
a·quat´ic
a·quat´i-cal·ly
aq´ue-duct
a´que-ous
aq´ui-fer
a-quiv´er
ar´a·ble
ar´bi-ter
ar´bi-trage
ar´bi-trag·er

ar´bi-trar-i·ly
ar´bi-trar·y
ar´bi-trate
ar´bi-trat-ing
ar-bi-tra´tion
ar´bi-tra-tive
ar´bi-tra-tor
ar´bi-tress
ar´bor
ar-bo´re·al
ar´bour (Br.)
ar-cade´
ar-cane´
ar-chae-ol´o-gist
ar-chae-ol´o·gy
ar-cha´ic
ar-cha´i-cal·ly
ar-che-o-log´ic
ar-che-o-log´i-cal
ar-che-ol´o-gist
ar-che-ol´o·gy
arch´er
ar´cher-fish
arch´er·y
ar´che-type
ar´chi-tect
ar-chi-tec´tur-al
ar´chi-tec-ture
ar-chi´val
ar´chive
ar´chi-vist
arch´way
arc´ing

ar´dent
ar´dent·ly
ar´dor
ar´du-ous
ar´du-ous·ly
ar´e·a-way
a·re´na
ar´go·sy
ar´gu-a·ble
ar´gue
ar´gued
ar´gu-ing
ar´gu-ment
ar-gu-men-ta´tion
ar-gu-men´ta-tive
a´ri·a
ar´id
a·rid´i·ty
ar´id-ness
a·right´
a´ri-ose
a·rise´
a·ris´en
a·ris´ing
ar-is-toc´ra·cy
a·ris´to-crat
a·ris-to-crat´ic
a·rith´me-tic *(n.)*
ar-ith-met´ic *(adj.)*
ar-ith-met´i-cal
ar-ma´da
ar´ma-ment
ar´ma-ture

18

arm´band
arm´chair
armed
arm´ful
ar´mies
ar´mil·lar·y
ar´mi·stice
ar·moire´
ar´mor
ar´mored
ar·mo´ri·al
armor–plated
ar´mo·ry
ar´mour (Br.)
arm´pit
arm´rest
ar´my
a·ro´ma
ar·o·mat´ic
ar·o·mat´i·cal·ly
a·ro´ma·tize
a·rose´
a·round´
a·rous´al
a·rouse´
a·rous´ing
ar·raign´
ar·raign´ment
ar·range´
ar·range´a·ble
ar·range´ment
ar·rang´er
ar·rang´ing

ar·ray´
ar·rayed´
ar·ray´ing
ar·rear´
ar·rear´age
ar·rest´
ar·rest´ed
ar·rest´er
ar·rest´ing
ar·res´tive
ar·riv´al
ar·rive´
ar·riv´ing
ar´ro·gance
ar´ro·gant
ar´ro·gate
ar´ro·gat·ing
ar·ro·ga´tion
ar´se·nal
ar´se·nate
ar´se·nic (n.)
ar·sen´ic (adj.)
ar´son
ar´son·ist
art´ful
art´ful·ly
ar´ti·cle
ar´ti·cled
ar·tic´u·late
ar·tic´u·lat·ed
ar·tic·u·la´tion
ar·tic´u·la·tor
ar´ti·fact

ar´ti·fice
ar·ti·fi´cial
ar·ti·fi·ci·al´i·ty
ar·ti·fi´cial·ly
ar´ti·san
art´ist
ar·tiste´
ar·tis´tic
ar·tis´ti·cal
ar·tis´ti·cal·ly
ar´tist·ry
art´less
art´work
art´y
as·cend´
as·cend´a·ble
as·cend´an·cy
as·cend´ant
as·cend´ing
as·cen´sion
as·cent´
as·cer·tain´
as·cer·tain´a·ble
as·cet´ic
as·cet´i·cism
as·crib´a·ble
as·cribe´
as·crip´tive
as·crip´tion
a·sex´u·al
a·shamed´
a·sham´ed·ly
ash´en

a·shore´
ash´tray
ash´y
a·side´
as´i-nine
as-i-nin´i·ty
a·skance´
a·skew´
a·slant´
a·sleep´
a-so´cial
as´pect
as´per-ate
as-per´i·ty
as-perse´
as-per´sion
as-phyx´i·a
as-phyx´i-ate
as´pic
as´pi-rant
as´pi-rate
as´pi-ra´tion
as´pi-ra-tor
as-pir´a-to·ry
as-pire´
as´pi-rin
as-pir´ing
as-pir´ing·ly
as-sail´
as-sail´a·ble
as-sail´ant
as-sas´sin
as-sas´si-nate

as-sas-si-na´tion
as-sas´si-na-tor
as-sault´
as-sault´er
as´say (n.)
as-say´ (v.)
as-say´er
as-sem´blage
as-sem´ble
as-sem´bler
as-sem´bling
as-sem´bly
as-sent´
as-sert´
as-ser´tion
as-ser´tive
as-sess´
as-sess´ment
as´ses´sor
as´set
as-sid´u-ous
as-sid´u-ous·ly
as-sign´
as-sign-a-bil´i·ty
as-sign´a·ble
as-sig-na´tion
as-sign·ee´
as-sign´er
as-sign´ment
as-sign´or
as-sim´i-late
as-sim´i-lat-ing
as-sim-i-la´tion

as-sim´i-la-tive
as-sim´i-la-tor
as-sist´
as-sist´ance
as-sist´ant
as-sist´ed
as-sist´er
as-sist´ing
as-so´ci-ate
as-so´ci-at-ing
as-so-ci-a´tion
as-sort´
as-sort´ed
as-sort´ment
as-suage´
as-suag´ing
as-sum´a·ble
as-sum´a·bly
as-sume´
as-sumed´
as-sum´er
as-sum´ing
as-sump´tion
as-sump´tive
as-sur´ance
as-sure´
as-sured´
as-sur´ed·ly
as-sur´ed-ness
as-sur´ing
as´ter-isk
a·stern´
as´ter-oid

a·stir´
as-ton´ish
as-ton´ished
as-ton´ish-ing
as-ton´ish-ing·ly
as-ton´ish-ment
as-tound´
as-tound´ed
as-tound´ing·ly
as´tral
a·stray´
a·stride´
as-trin´gen·cy
as-trin´gent
as´tro-dome
as´tro-labe
as-trol´o-ger
as-tro-log´i-cal·ly
as-trol´o·gy
as´tro-naut
as-tron´o-mer
as-tro-nom´ic
as-tro-nom´i-cal·ly
as-tron´o·my
as-tro-phys´i-cal
as-tro-phys´i-cist
as-tro-phys´ics
as-tute´
as-tute´ly
as-tute´ness
a·sun´der
a·sy´lum
a·sym-met´ric

a·sym-met´ri-cal
a·sym´me-try
a·te-lier´
a´the-ism
a´the-ist
a·the-is´tic
a·the-is´ti-cal·ly
ath´lete
ath-let´ic
ath-let´i-cal·ly
a·tin´gle
at´mo-sphere
at-mo-spher´ic
at´oll
at´om
a·tom´ic
at´om-iz·er
a·ton´al
a·ton-al-is´tic
a·to-nal´i·ty
a·tone´
a·tone´ment
a·ton´ing
a·top´
a-trem´ble
a´tri·um
a·tro´cious
a·tro´cious·ly
a·troc´i·ty
at-tach´
at-tach´a·ble
at-ta-ché´
at-tached´

at-tach´ment
at-tack´
at-tacked´
at-tack´er
at-tack´ing
at-tain´
at-tain-a·bil´i·ty
at-tain´a·ble
at-tain´a·ble-ness
at-tain´ment
at-tempt´
at-tend´
at-tend´ance
at-tend´ant
at-tend´ing
at-ten´tion
at-ten´tive
at-ten´tive·ly
at-ten´u-ate
at-ten-u-a´tion
at-test´
at´tic
at-tire´
at´ti-tude
at-ti-tu´di-nize
at-tor´ney
at-tract´
at-trac´tion
at-tract´ive·ly
at-tract´ive-ness
at-trib´ut-a·ble
at´tri-bute *(n.)*
at-trib´ute *(v.)*

at-tri-bu′tion
at-trib′u-tive
at-tri′tion
at-tri′tus
at-tune′
a·typ′i-cal
au′burn
auc′tion
auc-tion-eer′
au-da′cious
au-dac′i·ty
au-di·bil′i·ty
au′di·ble
au′di·bly
au′di-ence
au′di·o
au-di-o–vis′u·al
au′dit
au-di′tion
au′di-tor
au-di-to′ri·um
au′di-to·ry
au′ger
aug-ment′ (v.)
aug′ment (n.)
aug-ment′a·ble
aug-men-ta′tion
aug-men′ta-tive
au′gu·ry
au-gust′
au′ra
au′re-ole
au′ri-cle

au-ric′u-lar
au-ro′ra
aus′cul-tate
aus-cul-ta′tion
aus-pi′cial
aus-pi′cious
aus-pi′cious·ly
aus-tere′
aus-tere′ly
aus-ter′i·ty
au-then′tic
au-then′ti-cal·ly
au-then′ti-cate
au-then-ti-ca′tion
au-then-tic′i·ty
au′thor
au-thor-i-tar′i·an
au-thor′i-ta-tive
au-thor′i·ty
au-tho-ri-za′tion
au′tho-rize
au′tho-rized
au′tho-riz-ing
au′thor-ship
au′tism
au′to
au-to-bi-og′ra-phy
au-toc′ra·cy
au′to-crat
au-to-crat′ic
au-to-crat′i-cal·ly
au′to-graph
au-to-im-mune′

au′to-mate
au-to-mat′ic
au-to-mat′i-cal·ly
au-to-ma′tion
au-tom′a-ton
au-to-mo-bile′
au-to-mo′tive
au-ton′o-mist
au-ton′o-mous
au-ton′o·my
au′top·sy
au′tumn
au-tum′nal
aux-il′ia·ry
a·vail′
a·vail-a·bil′i·ty
a·vail′a·ble
a·vailed′
av′a-lanche
av′a-rice
av-a-ri′cious
a·venge′
a·venged′
a·veng′er
a·veng′ing
av′e-nue
a·ver′
av′er-age
a·verse′
a·ver′sion
a·vert′
a·vert′ed
a′vi-ar·y

a´vi-ate
a·vi-a´tion
a´vi-a-tor
a·vi-a´trix
av´id
a·vid´i·ty
av´id·ly
av-o-ca´tion
a·void´
a·void´a·ble
a·void´a·bly
a·void´ance
a·void´ed
a·vow´
a·vow´al
a·vowed´
a·vow´ed·ly
a·vul´sion
a·vun´cu-lar
a´wait´
a·wake´
a·wak´en-ing
a·wak´ing
a·ward´
a·ward´ed
a·ware´
a·ware´ness
a·wash´
a·way´
awe
a·weigh´
awe´some
awe´stricken

awe´struck
aw´ful
aw´ful·ly
a·while´
a·whirl´
awk´ward
awk´ward·ly
awk´ward-ness
aw´ning
a·woke´
a·wry´
ax´i·om
ax-i-o-mat´ic
ax-i-o-mat´i-cal·ly
ax´is
ax´le
az´i-muth
az´ure

B

bab´ble
bab´bler
bab´bling
babe
ba´bied
ba´bies
ba´by
ba´by-ish
baby–sit
bac-ca-lau´re-ate
bac´cha-nal
bac-cha-na´lia
bac-cha-na´lian

bach´e-lor
back´ache
back´bend
back´bite
back´bit-ing
back´board
back´bone
back´break-ing
back´date
back´drop
backed
back´er
back´field
back´fire
back´flip
back´gam-mon
back´ground
back´hand·ed
back´ing
back´lash
back´list
back´log
back´pack
back–pedal
back´rest
back´slap-ping
back´slash
back´slid-ing
back´stage´
back´stop
back´stretch
back´stroke
back´swing

back´talk
back´track
back´up
back´ward
back´ward-ness
back-woods´
back-yard´
ba´con
bac-te´ri·a
bac-te´ri·al
bad´ly
bad´min-ton
bad–mouth
bad–tem-pered
baf´fle
baf´fling
bag´a-telle´
ba´gel
bag´ful
bag´gage
bagged
bag´ger
bag´ging
bag´gy
bag´pipe
ba-guette´
bail
bailed
bai´liff
bai´li-wick
bail´ment
bail´or
bail´out

bake
bak´er
bak´er·y
bak´ing
bal´ance
bal´anc·er
bal´anc-ing
bal´co-nies
bal´co·ny
bal´der-dash
bald´head·ed
bald´ness
bale´ful
bal´er
bal´ing
balk´i·er
balk´ing
balk´y
bal´lad
bal´lad·ry
bal´last
bal-le-ri´na
bal´let
bal-loon´
bal-loon´ist
bal´lot
ball´room
bal´ly-hoo
balm´i-ness
balm´y
ba-lo´ney
bal´us-ter
bal-us-trade´

bam-boo´
bam-boo´zle
ba´nal
ba-nal´i·ty
ban´dage
ban´dag-ing
ban-dan´na
band´box
band´ed
band´er
ban´dit
ban´dit·ry
band´stand
band´wag·on
ban´dy
ban´dy-ing
bandy–legged
ban´gle
ban´ish
ban´ish-ment
ban´is-ter
ban´jo
ban´jos
bank
bank´a·ble
bank´er
bank´ing
bank´rupt
bank´rupt·cy
ban´ner
ban´quet
ban´tam
ban´ter

ban´ter-ing·ly
bap´tism
bap´tis´mal
bap-tize´
bap-tized´
bap-tiz´ing
bar
bar-bar´i·an
bar-bar´ic
bar-bar´i-cal·ly
bar´ba-rism
bar´ba-rous
bar´be-cue
bar´bell
bar´ber
bar´ber-shop
bare
bare´back
bared
bare´faced
bare´foot
bare–handed
bare´head·ed
bare´leg-ged
bare´ly
bar´gain
bar´gain·er
barge
bar´keep
bark´er
bark´ing
bar´maid
bar´man

bar mitz´vah
bar´na-cle
barn´dance
barn´storm
barn´yard
ba-rom´e-ter
bar-o-met´ric
ba-roque´
bar´rack
bar-rage´
barred
bar´rel
bar´ren
bar´ren-ness
bar-rette´
bar´ri-cade
bar´ri-cad´ing
bar´ri·er
bar´ring
bar´ris-ter
bar´room
bar´tender
bar´ter
ba´sal
base´ball
base´board
base´less
base´ly
base´ment
base´ness
bash´ful
bash´ful·ly
bash´ful-ness

bash´ing
ba´sic
ba´si-cal·ly
ba-sil´i·ca
ba´sin
ba´sin-like
ba´sis
bas´ket
bas´ket-ball
bas´ket-ful
bas´ket·ry
bas´ket-work
bas-si-net´
bas´tion
bath *(n.)*
bathe *(v.)*
bath´er
bath´house
bath´ing
bath´robe
bath´room
bath´tub
ba-ton´
bat-tal´ion
bat´ten
bat´ter
bat´ter-ies
bat´ter-ing
bat´ter·y
bat´ting
bat´tle
bat´tle-field
bat´tle-ground

bat´tle-ment
battle–scarred
bat´tle-ship
bat´ty
bau´ble
bawd´i-ness
bawd´y
bay´o-net
bay´ou
ba-zaar´
ba-zoo´ka
beach´ball
beach´comb·er
beach´front
beach´head
beach´wear
bea´con
bead´ed
bead´ing
bead´work
bead´y
beak
beaked
beak´er
beam
beamed
beam´ing
bean
bean´bag
bean´ie
bean´pole
bean´stalk
bear

bear´able
bear´a·bly
beard
beard´ed
beard´less
bear´er
bear´ing
bear´ish
bear´skin
beast
beast´li-ness
beast´ly
beat
beat´en
beat´er
be-at-i-fi-ca´tion
be-at´i-fied
be-at´i-fy
beat´ing
be-at´i-tude
beau´te-ous
beau-ti´cian
beau´ties
beau´ti-fi-ca´tion
beau´ti-fied
beau´ti-fi·er
beau´ti-ful·ly
beau´ti-fy-ing
beau´ty
be-calm´
be-came´
be-cause´
beck´on

beck´on-ing
be-cloud´
be-come´
be-com´ing
be-daub´
be-daz´zle
be-daz´zle-ment
be-daz´zling
bed´bug
bed´clothes
bed´ded
bed´ding
be-dev´il
bed´fel-low
bed´jack·et
bed´lam
bed´post
be-drag´gle
bed´rid-den
bed´rock
bed´roll
bed´room
bed´sheet
bed´side
bed´sore
bed´spread
bed´spring
bed´stead
bed´time
beef
beef´i-ness
beef´steak
beef·y

bee´hive
bee´keep·er
bee´keep-ing
bee´line
beep
beep´er
bees´wax
be-fall´
be-fall´en
be-fell´
be-fit´
be-fit´ting·ly
be-fog´
be-fogged´
be-fog´ging
be-fore´
be-fore´hand
be-fore´time
be-friend´
be-fud´dle
beg
be-gan´
beg´gar
beg´gar-li-ness
beg´gar·ly
beg´ging
be-gin´
be-gin´ner
be-gin´ning
be-grudge´
be-grudg´ing·ly
be-guile´ment
be-guil´er

be-guil´ing·ly
be-gun´
be-half´
be-hav´ior
be-hav´ior·al
be-hav´ior-al·ly
be-hav´ior-ism
be-head´
be-head´ed
be-held´
be-he´moth
be-hest´
be-hind´
be-hind´hand
be-hold´
be-hold´en
be-hold´er
be-hold´ing
be´ing
be-jew´el
be-jew´eled
be-la´bor
be-lat´ed
be-lat´ed·ly
be-lat´ed-ness
be-lay´
belch
be-lea´guer
be-lea´guered
be-lea´guer-ment
bel´fry
be-lie
belief´

be-li´er
be-liev-a·bil´i·ty
be-liev´a·ble
be-liev´a·bly
be-lieve´
be-lieved´
be-liev´er
be-liev´ing
be-lit´tle
be-lit´tle-ment
be-lit´tling
bel´li-cose
bel´li-cose·ly
bel´li-cose-ness
bel-li-cos´i·ty
bel-lig´er-ence
bel-lig´er-en·cy
bel-lig´er-ent
bel´low
bell–shaped
bell´tow·er
bell´weth·er
bel´ly
bel´ly-ache
bel´ly-but-ton
bel´ly-ful
be-long´
be-longed´
be-long´ing
be-long´ings
be-loved´
be-low´
belt

belt´ed	be-quest´	be-tray´al
belt´ing	be-rate´	be-tray´er
be-ly´ing	be-rat´ed	be-troth´
be-moan´	be-rat´ing	be-troth´al
be-moaned´	be-reave´	be-throthed´
be-moan´ing	be-reaved´	bet´ter
be-muse´	be-reave´ment	bet´ter–off
be-mused´	be-reav´ing	bet´ter-ment
be-mus´ed·ly	be-reft´	bet´ting
be-muse´ment	ber´ries	be-tween´
be-mus´ing	ber´ry	be-twixt´
bend´a·ble	ber´ry-like	bev´el
bend´ed	ber-serk´	bev´eled
bend´er	berth	bev´el-ing
bend´ing	berth´ing	bev´er-age
be-neath´	be-seech´	bev´ies
ben-e-dic´tion	be-seeched´	bev´y
ben-e-dic´to·ry	be-seech´er	be-wail´
ben´e-fac-tor	be-seech´ing·ly	be-wail´ing
ben´e-fice	be-set´	be-ware´
ben-e-fi´cial	be-side´	be-wil´der
ben-e-fi´cial·ly	be-smirch´	be-wil´dered
ben-e-fi´cia-ries	be-smirch´er	be-wil´der-ing·ly
ben-e-fi´cia·ry	best–known	be-wil´der-ment
ben´e-fit	best–liked	be-witch´
ben´e-fit·ed	be-stow´	be-witch´ing·ly
ben´e-fit-ing	be-stow´al	be-yond´
be-nev´o-lence	best–paid	bi-an´nu·al
be-nev´o-lent	be-stride´	bi-an´nu-al·ly
be-nign´	best–selling	bi´as
be-nign´ly	be-tide´	bi´ased
be-numb´	be-times´	bi´as-ing
be-queath´	be-tray´	bib-li-og´ra-phy

bib´li-o-phile
bi-cam´er·al
bi-cen-ten´a·ry
bi-cen-ten´ni·al
bick´er
bick´er-ing
bi´cy-cle
bi´cy-cler
bi´cy-clist
bid
bid´den
bid´der
bid´ding
bid´dy
bide
bid´ing
bi-di-rec´tion·al
bi-en´ni-al·ly
bi-fo´cals
bi´fur-cate
bi´fur-cat·ed
bi-fur-ca´tion
big´a-mist
big´a-mous
big´a·my
big´ger
big´heart·ed
big´heart-ed·ly
big´heart-ed-ness
big´ness
big´ot
big´ot·ed
big´ot·ry

big´wig
bike
bik´er
bi-ki´ni
bi-lat´er·al
bi-lat´er-al·ly
bi-lin´e·ar
bi-lin´gual
bil´ious
bil´ious·ly
bil´ious-ness
bill´board
bil´liards
bill´ing
bil´lion
bil´lion-aire
bil´lionth
bill of sale
bil´low
bil´low·y
bi-month´ly
bi´na·ry
bind
bind´er
bind´er·y
bind´ing
bin-oc´u-lars
bi·o-de-grad´a·ble
bi·o-feed´back
bi·o-gen´e-sis
bi-o-ge-net´ic
bi-og´ra-pher
bi·o-graph´ic

bi·o-graph´i-cal
bi-og´ra-phy
bi-o-log´i-cal·ly
bi-ol´o-gist
bi-ol´o·gy
bi-on´ic
bi-on´i-cal·ly
bi´o-rhythm
bi´o-sphere
bi-par´ti-san
bird´bath
bird´cage
bird´house
bird´seed
bird's–eye
birth´day
birth´place
birth´rate
birth´right
birth´stone
bis´cuit
bi·sect´
bi-sec´tion
bish´op
bish´op-ric
bite
bit´er
bit´ing
bit´ten
bit´ter
bit´ter-ness
bit´ter-sweet
biv´ouac

biv´ouacked
biv´ouack-ing
bi-week´ly
bizarre´
blab
blab´ber
black–eyed pea
black´mail
black´out
black´smith
blam´a·ble
blam´a·bly
blame
blamed
blame´ful·ly
blame´ful-ness
blame´less·ly
blame´less-ness
blame´wor-thy
blam´ing
blanch
blanch´er
blanch´ing
bland
blan´dish-ment
bland´ly
bland´ness
blank
blan´ket
blank´ly
blank´ness
blar´ney
bla-sé´

blas´pheme
blas´phem·er
blas´phem-ing
blas´phe-mous·ly
blas´phe·my
blast
blast´ed
blast´er
bla´tant
bla´tant·ly
blath´er
blath´er-ing
blaze
blazed
blaz´er
blaz´ing
bla´zon
bleak
bleak´ly
blear´i·ly
blear´i-ness
blear´y
blear´y–eyed
bleed
bleed´er
bleed´ing
blem´ish
blend
blend´er
blend´ing
bless
bless´ed·ly
bless´ing

blind´ing
blind´ing·ly
blind´ly
blind´ness
blink
blink´er
blink´ing
bliss
bliss´ful·ly
bliss´ful-ness
blis´ter
blis´ter-ing
blis´ter·y
bliz´zard
bloat
bloat´ed
bloat´er
block
block-ade´
block-ad´ed
block-ad´er
block-ad´ing
block´age
block´buster
block´head
blond, blonde
blood
blood´cur-dling
blood´hound
blood´i-est
blood´less
blood´let-ting
blood´shed

blood´stain	bluff	bob´bin
blood´suck·er	bluff´er	bob´bing
blood´thirst·y	bluff´ing	bob´ble
blood´y	blun´der	bob´sled
bloom	blun´der·er	bo-da´cious
bloom´ers	blun´der-ing·ly	bod´ice
bloom´ing	blunt	bod´i·ly
bloop´er	blunt´ly	bod´y
blos´som	blunt´ness	bod´y-build·er
blot	blur	bod´y-guard
blotch	blurred	body–search
blotch´y	blur´red-ness	bod´y-work
blot´ted	blur´ring	bog´gle
blot´ter	blur´ry	bo´gus
blot´ting	blurt	bo´gy
blouse	blurt´ed	boil
blow	blush	boil´er
blow–dry	blushed	boil´ing
blow–dryer	blush´er	bois´ter-ous
blow´er	blush´ing·ly	bois´ter-ous·ly
blown	blus´ter	bois´ter-ous-ness
blow´out	blus´ter-ing·ly	bold
blow´torch	blus´ter-ous	bold´face
bludg´eon	blus´ter·y	bold–faced
blue´berry	board´er	bold´ly
blue´bird	board´ing-house	bold´ness
blue–black	board´walk	bol´ster
blue–blooded	boast	bom-bard´
blue–collar	boast´er	bom-bard´ment
blue–eyed	boast´ful	bom-bas´tic
blue´grass	boast´ing·ly	bom-bas´ti-cal·ly
blue–pencil	boat´house	bo´na fide
blue´print	boat´ing	bo-nan´za

bond´age
bond´ed
bond´ing
bon´fire
bon´net
bon´ny
bo´nus
bon´y
book
book´bind-ing
book´case
book´end
book´ie
book´ing
book´ish-ness
book´keep·er
book´keep-ing
book´let
book´mak·er
book´mark
book´sell·er
book´sell-ing
book´shelf
book´store
book´worm
boor
boor´ish
boor´ish·ly
boor´ish-ness
boost
boost´er
boot
boot´black

boot´ed
boot´ie
boot´leg
boot´leg-ger
boot´leg-ging
boot´strap
boo´ty
booze
booz´er
booz´y
bop
bor´der
bor´dered
bor´der·er
bor´der-line
bore´dom
bor´er
bor´ing
born
borne
bor´ough
bor´row
bor´row·er
bor´row-ing
boss´i-ness
boss´y
bo-tan´i-cal
bo-tan´i-cal·ly
bot´a-nist
bot´a·ny
both´er
both´er-some
bot´tle

bot´tle–fed
bot´tle-neck
bot´tler
bot´tling
bot´tom
bot´tom-less
bought
boul´der
bou´le-vard
bounce
bounc´er
bounc´ing
bounc´y
bound
bound´a-ries
bound´a·ry
bound´ed
bound´er
bound´less-ness
boun´te-ous·ly
boun´te-ous-ness
boun´ti-ful·ly
boun´ti-ful-ness
boun´ty
bou-quet´
bour´bon
bour´geois,
  bour´geoise
bour´geoi-sie´
bourne
bou-tique´
bou´ton-niere´
bow´er

bow´er·y	brain´less	brawn´i·er
bow´ing	brain´pow·er	brawn´i-est
bow´leg-ged	brain´storm	brawn´i-ness
bowl´er	brain´storm-ing	brawn´y
bowl´ing	brain´teas·er	bra´zen
box´car	brain´wash	bra´zen·ly
box´er	brain´wash-ing	bra´zen-ness
box´ing	brain´y	braz´er
box´y	braise	bra´zier
boy´cott	braised	braz´ing
boy´friend	brais´ing	bread
boy´ish	bram´ble	bread´bas-ket
boy´ish-ness	bram´bly	bread´board
brace´let	bran´died	bread´box
brac´ing·ly	bran´dish	bread´crumb
brac´ing-ness	brand–new	bread´pan
brac´ing	bran´dy	breadth
brack´et	brash	bread´win-ner
brack´ish	brash´ly	break
brag	brash´ness	break´a·ble
brag-ga-do´ci·o	bras-siere´	break´age
brag´gart	brass´i-ness	break´a-way
bragged	brass´y	break´down
brag´ger	brave	break´er
brag´ging	brave´heart·ed	break–e´ven
braid	brave´ly	break´fast
braid´ing	brav´er·y	break–in
brain	brav´est	break´ing
brain´child	bra´vo	break´through
brain–dead	bra-vu´ra	break´up
brain´i·er	brawl	breath
brain´i·ly	brawl´er	breath´a·ble
brain´i-ness	brawn	breathe

breath´er
breath´ing
breath´less·ly
breath´less-ness
breath´tak-ing·ly
breed
breed´er
breed´ing
breeze
breeze´way
breez´i·ly
breez´i-ness
breez´y
breth´ren
brev´i·ty
brew
brew´er
brew´er·y
brew´ing
bribe
bribed
brib´er
brib´er·y
brib´ing
bric–a–brac
brick
brick´lay·er
brick´laying
brick´work
brick´yard
brid´al
bride´groom
brides´maid

bridge
bridge´a·ble
bridge´head
bridge´work
bridg´ing
brief
brief´case
brief´ing
brief´ly
bright
bright´en
bright´en·er
bright–eyed
bright´ly
bright´ness
bril´liance
bril´lian·cy
bril´liant
bril´liant·ly
bril´liant-ness
brim
brim´ful
brim´less
brimmed
brim´ming
bring
bring´ing
brin´y
brisk
brisk´ly
brisk´ness
bris´tle
bris´tling

bris´tly
brit´tle
brit´tle-ness
broad´cast
broad´cast-ing
broad´en
broad´ly
broad–mind·ed
broad–spectrum
bro-cade´
bro-cad´ed
bro-chure´
broil
broil´er
broke
bro´ken
broken–down
bro´ken-heart·ed
bro´ker
bro´ker-age
broth´el
broth´er-hood
brother–in–law
broth´er-li-ness
broth´er·ly
brou´ha·ha
brow´beat
brow´beat·er
brow´beat-ing
brown–bag
brown´out
brown´stone
browse

brows´er	buck´tooth	bulg´ing
brows´ing	bu-col´ic	bulg´y
bruise	bu-col´i-cal·ly	bulk´i·er
bruised	bud´ding	bulk´i-ness
bruis´er	bud´dy	bulk´y
bruis´ing	bud´get	bull´doze
brush	bud´get-ar·y	bull´doz·er
brushed	bud´get·ed	bull´doz-ing
brush–off	bud´get·er	bul´le-tin
brush´work	bud´get-ing	bul´let-proof
brusque	buff´er	bull´fight
brusque´ly	buf´fet *(strike)*	bull´fight·er
brusque´ness	buf-fet´ *(food)*	bull´fight-ing
bru´tal	buf-foon´	bull´head·ed
bru-tal´i·ty	buf-foon´er·y	bull´head-ed-ness
bru´tal-ize	buf-foon´ish	bull´horn
bru´tal·ly	bug´a-boo	bul´lied
brute	bug–eyed	bull´ish
brut´ish·ly	bug´gy	bull´ish-ness
brut´ish-ness	bu´gle	bull´pen
bub´ble	bu´gler	bull's–eye
bub´ble-gum	bu´gling	bul´ly
bub´ble-top	build	bul´ly-ing
bub´bli-ness	build´er	bum´ble
bub´bling	build´ing	bum´bler
bub´bly	build´up	bum´bling
buc´ca-neer	built	bum´mer
buck´et	built–in	bump´er
buck´le	built–up	bumper–to–
buck´ler	bul´bous	bumper
buck´ling	bul´bous·ly	bump´i·er
buck´shot	bulge	bump´i·ly
buck´skin	bulg´i-ness	bump´i-ness

bump´kin
bump´tious
bump´y
bun´dle
bun´dling
bun´ga-low
bun´gee
bun´gle
bun´gled
bun´gler
bun´gling
bunk´house
bunt´ing *(cloth)*
buoy´an-cy
buoy´ant
bur´den
bur´dened
bur´den-some
bu´reau
bu-reauc´ra·cy
bu´reau-crat
bu-reau-crat´ic
bur´geon
burg´er
bur´glar
bur´gla-ries
bur´glar-ize
bur´glar-proof
bur´gla·ry
bur´i·al
bur´ied
bur´ies
bur´lap

bur´lesque´
bur´li-ness
bur´ly
burn
burned
burn´er
burn´ish
burnt
bur´row
bur´row·er
burst
burst´ing
bur´y
bur´y-ing
bus´boy
bush
bushed
bush´el
bush´i·er
bush´i-ness
bush´y
bus´ied
bus´i·er
bus´i-est
bus´i·ly
bus´i-ness
bus´i-ness-like
bus´i-ness-man
bus´tle
bus´tled
bus´tler
bus´tling
bus´y

bus´y-bod·y
butch´er
butch´er·y
but´ler
butt
butte
but´ter *(spread)*
butt´er *(one who butts)*
but´ter-ball
but´ter-fat
but´ter-fin-gers
but´ter-i-ness
but´ter·y
but´ton
button–down
but´ton-hole
but´tress
bux´om
bux´om·ly
bux´om-ness
buy
buy´back
buy´er
buy´ing
buy´off
buy´out
buzz´er
buzz´ing
buzz´word
by
by–and–by
bye

by´gone
by´law
by–line
by´pass
by–product
by´stand·er
byte
by´way
by´word

C

ca-bal´
cab´a·la
cab-a-lis´tic
cab-a-ret´
cab´by
cab´driv·er
cab´in
cab´i-net
cab´i-net-mak·er
cab´i-net·ry
cab´i-net-work
ca´ble
ca´ble-cast
ca´ble-gram
ca´ble-vi-sion
ca´bling
ca-boose´
cab´o-tage
cab´stand
cache
cached
ca-chet´

cack´le
cack´ling
ca-coph´o-nous
ca-coph´o-nous·ly
ca-coph´o·ny
ca-dav´er
ca-dav´er-ous
cad´dy
ca´dence
ca´denced
ca-det´
ca-det´ship
cadge
cad´re
ca-fé´
caf-e-te´ri·a
caf´fein-at·ed
caf´feine
caf´tan
cage´ling
ca´gey
ca´gi·er
ca´gi·ly
cag´i-ness
ca-jole´
ca-jol´er·y
ca-jol´ing·ly
ca-lam´i-tous·ly
ca-lam´i-tous-ness
ca-lam´i·ty
cal´cu-la·ble
cal´cu-la-bly
cal´cu-late

cal´cu-lat·ed
cal´cu-lat-ed·ly
cal´cu-lat-ed-ness
cal´cu-lat-ing
cal´cu-lat-ing·ly
cal-cu-la´tion
cal´cu-la-tor
cal´cu·li
cal´cu-lous
cal´cu-lus
cal´en-dar
calf´skin
cal´i-ber
cal´i-brate
cal-i-bra´tion
cal´i-bra-tor
cal´i·co
cal´i-per
ca´liph
ca´liph-ate
cal-is-then´ics
calk
calk´ing
call
call´able
call´er
cal-lig´ra-pher
cal-lig´ra-phy
call´ing
cal-li´o·pe
cal´low
cal´low-ness
calm´ing·ly

37

calm´ly
calm´ness
ca-lor´ic
ca-lor´i-cal·ly
cal´o-rie
cal-o-rif´ic
ca-lum´ni-ate
ca-lum-ni-a´tion
ca-lum´ni-a-tor
cal´um-nies
cal´um·ny
ca-lyp´so
ca-ma-ra´de-rie
cam´bric
cam´cord·er
cam´er·a
cam´er·a-man
camera–ready
camera–shy
cam´i-sole
cam´ou-flage
cam-paign´
cam-paign´er
camp´er
camp´fire
camp´ground
camp´i-ness
camp´site
cam´pus
camp´y
ca-nal´
ca´na·pé
ca-nard´

can´cel
can´cel-a·ble
can´celed
can´cel·er
can´cel-ing
can-cel-la´tion
can´cer
can´cer-ous
can-de-la´bra
can-de-la´brum
can´did
can´di-da·cy
can´di-date
can´did·ly
can´did-ness
can´died
can´dies
can´dle
can´dle-light
can´dle-pow·er
can´dler
can´dle-shade
can´dle-stick
can´dor
can´dy
cane´brake
ca´nine
can´is-ter
can´ker
canned
can´ner
can´ner·y
can´ni-bal

can´ni-bal-ism
can-ni-bal-is´tic
can´ni-bal-ize
can´ni·ly
can´ni-ness
can´ning
can´non
can´non-ade´
can´non-ball
can´non-eer
can´not
can´ny
ca-noe´
ca-noe´ing
ca-noe´ist
ca-noes´
can´o·la
ca-non´i-cal
can-on-i-za´tion
can´on-ize
can´o-pies
can´o·py
can-tan´ker-ous
can-ta´ta
can-teen´
can´vas
can´vas-back
can´vass
can´vass·er
can´yon
ca-pa-bil´i-ties
ca-pa-bil´i·ty
ca´pa·ble

ca´pa·bly
ca-pa´cious
ca-pac´i-tate
ca-pac´i·ty
cap´ful
cap´i·ta
cap´i-tal
cap´i-tal-ism
cap´i-tal-ist
cap-i-tal-is´tic
cap´i-tal-ize
cap´i-tol
ca-pit´u-late
ca-pit-u-la´tion
cap-puc-ci´no
ca-price´
ca-pri´cious·ly
ca-pri´cious-ness
cap´size
cap´siz-ing
cap´su-lar
cap´sule
cap´tain
cap´tion
cap´tious
cap´tious·ly
cap´tious-ness
cap´ti-vate
cap´ti-vat-ing·ly
cap-ti-va´tion
cap´tive
cap-tiv´i·ty
cap´tor

cap´ture
cap´tur·er
cap´tur-ing
ca-rafe´
car´a-mel
car´a-mel-ize
car´at
car´a-van
car-a-van´sa·ry
car´barn
car-bo-hy´drate
car´bon
car-bon-a´tion
car´bun-cle
car´cass
card´board
card–carrying
card´case
car´di-nal
card´sharp
ca-reen´
ca-reer´
care´free
care´ful·ly
care´giv·er
care´less·ly
care´less-ness
ca-ress´
ca-ress´ing·ly
car´et
care´tak·er
care´worn
car´fare

car´go
car´goes
car´i-ca-ture
car´i-ca-tur-ist
car´il-lon
car´nage
car´nal
car´nal·ly
car-na´tion
car´ni-val
car´ni-vore
car-niv´o-rous
car´ol
car´ol·er
car´om
ca-rous´al
ca-rouse´
car-ou-sel´
ca-rous´ing
ca-rous´ing·ly
car´pen-ter
car´pen-try
car´pet
car´pet-ing
carp´ing
car´pool
car´port
car´riage
car´ri·er
car-rou-sel´
car´ried
car´ry
car´ry-all

car´ry–on
car´sick
cart´age
car-tel´
car-tog´ra-pher
car-tog´ra-phy
car´ton
car-toon´
car-toon´ist
car´tridge
cart´wheel
carve
carv´er
carv´ing
cas-cade´
case´book
case´ment
cash–and–carry
cash-ier´
cash´mere
cas´ing
cas´ket
cas´se-role
cas-sette´
cas-ta-net´
cast´a-way
cas´ti-gate
cas-ti-ga´tion
cas-ti-ga´tor
cast´ing
ca´su-al
ca´su-al·ly
ca´su-al-ness

ca´su-al·ty
cat´a-comb
cat´a-log, cat´a-
  logue
cat´a-log·er, cat´a-
  logu·er
cat´a-log-ing, cat´a-
  logu-ing
cat´a-lyst
cat-a-lyt´ic
cat-a-ma-ran´
cat´a-pult
ca-tas´tro-phe
cat-a-stroph´ic
cat-a-stroph´i-cal
catch´all
catch´er
catch´i·er
catch´ing
catch´word
catch´y
cat-e-gor´i-cal
cat-e-gor´i-cal·ly
cat-e-go-ri-za´tion
cat´e-go-rize
cat´e-go·ry
cat´e·nate
ca´ter
ca´ter·er
ca-the´dral
cath´ode
cat´nap
cat´nip

cat´sup
cat´ty
cau´cus
caul´dron
caulk´ing
caus´al
caus´al·ly
cau-sa´tion
caus´a-tive
cause
caus´er
cause´way
caus´ing
caus´tic
caus´ti-cal·ly
cau´tion
cau´tion-ar·y
cau´tious·ly
cau´tious-ness
cav´al-cade´
cav´a-lier´
cav-a-lier´ly
cav´al·ry
ca´ve·at
cave–in
cave´man
cav´ern
cav´ern-ous
cav´il
cav´i·ty
cavort´
ca-vort´ing
cease´less

cease´less·ly
ceas´ing
cede
ced´ed
ced´ing
ceil´ing
ceil´inged
cel´e-brate
cel´e-brat·ed
cel-e-bra´tion
cal´e-bra-tive
cel´e-bra-tor
cel´e-bra-to·ry
ce-leb´ri·ty
ce-ler´i·ty
ce-les´tial
cel´i-ba·cy
cel´i-bate
cel´lar
cell´mate
cel´lo
cel´lo-phane
cel´lu-lar
cel´lu-lite
ce-ment´
cem´e-ter-ies
cem´e-ter·y
cen´sor
cen´sor-a·ble
cen-so´ri·al
cen-so´ri-ous·ly
cen´sor-ship
cen´sur-a·ble

cen´sure
cen´sured
cen´sur-ing
cen´sus
cen-te-nar´i·an
cen-ten´ni·al
cen´ter
cen´ter-fold
cen´ter-line
cen´ter-piece
cen´ti-grade
cen´ti-gram
cen´ti-me-ter
cen´tral
cen-tral-i-za´tion
cen´tral-ize
cen´tral·ly
cen´tre (Br.)
cen´tric
cen-tric´i·ty
cen-trif´u-gal
cen´tri-fuge
cen´trist
cen´tu·ry
ce-ram´ic
ce´re-al
cer-e-mo´ni·al
cer-e-mo´ni-al·ly
cer´e-mo-nies
cer-e-mo´ni-ous
cer-e-mo´ni-ous·ly
cer´e-mo·ny
cer´tain

cer´tain·ly
cer´tain·ty
cer´ti-fi-a·ble
cer´ti-fi-a·bly
cer-tif´i-cate
cer-ti-fi-ca´tion
cer´ti-fied
cer´ti-fies
cer´ti-fy
cer´ti-fy-ing
ces-sa´tion
cess´pool
cha-grin´
cha-grined´
chair
chair´lift
chair´per-son
chaise
chal-ced´o·ny
chal´dron
cha´let
chal´ice
chalk
chalk´y
chal´lenge
chal´leng·er
chal´leng-ing
cham´ber
cham´ber-maid
cham´ois
cham´o-mile
cham-pagne´
cham´pi·on

cham´pi-on-ship
chan´cel
chan´cel-lor
chanc´i-ness
chanc´y
chan´de-lier´
change´a·ble
change´a·ble-ness
change´a·bly
changed
change´less·ly
change´less-ness
change´ling
chang´er
chang´ing
chan´nel
chan´neled
chan´nel-ing
chant
chant´er
cha´os
cha-ot´ic
cha-ot´i-cal·ly
chap´el
chap´er·on
chap´lain
chap´lain·cy
chap´ter
char´ac-ter
char-ac-ter-is´tic
char-ac-ter-i-
   za´tion
char´ac-ter-ize

cha-rade´
char´coal
charge´a·ble
charge´a·bly
charged
charg´er
charg´ing
cha-ris´ma
char´is-mat´ic
char´i-ta·ble
char´i-ta·ble-ness
char´i-ta·bly
char-i-ties
char´i·ty
char´la-tan
charm
charmed
charm´er
charm´ing·ly
char´ter *(grant)*
chart´er *(planner)*
chartreuse´
chase
chased
chas´er
chas´ing
chasm
chas´sis
chaste
chaste´ly
chaste´ness
chas´ten
chas-tise´ment

chas-tis´er
chas´ti·ty
châ-teau´
cha-teaux´ *(pl.)*
chat´tel
chat´ter
chat´ter-box
chat´ter·er
chat´ti·ly
chat´ti-ness
chat´ting
chat´ty
chauf´feur
chau´vin-ism
chau´vin-ist
chau-vin-is´ti-cal·ly
cheap
cheap´en
cheap´ened
cheap´ly
cheap´skate
cheat
cheat´er
check´book
checked
cheek´er
check´er-board
check´ered
check´ers
check´list
check–out
check´point
check´up

42

cheek´bone

cheek´y

cheer´ful

cheer´ful·ly

cheer´ful-ness

cheer´i·ly

cheer´i-ness

cheer´lead·er

cheer´less

cheer´y

chees´y

chem´i-cal

chem´i-cal·ly

che-mise´

chem´ist

chem´is-try

cher´ish

cher´ish-a·ble

cher´ish·er

cher´ish-ing·ly

cher´ub

che-ru´bic

cher´u-bim *(pl.)*

chest

chest´ed

chest´ful

chest´i·ly

chest´nut

chest´y

chev´ron

chew´a·ble

chew´ing

chew´y

chew´i-ness

chi-ca´ner·y

chi´cle

chide

chid´ing·ly

chief

chief´ly

chief of state

chief´tain

chif-fon´

chif-fo-nade´

chi´gnon

child

child´bear-ing

child´birth

child´hood

child´ish·ly

child´ish-ness

child´like

chil´dren

chill´i-ness

chill´ing·ly

chill´y

chime

chimed

chim´er

chi-me´ra

chi-mer´i-cal

chim´ing

chim´ney

chi´na-ware

chintz

chintz´y

chip´board

chip´per

chis´el

chis´el·er

chis´el-ing

chit´chat

chi-val´ric

chiv´al-rous·ly

chiv´al-rous-ness

chiv´al·ry

choc´o-late

choice

choic´est

choir

choir´boy

choir´mas-ter

choke

choked

chok´er

chok´ing

chol´er

cho-les´ter·ol

cho´line

choose

choos´y

choos´ing

chop

chop´per

chop´pi-ness

chop´ping

chop´py

chop´stick

cho´ral

cho-rale´
cho´re-o-graph
cho-re-og´ra-pher
cho-re-o-graph´ic
cho-re-og´ra-phy
cho´ris-ter
chor´tle
chor´tling
cho´rus
chose
cho´sen
chow´der
chris´ten
chris´ten-ing
chron´ic
chron´i-cal·ly
chron´i-cle
chron´i-cler
chron´i-cling
chron-o-log´ic
chron-o-log´i-cal
chro-nol´o·gy
chro-nom´e-ter
chub´by
chuck´le
chuck´led
chuckle-head
chuck´ling
chum´mi·ly
chum´mi-ness
chum´my
chunk´i·ly
chunk´i-ness

chunk´y
church
church´go·er
church´ly
church´yard
churl
churl´ish
churl´ish·ly
churl´ish-ness
churn
churn´er
chutz´pa
ci-gar´
cig-a-rette´,
　cig-a-ret´
cigar–shaped
cinc´ture
cin´der
cin´e-ma
cin-e-ma-theque´
cin-e-mat´ic
cin-e-mat´i-cal·ly
ci´pher
ci´pher-a·ble
cir´cle
cir´cled
cir´clet
cir´cling
cir´cuit·ry
cir-cu´i·ty
cir-cu´i-tous
cir´cu-lar
cir-cu-lar´i·ty

cir´cu-lar-ize
cir´cu-late
cir-cu-la´tion
cir´cu-la-tor
cir´cu-la-to·ry
cir-cum´fer-ence
cir-cum-fer-en´tial
cir-cum-lo-cu´tion
cir-cum-nav´i-gate
cir´cum-scribe
cir-cum-scrip-tion
cir´cum-spect
cir-cum-spec´tion
cir-cum-spec´tive
cir´cum-stance
cir´cum-stanced
cir-cum-stan´tial
cir-cum-stan´tial·ly
cir-cum-stan´ti-ate
cir´cum-vent
cir-cum-ven´tion
cir´cus
cis´tern
cit´a-del
ci-ta´tion
ci-ta´tion-al
cit´ies
cit´ied
cit´i-fied
cit´i-fy
cit´ing
cit´i-zen
cit´i-zen·ry

cit´i-zen-ship
cit´y
cit´y-scape
city–state
cit´y-wide
civic–minded
civ´ics
civ´il
ci-vil´ian
ci-vil´i-ty
civ-i-li-za´tion
civ´i-lize
civ´i-lized
civ´i-liz-ing
civ´il·ly
claim
claim´ant
claim´er
clair-voy´ance
clair-voy´ant
clair-voy´ant·ly
clam´ber
clam´mi·ly
clam´mi-ness
clam´my
clam´or
clam´or·er
clam´or-ous
clam´or-ous·ly
clam´or-ous-ness
clamp
clan-des´tine
clan-des´tine·ly

clan-des´tine-ness
clang
clang´er
clang´or-ous
clan´nish
clans´man
clap
clapped
clap´per
clap´ping
clap´trap
clar-i-fi-ca´tion
clar´i-fied
clar´i-fy
clar´i-fy-ing
clar´i-on
clar´i-ty
clasp
clasp´er
clas´sic
clas´si-cal·ly
clas´si-fi-a·ble
clas-si-fi-ca´tion
clas´si-fied
clas´si-fi-er
clas´si-fy
clas´si-fy-ing
class´mate
class´room
class´y
clat´ter
clat´tered
clat´ter·er

clat´ter-ing
clau-di-ca´tion
claus´al
clause
claus-tro-pho´bi·a
claus-tro-pho´bic
cla-vier´
clay
clay´ey
clean
clean–cut
clean´er
clean–handed
clean´li-ness
clean´ly
clean´ness
cleanse
cleansed
cleans´er
clean–shaven
cleans´ing
clean´up
clear´ance
clear–cut
clear–eyed
clear´head·ed
clear´head-ed-ness
clear´ing-house
clear´ly
clear–sight´ed
clear´wing
cleav´age
cleave

cleaved
cleav´er
cleav´ing
clem´en·cy
clem´ent
clem´ent·ly
cler´gy
cler´gy-man
cler´ic
cler´i-cal
clev´er
clev´er·ly
clev´er-ness
cli-che´
cli-ched´
click
click´er
cli´ent
cli´en-tele´
cliff
cliff´hang·er
cliff´y
cli-mac´tic
cli-mac´ti-cal·ly
cli´mate
cli-mat´ic
cli´ma-tize
cli-ma-tol´o·gy
cli´max
climb
climb´a·ble
climbed
climb´er

climb´ing
clinch
clinch´er
cling
cling´er
cling´i-ness
cling´ing
cling´y
clin´ic
clin´i-cal·ly
cli-ni´cian
clink
clink´er
clip
clip´board
clip–on
clipped
clip´per
clip´ping
clique
cli´quish
cli´quish-ness
cloak
cloak–and–dagger
clob´ber
cloche
clock´mak·er
clock´mak-ing
clock´wise
clock´work
clod
clod´hopper
clod´dish

clois´ter
clois´tered
clois´tral
close
close–by
close call
closed
closed–circuit
closed–door
close–fisted
close–fitting
close–knit
close´ly
close´mouthed
close´ness
close´out
clos´est
clos´et
clos´et-ful
close–up
clos´ing
clo´sure
cloth
clothe
clothes´horse
clothes´line
clothes´pin
cloth´ier
cloth´ing
clo´ture
cloud´burst
cloud´i-ness
cloud´less

cloud´y

clo´ver-leaf

clown

clown´ish

clown´ish·ly

cloy´ing·ly

club

clubbed

club´ber

club´bi-ness

club´bing

club´by

club´house

clum´si·er

clum´si·ly

clum´si-ness

clum´sy

clunk

clunk´er

clunk´y

clus´ter

clus´ter·y

clutch

clut´ter

co-ag´u-lant

co-ag´u-late

co-ag-u-la´tion

co-a-lesce´

co-a-les´cence

co-a-les´cent

co-a-lesc´ing

co-a-li´tion

co-an´chor

co´apt

coarse´ly

coars´en

coarse´ness

coast´al

coast´er

coast´line

coast–to–coast

coat

coat´ed

coat´ing

coat´rack

coat´room

coat´tail

co-au´thor,

  co–au´thor

coax

co-ax´i·al

coax´ing

coax´ing·ly

cob´bler

cob´ble-stone

cob´web

cock´eyed

cock´i·ly

cock´i-ness

cock´tail

cock´y

co-coon´

cod´dle

code

cod´ed

co-de-fend´ant

co-de-pend´ence

co-de-pend´en·cy

co-de-pend´ent

codg´er

cod´i-cil

cod-i-fi-ca´tion

cod´i-fied

cod´i·fy

cod´ling

co´ed

co-ed-u-ca´tion·al

co´ef-fi´cient

co-erce´

co-erc´i·ble

co-erc´ing

co-er´cion

co-er´cive·ly

co-er´cive-ness

co-ex-ist´

co-ex-is´tence

cof´fee-cake

cof´fee-house

cof´fee-pot

cof´fer

cof´fin

co´gent

cog´i-tate

cog´i-tat-ing

cog-i-ta´tion

cog´i-ta-tor

cog-ni´tion

cog´ni-tive

co-hab´it

co-hab´i-tate
co-hab-i-ta´tion
co-here´
co-her´ence
co-her´ent·ly
co-he´sion
co-he´sive·ly
co-he´sive-ness
co´hort
co–host´
coin´age
co-in-cide´
co-in´ci-dence
co-in´ci-dent
co-in-ci-den´tal
co-in-ci-den´tal·ly
co-in-cid´ing
coin–operated
co-in-sur´ance
co-in-sure´
col´an-der
cold´–blood´ed
cold´heart´ed
cold´ly
cold´ness
col´ic
col´ick·y
col-i-se´um
col-lab´o-rate
col-lab´o-rat-ing
col-lab-o-ra´tion
col-lab´o-ra-tive
col-lab´o-ra-tor

col-lage´
col-lapse´
col-lapsed´
col-laps´i·ble
col-laps´ing
col´lar-bone
col´lar but-ton
col-late´
col-lat´er-al
col-lat´er-al-ize
col-lat´ing
col-la´tion
col-la´tor
col´league
col-lect´
col-lect´ed
col-lect´i·ble
col-lec´tion
col-lec´tive·ly
col-lec´tor
col´leen
col´lege
col-le´gi·al
col-le´gian
col-le´giate
col-lide´
col-lid´ing
col-li´sion
col-lo´qui·al
col-lo´qui-al-ism
col-lo´qui-al·ly
col´lo-quy
col-lude´

col-lud´ing
col-lu´sion
col-lu´sive
co-logne´
co´lon
col´o-nel
co-lo´ni·al
co-lo´ni-al-ism
col-o-ni-za´tion
col´o-nize
col-on-nade´
col´o-phon
col´or
col´or-ant
col-or-a´tion
col´or-bear·er
color–blind
color–code
col´ored
col´or-fast
col´or-ful
col´or-ist
col´or-ize
col-or-i-za´tion
col´or-less
co-los´sal
co-los´sus
col´our (Br.)
colt´ish
col´umn
co-lum´nar
col´um-nist
co´ma

co´ma-tose
com´bat *(n., v.)*
com-bat´ *(v.)*
com-bat´ant
com-bat´ing
com-bat´ive
comb´er
com-bin´a·ble
com-bin-a·bil´i·ty
com-bi-na´tion
com-bine´ *(to join)*
com´bine *(n. harvester)*
com-bin´ing
com´bo
com-bust´
com-bus´ti·ble
com-bus´tion
come´back
co-me´di·an
co-me´dic
com´e-dies
com´e·dy
come–hither
come´li-ness
come·ly
come–on
co-mes´ti·ble
com´et
come-up´pance
com´fit
com´fort
com´fort-a·ble

com´fort-a·bly
com´fort·er
com´fy
com´ic
com´i-cal·ly
com´ing
coming–out
com´ma
com-mand´
com´man-dant
com´man-deer´
com-mand´er
com-mand´ing
com-mand´ing·ly
com-mand´ment
com-man´do
com-man´dos
com-mem´o-rate
com-mem´o-rat-ing
com-mem-o-ra´tion
com-mem´o-ra-tive
com-mem´o-ra-to·ry
com-mence´
com-mence´ment
com-menc´ing
com-mend´a·ble
com-mend´a·bly
com-men-da´tion
com-men´su-rate
com´ment
com´men-tar·y
com´men-ta-tor

com´merce
com-mer´cial
com-mer´cial-ism
com-mer-ci-al´i-ty
com-mer-cial-i-za´tion
com-mer´cial-ize
com-mer´cial-ized
com-mer´cial·ly
com-min´gle
com-min´gling
com-mis´er-ate
com-mis-er-a´tion
com´mis-sar·y
com-mis´sion
com-mis´sion-a·ble
com-mis´sioned
com-mis´sion·er
com-mit´ment
com-mit´ted
com-mit´tee
com-mit´ting
com-mo´di-ous
com-mo´di-ous·ly
com-mod´i-ties
com-mod´i·ty
com´mo-dore
com´mon
com-mon-al´i·ty
com´mon-al·ty
com´mon·er
com´mon·ly
com´mon-place

com´mon-weal
com´mon-wealth
com-mo´tion
com-mu´nal
com-mu´nal·ly
com-mu-nal-is´tic
com-mu-nal´i·ty
com-mu´nal-ize
com-mune´ *(v.)*
com´mune *(n.)*
com-mu´ni-ca·ble
com-mu´ni-cate
com-mu´ni-cat-ing
com-mu´ni-ca´tion
com-mu´ni-ca´-
　tion·al
com-mu´ni-ca-tive
com-mu´ni-ca-tor
com-mu´nion
com´mu-nism
com´mu-nist
com´mu-nis´tic
com-mu´ni-ties
com-mu´ni·ty
com-mu-ta´tion
com-mute´
com-mut´er
com-mut´ing
com´pact *(n.)*
com-pact´ *(adj., v.)*
com-pact´ed
com-pact´ly
com-pact´ness

com-pac´tor
com´pa-nies
com-pan´ion
com-pan´ion-ship
com´pa·ny
com-pa-ra-bil´i·ty
com´pa-ra·ble
com´pa-ra·bly
com-par´a-tive·ly
com-pare´
com-par´ing
com-par´i-son
com-par´i-son–
　shop
com-part´ment
com-part-men´tal
com-part-men´tal-
　ize
com´pass
com´pass·es
com-pas´sion
com-pas´sion-ate
com-pat-i-bil´i·ty
com-pat´i·ble
com-pat´i·bly
com-pa´tri·ot
com-pel´
com-pel´la·bly
com-pelled´
com-pel´ling
com-pel´ling·ly
com-pen´di-ous
com-pen´di-ous·ly

com-pen´di·um
com´pen-sate
com´pen-sat-ing
com-pen-sa´tion
com-pen-sa´tion·al
com-pen´sa-to·ry
com-pete´
com´pe-tence
com´pe-ten·cy
com´pe-tent
com´pe-tent·ly
com-pet´ing
com-pe-ti´tion
com-pet´i-tive
com-pet´i-tive·ly
com-pet´i-tive-ness
com-pet´i-tor
com-pi-la´tion
com-pile´
com-pil´er
com-pil´ing
com-pla´cence
com-pla´cen-cy
com-pla´cent·ly
com-plain´
com-plain´ant
com-plain´ing·ly
com-plaint´
com-plai´sance
com-plai´sant·ly
com-plect´ed
com´ple-ment
com-ple-men´ta·ry

com-plete
com-plet´ed
com-plete´ly
com-plete´ness
com-ple´tion
com´plex
com-plex´ion
com-plex´ioned
com-plex´i·ty
com-plex´ness
com-pli´a·ble
com-pli´ance
com-pli´ant
com´pli-cate
com´pli-cat·ed
com´pli-ca´tion
com-plic´i·ty
com-plied´
com´pli-ment
com´pli-men´ta·ry
com-ply´ing
com-po´nent
com-port´ment
com-pos´a·ble
com-pose´
com-posed´
com-pos´er
com-pos´ite
com-po-si´tion
com-pos´i-tor
com´post
com-po´sure
com´pote

com´pound (n., adj.)
com-pound´ (v., adj.)
com-pre-hend´
com-pre-hend´i·ble
com-pre-hen´si·ble
com-pre-hen´sion
com-pre-hen´sive
com´press (n.)
com-press´ (v.)
com-pressed´
com-press´i·ble
com-pres´sion
com-prise´
com-pris´ing
comp-trol´ler
comp-trol´ler-ship
com-pul´sion
com-pul´sive·ly
com-pul´sive-ness
com-pul´so·ry
com-punc´tion
com-punc´tious
com-pu-ta´tion
com-put´a·ble
com-put´a·bly
com-put-a-bil´i·ty
com-pute´
com-put´er
com-put´er-ize
com-put-er-i-za´- tion

com-put´ing
com´rade
com´rade·ly
com´rade-ship
con-cat´e-nate
con-cat-e-na´tion
con´cave
con´cave´ly
con-cave´ness
con-cav´i·ty
con-ceal´a·ble
con-ceal-a·bil´i·ty
con-ceal´ment
con-cede´
con-ced´ed·ly
con-ced´er
con-ced´ing
con-ceit´
con-ceit´ed
con-ceiv-a·bil´i·ty
con-ceiv´a·ble
con-ceiv´a·bly
con-ceive´
con-ceiv´ing
con´cen-trate
con´cen-trat·ed
con´cen-trating
con´cen-tra´tion
con´cen-tra-tive
con-cen´tric
con-cen´tri-cal·ly
con-cen-tric´i·ty
con´cept

con-cep´tive
con-cep´tu·al
con-cep´tu·al-ize
con-cep-tu·al-i-za´-
  tion
con-cep´tu·al·ly
con-cern´
con-cerned´
con-cern´ing
con´cert (n.)
con-cert´ (v.)
con-cert´ed
con-cer´to
con-ces´sion
con-ces´sion-aire´
con-cierge´
con-cil´i-ate
con-cil´i-at-ing
con-cil-i-a´tion
con-cil´i-a-tor
con-cil´ia-to·ry
con-cise´ly
con-cise´ness
con´clave
con-clude´
con-clud´ing
con-clu´sion
con-clu´sive·ly
con-clu´sive-ness
con-coct´
con-coc´tion
con-com´i-tance
con-com´i-tan·cy

con-com´i-tant
con´cord (n.)
con-cord´ (v.)
con-cor´dance
con-cor´dant
con´course
con´crete,
  con-crete´
con-crete´ly
con-crete´ness
con´cu-bine
con-cur´
con-curred´
con-cur´rence
con-cur´ren·cy
con-cur´rent·ly
con-cur´ring·ly
con-cus´sion
con-demn´
con-dem´na·ble
con-dem-na´tion
con-demned´
con-demn´er
con-demn´ing
con-dens´a·ble
con-den´sate
con-den-sa´tion
con-dense´
con-densed´
con-dens´er
con-dens´ing
con-de-scend´
con-de-scend´ence

con-de-scend´ing·ly
con-de-scen´sion
con´di-ment
con-di´tion·al
con-di´tion-al·ly
con-di´tioned
con-di´tion·er
con-di´tion-ing
con-do´lence
con-dol´ing
con´dom
con-do-min´i·um
con-don´a·ble
con-done´
con-duce´
con-du´cive
con´duct (n.)
con-duct´ (v.)
con-duct´ed
con-duc´tion
con-duc-tiv´i·ty
con-duc´tor
con´duit
con-fab´u-late
con-fab-u-la´tion
con-fec´tion-ar·y
con-fec´tion·er
con-fec´tion-er·y
con-fed´er-a·cy
con-fed´er-ate
con-fed-er-a´tion
con-fer´
con´fer·ee´

con'fer-ence
con-fer'ment
con-ferred'
con-fer'ring
con-fess'
con-fessed'
con-fess'ed·ly
con-fes'sion
con-fes'sion·al
con-fes'sor
con'fi-dant
con-fide'
con-fid'ed
con'fi-dence
con'fi-dent
con-fi-den'tial
con-fi-den-ti-al'i·ty
con-fi-den'tial·ly
con'fi-dent·ly
con-fid'ing·ly
con-fig-u-ra'tion
con-fig-u-ra'tive
con-fig'ure
con-fin'a·ble
con-fine' (v.)
con'fine (n.)
con-fined'
con-fine'a·ble
con-fin'ed-ness
con-fine'ment
con-fin'er
con-fin'ing
con-firm'

con-firm'a·ble
con-firm-a·bil'i·ty
con-fir-ma'tion
con-fis'ca·ble
con'fis-cate
con'fis-ca'tion
con-fis'ca-to·ry
con-fla-gra'tion
con'flict (n.)
con-flict' (v.)
con-flict'ing
con-flic'tive
con-flic'to·ry
con'flu-ence
con'flu'ent
con-form'
con-form'a·ble
con-form'ance
con-for-ma'tion
con-for-ma'tion·al
con-form'ist
con-form'i·ty
con-found'
con-found'a·ble
con-found'ed
con-fra-ter'ni·ty
con-front'
con-fron-ta'tion·al
con-fus'a·ble
con-fus'a·bly
con-fuse'
con-fused'
con-fus'ing·ly

con-fu'sion
con-fu-ta'tion
con-fute'
con-geal'
con-geal'a·ble
con'ge-ner
con-ge-ner'ic
con-ge'nial
con-ge-ni·al'i·ty
con-gen'i-tal
con-gen'i-tal·ly
con-gest'
con-gest'ed
con-ges'tion
con-ges'tive
con-glom'er-ate
con-glom-er-a'tion
con-grat'u-late
con-grat'u-lat-ing
con-grat-u-la'tion
con-grat'u-la-to·ry
con'gre-gate
con-gre-ga'tion·al
con'gress
con-gres'sio-nal
con'gress-man
con'gress-per-son
con'gress-wom·an
con-gru'ence
con-gru'en-cy
con-gru'ent·ly
con-gru'i·ty
con'gru-ous·ly

53

con´ic
con´i-cal
con-jec´tur-a·bly
con-jec´tur·al
con-jec´ture
con-join´
con´ju-gal
con´ju-gal·ly
con-junc´tion
con-junc´tive
con-junc´ture
con´jure, con-jure´
con´jur·er
con-nect´
con-nect-a·bil´i·ty
con-nect´a·ble
con-nect´ed
con-nect´er
con-nect-i·bil´i·ty
con-nect´i·ble
con-nec´tion
con-nec´tive
con-nec-tiv´i·ty
con-nec´tor
con-nip´tion
con-niv´ance
con-nive´
con-niv´er·y
con´nois-seur´
con´no-ta´tion
con´no-ta-tive
con´no-ta-tive·ly
con-note´

con-not´ing
con-nu´bi·al
con´quer
con´quer-a·ble
con´quered
con´quer-ing
con´quer·or
con´quest
con-quis´ta-dor
con-san-guin´e·ous
con-san-guin´-
    e·ous·ly
con-san-guin´i·ty
con´science
con-sci-en´tious
con-sci-en´tious·ly
con-sci-en´tious-
    ness
con´scion-a·ble
con´scion-a·bly.
con´scious·ly
con´scious-ness
con-scribe´
con´script (n.)
con-script´ (v.)
con-scrip´tion
con´se-crate
con´se-crat-ing
con-se-cra´tion
con´se-cra-tor
con-sec´u-tive·ly
con-sen´su-al·ly
con-sen´sus

con-sent´ing·ly
con-sent´er
con-sen´tient·ly
con´se-quence
con´se-quent
con-se-quen´tial
con-se-quen´tial·ly
con´se-quent·ly
con-serv´an·cy
con-ser-va´tion·al
con-serv´a-tism
con-serv´a-tive·ly
con-serv´a-tive-
    ness
con´ser-va-tor
con-serv´a-to·ry
con-serve´
con-serv´ing
con-sid´er
con-sid´er-a·ble
con-sid´er-a·bly
con-sid´er-ate·ly
con-sid-er-a´tion
con-sid´ered
con-sid´er-ing
con-sign´
con-sign´a·ble
con-sig-na´tion
con´sign·ee´
con-sign´ment
con-sign´or
con-sist´
con-sist´ence

con-sist´en·cy

con-sist´ent·ly

con-sis´to·ry

con-sol´a·ble

con-so-la´tion

con-sole´ *(v.)*

con´sole *(n.)*

con-sol´i-date

con-sol´i-dat-ing

con-sol-i-da´tion

con-sol´ing

con-sol´ing·ly

con´so-nance

con´so-nant

con-sort´ *(v.)*

con´sort *(n.)*

con-sor´ti·al

con-sor´ti·um

con-spic´u-ous

con-spic´u-ous·ly

con-spic´u-ous-ness

con-spir´a·cy

con-spir´a-tive

con-spir´a-tor

con-spir´a-to´ri-
al·ly

con-spire´

con-spir´ing

con´sta·ble

con-stab´u-lar·y

con´stan·cy

con´stant

con´stant·ly

con-stel-la´tion

con´ster-nate

con-ster-na´tion

con´sti-pate

con´sti-pat·ed

con-sti-pa´tion

con-stit´u-en·cy

con-stit´u-ent

con´sti-tute

con-sti-tu´tion

con-sti-tu´tion·al

con -sti-tu´-tion-
al·ly

con-strain´

con-strain´a·ble

con-strained´

con-strain´ing

con-straint´

con-strict´

con-stric´tion

con-stric´tive

con-stric´tor

con-strin´gen·cy

con-strin´gent

con-stru´a·ble

con-stru´al

con-struct´ *(v.)*

con´struct *(n.)*

con-struct´i·ble

con-struc´tion

con-struc´tive

con-struc´tive·ly

con-struc´tor

con-strue´

con-strued´

con-stru´ing

con´sul

con´sul·ar

con´sul-ate

con-sult´

con-sult´an·cy

con-sult´ant

con-sul-ta´tion

con-sult´ing

con-sul´tor

con-sum´a·ble

con-sume´

con-sumed´

con-sum´er

con-sum´er-ism

con-sum´ing

con-sum´mate
    (adj.)

con´sum-mate
    (v., adj.)

con-sum-ma´tion

con-sump´tion

con´tact

con-ta´gion

con-ta´gious

con-ta´gious-ness

con-tain´

con-tain´a·ble

con-tained´

con-tain´er-ize

con-tain´ing

con-tain´ment
con-tam´i-na·ble
con-tam´i-nant
con-tam´i-nate
con-tam´i-nat·ed
con-tam´i-nat-ing
con-tam-i-na´tion
con-tam´i-na-tive
con-tam´i-na-tor
con-temn´
con-temn´er
con-tem´pla·ble
con´tem-plate
con´tem-plat-ing
con-tem-pla´tion
con-tem´pla-tive
con-tem-po-ra-ne´-
  i·ty
con-tem-po-ra´ne-
  ous
con-tem-po-ra´ne-
  ous·ly
con-tem-po-ra´ne-
  ous-ness
con-tem´po-rar·y
con-tem´po-rize
con-tempt´
con-tempt-i-bil´i·ty
con-tempt´i·ble
con-tempt´i·ble-
  ness
con-temp´tu-ous
con-temp´tu-ous·ly

con-tend´
con-tend´er
con-tent´ *(adj., v.,*
  n.)
con´tent *(n.)*
con-tent´ed
con-tent´ed·ly
con-tent´ed-ness
con-ten´tion
con-ten´tious·ly
con-ten´tious-ness
con-tent´ly
con-tent´ment
con-tent´ness
con´tents
con-ter´mi-nous
con-ter´mi-nous·ly
con-ter´mi-nous-
  ness
con´test *(n.)*
con-test´ *(v.)*
con-test´a·ble
con-test´a·bly
con-tes´tant
con´text
con-tex´tu-al
con-tex´tu-al·ly
con-ti-gu´i·ty
con-tig´u-ous
con-tig´u-ous·ly
con-tig´u-ous-ness
con´ti-nence
con´ti-nent

con-ti-nen´tal
con-ti-nen´tal·ly
con´ti-nent·ly
con-tin´gence
con-tin´gen·cy
con-tin´gent·ly
con-tin´u-a·ble
con-tin´u-al
con-tin´u-al·ly
con-tin´u-ance
con-tin-u-a´tion
con-tin´ue
con-tin´u-ing
con-ti-nu´i·ty
con-tin´u-ous·ly
con-tin´u-ous-ness
con-tin´u·um
con-tort´
con-tort´ed
con-tor´tion
con-tor´tion-ist
con´tour
con´tra
con´tra-band
con´tra-cep´tion
con´tra-cep´tive
con´tract *(n., v.)*
con-tract´ *(v.)*
con-tract´ed
con-tract-i-bil´i·ty
con-tract´i·ble
con-trac´tion
con´trac-tor

con-trac´tu·al
con-trac´tu-al·ly
con-tra-dict´a·ble
con-tra-dict´
con-tra-dic´tion
con-tra-dic´tive·ly
con-tra-dic´tive-
  ness
con-tra-dic´to·ry
con-tra-dis-tinc´-
  tion
con-tra-dis-tinc´-
  tive
con-tral´to
con-trap´tion
con´trar-i-ness
con´trar·i-wise
con´trar·y
con-trast´ *(v.)*
con´trast *(n.)*
con-trast´a·bly
con-trast´ing·ly
con-trast´y
con-tra-vene´
con-tra-ven´tion
con´tre-temps
con-trib´ut-a·ble
con-trib´ute
con-trib´ut-ing
con-tri-bu´tion
con-trib´u-tive
con-trib´u-tor
con-trib´u-to·ry

con-trite´
con-trite´ly
con-trite´ness
con-tri´tion
con-triv´a·ble
con-triv´ance
con-trive´
con-trived´
con-triv´er
con-triv´ing
con-trol´
con-trol´la·ble
con-trol´la·bly
con-trol-led´
con-trol´ler
con-trol´ling
con-tro-ver´sial
con-tro-ver´sial·ly
con´tro-ver·sy
con´tro-vert
con-tro-vert´i·ble
con-tro-vert´i·bly
con-tu-ma´cious
con-tu-ma´cious·ly
con-tu-ma´cious-
  ness
con-tu´ma·cy
con-tu-me´li-ous
con-tu-me´li-ous·ly
con-tu´me·ly
con-tu´sion
co-nun´drum
con-va-lesce´

con-va-les´cence
con-va-les´cent
con-va-lesc´ing
con-vect´
con-vec´tion
con-vec´tion·al
con-vene´
con-ve´nience
con-ve´nient
con-ve´nient·ly
con-ven´ing
con´vent
con-ven´tion
con-ven´tion·al
con-ven´tion-al´i·ty
con-ven´tion-al·ly
con-ven-tion-eer´
con-verge´
con-ver´gence
con-ver´gen·cy
con-ver´gent
con-verg´ing
con-ver´sance
con-ver´sant
con-ver-sa´tion
con-ver-sa´tion·al
con-ver-sa´tion-al-
  ist
con´verse
  (reversed)
con-verse´ *(speak)*
con-verse´ly
con-vers´ing

con-ver´sion
con´vert (n.)
con-vert´ (v.)
con-vert´i·ble
con´vex
con-vex´i·ty
con-vey´
con-vey´a·ble
con-vey´ance
con-vey´ing
con-vey´or
con´vict (n.)
con-vict´ (v.)
con-vict´a·ble
con-vic´tion
con-vince´
con-vinc´i·ble
con-vinc´ing·ly
con-viv´i·al
con-viv-i-al´i·ty
con-viv´i-al·ly
con-vo-ca´tion
con-vo-ca´tion·al
con-voke´
con-vok´ing
con´vo-lute
con´vo-lut·ed
con´vo-lute·ly
con-vo-lu´tion
con-vo-lu´tion·al
con´voy
con-vulse´
con-vul´sion

con-vul´sive
con-vul´sive·ly
cook´book
cook´er
cook´er·y
cook´ie
cook´ing
cook´off
cook´out
cook´stove
cook´ware
cool´ant
cool´er
coo´lie
cool´ly
cool´ness
coop´er-age
co-op´er-ate
co-op-er-a´tion
co-op´er-a-tive·ly
co-or´di-nate
co-or-di-na´tion
co-or´di-na-tor
cop´i·er
cop´ies
co´pi´lot
cop´ing
co´pi-ous
co´pi-ous·ly
co´pi-ous-ness
cop–out
cop´per-plate
copse

cop´ter
cop´u-late
cop-u-la´tion
cop´y
cop´y-cat
cop´y-ed-i-tor
cop´y-ing
cop´y-right
cop´y-right·ed
cor´dial
cor-dial´i·ty
cor´dial·ly
cord´less
cor´du-roy
co-re-la´tion
co-re-spon´dent
cork´age
cork´board
cork´screw
cork´y
cor´ner
cor´nered
cor´ner-stone
cor-net´
corn´fed
corn´field
cor´nice
corn´stalk
cor-nu-co´pi·a
corn´y
cor´o-nar·y
cor-o-na´tion
cor´o-ner

cor-o-net´
cor´po-rate
cor´po-rate·ly
cor-po-ra´tion
cor-po´re·al
corps
corpse
cor´pu-lence
cor´pu-lent
cor-ral´
cor-rect´
cor-rect´a·ble
cor-rec´tion
cor-rec´tion·al
cor-rec´tive
cor-rect´ly
cor-rect´ness
cor´re-late
cor-re-la´tion·al
cor-rel´a-tive
cor-re-spond´
cor-re-spon´dence
cor-re-spon´dent
cor-re-spond´ing
cor-re-spon´sive
cor´ri-dor
cor-ri-gi·bil´i·ty
cor´ri-gi·ble
cor-rob´o-rate
cor-rob-o-ra´tion
cor-rob´o-ra-tive
cor-rob´o-ra-tor
cor-rode´

cor-rod´i·ble
cor-rod´ing
cor-ro´sion
cor-ro´sive
cor-ro´sive·ly
cor-ro´sive-ness
cor´ru-gate
cor´ru-gat·ed
cor-ru-ga´tion
cor-rupt´
cor-rupt´er
cr-rupt´i·ble
cor-rup´tion
cor-rup´tive
cor-rupt´ly
cor-rupt´ness
cor-sage´
cor´set
cor´tege
cor´us-cate
cor-us-ca´tion
co´sign
co-sig´na-to·ry
co´sign·er
cos-met´ic
cos-met´i-cal·ly
cos-me-tol´o·gy
cos´mic
cos´mi-cal·ly
cos-mo-log´i-cal
cos-mol´o·gy
cos´mo-naut
cos-mo-pol´i-tan

cos´mos
cost´li-ness
cost´ly
cos´tume
cos´tum·er
co-ten´an·cy
co-ten´ant
co´te-rie
co-ter´mi-nous
co-ter´mi-nous·ly
co-til´lion
cot´tage
cot´ter
cot´ton
cot´ton-seed
cough
could
cou´lee
coun´cil
coun´sel
coun´sel-lor (Br.)
coun´sel·or
coun´te-nance
coun´ter (contra)
count´er (ledge)
coun´ter-act´
coun´ter-bal-ance
coun´ter-claim
coun´ter-clock´wise
coun´ter-cul-ture
coun´ter-feit·er
coun´ter-mand
coun´ter-mine

coun´ter-of-fer	cour´te-san	coy
coun´ter-part	cour´te·sy	coy´ly
coun´ter-point	court´house	coy´ness
coun-ter-pro-duc´-tive	cour´tier	co´zi-est
	court´li-ness	co´zi·ly
coun´ter-sign	court´ly	co´zi-ness
coun´ter-suit	court´room	co´zy
count´er-top	court´ship	crab´bi-ness
count´ess	court´yard	crab´by
coun´ties	cous´in	crack´down
count´less	cov´en	cracked
coun´tries	cov´e-nant	crack´er
coun´tri-fied	cov´er	cracker–barrel
coun´try	cov´er-age	crack´ing
coun´try-man	cov´er-all	crack´le
coun´try-side	cov´ered	crack´ling
coun´ty	cov´er-ing	crack´pot
cou´ple	cov´er-let	crack–up
cou´pler	cov´ert	cra´dle
cou´plet	co´vert·ly	craft
cou´pling	co´vert-ness	craft´i·ly
cou´pon	cov´er–up	craft´i-ness
cour´age	cov´et	crafts´man-ship
cou-ra´geous·ly	cov´e-tous·ly	craft´y
cou-ra´geous-ness	cov´e-tous-ness	crag´gi-ness
cou´ri·er	cov´ey	crag´gy
course	cow´ard	cram
cours·er	cow´ard-ice	crammed
cours´ing	cow´ard·ly	cram´ming
court	cow´er	cramp
cour´te-ous	cowl	cramped
cour´te-ous·ly	cowl´ing	crane
cour´te-ous-ness	co–worker	craned

cran´ing
crank
crank´case
crank´i-ness
crank´shaft
crank´y
cran´ny
crash´ing
crash–land
crass´ly
crass´ness
crater (chasm)
crat´ing
cra-vat´
crave
cra´ven
crav´ing
craw
craw´dad
craw´fish
crawl
crawl´ing
crawl´space
crawl´y
cray´fish
cray´on
craze
crazed
cra´zi·ly
cra´zi-ness
cra´zy
creak
creak´i·ly

creak´i-ness
creak´y
cream
cream–colored
cream´er
cream´er·y
cream´i-ness
cream´y
cre-ate´
cre-at´ing
cre-a´tion-ism
cre-a´tive
cre-a´tive·ly
cre-a-tiv´i·ty
cre-a´tor
crea´ture
cre´dence
cre-den´tial
cre-den´za
cred-i·bil´i·ty
cred´i·ble
cred´it
cred´it-a·ble
cred´i-tor
cre´do
cre-du´li·ty
cred´u-lous
cred´u-lous·ly
creed
creel
creek
creep
creep´er

creep´i-ness
creep´ing
creep´y
cre´mate
cre-ma´tion
cre-ma-to´ri·um
cre´o-sote
crêpe
cre-scen´do
cres´cent
crest
crest´ed
crest´fall·en
crest´ing
crev´ice
crev´iced
crew´el-work
crew´man
crib´bage
crib´bing
crick´et
crick´et·er
cried
cri´er
crime
crim´i-nal
crim-i-nal´i·ty
crim´i-nal·ly
crim-i-nol´o-gist
crim-i-nol´o·gy
crimp
crim´son
cringe

61

cringed
cring´ing
crin´kle
crin´kly
crin´o-line
crip´ple
crip´pled
crip´pler
crip´pling
cri´sis
crisp´er
crisp´i-ness
crisp´ly
crisp´ness
crisp´y
criss´cross
cri-te´ri-on
crit´ic
crit´i-cal
crit´i-cal·ly
crit´i-cism
crit´i-ciz-a·ble
crit´i-cize
crit´i-ciz-ing
cri-tique´
crit´ter
cro-chet´
cro-cheted´
cro-chet´er
cro-chet´ing
crock´er·y
crock´et
cro´cus

crois-sant´
cro´ny
cro´ny-ism
crook´ed (v.)
crooked (adj.)
croon´er
cross
cross´bar
cross´bow
cross´–coun´try
cross´cur-rent
cross´–ex-am´ine
cross´hatch
cross´ing
cross´–leg´ged
cross´ness
cross´o·ver
cross´patch
cross´–pol-li-na´-
   tion
cross´–pur´pose
cross´–ref´er-ence
cross´walk
crotch´et
crow´bar
crowd´ed
crowned
crow's–nest
cru´cial
cru´ci·ble
cru´ci-fix
cru´ci·fy
crude

crude´ly
cru´el
cru´el·ly
cru´el·ty
cru´et
cruise
cruised
cruis´er
cruis´ing
crumb
crum´ble
crum´bling
crum´bly
crumb´y
crum´my
crum´ple
crum´pling
crunch
crunch´ing
cru-sade´
cru-sad´er
cru-sad´ing
crush
crush´a·ble
crus-ta´cean
crust´ed
crust´i·ly
crust´i-ness
crust´y
crutch
crux
cry´ba·by
cry´ing

62

cry-o-gen´ics
cry-on´ics
crypt
cryp´tic
cryp´to-gram
cryp-tog´ra-pher
cryp-tog´ra-phy
crys´tal
crys´tal-line
crys-tal-li-za´tion
crys´tal-lize
cub´by-hole
cube
cubed
cu´bic
cu´bi-cal *(adj.)*
cu´bi-cle *(n.)*
cub´ism
cub´ist
cud´dle
cud´dled
cud´dling
cud´dly
cud´gel
cui-sine´
cul´–de–sac
cul´i-nar·y
cul´mi-nate
cul-mi-na´tion
cu-lotte´
cul-pa-bil´i·ty
cul´pa·ble
cul´pa·bly

cul´prit
cult
cul´ti-vate
cul´ti-vat·ed
cul-ti-va´tion
cul´ti-va-tor
cul´tur·al
cul´ture
cul´tured
cul´vert
cum´ber-some
cu´mu-la-tive
cu´mu-la-tive·ly
cup´ful
cu-pid´i·ty
cu´po·la
cupped
cup´ping
cur´a·ble
cu´ra-tive
cu-ra´tor
curb´ing
curb´side
curb´stone
curd
cur´dle
cur´dling
cure–all
cur´few
cu´ri·o
cu-ri-os´i·ty
cu´ri-ous
cu´ri-ous·ly

curl´er
cur´li-cue
curl´i-ness
curl´ing
curl´y
cur-mud´geon
cur´ren·cy
cur´rent
cur´rent·ly
curse
cursed
curs´ing
cur´sive
cur´sive·ly
cur´sive-ness
cur´sor
cur´so·ry
curt
cur-tail´
cur-tail´ment
cur´tain
curt´ly
curt´ness
curt´sy, curt´sey
cur-va´ceous
cur-va´ceous-ness
cur´va-ture
curve
curved
curv´ing
cush´ion
cush´y
cuss´ed-ness

cus·to´di·al
cus·to´di·an
cus´to·dy
cus´tom
cus´tom-ar´i·ly
cus´tom-ar·y
cus´tom–built´
cus´tom·er
cus´tom-ize
cus´tom–made´
cut´a·way
cut´back
cut´down
cute
cute´ly
cute´ness
cute´sy
cu´ti·cle
cut´ie
cut´ler·y
cut´off
cut´–rate´
cut´ter
cut´throat
cut´ting
cut´up
cy-ber-net´ics
cy´ber-space
cy´cle
cy´clic, cy´cli-cal
cy´cling
cy´clist
cy´clone

cyl´in-der
cy-lin´dri-cal·ly
cym´bal
cyn´ic
cyn´i-cal·ly
cyn´i-cism

D

dab´ble
dab´bling
dad´dy
daf´fo-dil
daf´fy
dag´ger
dai´lies
dai´ly
dain´ti·ly
dain´ti-ness
dain´ty
dai´qui·ri
dair´ies
dair´y
dair´y-man
dai-shi´ki
dal´li-ance
dal´lied
dal´li·er
dal´ly
dal´ly-ing
dam´age
dam´age-a·ble
dam´ag-ing
dam´ask

dam-na´tion
damned
damn´ing
damp´en
damp´en·er
damp´er
damp´ing
damp´ish
damp´ness
dam´sel
dance´a·ble
danced
danc´er
danc´er-cise
danc´ing
dan´der
dan´di-fied
dan´di·fy
dan´druff
dan´dy
dan´ger
dan´ger-ous·ly
dan´gle
dan´gled
dan´gling
dank´ness
dap´per
dap´ple
dare´dev·il
dare´say
dar´ing
dar´ing·ly
dark´en

dark´ly

dark´ness

dark´room

dar´ling

darn

darned

darn´ing

dash´board

dashed

dash´er

da-shi´ki

dash´ing

das´tard·ly

da´ta

da´ta-base

date

date´book

dat´ed

date´line

dat´ing

da´tum

daub´er

daugh´ter

daugh´ter-in-law

daunt

daunt´ing·ly

daunt´less·ly

daunt´less-ness

dav´en-port

daw´dle

daw´dler

daw´dling

dawn

day´bed

day´break

day´dream

day´light

day´time

day-to-day

dazed

daz´ed·ly

daz´zle

daz´zling

daz´zling·ly

dea´con

dea´con-ess

de-ac´ti-vate

de-ac-ti-va´tion

de-ac´ti-va-tor

dead´beat

dead´bolt

dead´en

dead´en-ing

dead´li·er

dead´line

dead´li-ness

dead´lock

dead´ly

dead´pan

deaf´en

deaf´en-ing

deaf´ness

deal´er

deal´er-ship

deal´ing

dealt

dear´ie

dear´ly

death´bed

death-dealing

death´less

death´ly

death´trap

de-ba´cle

de-bar´

de-bark´

de-bar-ka´tion

de-based´

de-bas´ing

de-bat´a·ble

de-bate´

de-bat´er

de-bat´ing

de-bauch´

de-bauched´

de-bauch´er

de-bauch´er·y

de-ben´ture

de-bil´i-tate

de-bil´i-tat·ed

de-bil-i-ta´tion

deb´it

deb´o-nair´

de-bone´

debt´or

de-bug´

de´but

deb´u-tante

dec´ade

dec´a-dence
dec´a-dent
de-caf´fein-ate
de´cal
de-cant´
de-cant´er
de-cap´i-tate
de-cap-i-ta´tion
de-cay´
de-cayed´
de-cay´ing
de-ceased´
de-ce´dent
de-ceit´
de-ceit´ful·ly
de-ceit´ful-ness
de-ceiv´a·ble
de-ceiv´a·bly
de-ceive´
de-ceiv´er
de-cel´er-ate
de-cel-er-a´tion
de´cen·cy
de´cent
de´cent·ly
de-cen-tral-i-za´-
   tion
de-cen´tral-ize
de-cep´tion
de-cep´tive·ly
de-cer´ti·fy
dec´i-bel
de-cide´

de-cid´ed·ly
de-cid´ing
de-cid´u-ous
de-cid´u-ous·ly
dec´i-mal
dec´i-mate
dec-i-ma´tion
de-ci´pher
de-ci´pher-a·ble
de-ci´sion
de-ci´sive·ly
de-ci´sive-ness
deck´le
de-claim´
dec-la-ma´tion
de-clam´a-to·ry
dec-la-ra´tion
de-clare´
de-clas´si·fy
de-claw´
de-cline´
de-clined´
de-clin´ing
de-cliv´i·ty
de-code´
de-cod´er
de-cod´ing
dé-col-le-tage´
de-com-mis´sion
de-com-pose´
de-com-press´
de-com-pres´sion
de-con-tam´i-nate

de-cor´
dec´o-rate
dec-o-ra´tion
dec´o-ra-tive·ly
dec´o-ra-tor
dec´o-rous·ly
de-co´rum
dé-cou-page´
de´-coy
de´coyed
de´crease *(n.)*
de-crease´ *(v.)*
de-creas´ing·ly
de-cree´
de-creed´
de-cree´ing
de-crep´it
de-cried´
de-crim´i·nal-ize
de-cry´
ded´i-cate
ded´i-cat·ed
ded-i-ca´tion
ded´i-ca-to·ry
de-duce´
de-duced´
de-duc´i·ble
de-duc´i·bly
de-duc´ing
de-duct´
de-duct-i-bil´i·ty
de-duct´i·ble
de-duc´tion

de-duc´tive
de-duc´tive·ly
deed
deem
de–em´pha-size
de–em´pha-sis
deep´en
deep–freeze
deep–fry
deep–rooted
deep–seated
deer´skin
de-face´
de-faced´
de-face´ment
de-fac´ing
de fac´to
def-a-ma´tion
de-fam´a-to·ry
de-fame´
de-fault´
de-fault´er
de-feat´ed
de-feat´ist
def´e-cate
def-e-ca´tion
de´fect (n.)
de-fect´ (v.)
de-fect´ed
de-fec´tion
de-fec´tive
de-fec´tor
de-fend´

de-fend´a·ble
de-fend´ant
de-fend´er
de-fense´
de-fense´less
de-fen´si·ble
de-fen´si·bly
de-fen´sive
de-fen´sive·ly
de-fer´
def´er-ence
def´er-ent
def-er-en´tial
def-er-en´tial·ly
de-fer´ment
de-ferred´
de-fi´ance
de-fi´ant·ly
de-fi´cien·cy
de-fi´cient
de-fi´cient·ly
def´i-cit
de-fied´
de-fi´er
de-file´
de-file´ment
de-fil´er
de-fil´ing
de-fin´a·ble
de-fin´a·bly
de-fine´
de-fin´ing
def´i-nite

def´i-nite·ly
def-i-ni´tion
de-fin´i-tive
de-fin´i-tive·ly
de-flate´
de-fla´tion
de-fla´tion-ar·y
de-fla´tor
de-flect´
de-flect´a·ble
de-flec´tion
de-flec´tive
de-flec´tor
de-fog´ger
de-fo´li-ant
de-fo´li-ate
de-for-est-a´tion
de-form´
de-for-ma´tion
de-formed´
de-for´mi·ty
de-fraud´
de-fraud´ed
de-fray´
de-frayed´
de-fray´ing
de-frock´
de-frost´er
deft´ly
deft´ness
de-funct´
de-fuse´
de-fy´

de-fy´ing
de-gen´er-a·cy
de-gen´er-ate
de-gen-er-a´tion
de-gen´er-a-tive
de-glaze´
deg-ra-da´tion
de-grade´
de-grad´ed
de-grad´ing
de-grease´
de-gree´
de-hu´man-ize
de-hu-mid´i-fi·er
de-hy´drate
de-hy-dra´tion
de-ice´
de-ic´er
de-i-fi-ca´tion
de´i-fied
de´i·fy
deign
de´i-ties
de´i·ty
de-ject´
de-ject´ed
de-ject´ed·ly
de-jec´tion
de-lam´i-nate
de-lam-i-na´tion
de-lay´
de-layed´
de-lay´ing

de-lec´ta·ble
de-lec´ta·bly
del´e-ga·cy
del´e-gate
del-e-ga´tion
de-lete´
de-let´ed
del-e-te´ri-ous
de-le´tion
del´i
de-lib´er-ate·ly
de-lib-er-a´tion
de-lib´er-a-tive
del´i-ca-cies
del´i-ca·cy
del´i-cate
del´i-cate·ly
del´i-cate-ness
del-i-ca-tes´sen
de-li´cious
de-li´cious·ly
de-light´ed·ly
de-light´ful·ly
de-lim´it
de-lim´it·er
de-lin´e-ate
de-lin-e-a´tion
de-lin´e-a-tor
de-lin´quen·cy
de-lin´quent
de-lin´quent·ly
de-lir´i-ous
de-lir´i-ous·ly

de-lir´i·um
de-liv´er
de-liv´er-ance
de-liv´er·er
de-liv´er-ies
de-liv´er·y
de-louse´
de-lude´
de-lud´ed
de-lud´ing
del´uge
del´uged
de-lu´sion
de-lu´sion·al
de-luxe´
delved
delv´er
delv´ing
de-mag´net-ize
dem´a-gog´ic
dem´a-gogue
de-mand´
de-mand´ed
de-mand´ing
de-mar-ca´tion
de-ma-te´ri-al-ize
de-mean´
de-mean´or
de-ment´ed
de-men´tia
de-mer´it
de-mil´i-ta-rize
de-mise´

dem´i-tasse
dem´o
de-mo´bi-lize
de-moc´ra·cy
dem´o-crat
dem´o-crat´ic
dem´o-crat´i-cal·ly
de-moc´ra-tize
de-mod´u-late
de-mod-u-la´tion
de-mod´u-la-tor
de´mo-graph´ics
de-mol´ish
dem-o-li´tion
de´mon
de-mon´ic
de-mon-ol´o·gy
de-mon´stra·ble
de-mon´stra·bly
dem´on-strate
dem´on-strat-ing
dem-on-stra´tion
de-mon´stra-tive
dem´on-stra-tor
de-mor-al-i·za´tion
de-mor´al-ize
de-mor´al-iz-ing
de´mos
de-mote´
de-mot´ed
de-mo´tion
de-mur´ *(v.)*
de-mure´ *(adj.)*

de-mure´ly
de-mys´ti·fy
de-my-thol´o-gize
de-na´tion-al-ize
de-nat´u-ral-ize
de-na´tured
de-ni´a·ble
de-ni´al
de-nied´
de-nies´
den´i-grate
den-i-gra´tion
den´i-gra-tor
den´im
den´i-zen
de-nom-i-na´tion
de-nom-i-na´tion·al
de-nom´i-na-tor
de-note´
de-not´ing
de-no´tive
de-noue-ment´
de-nounced´
de-nounc´ing
dense´ly
dense´ness
den´si·ty
den´tal
den´tist
den´tis-try
den´ture
de-nude´
de-nun´ci-ate

de-nun-ci-a´tion
de-ny´ing
de-o´dor-ant
de-o´dor-ize
de-o´dor-iz·er
de-part´ed
de-part´ment
de-part-men´tal-ize
de-par´ture
de-pend´
de-pend-a·bil´i·ty
de-pend´a·ble
de-pen´dence
de-pen´dent
de-per-son-a-li-za´-
  tion
de-per´son-al-ize
de-pict´
de-pic´tion
de-pil´a-to·ry
de-ple´tion
de-plor´a·ble
de-plor´a·bly
de-plore´
de-plored´
de-plor´ing·ly
de-ploy´ment
de-po´lar-ize
de-pop´u-late
de-pop-u-la´tion
de-port´
de-por-ta´tion
de-port´ed

de-port-ee′
de-port′ment
de-pose′
de-posed′
de-pos′ing
de-pos′it
de-pos′it·ed
dep-o-si′tion
de-pos′i-to·ry
de′pot
dep-ra-va′tion
de-praved′
de-prav′i·ty
dep′re-cate
dep′re-cat-ing
dep-re-ca′tion
de-pre′cia·ble
de-pre′ci-ate
de-pre-ci-a′tion
de-press′
de-pres′sant
de-pressed′
de-press′ing
de-pres′sion
de-pres′sur-ize
de-pres-sur-i-za′-
  tion
dep-ri-va′tion
de-prive′
de-prived′
de-priv′ing
depth
dep-u-ta′tion

dep′u-ties
dep′u-tize
dep′u·ty
de-rail′ment
de-range′ment
de-rang′ing
der′by
de-reg′u-late
der′e-lict
der-e-lic′tion
de-ride′
de-rid′ing
de-ri′sion
de-ri′sive
de-ri′sive·ly
de-ri′sive-ness
der-i-va′tion
de-riv′a-tive
de-rive′
de-rived′
de-riv′ing
der-ma-tol′o-gist
der-ma-tol′o·gy
der′o-gate
der-o-ga′tion
de-rog′a-tive
de-rog′a-tive·ly
de-rog′a-to·ry
der′rick
der′ring·do
de-scend′ed
de-scend′ent
de-scend′er

de-scrib′a·ble
de-scribe′
de-scribed′
de-scrip′tion
de-scrip′tive
de-scrip′tor
des-cry′
des-cry′ing
des′e-crate
des-e-cra′tion
des′e-cra-tor
de-seg′re-gate
de-seg-re-ga′tion
de-se-lect′
de-sen-si-ti′za-tion
de-sen′si-tize
des′ert *(wasteland)*
de-sert′ *(forsake)*
de-sert′er
de-sert-i-fi-ca′tion
de-ser′tion
de-served′
de-serv′ed·ly
de-serv′ing
de-sign′
des′ig-nate
des-ig-na′tion
des′ig-na-tor
de-sign′er
de-sign′ing
de-sir-a-bil′i·ty
de-sir′a·ble
de-sir′a·bly

de-sire´	des-sert´	de-ter´gent
de-sir´ous	de-sta´bi-lize	de-te´ri-o-rate
de-sist´	des-ti-na´tion	de-te-ri-o-ra´tion
desk´top	des´tined	de-ter´ment
des´o-late	des´ti-nies	de-ter´min-a·ble
des´o-late-ness	des´ti·ny	de-ter´mi-nant
des-o-la´tion	des´ti-tute	de-ter-mi-na´tion
de-sorb´	des-ti-tu´tion	de-ter´mined
de-spaired´	de-stroyed´	de-terred´
de-spair´ing	de-stroy´er	de-ter´rence
de-spair´ing·ly	de-struct´	de-ter´rent
des-per-a´do	de-struc´ti·ble	de-test´
des-per-a´does	de-struc´tion	de-test´a·ble
des´per-ate	de-struc´tive·ly	de-test´a·bly
des´per-ate·ly	de-struc´tive-ness	de-tes-ta´tion
des´per-ate-ness	des´ul-to·ry	de-throne´
des-per-a´tion	de-tach´	det´o-nate
de-spic´a·ble-ness	de-tach´a·ble	det-o-na´tion
de-spic´a·bly	de-tached´	det´o-na-tor
de-spis´a·ble	de-tach´ment	de´tour
de-spised´	de-tail´, de´tail	de-tox-i-fi-ca´tion
de-spis´er	de-tailed´	de-tox´i·fy
de-spis´ing	de´tail-ing	de-tract´
de-spite´	de-tain´	de-trac´tion
de-spoil´er	de-tain´ment	de-trac´tor
de-spoil´ing	de-tect´	de-train´
de-spond´	de-tect´a·ble	det´ri-ment
de-spon´dence	de-tec´tion	det-ri-men´tal
de-spon´den·cy	de-tec´tive	deuce
de-spon´dent	de-tec´tor	deuc´ed
des´pot	dé-tente	deuc´ed·ly
des-pot´ic	de-ten´tion	de-val´u-ate
des´po-tism	de-ter´	de-val-u-a´tion

de-val´ue
dev´as-tate
dev´as-tat·ed
dev´as-tat-ing
dev´as-tat-ing·ly
dev-as-ta´tion
de-vel´op
de-vel´oped
de-vel´op·er
de-vel´op-ing
de-vel´op-ment
de-vel´op-men´tal
de´vi-ance
de´vi-ant
de´vi-ate
de-vi-a´tion
de-vice´
dev´il
dev´il-ish·ly
dev´il-ment
dev´il-try
de´vi-ous·ly
de´vi-ous-ness
de-vise´
de-vi-tal-i·za´tion
de-vi´tal-ize
de-void´
de-vote´
de-vot´ed
de-vot´ed·ly
de-vot´ed-ness
dev´o-tee´
de-vo´tion

de-vo´tion·al
de-vour´
de-vout´
de-vout´ly
de-vout´ness
dew´i-ness
dew´lap
dew´point
dew´y
dew´y–eyed
dex-ter´i·ty
dex´ter-ous
dex´ter-ous·ly
dex´ter-ous-ness
dex´trous
di-a-bol´ic
di-a-bol´i-cal
di-a-bol´i-cal·ly
di´ag-nose
di-ag-no´sis
di-ag-nos-ti´cian
di´ag-nos-tics
di-ag´o-nal
di-ag´o-nal·ly
di´a-gram
di´a-gram-mat´ic
di´al
di´a-lect
di´aled
di´al·er
di´al-ing
di´a-logue
di-am´e-ter

di-a-met´ric
di-a-met´ri-cal·ly
di´a-per
di-aph´a-nous
di´a-ries
di´a-rist
di´a·ry
di-as´po·ra
di´a-spore
di´a-tribe
dic´ey
di-chot´o·my
dick´er
dick´ey
dic´tate
dic´tat-ing
dic-ta´tion
dic´ta-tor
dic-ta-to´ri·al
dic-ta´tor-ship
dic´tion
dic´tio-nar-ies
dic´tio-nar·y
dic´tum
di-dac´tic
di-dac´ti-cal·ly
die´sel
di´et
di´e-tar·y
di´et·er
di-e-tet´ic
di-e-ti´tian
dif´fered

dif´fer-ence

dig´ni-fy-ing

dined

dif´fer-ent

dig´ni-tar-ies

din´er

dif-fer-en´tia·ble

dig´ni-tar·y

di-nette´

dif-fer-en´tial

dig´ni-ties

din´gi-ness

dif-fer-en´ti-ate

dig´ni·ty

din´gy

dif´fer-ent·ly

di-gress´

din´ing

dif´fi-cult

di-gres´sion

din´ner

dif´fi-cul-ties

di-gres´sive

din´ner-time

dif´fi-cult·ly

di-lap´i-date

din´ner-ware

dif´fi-cul·ty

di-lap´i-dat·ed

di´no-saur

dif´fi-dence

di-late´

di´o-cese

dif´fi-dent

di-lat´ing

di´ode

dif´fi-dent·ly

di-la´tion

di-o-ram´a

dif-fract´

di-lem´ma

diph´thong

dif-frac´tion

dil-et-tante´

di-plo´ma

dif-fuse´

dil´i-gence

di-plo´ma·cy

dif-fus´i·ble

dil´i-gent

dip´lo-mat

dif-fu´sion

dil´i-gent·ly

dip-lo-mat´ic

dif-fu´sive

dil´ly-dal·ly

dip-lo-mat´i-cal·ly

di´gest *(n.)*

di-lute´

dipped

di-gest´ *(v.)*

di-lut´ing

dip´per

di-gest-i·bil´i·ty

di-lu´tion

dip-so-ma´ni·a

di-gest´i·ble

di-men´sion·al

dip-so-ma´ni·ac

di-ges´tion

di-min´ish

dip´stick

di-ges´tive

dim-i-nu´tion

di-rect´

dig´ger

dim´ly

di-rect´ed

dig´gings

dimmed

di-rec´tion

dig´it

dim´mer

di-rec´tive

dig´i-tal

dim´ming

di-rect´ly

dig´it-al·ly

dim´ness

di-rect´ness

dig´i-tize

dim´ple

di-rec´tor

dig´ni-fied

dim´pling

di-rec´tor-ate

dig´ni·fy

dim´wit

di-rec´to·ry

dire´ly
dirge
dir´i·gi·ble
dirt´i·er
dirt´i-ness
dirt´–poor´
dirt´y
dis-a·bil´i·ty
dis-a´ble
dis-a´bled
dis-a´bling
dis´a·buse´
dis-ad-van´taged
dis-ad-van-ta´geous
dis-af-fect´ed
dis-af-fil-i-a´tion
dis-af-firm´
dis-a·gree´
dis-a·gree-a·bil´i·ty
dis-a·gree´a·ble
dis-a·gree´a·bly
dis-a·gree´ment
dis-al-low´
dis-al-low´ance
dis-ap-pear´
dis-ap-pear´ance
dis-ap-peared´
dis-ap-point´
dis-ap-point´ed·ly
dis-ap-point´ing
dis-ap-point´ment
dis-ap-pro-ba´tion
dis-ap-prov´al

dis´ap-prove´
dis´ap-prov´ing
dis´ap-prov´ing·ly
dis-arm´
dis-ar´ma-ment
dis-arm´ing
dis-arm´ing·ly
dis-ar-ray´
dis-as-so´ci-ate
di-sas´ter
di-sas´trous·ly
dis-a·vow´
dis-a·vow´al
dis-a·vow´ed·ly
dis-band´
dis-bar´
dis-bar´ment
dis-be-lief´
dis-be-lieve´
dis-be-liev´er
dis-burs´a·ble
dis-burse´
dis-burse´ment
dis-burs´ing
dis´card *(n.)*
dis-card´ *(v.)*
dis-cern´i·ble
dis-cern´i·bly
dis-cern´ing
dis-cern´ment
dis´charge *(n.)*
dis-charge´ *(n., v.)*
dis-ci´ple

dis-ci-pli-nar´i·an
dis´ci-pli-nar·y
dis´ci-pline
dis-claim´er
dis-close´
dis-clos´ing
dis-clo´sure
dis´co
dis-col-or-a´tion
dis-com-bob´u-late
dis-com´fit
dis-com´fi-ture
dis-com´fort
dis-con-cert´
dis-con-cert´ed
dis-con-cert´ing
dis-con-nect´ed
dis-con´so-late
dis-con-so-la´tion
dis-con-tent´
dis-con-tent´ed
dis-con-tent´ment
dis-con-tin-u-a´tion
dis-con-tin´ue
dis´cord
dis-cor´dance
dis-cor´dant·ly
dis´co-theque
dis´count
dis-cour´age
dis-cour´age-ment
dis-cour´ag-ing
dis-cour´ag-ing·ly

dis´course (n.)
dis-course´ (v.)
dis-cour´te-ous·ly
dis-cour´te-ous-
 ness
dis-cour´te·sy
dis-cov´er
dis-cov´er·er
dis-cov´er-ies
dis-cov´er·y
dis-cred´it
dis-cred´it-a·ble
dis-creet´ (prudent)
dis-creet´ly
dis-creet´ness
dis-crep´an·cy
dis-crete´ (distinct)
dis-cre´tion
dis-cre´tion-ar·y
dis-crim´i-nate
dis-crim´i-nat-ing
dis-crim-i-na´tion
dis-cuss´
dis-cussed´
dis-cus´sion
dis-dain´ful·ly
dis-dain´ful-ness
dis-eased
dis-em-bark´
dis-em-bar-ka´tion
dis-em-bod´y
dis-en-chant´
dis-en-chant´ing

dis-en-chant´ment
dis-en-fran´chise
dis-en-gage´
dis-en-gage´ment
dis-en-tan´gle
dis-fa´vor
dis-fig-u-ra´tion
dis-fig´ure
disfig´ur-ing
dis-gorge´
dis-grace´
dis-grace´ful·ly
dis-grun´tled
dis-guise´
dis-gust´ed
dis-gust´ed·ly
dis-gust´ing·ly
dis-ha·bille´
dis-har´mo·ny
dish´cloth
dis-heart´en
dis-heart´en-ing
dished
di-shev´eled
di-shev´el-ment
dish´mop
dis-hon´est
dis-hon´est·ly
dis-hon´es·ty
dis-hon´or
dis-hon´or-a·ble
dis-hon´or-a·bly
dish´pan

dish´wash·er
dish´wa´ter
dis-il-lu´sion
dis-in-cli-na´tion
dis-in-cline´
dis-in-clined´
dis-in-fect´
dis-in-fec´tant
dis-in-gen´u-ous
dis-in-her´it
dis-in´te-grate
dis-in-te-gra´tion
dis-in-ter´
dis-in´ter-est
dis-in´ter-est·ed
dis-join´
dis-joint´ed
disk
disk-ette´
dis-like´
dis´lo-cate
dis-lo-ca´tion
dis-lodge´
dis-loy´al
dis-loy´al·ly
dis-loy´al·ty
dis´mal
dis´mal·ly
dis-man´tle
dis-man´tling
dis-may´
dis-mem´ber-ment
dis-miss´

dis-mis´sal
dis-miss´ive
dis-mount´
dis-o·be´di-ence
dis-o·be´di-ent·ly
dis-o·bey´
dis-o·beyed´
dis-or´der
dis-or´dered
dis-or´der·ly
dis-or-ga-ni-za´tion
dis-or´ga-nize
dis-o´ri-ent
dis-o-ri-en-ta´tion
dis-own´
dis-par´age-ment
dis-par´ag-ing·ly
dis-par´i·ty
dis-patch´er
dis-pel´
dispelled´
dis-pel´ling
dis-pens´a·ble
dis-pen´sa·ry
dis-pen-sa´tion
dis-pense´
dis-pens´er
dis-per´sal
dis-per´sant
dis-perse´
dis-per´sion
di-spir´it·ed
dis-place´

dis-placed´
dis-place´ment
dis-play´
dis-please´
dis-pleas´ing
dis-plea´sure
dis-pos´a·ble
dis-pos´al
dis-pose´
dis-posed
dis-po-si´tion
dis-pos-sessed´
dis-proof´
dis-pro-por´tion
dis-pro-por´tion·al
dis-pro-por´tion-
　al·ly
dis-pro-por´tion-
　ate·ly
dis-prove´
dis-put´a·ble
dis-put´a·bly
dis-pu´tant
dis-pu-ta´tion
dis-pute´
dis-qual-i-fi-ca´tion
dis-qual´i-fied
dis-qual´i·fy
dis-qui´et
dis-re-gard´
dis-re-pair´
dis-rep´u-ta·ble
dis-re-pute´

dis-re-spect´
dis-re-spect´ful
dis-robe´
dis-rupt´
dis-rup´tion
dis-rup´tive
dis-sat-is-fac´tion
dis-sat´is-fied
dis-sat´is·fy
dis-sect´
dis-sect´ed
dis-sec´tion
dis-sem´blance
dis-sem´ble
dis-sem´i-nate
dis-sem-i-na´tion
dis-sen´sion
dis-sent´er
dis-sen´tious
dis-ser-ta´tion
dis-serv´ice
dis´si-dence
dis´si-dent
dis-sim´i-lar
dis-sim-i-lar´i·ty
dis-sim´i-lar·ly
dis´si-pate
dis´si-pat·ed
dis-si-pa´tion
dis-so´ci-ate
dis-so-ci-a´tion
dis´so-lute
dis´so-lute·ly

dis-so-lu´tion
dis-solv´a·ble
dis-solve´
dis-solv´ing
dis´so-nance
dis´so-nant
dis-suade´
dis-sua´sion
dis-sua´sive
dis´taff
dis´tance
dis´tant·ly
dis-taste´ful
dis-tem´per
dis-tend´ed
dis-tend´er
dis-till´
dis´til-late
dis-til-la´tion
dis-till´er
dis-till´er·y
dis-till´ing
dis-tinct´
dis-tinc´tion
dis-tinc´tive·ly
dis-tinc´tive-ness
dis-tinct´ly
dis-tinct´ness
dis-tin´guish
dis-tin´guish-a·ble
dis-tin´guished
dis-tort´ed
dis-tor´tion

dis-tract´
dis-tract´ed
dis-tract´ed·ly
dis-tract´ed-ness
dis-tract´ing·ly
dis-trac´tion
dis-trac´tive
dis-traught´
dis-tressed´
dis-tress´ful
dis-tress´ing
dis-tress´ing·ly
dis-trib´ute
dis-tri-bu´tion
dis-trib´u-tor
dis´trict
dis-trust´ful
dis-turb´
dis-tur´bance
dis-turbed´
dis-turb´er
dis-use´
ditch
dit´to
dit´ty
di´va
di-van´
dive
div´er
di-verge´
di-ver´gence
di-ver´gent
di-ver´gent·ly

di´vers *(disparate)*
di-verse´
di-ver´si-fied
di-ver´sion
di-ver´sion-ar·y
di-ver´si·ty
di-vert´
di-vert´ing
di-vest´
di-vest´i-ture
di-vide´
di-vid´ed
div´i-dend
di-vid´er
div-i-na´tion
di-vine´
di-vine´ly
div´ing
di-vin´i·ty
di-vis´i·ble
di-vi´sion
di-vi´sive
di-vi´sive·ly
di-vi´sive-ness
di-vorce´
div´ot
di-vulge´
di-vulg´ing
diz´zi·ly
diz´zi-ness
diz´zy
do´a·ble
doc´ile

doc′ile·ly

dock′et

dock′side

dock′yard

doc′tor

doc′tor-al

doc′tor-ate

doc′tri-naire′

doc′tri-nal

doc′trine

doc′u-dra·ma

doc′u-ment

doc′u-men′ta·ry

doc-u-men-ta′tion

dod′der

dod′dered

dod′der-ing

dodge

dodg′er

dodg′ing

doe

do′er

doe′skin

does′n't

doff

dog′bite

dog′catch·er

dog-eared

dog′ged·ly

dog′ged-ness

dog′ger·el

dog′gy

dog′house

dog′leg

dog′ma

dog-mat′ic

dog′ma-tism

doi′lies

doi′ly

do′ing

do–it–yourself

dole′ful·ly

dole′ful-ness

dol′lar

dol′lop

dol′ ly

do′lo-rous·ly

do′lo-rous-ness

do-main′

domed

do-mes′tic

do-mes′ti-cate

do-mes′ti-cal·ly

do-mes-tic′i·ty

dom′i-cile

dom′i-nance

dom′i-nant

dom′i-nate

dom-i-na′tion

dom′i-neer′ing

do-min′ion

do-nate′

do-nat′ing

do-na′tion

done

done′ness

don′ny-brook

do′nor

do–nothing

don't

doo′dad

doo′dle

doo′dling

doo′fus

doo′hick·ey

doom

doom′say·er

dooms′day

door′bell

do–or–die

door′frame

door′jamb

door′keep·er

door′mat

door′stop

door–to–door

door′way

doo′zie

dop′ey

dork′y

dor′man·cy

dor′mant

dor′mi-to-ries

dor′mi-to·ry

dos′age

dosed

dos′ing

dos′sier

dot′age

dote
dot´ed
dot´ing
dot´ish
dot´ted
dot´ty
dou´ble
dou´ble–deck´er
dou´ble-head´er
dou´bly
doubt´ful
doubt´ful·ly
doubt´less
dough´nut
dough´ti·ly
dough´ty
dough´y
dour´ly
doused
dous´ing
dove´tail
dow´a-ger
dowd´y
dow´el
dow´er
down–and–out
down´beat
down´cast
down´draft
down´er
down´fall
down´grade
down´heart·ed

down´hill´
down´pour
down´right
down´size
down´stairs´
down´time
down–to–earth
down´town´
down´trod´den
down´turn
down´ward
down´y
dow´ries
dow´ry
dowse
dows´er
dox-ol´o·gy
doze
doz´en
doz´er
doz´ing
drab´ness
draft´i-ness
draft´y
drag
dragged
drag´ging
drag´net
drag´on
drain´age
drain´er
dra´ma
dra-mat´ic

dra-mat´i-cal·ly
dram´a-tist
dram´a-tize
dram´shop
drap´er·y
drap´ing
dras´tic
dras´ti-cal·ly
draw´back
draw´bridge
draw´er
draw´ing
drawl´er
drawl´ing
drawn
draw´string
dray´age
dread´ful
dread´ful·ly
dread´ful-ness
dread´locks
dread´nought
dream´er
dream´i·ly
dream´i-ness
dream´ing
dreamt
dream´y
drear´i·ly
drear´i-ness
drear´i-some
drear´y
dredge

dredg´er	droop´i-ness	du´al
dredg´ing	droop´ing	du-al´i·ty
drench	droop´y	du´al·ly
dress´er	drop´let	dub´bing
dress´ing	drop´out	du´bi-ous
dress´mak·er	dropped	duck´ling
dress´mak-ing	drop´per	duck´y
dress´y	drop´ping	dud´geon
drib´bled	dross	du´el
drib´let	drowse	du-et´
drift´er	drows´i·ly	duf´fer
drift´ing	drows´i-ness	duf´fle
drift´wood	drows´y	dug´out
dri´ly	drub´bing	dul´cet
drink´a·ble	drudge	dull
drink´er	drudg´er·y	dul´lard
drink´ing	drug	dull´ish
dripped	drugged	du´ly
drip´ping	drug´gist	dumb´bell
drip´py	drug´store	dumb´found
drive	drum´beat	dumb´ly
driv´el	drummed	dumb´struck
driv´en	drum´mer	dum´found
driv´er	drum´ming	dum·my
drive´way	drum´stick	dump´i-ness
driv´ing	drunk´ard	dump´ling
driz´zle	drunk´en	dump´y
driz´zling	drunk´en-ness	dunce
driz´zly	dry´er	dun´der-head
droll´er·y	dry´goods	dun-ga-ree´
drone	dry´ing	dun´geon
dron´ing	dry´ly	dun´nage
drool	dry´ness	dunned

dun´ning
duped
dup´ing
du´plex
du´pli-cate
du-pli-ca´tion
du´pli-ca-tor
du-plic´i-tous
du-plic´i-ty
du-ra-bil´i-ty
du´ra-ble
du´ra-bly
du-ra´tion
dur´ing
dusk´i-ness
dusk´y
dust´bin
dust´cloth
dust´er
dust´i-ness
dust´pan
dust´y
du´ties
du´ti-ful
du´ti-ful-ly
du´ty
dut´y–free´
dwarf
dwarf´ish
dwell´er
dwell´ing
dwelt
dwin´dle

dwin´dling
dye
dyed
dye´ing
dye´stuff
dy´ing
dy-nam´ic
dy-nam´i-cal-ly
dy´na-mism
dy´na-mite
dy´na-mit-ed
dy´na-mit-er
dy´na-mo
dy-nas´tic
dy´nas-ty

E

each
each other
ea´ger
ea´ger-ly
ea´ger-ness
ear
ear´ache
ear´drop
ear´drum
eared
ear´flap
ear´ful
ear´li-er
ear´li-est
ear´li-ness
ear´lobe

ear´ly
ear´mark
ear´muff
earn
earn´er
ear´nest
ear´nest-ly
ear´nest-ness
earn´ing
ear´piece
ear´phone
ear´plug
ear´ring
ear´shot
ear´split-ting
earth
earth´born
earth´bound
earth´en
earth´en-ware
earth´i-er
earth´i-ly
earth´i-ness
earth´li-ness
earth´ling
earth´ly
earth´mov-er
earth´mov-ing
earth´quake
earth´rise
earth´shak-ing
earth´y
ease

eased	ebb	ec-o-nom´ics
ease´ful	ebbed	e·con´o-mies
ease´ful·ly	ebb´ing	e·con´o-mist
ease´ful-ness	ebb tide	e·con´o-mize
ea´sel	eb´o·ny	e·con´o-miz·er
ease´ment	e·bul´lience	e·con´o-miz-ing
eas´i·er	e·bul´lien·cy	e·con´o·my
eas´i-est	e·bul´lient	ec´o-sphere
eas´i·ly	e·bul´lient·ly	ec´o-sys-tem
eas´i-ness	ec-cen´tric	ec´ru
eas´ing	ec-cen´tri-cal	ec´sta-sies
east	ec-cen´tri-cal·ly	ec´sta·sy
east´bound	ec-cen-tric´i·ty	ec-stat´ic
east´er·ly	ec-cle-si-as´tic	ec-stat´i-cal·ly
east´ern	ec-cle-si-as´ti-cal	ec-u-men´i-cal
east´ern·er	ech´o	ec-u-men´i-cal·ly
east´ern-most	ech´oed	ed´died
east´ward	ech´oes	ed´dies
east´ward·ly	ech´o-ing	ed´dy
eas´y	ech-o-lo-ca´tion	ed´dy-ing
eas´y chair	é´clair	e·de´ma
eas´y-go-ing	e·clat´	edge
eat	ec-lec´tic	edged
eat´a·ble	ec-lec´ti-cal	edge´less
eat´en	ec-lec´ti-cal·ly	edg´er
eat´er	e·clipse´	edge´ways
eat´er·y	e·clips´ing	edge´wise
eat´ing	ec-o-log´ic	edg´i·ly
eave	ec-o-log´i-cal	edg´i-ness
eaves	e·col´o·gy	edg´ing
eaves´drop	ec-o-nom´ic	edg´y
eaves´drop-per	ec-o-nom´i-cal	ed´i·ble
eaves´drop-ing	ec-o-nom´i-cal·ly	e´dict

ed-i-fi-ca´tion

ed´i-fice

ed´i-fy

ed´i-fy-ing

ed´it

ed´it-a·ble

e·di´tion

ed´i-tor

ed-i-to´ri-al

ed-i-to´ri-al-ize

ed-i-to´ri-al-ly

ed´u-ca·ble

ed´u-cate

ed´u-cat·ed

ed´u-cat-ing

ed-u-ca´tion

ed-u-ca´tion·al

ed´u-ca-tor

e·duce´

e·duc´i·ble

e·duc´tion

e·duc´tive

e·duc´tor

e´duct

eel´grass

ee´rie

ee´ri·ly

ee´ri-ness

ef´fa·ble

ef-face´

ef-face´a·ble

ef-face´ment

ef-fac´ing

ef-fect´

ef-fect´i·ble

ef-fec´tive

ef-fec´tive·ly

ef-fec´tive-ness

ef-fec´tor

ef-fects´

ef-fec´tu·al

ef-fec´tu-al·ly

ef-fec´tu-ate

ef-fem´i-na·cy

ef-fem´i-nate

ef-fem´i-nate·ly

ef´fer-ent

ef-fer-vesce´

ef-fer-ves´cence

ef-fer-ves´cent

ef-fer-vesc´ing

ef-fete´

ef-fete´ly

ef-fete´ness

ef-fi-ca´cious

ef-fi-ca´cious·ly

ef´fi-ca·cy

ef-fi´cien·cy

ef-fi´cient

ef-fi´cient·ly

ef´fi·gy

ef´flu-ence

ef´flu-ent

ef-flu´vi·al

ef-flu´vi·um

ef´flux

ef´fort

ef´fort-less

ef´fort-less·ly

ef-fron´ter·y

ef-ful´gent

ef-fuse´

ef-fu´sion

ef-fu´sive

ef-fu´sive·ly

ef-fu´sive-ness

e·gal-i-tar´i·an

egg´beat·er

egg´cup

egg´head

egg´shaped

egg´shell

e´go

e´go-cen´tric

ego ideal

e´go-ism

e´go-ist

e´go-is´tic

e´go-is´ti-cal·ly

e·go-ma´ni·a

e·go-ma´ni·ac

e´go-tism

e´go-tist

e´go-tis´tic

e´go-tis´ti-cal

e´go-tis´ti-cal·ly

e·gre´gious

e·gre´gious·ly

e·gre´gious-ness

e´gress
eight
eight´ball
eigh-teen´
eigh-teenth´
eighth
eighth rest
eight´i-eth
eight´y
ei´ther
e·jac-u-la´tion
e·jac´u-la-to·ry
e·ject´
e·jec´tion
eke
eked
ek´ing
e·lab´o-rate
e·lab´o-rate·ly
e·lab´o-rate-ness
e·lab´o-rat-ing
e·lab-o-ra´tion
e·lab´o-ra-tive
e·lapse´
e·laps´ing
e·las´tic
e·las´ti-cal·ly
e·las-tic´i·ty
e·las´ti-cize
e·late´
e·lat´ed
e·lat´ed·ly
e·lat´ed-ness

e·la´tion
el´bow
el´bow-room
el´der
el´der-ber·ry
el´der·ly
el´dest
e·lect´
e·lec-tee´
e·lec´tion
e·lec´tion-eer´
e·lec´tive
e·lec´tor
e·lec´tor-al
e·lec´tor-ate
e·lec´tric
e·lec´tri-cal
e·lec´tri-cal·ly
e·lec-tri´cian
e·lec-tric´i·ty
e·lec-tri-fi-ca´tion
e·lec´tri-fied
e·lec´tri·fy
e·lec´tro-cute
e·lec-tro-cu´tion
e·lec´trode
e·lec-trol´y-sis
e·lec´tro-lyte
e·lec´tron
e·lec-tron´ic
e·lec-tron´i-cal·ly
e·lec-tron´ics
el-ee-mos´y-nar·y

el´e-gance
el´e-gant
el´e-gant·ly
el´e-gize
el´e·gy
el´e-ment
el-e-men´tal·ly
el-e-men´ta·ry
el´e-phan´tine
el´e-vate
el´e-vat·ed
el-e-va´tion
el´e-va-tor
e·lev´en
e·lev´enth
elf´in
elf´ish
e·lic´it
e·lic´i-tor
e·lide´
e·lid´i·ble
e·lid´ing
el-i-gi-bil´i·ty
el´i-gi-ble
el´i-gi-bly
e·lim´i-nate
e·lim-i-na´tion
e·lim´i-na-tor
e·lite´
e·lit´ism
e·lit´ist
e·lix´ir
el-lipse´

el-lip´tic
el-lip´ti-cal
el-o-cu´tion
el-o-cu´tion-ar·y
e·loge´
e·lon´gate
e·lon´gat·ed
e·lon-ga´tion
e·lope´
e·lope´ment
e·lop´ing
el´o-quence
el´o-quent·ly
else´where
e·lu´ci-date
e·lu-ci-da´tion
e·lu´ci-da-tive
e·lude´
e·lud´er
e·lu´sive
e·lu´sive·ly
e·lu´so·ry
e·lu´vi·al
e·lu´vi-ate
e·lu´vi-a´tion
e·lu´vi·um
e·ma´ci-ate
e·ma´ci-at·ed
E´–mail
em´a-nate
em-a-na´tion
em-a-na´tion·al
em´a-na-tive

em´a-na-tor
e·man´ci-pate
e·man´ci-pat·ed
e·man-ci-pa´tion
e·man´ci-pa-tor
e·mas´cu-late
e·mas-cu-la´tion
em-balm´
em-balm´er
em-bank´
em-bank´ment
em-bar´go
em-bar´goes
em-bark´
em-bar-ka´tion
em-bar´rass
em-bar´rassed
em-bar´rass·es
em-bar´rass-ing·ly
em-bar´rass-ment
em´bas-sies
em´bas·sy
em-bat´tle
em-bed´ded
em-bel´lish
em-bel´lish-ment
em´ber
em-bez´zle
em-bez´zled
em-bez´zle-ment
em-bez´zler
em-bit´ter
em-blaze´

em-bla´zon
em´blem
em´blem-at´ic
em-blem-at´i-cal
em-bod´i·er
em-bod´i-ment
em-bod´y
em-bold´en
em-boss´
em-bossed´
em-boss´ing
em-bow´el
em-brace´
em-brace´a·ble
em-brac´er
em-brac´ing
em-bra´sure
em-broi´der
em-broi´der·y
em-broil´
em´cee
e·mend´
e·mend´er
e·merge´
e·mer´gence
e·mer´gen-cies
e·mer´gen-cy
e·mer´gent
e·mer´gent·ly
e·merg´ing
e·mer´i-tus
e·mersed´
e·mer´sion

em´er·y
em´i-grant
em´i-grate
em´i-grat-ing
em-i-gra´tion
em-i-gra´tion·al
em´i-gra-tive
e·mi-gre´
em´i-nence
em´i-nen·cy
em´i-nent
em´i-nent·ly
em´is-sar-ies
em´is-sar·y
e·mis´sion
e·mis´sive
e·mis-siv´i·ty
e·mit´
e·mit´ted
e·mit´ter
e·mit´ting
e·mol´lience
e·mol´lient
e·mol´u-ment
e·mote´
e·mot´er
e·mot´ing
e·mo´tion
e·mo´tion·al
e·mo´tion-al·ly
e·mo´tive
em-pan´el
em-pan´el-ing

em-path´ic
em-path´i-cal·ly
em-pa-thet´i-cal·ly
em´pa-thize
em´pa-thy
em´per·or
em´pha-ses
em´pha-sis
em´pha-size
em´pha-siz-ing
em-phat´ic
em-phat´i-cal·ly
em´pire
em-pir´i-cal
em-pir´i-cism
em-place´ment
em-ploy´
em-ploy-a·bil´i·ty
em-ploy´a·ble
em-ploy·ee´
em-ploy´er
em-ploy´ment
em-po´ri·um
em-pow´er
em-pow´er-ment
em´press
emp´tied
emp´ti·er
emp´ties
emp´ti·ly
emp´ti-ness
emp´ty
emp´ty—hand´ed

emp´ty-ing
em´u-late
em-u-la´tion
em´u-la-tor
e·mul-si-fi-ca´tion
e·mul´si-fied
e·mul´si-fi·er
e·mul´si·fy
e·mul´sion
en-a´ble
en-a´bler
en-a´bling
en-act´
en-ac´tor
en-am´el
en-am´eled
en-am´el-ware
en-am´or
en-am´ored
en-camp´
en-cap´su-late
en-case´
en-chant´
en-chant´er
en-chant´ing
en-chant´ing·ly
en-chant´ment
en-chant´ress
en-cir´cle
en-cir´cling
en´clave
en-close´
en-clo´sure

en-code´
en-co´mi·um
en-com´pass
en´core
en-coun´ter
en-cour´age
en-cour´age-ment
en-cour´ag-ing
en-croach´
en-crust´
en-crus-ta´tion
en-crypt´
en-cum´ber
en-cum´brance
en-cy-clo-pae´di·a (Br.)
en-cy-clo-pe´di·a
en-cy-clo-pe´dic
end
en-dan´gered
en-dan´ger-ment
en-dear´
en-dear´ing
en-dear´ment
en-deav´or
en-deav´our (Br.)
en-dem´ic
en-dem´i-cal·ly
end´ing
end´less·ly
end´most
en-dorse´
en-dors-ee´
en-dorse´ment

en-dors´er
en-dors´ing
en-dow´
en-dow´er
en-dow´ment
en-due´
en-dur´a·ble
en-dur´a·bly
en-dur´ance
en-dure´
en-dur´ing
end´ways
end´wise
en´e-mies
en´e·my
en-er-get´ic
en´er-gize
en´er-giz·er
en´er·gy
en´er-vate
en-er-va´tion
en-fee´ble
en-fee´bling
en-fold´
en-force´
en-force´a·ble
en-force´ment
en-forc´er
en-forc´ing
en-fran´chise
en-gage´
en-gaged´
en-gage´ment

en-gag´er
en-gag´ing
en-gag´ing·ly
en-gen´der
en´gine
en-gi-neer´ing
en-gorge´
en-grain´
en-grave´
en-grav´er
en-grav´ing
en-gross´
en-gross´ed·ly
en-gross´er
en-gross´ing
en-gulf´
en-hance´
en-hance´ment
en-hanc´ing
e·nig´ma
e ·nig-mat´ic
en-join´
en-join´der
en-join´er
en-joy´
en-joy´a·ble
en-joy´a·bly
en-joy´ment
en-large´
en-large´a·ble
en-large-ment
en-light´en
en-light´en·er

en-light´en-ment
en-list´
en-list´ed
en-list´ment
en-liv´en
en-liv´en·er
en-liv´en-ing
en´mi-ties
en´mi·ty
en-no´ble
en-no´bler
en-no´bling
en-nui´
e·nor´mi·ty
e·nor´mous·ly
e·nough´
en-rage´
en-rapt´
en-rap´ture
en-rich´
en-rich´ment
en-robe´
en-roll´
en-rolled´
en-roll·ee´
en-roll´ing
en-roll´ment
en-rol´ment
en-sem´ble
en-shrine´
en-shrine´ment
en-slave´

en-snare´
en-sue´
en-su´ing
en-tail´ment
en-tan´gle
en-tan´gle-ment
en-tan´gling
en-tente´
en´ter
en-ter´ic
en-ter-i´tis
en´ter-prise
en´ter-pris-ing
en´ter-pris-ing·ly
en-ter-tain´
en-ter-tain´er
en-ter-tain´ing
en-ter-tain´ment
en-thrall´er
en-thrall´ing·ly
en-throne´ment
en-thuse´
en-thu´si-asm
en-thu´si-ast
en-thu-si-as´tic
en-tice´ment
en-tic´ing
en-tic´ing·ly
en-tic´ing-ness
en-tire´ly
en-tire´ty
en-ti´tle
en-ti´tle-ment

en´ti·ty
en-tomb´ment
en-to-mo-log´ic
en-to-mo-log´i-cal
en-to-mol´o-gist
en-to-mol´o·gy
en´tou-rage´
en´trance *(n.)*
en-trance´ *(v.)*
en-tranc´ing
en´trant
en-trap´ment
en´tre
en-treat´
en-treat´ies
en-treat´ing
en-treat´y
en´trée
en´tre-pre-neur´
en´tre-pre-neur´i·al
en´tries
en-trust´
en´try
en´try—lev´el
en´try-way
en-twine´
e·nu´mer-ate
e·nu-mer-a´tion
e·nun´ci-ate
e·nun-ci-a´tion
en-ure´
en-vel´op
en´ve-lope

88

en-vel´oped
en-vel´op-ing
en-vel´op-ment
en´vi-a·ble
en´vi-a·bly
en´vied
en´vi·er
en´vies
en´vi-ous
en´vi-ous·ly
en-vi´ron
en-vi´ron-ment
en-vi´ron-men´-
  tal·ly
en-vi´ron-men´tal-
  ist
en-vi´rons
en-vis´age
en-vi´sion
en´voy
en´vy
en´vy-ing
e´on
e·phem´er·al
e·phem´er-al·ly
ep´ic
ep´i-cen´ter
ep´i-cure
ep´i-cu-re´an
ep´i-dem´ic
ep´i-gram
ep´i-logue
ep´i-sode

ep-i-sod´ic
e·pis´tle
ep´i-taph
ep´i-thet
e·pit´o·me
e·pit-o-mize
ep´och
ep´och·al
ep-ox´y
eq´ua·ble
eq´ua·bly
e´qual
e´qualed
e´qual-ing
e·qual´i·ty
e´qual-ize
e´qual-iz·er
e´qual·ly
e·qua-nim´i·ty
e·qua´tion
e·qua´tor
e·qua-to´ri·al
e·ques´tri·an
e´qui-dis´tant
e´quine
e·quip´ment
e·quipped´
e·quip´ping
eq´ui-ta·ble
eq´ui-ta·bly
eq´ui·ty
e·quiv´a-lence
e·quiv´a-len·cy

e·quiv´a-lent·ly
e·quiv´o-ca·cy
e·quiv´o-cal
e·quiv´o-cal·ly
e·quiv´o-cate
e·quiv´o-ca´tion
e·quiv´o-ca-tor
e·rad´i-cate
e·rad-i-ca´tion
e·rase´
e·rased
e·ras´er
e·ras´ing
e·ra´sure
e·rect´
e·rec´tion
ere-now´
er-go-nom´ic
er-go-nom´i-cal·ly
er-go-nom´ics
e·rode´
e·rod´i·ble
e·rog´e-nous
e·ro´sion
e·ro´sive
e·rot´ic
e·rot´i·ca
e·rot´i-cism
er´ran·cy
er´rand
er´rant
er´rant·ly
er-rat´ic

err´ing
err´ing·ly
er-ro´ne-ous
er-ro´ne-ous·ly
er-ro´ne-ous-ness
er´ror
er´satz
erst´while´
er´u-dite
er-u-di´tion
e·rupt´
e·rup´tion
e·rup´tive
es´ca-late
es-ca-la´tion
es´ca-la-tor
es´ca-pade
es-cape´
es-caped´
es-cap·ee´
es-cap´ing
es-cap´ist
es-chew´
es´cort (n.)
es-cort´ (v.)
es´crow
es´o-ter´ic
es-o-ter´i-cal·ly
es-pe´cial
es-pe´cial·ly
es´pi-o-nage
es´pla-nade
es-pous´al

es-pouse´
es-pous´er
es-pous´ing
es´quire
es´say (n.)
es-say´ (v.)
es-say´er
es´say-ist
es´sence
es-sen´tial
es-sen´tial·ly
es-tab´lish
es-tab´lish-a·ble
es-tab´lished
es-tab´lish-ment
es-tate´
es-teem´
es´ti-ma·ble
es´ti-mate
es-ti-ma´tion
es´ti-ma-tor
es-trange´
es-trange´ment
es-trang´ing
es´tu-ar·y
etch´ing
e·ter´nal·ly
e·ter´ni·ty
e·the´re·al
e·the´re-al·ly
eth´ic
eth´i-cal·ly
eth´ics

eth´nic
eth´ni-cal·ly
eth-nic´i·ty
eth´no-cen´tric
et´i-quette
e´tude
et-y-mol´o·gy
eu´lo·gy
eu´phe-mis´tic
eu´phe-mize
eu·pho´ri·a
eu·phor´ic
eu-tha-na´sia
e·vac´u-ate
e·vac-u-a´tion
e·vade´
e·vad´ing
e·val´u-ate
e·val-u-a´tion
e´van-gel´ic
e´van-gel´i-cal
e·van´ge-lism
e·van´ge-list
e·van´ge -lis´tic
e·vap´o-rate
e·vap´o-rat-ing
e·vap-o-ra´tion
e·vap´o-ra-tor
e·va´sion
e·va´sive
e·va´sive·ly
e·va´sive-ness
e´ven-hand·ed

e´ven-ing *(equating)*
eve´ning *(night)*
e´ven·ly
e´ven-ness
e·vent´
e·ven–temp´ered
e·vent´ful
e·ven´tu·al
e·ven´tu-al´i·ty
e·ven´tu-al·ly
e·ven´tu-ate
ev´er-green
ev-er-last´ing
ev-er-more´
e·vert´
ev´er·y-bod·y
ev´er·y-day
ev´er·y-one
ev´er·y-thing
ev´er·y-where
e·vic´tion
ev´i-dence
ev´i-denc-ing
ev´i-dent
ev´i-den´tial
ev-i-den´ti-a·ry
ev´i-dent·ly
ev´i-dent-ness
e´vil
e´vil-do·er
e´vil-do-ing
e´vil·ly
e´vil–mind´ed

e·vince´
e·vinc´ing
e·vis´cer-ate
e·vis-cer-a´tion
ev´i-ta·ble
e·voke´
e·vok´ing
ev-o-lu´tion
ev-o-lu´tion-ar·y
ev-o-lu´tion-ist
e·volve´
e·volv´ing
e·vul´sion
ex-ac´er-bate
ex-ac´er-bat-ing
ex-act´
ex-act´ing
ex-ac´ti-tude
ex-act´ly
ex-act´ness
ex-ac´tor
ex-ag´ger-ate
ex-ag´ger-at·ed
ex-ag-ger-a´tion
ex-alt´
ex-al-ta´tion
ex-alt´ed
ex-alt´ed·ly
ex-am´
ex-am-i-na´tion
ex-am´ine
ex-am´in·er
ex-am´ple

ex-as´per-ate
ex-as´per-at-ing
ex-as-per-a´tion
ex´ca-vate
ex´ca-va´tion
ex´ca-va-tor
ex-ceed´
ex-ceed´ing·ly
ex-cel´
ex-celled´
ex´cel-lence
ex´cel-lent
ex-cel´ling
ex-cept´a·ble
ex-cept´ing
ex-cep´tion
ex-cep´tion-al
ex´cerpt *(n.)*
ex-cerpt´ *(v.)*
ex-cess´ *(n.)*
ex´cess *(adj.)*
ex-ces´sive·ly
ex-change´
ex-change´a·ble
ex-chang´ing
ex´che-quer
ex´cise *(n. tax)*
ex-cise´ *(v. cut out)*
ex-ci´sion
ex-cit´a·ble
ex-ci-ta´tion
ex-cite´
ex-cit´ed·ly

ex-cite′ment
ex-cit′er
ex-cit′ing
ex-claim′
ex-claim′er
ex-cla-ma′tion·al
ex-clam′a-to·ry
ex-clude′
ex-clud′ing
ex-clu′sion-ar·y
ex-clu′sive·ly
ex-clu-siv′i·ty
ex-com-mu′ni-cate
ex-com-mu-ni-ca′-
  tion
ex-co′ri-ate
ex-co-ri-a′tion
ex′cre-ment
ex-crete′
ex-cru′ci-at-ing·ly
ex′cul-pate
ex-cul′pa-to·ry
ex-cur′sion
ex-cus′a·ble
ex-cus′a·bly
ex-cuse′
ex-cus′ing
ex-ec′
ex′e-crate
ex-e-cra′tion
ex′e-cute
ex-e-cu′tion
ex-ec′u-tive

ex-ec′u-tor
ex-em′pla·ry
ex-em′pli·fy
ex-empt′
ex-emp′tion
ex′er-cise
ex′er-cis·er
ex-ert′
ex-er′tion
ex-ert′ive
ex-fo′li-ate
ex′hal′ant
ex-ha-la′tion
ex′hale
ex-haust′ed
ex-haust′i·ble
ex-haus′tion
ex-hib′it
ex-hi-bi′tion-ism
ex-hi-bi′tion-ist
ex-hib′i-tor
ex-hil′a-rate
ex-hil-a-ra′tion
ex-hil′a-ra-tor
ex-hort′
ex-hor-ta′tion
ex-hu-ma′tion
ex-hume′
ex′i-gen-cies
ex′i-gen·cy
ex-ig′u-ous
ex′ile
ex-ist′

ex-is′tence
ex-is′tent
ex-is-ten′tial
ex-is-ten′tial-ism
ex′o-dus
ex-on′er-ate
ex-on-er-a′tion
ex-or′bi-tance
ex-or′bi-tant
ex-or′bi-tant·ly
ex′or-cise
ex′or-cism
ex′or-cist
ex-ot′ic
ex-ot′i·ca
ex-pand′
ex-pand′a·ble
ex-pand′ed
ex-panse′
ex-pan′sion
ex-pan′sion-ar-y
ex-pan′sive·ly
ex-pa′tri-ate
ex-pa-tri-a′tion
ex-pect′an·cy
ex-pect′ant·ly
ex-pec-ta′tion
ex-pec′to-rant
ex-pec′to-rate
ex-pe′di-ence
ex-pe′di-en·cy
ex-pe′di-ent
ex-pe′di-ent·ly

ex´pe-dite
ex´pe-dit·er
ex´pe-dit-ing
ex-pe-di´tion
ex-pe-di´tion-ar·y
ex-pe-di´tious·ly
ex-pel´
ex-pelled´
ex-pel´ling
ex-pend´
ex-pend´a·ble
ex-pend´i-ture
ex-pense´
ex-pen´sive·ly
ex-pe´ri-ence
ex-pe´ri-enced
ex-pe´ri-enc-ing
ex-per´i-ment
ex-per´i-men´tal
ex-per´i-men´tal·ly
ex-per-i-men-ta´-
    tion
ex-pert´ *(adj.)*
ex´pert *(n., adj.)*
ex-per-tise´
ex´pert·ly
ex´pi-ate
ex-pi-ra´tion
ex-pire´
ex-pired´
ex-pir´ing
ex-plain´
ex-pla-na´tion

ex-plan´a-to·ry
ex´ple-tive
ex-plic´a·ble
ex´pli´ca·bly
ex´pli-cate
ex-pli-ca´tion
ex-plic´it
ex-plic´it·ly
ex-plode´
ex-plod´ing
ex-ploit´ *(v.)*
ex´ploit *(n.)*
ex-ploit´a·ble
ex-ploi-ta´tion
ex-ploit´er
ex-ploit´ive
ex-plo-ra´tion
ex-plor´a·tive
ex-plor´a-to·ry
ex-plore´
ex-plor´er
ex-plor´ing
ex-plo´sion
ex-plo´sive
ex-po´nent
ex-po-nen´tial
ex-po-nen´tial·ly
ex´port *(n., v.)*
ex-port´ *(v.)*
ex-por-ta´tion
ex-port´er
ex-pose´
ex-po-sé´

ex-posed´
ex-pos´ing
ex-pos´tu-late
ex-po´sure
ex-press´
ex-press´ing
ex-pres´sion
ex-pres´sion-ism
ex-pres´sion-less
ex-pres´sive·ly
ex-press´ly
ex-press´way
ex-pro´pri-ate
ex-pro-pri-a´tion
ex-pul´sion
ex-punge´
ex´pur-gate
ex-pur-ga´tion
ex-quis´ite·ly
ex´tant
ex-tem-po-ra´ne-
    ous
ex-tem-po-ra´ne-
    ous·ly
ex-tem´po-rar·y
ex-tem´po-rize
ex-tend´ed
ex-tend´er
ex-ten´si·ble
ex-ten´sion
ex-ten´sive·ly
ex-tent´
ex-ten´u-ate

ex-ten´u-at-ing
ex-ten-u-a´tion
ex-te´ri-or
ex-ter´mi-nate
ex-ter-mi-na´tion
ex-ter´mi-na-tor
ex-ter´nal
ex-ter´nal-ize
ex-ter´nal·ly
ex-tinct´
ex-tinc´tion
ex-tin´guish
ex-tin´guish-a·ble
ex-tin´guish·er
ex´tir-pate
ex-tol´
ex-tolled´
ex-tol´ling
ex-tort´
ex-tort´ed
ex-tor´tion
ex-tor´tion·er
ex-tor´tion-ist
ex´tra
ex´tract *(n.)*
ex-tract´ *(v.)*
ex-trac´tion
ex´tra-cur-ric´u-lar
ex´tra-dite
ex-tra-di´tion
ex-tra-le´gal
ex´tra-mar´i-tal
ex-tra´ne-ous

ex-tra´ne-ous·ly
ex-traor´di-nar´i·ly
ex-traor´di-nar·y
ex-trap´o-late
ex-trap-o-la´tion
ex-tra-sen´so·ry
ex-tra-ter-res´tri·al
ex-trav´a-gance
ex-trav´a-gant·ly
ex-trav-a-gan´za
ex-treme´ly
ex-trem´ist
ex-trem´i·ty
ex-tric´a·ble
ex´tri-cate
ex-tri-ca´tion
ex´tro-vert
ex-trude´
ex-trud´er
ex-trud´ing
ex-tru´sion
ex-tru´sive
ex-ude´
ex-ult´
ex-ul-ta´tion
ex´urb
ex-ur´ban-ite
ex-ur´bi·a
eye´ball
eye´brow
eye´ful
eye´glass
eye´ing

eye´lash
eye´let
eye´lid
eye´lin·er
eye´o-pen·er
eye´sight
eye´sore

F

fa´ble
fa´bled
fab´ric
fab´ri-cate
fab-ri-ca´tion
fab´u-list
fab´u-lous
fab´u-lous·ly
fab´u-lous-ness
fa-çade´
face´less
face´lift
face´–off
face´plate
fac´et
fac´et-ed
fa-ce´tious
fa-ce´tious·ly
fa-ce´tious-ness
face´–to–face´
fa´cial
fac´ile
fa-cil´i-tate
fa-cil´i-ties

fa-cil'i·ty
fac'ing
fac-sim'i·le
fact'find-ing
fac'tion
fac'tion·al
fac'tious
fac'tious·ly
fac-ti'tious
fac'tor
fac'to-ries
fac-tor'ing
fac'to·ry
fac-to'tum
fac'tu·al
fac'ul-ties
fac'ul·ty
fad'dish
fad'er
fail'ing
fail'ure
faint'ed
faint'heart·ed
faint'ly
fair'ground
fair'ies
fair'ly
fair–mind'ed
fair'ness
fair'way
fair'y
fair'y-land
fair'y tale

faith'ful·ly
faith'ful-ness
faith'less
faith'less·ly
fake
fak'er
fak'er·y
fal'la-cies
fal-la'cious
fal'la·cy
fall'ing
fall'out
fal'low
false'hood
false'ly
fal-si-fi-ca'tion
fal'si-fied
fal'si·fy
fal'ter
fal'ter-ing
fame
famed
fa-mil'ial
fa-mil'iar
fa-mil-iar'i·ty
fa-mil-iar-i·za'tion
fa-mil'iar-ize
fa-mil'iar·ly
fam'i-lies
fam'i·ly
fam'ine
fam'ish
fam'ished

fa'mous
fa'mous·ly
fa-nat'ic
fa-nat'i-cal·ly
fa-nat'i-cism
fan'cied
fan'ci·er
fan'cies
fan'ci-ful
fan'cy
fan'fare
fan'fold
fang
fanged
fan'gled
fanned
fan'ning
fan'ta-size
fan-tas'tic
fan'ta·sy
far'ci-cal
fare-well'
far'fetched
farm'er
farm'hand
farm'house
farm'ing
farm'land
farm'yard
far'sight·ed
far'ther
far'thest
fas'ci·a

fas´ci-nate
fas´ci-nat·ed
fas´ci-nat-ing
fas-ci-na´tion
fash´ion
fash´ion-a·ble
fash´ion-a·bly
fast´ten
fas´ten·er
fas´ten-ing
fas-tid´i-ous
fas-tid´i-ous·ly
fast´ing
fa´tal-ist
fa-tal-is´tic
fa-tal-is´ti-cal·ly
fa-tal´i·ty
fa´tal·ly
fate´ful
fat´head
fa´ther
fa´ther-land
fa´ther-less
fa´ther·ly
fath´om
fath´om-a·ble
fath´om-less
fa-tigue´
fa-tigued´
fa-tigu´ing
fat´ten
fat´ten·er
fat´ty

fa-tu´i·ty
fat´u-ous
fat´u-ous·ly
fau´cet
fault´find-ing
fault´i·er
fault´i·ly
fault´less·ly
fault´y
fau´na
fa´vor
fa´vor-a·ble
fa´vor-a·bly
fa´vor-ite
fa´vor-it-ism
fa´vour (Br.)
fawn´ing·ly
fe´al·ty
fear´ful
fear´less·ly
fea´sance
fea-si-bil´i·ty
fea´si·ble
fea´si·bly
feast
feath´er
feath´er-bed-ding
feath´er-brain
feath´ered
feath´er-weight
feath´er·y
fea´ture
fea´tured

feb´rile
feck´less
feck´less·ly
fed´er-al
fed´er-al-ist
fed-er-a´tion
fe-do´ra
fee´ble
fee´ble-ness
feed´back
feed´er
feed´ing
feed´stuff
feel´er
feel´ing
feet´first´
feign
feigned
feign´ing
feint
feist´i-ness
feist´y
fe-lic-i-ta´tion
fe-lic´i-tous·ly
fe-lic´i·ty
fe´line
fel´low
fel´low-ship
fel´on
fe-lo´ni-ous·ly
fel´o·ny
fe´male
fem´i-na·cy

fem´i-nine·ly
fem-i-nin´i·ty
fem´i-nism
fem´i-nist
fem´i-nize
fenc´ing
fend´er
fe´ral
fer-ment´
fer-men-ta´tion
fe-ro´cious·ly
fe-roc´i·ty
fer´ried
fer´ries
fer´ry
fer´ry-boat
fer´ry-ing
fer´tile
fer-til´i·ty
fer-til-i·za´tion
fer-til-i·za´tion·al
fer´til-ize
fer´til-iz·er
fer´vent
fer´vent·ly
fer´vid
fer´vid·ly
fer´vor
fes´ter
fes´ti-val
fes´tive
fes-tiv´i·ty
fes-toon´

fe´tal
fetch´ing
fet´id
fet´ish
fet´ter
fet´tle
fe´tus
feud
feu´dal
feu-dal-is´tic
fe´ver
fe´ver-ish
fe´ver-ish·ly
few´er
fi-as´co
fi´at
fib´bing
fi´brous
fick´le
fic´tion-al-ize
fic-ti´tious·ly
fid´dle
fid´dler
fid´dle-sticks
fid´dling
fi-del´i·ty
fid´get
fi-du´ci-ar·y
fief´dom
field´er
field´stone
fiend´ish·ly
fierce´ly

fi´er·y
fi-es´ta
fif-teen´
fif-teenth´
fifth
fif´ti-eth
fif´ty
fight´er
fight´ing
fig´ment
fig´ure
fig´ured
fig´ure-head
fil´a-ment
filch´er
fi-let´
fil´i·al
fil´i-bus-ter
fil´i-gree
fill
fill´er
fil´let
fill´ing
fil´ly
film´i·er
film´i·ly
film´i-ness
film´y
fil´ter
filth
filth´i·er
filth´i-ness
filth-y

fil´trate
fil-tra´tion
fi-na´gle
fi-na´gler
fi-na´gling
fi´nal
fi-nal´e
fi´nal-ist
fi-nal´i·ty
fi´na-lize
fi-na-li-za´tion
fi´nal·ly
fi-nance´
fi-nan´cial·ly
fin-an-cier´
fi-nanc´ing
find´er
find´ing
fine´ly
fine´ness
fin´er·y
fi-nesse´
fin´ger
fin´gered
fin´ger-ing
fin´ger-ling
fin´ger-nail
fin´ger-print
fin´i·al
fin´ick·y
fin´is
fin´ish
fin´ished

fin´ish·er
fi´nite
fin´nick·y
fire´arm
fire´brand
fire´crack·er
fire´fight
fire´fly
fire´man
fire´place
fire´proof
fire´side
fire´works
fir´ing
fir´ma-ment
firm´er
firm´ly
fir´ry
first´born
first´ly
fis´cal·ly
fish´bowl
fish´er-man
fish´er·y
fish´hook
fish´ing
fish´mon-ger
fish´net
fish´y
fis´sion
fis´sion-a·ble
fis´sure
fist´fight

fist´ful
fit´ful·ly
fit´ness
fit´ted
fit´ting·ly
fiv´er
fix´ate
fix-a´tion
fix´a-tive
fixed
fix´ing
fix´ture
fiz´zle
fiz´zling
fizz´y
flab´ber-gast
flab´bi-ness
flab´by
flac´cid
flac-cid´i·ty
flag´el-late
flagged
flag´ging
flag´on
fla´grance
fla´gran·cy
fla´grant
fia´grant·ly
flake
flaked
flak´i·er
flak´i-ness
flak´ing

flak´y
flam-boy´ant
flam-boy´ant·ly
flame
flamed
flam´ing
flam´ma·ble
flange
flanged
flank
flank´er
flan´nel
flap´jack
flap´pa·ble
flapped
flap´per
flap´ping
flare
flare´–up
flar´ing
flash
flash´back
flash´bulb
flash´ing
flash´light
flash´y
flat´car
flat´foot
flat–footed
flat´ly
flat´ten
flat´ter
flat´ter·er

flat´ter-ing
flat´ter·y
flat´top
flat´ware
flaunt´ing
fla´vor
fla´vor-ful
fla´vour (Br.)
flaw´less·ly
flea´bag
flea´bite
flea´–bit-ten
fledged
flee´ing
fleet–foot´ed
fleet´ing·ly
fleet´ness
flesh´i-ness
flesh´y
flex-i-bil´i·ty
flex´i·ble
flex´i·bly
flex´time
flick´er·y
fli´er
flight´i-ness
flight´less
flight´y
flim´flam
flim´si·ly
flim´si-ness
flim´sy
flinch´ing

fling´ing
flip´pant
flipped
flip´per
flip´ping
flirt
flir-ta´tion
flir-ta´tious·ly
flirt´er
flirt´y
flit´ting
fliv´ver
float´er
float´ing
flocked
flock´ing
flog´ging
flood´light
floor´board
floor´ing
floor´walk·er
flop´house
flop´pier
flop´ping
flop´py
flo´ra
flo´ral
flo-res´cence
flo-res´cent
flor´id
flor´id·ly
flo´rist
flo-ta´tion

flo-til´la
flot´sam
flounced
flounc´ing
flounc´y
flour´ish
flour´ished
flour´ish-ing
flour´y
flout´ed
flout´ing
flow´ered
flow´er-et
flow´er-ing
flow´er-pot
flow´er-y
flow´ing
flown
fluc´tu-ate
fluc´tu-at-ed
fluc´tu-at-ing
fluc-tu-a´tion
flu´en-cy
flu´ent-ly
fluff´i·er
fluff´i-ness
fluff´y
flu´id
fluke
fluk´y
flum´mer·y
flunk´out
flu-o-res´cence

flu-o-res´cent
flu-o-resc´ing
flu-o-ri-da´tion
flu´o-ride
flur´ry
flus´ter
flut´ed
flut´ing
flut´ist
flut´tered
flut´ter-ing
flut´ter·y
fly´–by–night
fly´catcher
fly´er
fly´ing
fly´wheel
foam´i·er
foam´i-ness
foam´ing
foam´y
fo´cal
fo´cus
fo´cused
fo´cus-ing
fod´der
fog´bound
fog´gi·er
fog´gi-ness
fog´gy
fog´horn
fo´gy
foi´ble

foiled
foil´ing
foist´ed
fold´ed
fold´er
fold´ing
fold´out
fo´li-age
fo-li-a´tion
folk´lore
folk´lor·ic
folks·y
folk´way
fol´low
fol´lowed
fol´low·er
fol´low-ing
fol´low–through
fol´low–up
fo-ment´
fon´dled
fon´dler
fon´dling
fond´ly
fond´ness
food´stuff
fool´er·y
fool´har·dy
fool´ing
fool´ish·ly
fool´ish-ness
fool´proof
foot´age

foot´ed
foot´er
foot´fall
foot´hill
foot´hold
foot´ing
foot´light
foot´print
foot´sie
foot´step
fop´per·y
fop´pish
for´age
for´aged
for´ag·er
for´ag·ing
for´ay
for-bear´
for-bear´ance
for-bid´den
for-bid´ding
forced
force´ful
forc´i·bly
forc´ing
fore´arm
fore-bod´ing
fore´cast
fore´cast·er
fore-close´
fore-clo´sure
fore´fa·ther
fore´go

fore´go·ing
fore´gone´
fore´ground
fore´head
for´eign
for´eign·er
fore´knowl-edge
fore´most
fo-ren´sic
fore-or-dain´
fore´run-ner
fore-see´a·ble
fore-seen´
fore-shad´ow-ing
fore-short´en
fore´sight·ed
fore´sight-ed-ness
for´est
for-est-a´tion
for´est·ed
for´est·ry
fore-tell´
for-ev´er
fore-warn´
fore´word
for´feit
for´fei-ture
forg´er
for´ger·y
for-get´ful
for-get´ful-ness
for-get´ta·ble
for-get´ting

forg´ing
for-give´
for-giv´en
for-give´ness
for-giv´ing
for-go´ing
for-got´ten
fork´ful
for-lorn´ly
for´mal
for-mal´i·ty
for´mal-ize
for´mal-wear
for´mat
for-ma´tion
form´a-tive·ly
for´mer *(bygone)*
for´mer·ly
for´mi-da·ble
for´mi-da·bly
form´less
for´mu·la
for´mu-late
for-mu-la´tion
for´ni-cate
for-sake´
for-sak´en
for-sook´
for-swear´
forth´com-ing
forth´right
for´ti-eth
for-ti-fi-ca´tion

101

for´ti·fied
for´ti·fi·er
for´ti·fy
for´ti·tude
for´tress
for·tu´i·tous·ly
for·tu´i·ty
for´tu·nate·ly
for´tune
for´ty
fo´rum
for´ward
for´ward·er
fos´sil
fos´sil-ize
fos´ter
foul´ly
foun-da´tion
found´er *(n.)*
foun´der *(v.)*
found´ling
found´ries
found´ry
foun´tain
foun´tain-head
four´flush·er
four´fold
four´some
four-teen´
four-teenth´
fourth
fowl´er
fox´i-ness

fox´y
foy´er
fra´cas
frac´tal
frac´tion
frac´tious·ly
frac´ture
frag´ile
fra-gil´i·ty
frag´ment
frag´men-tar·y
frag´ment·ed
fra´grance
fra´gran·cy
fra´grant
fra´grant·ly
frail´ties
frail´ty
frame´a·ble
frame´a·ble-ness
framed
fram´er
frame´work
fram´ing
fran´chise
fran-chi-see´
fran´chis·er
fran´gi·ble
fran´gi·ble-ness
frank´ly
frank´ness
fran´tic
fran´ti-cal·ly

fran´tic·ly
fra-ter´nal-ism
fra-ter´nal·ly
fra-ter´ni·ty
frat´er-nize
frat´ri-ci-dal
frat´ri-cide
fraud´u-lence
fraud´u-len·cy
fraud´u-lent·ly
fraught
frayed
fraz´zle
freak´ish
freak´y
freck´led
free´bie
free´dom
free´ly
fre´er
free´stand´ing
free´think·er
free-wheel´ing
free´will
freez´er
freez´ing
freight´er
fre-net´ic
fren´zied
fren´zy
fre´quen·cy
fre´quent
fre´quent·er

fre´quent·ly
fre´quent-ness
fres´co
fres´coes
fresh´en
fresh´ly
fresh´man
fresh´man-ship
fret´ful
fret´ful-ness
fri-a·bil´i·ty
fri´a·ble
fri´ar
fri´ar·y
fric´tion
friend´less
friend´li·er
friend´li-ness
friend´ly
fright´en
fright´ened
fright´en-ing
fright´ful·ly
frig´id
fri-gid´i·ty
frill´i-ness
frill´y
fringed
frisk´i·er
frisk´i-ness
frisk´y
frit´ter
fri-vol´i·ty

friv´o-lous·ly
friz´zle
friz´zly
frol´ic
frol´icked
frol´ick-ing
frol´ic-some
front´age
fron´tal
front´al·ly
fron-tier´
fron´tis-piece
frost´bite
frost´bit-ten
frost´ed
frost´i·ly
frost´ing
frost´y
froth´i·er
froth´i-ness
froth´y
frowned
frown´ing
frow´zy
fro´zen
fru´gal
fru-gal´i·ty
fru´gal-ness
fruit´cake
fruit´ful
fruit´i-ness
fru-i´tion
fruit·y

frump´y
frus´trate
frus´trat-ed
frus´trat-ing
frus-tra´tion
fu´el
fu´gi-tive
fugue
ful´crum
ful-fill´ing
ful-fill´ment
ful´gent
full´ness
ful´ly
ful´mi-nate
ful-mi-na´tion
ful´some
fum´ble
fum´bling
fu´mi-gant
fu´mi-gate
fu´mi-gat-ing
fu-mi-ga´tion
fu´mi-ga-tor
fum´ing
func´tion
func´tion-al
func´tion-al·ly
func´tion-ar·y
fun-da-men´tal
fun-da-men´tal·ly
fu´ner-al
fu´ner-ar·y

fu-ne´re-al
fun´gi-cide
fun´gus
fun´neled
fun´nel-ing
fun´ny
fu´ri-ous
fu´ri-ous·ly
fu´ri-ous-ness
fur´lough
fur´nace
fur´nish-ings
fur´ni-ture
fu´ror
fur´row
fur´ry
fur´ther-ance
fur´ther-more
fur´thest
fur´tive·ly
fu´ry
fu´se-lage
fu´si·ble
fu´sion
fuss´budg·et
fuss´i·ly
fuss´i-ness
fuss´y
fu´tile·ly
fu´tile-ness
fu-til´i·ty
fu´ton
fu´ture

fu-tur-is´tic
fuzz´y

G

gab´ar-dine
gab´bing
gab´ble
gab´by
ga´bled
ga´bling
gad´a·bout
gad´fly
gad´get
gad´get·ry
gaffe
gag
ga´ga
gagged
gag´ging
gag´gle
gai´e·ty
gai´ly
gain´a·ble
gai´ner (dive)
gain´ful·ly
gain´ly
gain´say·er
gait´ed
ga´la
ga-lac´tic
ga-lax´i·al
gal´ax·y
gal´lant

gal´lant·ly
gal´lant·ry
gal´le·on
gal-le-ri´a
gal´ler·y
gal´ley
gall´ing
gal´li-vant
gal´lon
gal´loped
gal´lop·er
gal´lop-ing
gal´lows
gall´stone
ga-loot´
ga-lore´
gal-va-ni-za´tion
gal´va-nize
gam´bler
gam´bling
gam´bol
gam´boled
gam´bol-ing
game´keep·er
game´ly
games´man-ship
gam´ey
gam´i·ly
gam´y
gan´der
gang´bust·ers
gan´gly
gang´ster

104

gang′way
ga-rage′
gar′bage
gar′ble
gar′bled
gar′den
gar′den·er
gar-gan′tu·an
gar′gled
gar′gling
gar′goyle
gar′ish·ly
gar′ish-ness
gar′land
gar′lic
gar′lick·y
gar′ment
gar′ner
gar′nish
gar′nish·ee′
gar′nish·er
gar′nish-ment
gar′ret
gar′ri-son
gar′ru-lous
gar′ru-lous-ness
gar′ter
gas′e-ous
gas-o-line′
gasp′ing
gas′tric
gate′house
gate′keep·er

gath′ered
gath′er-ing
gauche
gaud′i·ly
gaud′y
gauged
gaug′ing
gaunt′let
gaunt′ness
gauze
gav′el·er
gay′ly
gazed
ga-zette′
gaz′et-teer′
gaz′ing
gear′box
gear′shift
gee′zer
gel′a-tin
gel′a-tine
ge-lat′i-nous
gel′id
gelled
gel′ling
gen-e-al′o·gy
gen′er·al
gen-er-al′i·ty
gen-er-al-i·za′tion
gen′er-al-ize
gen′er-al·ly
gen′er-ate
gen′er-at-ing

gen-er-a′tion
gen′er-a-tive
gen′er-a-tor
ge-ner′ic
ge-ner′i-cal·ly
gen′er-os′i·ty
gen′er-ous·ly
ge-net′ic
ge-net′i-cal·ly
ge′nial
ge-ni-al′i·ty
ge′nie
ge′nius
gen′o-cide
gen′re
gen-teel′ly
gen′tile
gen-til′i·ty
gen′tle
gen′tle-man·ly
gen′tle-wom·an
gen′tlest
gent′ly
gen-tri-fi-ca′tion
gen′try
gen′u-flect
gen-u-flec′tion
gen′u-ine·ly
ge′ode
ge-o-graph′ic
ge-o-graph′i-cal·ly
ge-og′ra-phy
ge-o-log′ic

105

ge-o-log´i-cal
ge-ol´o-gist
ge-ol´o-gy
ge-o-met´ric
ge-o-met´ri-cal·ly
ge-om´e-try
ge-o-po-lit´i-cal
ger-i-at´rics
ger-mane´
ger´mi-cide
ger´mi-nate
ges´tur·al
ges´ture
ges´tur·er
ges´tur-ing
get´a·way
get´ter
get´ting
gey´ser
ghast´li-ness
ghast´ly
gher´kin
ghet´to
ghost´li-ness
ghost´ly
ghost´writ·er
ghoul´ish
gi´ant
gib´ber-ish
gibe
gib´ing
gid´di·ly
gid´di-ness

gid´dy
gift´ed
gig´a-byte
gi-gan´tic
gi-gan´ti-cal·ly
gig´gle
gig´gling
gig´gly
gild´ing
gim´let
gim´mick·ry
gim´mick·y
gin´ger
gin´ger-bread
gin´ger·ly
gin´ger-snap
gird´er
gird´ing
gir´dle
girl´friend
gis´mo
give´a·way
giv´en
giv´er
giv´ing
gla´cial
gla´cier
glad´den
glade
glad´i-a-tor
glad´i-a-to´ri·al
glad´ly
glad´ness

glam´or-ize
glam´o-rous·ly
glam´our
glance
glanc´ing
glan´du-lar
glar´ing
glass´es
glass´mak-ing
glass´ware
glass´y
gleam´ing
glee´ful·ly
glib´ly
glid´er
glid´ing
glim´mer-ing
glimpse
glimps´ing
glis´ten
glitch
glit´ter
glit-te-ra´ti
glit´ter-ing
glit´ter´y
glitz´y
gloat´ing
glob´al-ism
glob-al-i-za´tion
glob´al·ly
glob´u-lar
glob´ule
gloom´i·ly

gloom´i-ness

gloom´y

glo-ri-fi-ca´tion

glo´ri-fied

glo´ri-fi·er

glo´ri·fy

glo´ri-fy-ing

glo´ri-ous·ly

glo´ry

glos´sa·ry

glos´si-ness

gloss´y

gloved

glow´er-ing

glow´ing·ly

glued

glum´ly

glut´ted

glut´ton-ous

glut´ton·y

gnarl

gnarled

gnarl´y

gnaw´er

gnaw´ing

gnome

gnos´tic

goad´ed

goal´keep·er

goal´tend·er

goal´tend-ing

gob´ble-dy-gook

gob´bler

gob´bling

gob´let

gob´lin

god´dess

god´fa-ther

god´less

god´like

god´li-ness

god´ly

god´moth·er

god´par-ent

god´send

gold´en

golf´er

gol´ly

gon´do·la

gon-do-lier´

gone

gon´er

good–by´

good-bye´

good–bye´

good´heart´ed

good´ies

good´ness

good´y

goo´ey

goof´i-ness

goof´y

goon´y

gorge

gor´geous·ly

gor´geous-ness

gor´mand-ize

gor´y

gos´pel

gos´sa-mer

gos´sip-ing

gos´sip-mon-ger

gos´sip·y

goth´ic

goth´i-cal·ly

got´ten

gouge

goug´er

goug´ing

gour´mand

gour´man-dise´

gour´met

gout´y

gov´ern-a·ble

gov´ern-ance

gov´er-ness

gov´ern-ment

gov´er-nor

grab´ber

grab´bing

grab´by

grace´ful·ly

grace´ful-ness

grace´less

gra´cious·ly

gra´cious-ness

gra-da´tion

grad´ed

grad´er

gra´di-ent
grad´ing
grad´u-al·ly
grad´u-at·ed
grad´u-at-ing
grad-u-a´tion
graf-fi´ti
graf-fi´to
graft´ing
grain´i-ness
grain´y
gram-mat´i-cal·ly
gra´na·ry
grand-child
grand´chil-dren
grand´dad
grand-daugh-ter
gran-dee´
gran´deur
grand´fa-ther
gran-dil´o-quence
gran-dil´o-quent
gran´di-ose
grand´ly
grand´ma
grand´moth·er
grand´neph·ew
grand´niece
grand´pa
grand´par-ent
grand´son
grand´stand
grang´er

gran´ny
grant´er
grant´or
gran´u-lar
gran-u-lar´i·ty
gran´u-lat·ed
gran-u-la´tion
gran´ule
grape´vine
graph´ic
graph´i-cal·ly
grap´ple
grasped
grasp´ing
grass´i-ness
grass´land
grass´y
grate´ful·ly
grate´ful-ness
grat´er
grat-i-fi-ca´tion
grat´i-fied
grat´i-fy
grat´i-fy-ing
grat´ing
gra´tis
grat´i-tude
gra-tu´i-ties
gra-tu´i-tous·ly
gra-tu´i·ty
grav´el
grav´el·ly
grave´ly

grav´en
grav´i-tate
grav´i-tat-ing
grav-i-ta´tion·al
grav´i·ty
gra-vure´
gra´vy
gray´beard
gray´ish
gray´ness
graz´er
graz´ing
grease´less
greas´y
great´en
great´ly
great´ness
greed´i·ly
greed´i-ness
greed´y
green´er·y
green´gro-cer
green´ish
greet´ing
gre-gar´i-ous
grid´dle
grid´lock
grief´strick·en
griev´ance
grieve
griev´er
griev´ing
griev´ous·ly

grim´ace	group´ie	guid´ance
grime	grov´el	guide´book
grim´y	grov´eled	guide´post
grind´er	grov´el·er	guile´ful
grind´ing	grov´el-ing	guile´less
grind´stone	grow´er	guilt´i·ly
gripe	grow´ing	guilt´less
grip´er	grown	guilt´y
grip´ing	growth	guise
grippe	grub´by	gull´i·ble
gris´ly	grudg´ing·ly	gull´i·bly
grist	grue´some	gum´mi-ness
gris´tle	grum´bler	gum´my
grit´ty	grum´bling	gump´tion
griz´zled	grum´bly	gun´fight·er
groaned	grump´i·ly	gun´fire
groan´ing	grump´i-ness	gun´ner·y
gro´cer	grump´ish	gun´ny-sack
gro´cer-ies	grump´y	gun´shot
gro´cer·y	grun´gy	gur´gle
grog´gy	guar´an-tee´	gur´gling
grooms´man	guar´an-ties	gush´er
gros´grained	guar´an-tor	gush´i-ness
gross´ly	guar´an·ty	gush´ing·ly
gross´ness	guard´ed·ly	gush´y
gro-tesque´ly	guard´i·an	gust´i·ly
grouch´i-ness	guard´i-an-ship	gust·to
grouch´y	guess´er	gust´y
ground´break·er	guess´ing	gut´less
ground´break-ing	guess´ti-mate	guts´y
ground´less	guess´work	gut´ted
grounds´keep·er	guest´house	gut´ter
ground´swell	guf-faw´	gut´tur·al

guz´zle

guz´zling

gym-na´si·um

gym´nast

gym-nas´tics

gy-ne-col´o-gist

gy-ne-col´o·gy

gyp´sy

gy´rate

gy-ra´tion

gy´rat-ing

gy´ro-scope

gy -ro-scop´ic

H

ha-bil-i-ta´tion

hab´it

hab´i-tat

hab-i-ta´tion

ha-bit´u-al·ly

ha-bit´u-ate

ha-bit-u-a´tion

ha-bit´u·é

hab´it·us

hack´er

hack´le

hack´neyed

hag´gard

hag´gle

hair´do

hair´line

hairs´breadth

hair´spring

hair´style

hair´y

half´heart·ed

half´way

hal-i-to´sis

hal-le-lu´jah

hal´lowed

hal-lu-ci-na´tion

hal-lu´ci-na-to·ry

ham´let

ham´per

hand´bas-ket

hand´ful

hand´i-cap

hand´i-capped

hand´i-cap-per

hand´i-craft

hand´i·ly

hand´i-ness

hand´ker-chief

han´dle

han´dler

han´dling

hand´rail

hand´shake

hand´some·ly

hand´stand

hand´wo´ven

hand´writ-ing

hand´y

hang´ing

hang´o·ver

hang´–up

han´ker-ing

han´ky

hap-haz´ard·ly

hap´less

hap´pen-ing

hap´pen-stance

hap´pi·ly

hap´pi-ness

hap´py

ha-rangue´

ha-rangu´ing

ha-rass´

ha-rassed´

ha-rass´ing

ha-rass´ment

har´bin-ger

hard´en

hard´ened

hard´en·er

hard´en-ing

hard´head·ed

har´di·ly

har´di-ness

hard´ly

hard´ness

hard´ship

har´dy

harm´ful

harm´ful-ness

harm´less·ly

harm´less-ness

har-mon´ic

har-mon´i·ca

har-mon´i-cal·ly	ha´zel-nut	heart´y
har-mo´ni-ous·ly	haz´ing	heat´ed
har´mo-nize	ha´zy	heat´ed·ly
har´mo-niz-ing	head´ache	heat´er
har´mo·ny	head´ach·y	hea´then
harp´si-chord	head´dress	heat´stroke
har´ri-dan	head´er	heav´en·ly
harsh´ly	head´hunt·er	heaven–sent
harsh´ness	head´ing	heav´en-ward
har´vest	head´quar-ters	heav´i·er
har´vester	head´strong	heav´i·ly
has´sle	head´wait´er	heav´y
has´sled	head´y	heav´y-set
haste	heal´er	heck´le
has´ten	heal´ing	heck´ler
hast´i·ly	health´ful	heck´ling
hast´y	health´i·er	hec´tic
hate´ful	health´i-est	hedg´er
hate´mon-ger	health´i-ness	hedg´ing
ha´tred	health´y	he´do-nism
haugh´ti·ly	hear´ing	he´do-nist
haugh´ti-ness	hark´en	heed´ful
haugh´ty	hear´say	heed´less
haunt´ed	hearse	heft´i·er
haunt´ing	heart´ache	heft´i-est
hav´oc	heart´beat	heft´i·ly
hawk´er	heart´bro-ken	heft´y
hawk´ish	heart´burn	heif´er
haw´ser	heart´en	height´en
hay´mow	heart´felt	hei´nous
hay´ride	heart´less	heir´loom
haz´ard	heart´sick	heist
haz´ard-ous	heart´warm-ing	hel´i-cop-ter

he´li·um
he´lix
hel´lion
hell´ish
hel´lo´
hel´met·ed
helms´man
help´er
help´ful
help´ing
help´less·ly
help´less-ness
hem´i-sphere
hem´line
hem´lock
hence´forth´
hench´man
her´ald
he-ral´dic
her´ald·ry
her-ba´ceous
herb´al
her´bi-cide
her´biv-ore
here-af´ter
here´by
he-red´i-tar·y
he-red´i·ty
here´in-af´ter
here-of´
her´e·sy
her´e-tic
here´to-fore´

her´i-tage
her-maph´ro-dite
her´mit-age
her´ni·a
her´ni-ate
he´ro
he´roes
he-ro´ic
he-ro´i-cal·ly
her´o-ism
her-self´
hes´i-tan·cy
hes´i-tant
hes´i-tant·ly
hes´i-tate
hes´i-tat-ing·ly
hes-i-ta´tion
het-er-o-sex´u-al
heu-ris´tic
heu-ris´ti-cal·ly
hex-a-dec´i-mal
hex´a-gon
hex-ag´o-nal
hi-a´tus
hi´ber-nate
hi´ber-nat-ing
hi-ber-na´tion
hic´cough
hic´cup
hid´den
hide´a-way
hide´bound
hid´e-ous·ly

hid´ing
hi´er-ar´chal
hi´er-ar´chi-cal·ly
hi´er-ar-chy
hi´er-o-glyph´ic
high´born
high´bred
high´brow
high´lev´el
high´life
high´light
high´way
hik´er
hik´ing
hi-lar´i-ous·ly
hi-lar´i·ty
hill´i-ness
hill´side
hill´top
hill´y
him-self´
hind´most
hin´drance
hind´sight
hip´po-drome
hire´ling
hir´sute
his-to´ri·an
his-tor´ic
his-tor´i-cal
his-tor´i-cal·ly
his´to-ries
his´to·ry

his-tri-on´ics	home´less	hoop´la
hitch´hike	home´li-ness	hoo-ray´
hitch´hik·er	home´ly	hoose´gow
hoa´gy	home´mak·er	hoot´en-an·ny
hoard´ing	ho´me·o-path´ic	hoot´er
hoarse·ly	home´sick-ness	hope´ful·ly
hoarse-ness	home´stretch	hope´less·ly
hoar´y	home´ward	hope´less-ness
hoax	hom´ey-ness	hop´per
hob´ble	hom´i-ci-dal	hop´ping
hob´by	hom´i-cide	ho-ri´zon
hob´by-ist	hom´i-lies	hor´i-zon´tal·ly
hob´nob-bing	hom´i·ly	hor´mone
hock´ey	hom´i·ny	hor´o-scope
hodge´podge	ho-mo-ge´ne·ous	hor-ren´dous·ly
hoist´ed	ho-mog´e-nize	hor´ri·ble
hold´ing	ho-mo-sex´u·al	hor´ri·bly
hold´out	hon´est·ly	hor´rid
hol´i-day	hon´es·ty	hor-rif´ic
ho´li-ness	hon´ey-moon	hor-rif´i-cal·ly
ho-lis´tic	hon´or-a·ble	hor´ri-fied
ho-lis´ti-cal·ly	hon´or-a·bly	hor´ri·fy
hol´low	hon-o-rar´i·um	hor´ror
hol´o-caust	hon´or-ar·y	hors d'oeuvre
hol´o-gram	hon´our (Br.)	horse´pow·er
hol´o-graph	hood´ed	hors´y
ho-log´ra-phy	hood´lum	hor-ti-cul´tur·al
hol´ster	hood´wink	hor´ti-cul-ture
ho´ly	hoofed	hor´ti-cul´tur-ist
hom´age	hoof´er	ho´sier·y
home´bod·y	hook´ed	hos´pice
home´buy·er	hook´y	hos-pit´a·ble-ness
home´com-ing	hoo´li-gan	hos-pit´a·bly

hos´pi-tal	hub´bub	hu´mor-ist
hos-pi-tal´i·ty	hu´bris	hu´mor-less
hos´pi-tal-ize	huck´ster	hu´mor-ous·ly
hos´tage	hud´dle	hu´mour (Br.)
hos´tel	huff´i-ness	hump´backed
host´ess	huff´y	hunch´back
hos´tile·ly	huge´ly	hun´dred
hos-til´i·ty	hug´ging	hun´dred-fold
hos´tler	hulk´ing	hun´dredth
hot´bed	hu´man	hun´ger-ing
ho-tel´	hu-mane´ly	hun´gri·er
hot´head·ed	hu-man-i-tar´i·an	hun´gri·ly
hot´house	hu-man´i·ty	hun´gry
hot´ly	hu´man-ize	hunt´er
hot´shot	hu´man·ly	hunt´ing
hound´er	hu´man-oid	hur´dle
hour´glass	hum´ble	hurl´er
hour´ly	hum´bling	hurl´ing
house´bro-ken	hum´bly	hur-rah´
house´clean´ing	hum´bug	hur´ri-cane
house´ful	hum´ding´er	hur´ried·ly
house´keep·er	hum´drum	hur´ry
house´top	hu´mid	hur´ry-ing·ly
house´wares	hu-mid´i-fi·er	hurt´ful·ly
house´warm-ing	hu-mid´i·fy	hurt´ful-ness
house´work	hu-mid´i·ty	hurt´ing
hous´ing	hu´mi-dor	hur´tle
hov´el	hu-mil´i-ate	hur´tling
hov´er	hu-mil´i-at-ing	hus´band
hov´er-ing	hu-mil-i-a´tion	hus´band·ly
how´dy	hu-mil´i·ty	hus´band·ry
how-ev´er	hum´ming	husk´i·ly
howl´ing	hu´mor	husk´i-ness

114

husk´y
hus´sy
hus´tler
hus´tling
hy´brid
hy´drant
hy´drate
hy-dra´tion
hy-drau´lic
hy-drau´li-cal·ly
hy-dro-e·lec´tric
hy´dro-foil
hy´dro-gen
hy´giene
hy´gien´ist
hymn
hym´nal
hype
hyp´er
hy´per-link
hy-per-sen´si-tive
hy´per-text
hy´phen
hy´phen-ate
hy´phen-at·ed
hy-phen-a´tion
hyp-no´sis
hyp-no-ther´a·py
hyp-not´ic
hyp´no-tism
hyp´no-tist
hyp´no-tize
hy-po-chon´dri·ac

hy-poc´ri·sy
hyp-o-crit´i-cal
hy-poth´e-ses
hy-poth´e-sis
hy-poth´e-size
hy-po-thet´i-cal·ly
hys-ter´i-cal·ly
hys-ter´ics

I

i-bu-pro´fen
ice´berg
ice´break·er
ice´mak·er
ic´i-cle
ic´i·ly
ic´ing
ick´y
i´con
i·con´o-clast
ic´y
i·de´a
i·de´al
i·de´al-ism
i·de´al-ist
i·de´al-is´tic
i·de-al-is´ti-cal·ly
i·de´al·ly
i´de-ate
i·de-a´tion
i·den´ti-cal·ly
i·den´ti-fi-a·ble
i·den-ti-fi-ca´tion

i·den´ti-fied
i·den´ti-fies
i·den´ti·fy
i·den´ti·ty
i·de-o-log´ic
i·de-o-log´i-cal
i·de-ol´o·gy
id´i-o·cy
id´i·om
id´i-o-mat´ic
id-i-o-syn´cra·sy
id´i-ot
id-i-ot´ic
i´dled
i´dle-ness
i´dler
i´dling
i´dly
i´dol
i·dol´a-ter
i·dol´a-trous
i·dol´a-try
i´dol-ize
i´dyll
i·dyl´lic
if´fy
ig-nite´
lg-nit´ing
ig-ni´tion
ig-no´ble
ig-no´bly
ig-no-min´i-ous·ly
ig-no-ra´mus

ig´no-rance
ig´no-rant
ig-nore´
ill´-ad-vised´
il-le´gal
il-le-gal´i-ty
il-le´gal·ly
il-leg´i·ble
il-le-git´i-ma·cy
il-le-git´i-mate
il-lic´it
il-lic´it·ly
il-lit´er-a·cy
il-lit´er-ate
ill´ness
il´log´i-cal
il-lu´mi-nate
il-lu-mi-na´ti
il-lu-mi-na´tion
il-lu´mi-nat-ing
il-lu-mi-na´tion
il-lu´sion·al
il-lu´sion-ar·y
il-lu´sion-ist
il-lu´sive·ly
il-lu´so·ry
il´lus-trate
il´lus-trat-ing
il-lus-tra´tion
il-lus´tra-tive
il´lus-tra-tor
il-lus´tri-ous·ly
im´age

im´ag-e·ry
im-ag´i-nar·y
im-ag´i-na´tion
im-ag´i-na-tive·ly
im-ag´ine
im-ag´ing
im-ag´in-ing
im-bal´ance
im´be-cile
im-be-cil´ic
im-bibe´
im-bib´er
im-bro´glio
im-bue´
im-bu´ing
im´i-tate
im-i-ta´tion
im´i-ta-tive
im-mac´u-late·ly
im-ma-te´ri-al
im-ma-ture´
lm-ma-tur´i·ty
im-mea´sur-a·ble
im-mea´sur-a·bly
im-me´di-a·cy
im-me´di-ate·ly
im-mense´ly
im-mersed´
im-mers´i·ble
im-mers´ing
im-mer´sion
im´mi-grant
im-mi-gra´tion

im´mi-nent
im-mo´bile
im-mo´bi-lize
im-mod´er-a·cy
im-mod´er-ate
im-mod´er-ate·ly
im-mod´est·ly
im-mod´es·ty
im-mo-la´tion
im-mor´al
im-mo-ral´i·ty
im-mor´al·ly
im-mor´tal
im-mor-tal´i·ty
im-mor´tal-ize
im-mov´a·ble
im-mune´
im-mu-ni-za´tion
im´mu-nize
im-mu-nol´o-gist
im-mu-nol´o-gy
im-mu´ta·ble
im´pact
im-pact´ed
im-pair´ment
im-pale´
im-part´
im-par´tial
im-par-ti-al´i·ty
im-par´tial·ly
im-pass´a·ble
im´passe
im-pas´sioned

116

im-pas´sive·ly
im-pa´tience
im-pa´tient·ly
im-peach´a·ble
iin-peach´ment
im-pec´ca·ble
im-pec´ca·bly
im-pe-cu´ni·ous
im-ped´ance
im-pede´
im-ped´i-ment
im-ped´ing
im-pel´
im-pend´ing
im-pen´e-tra·ble
im-pen´e-tra·bly
im-pen´i-tent
im-per´a-tive
im-per-cep´ti·ble
im-per-cep´ti·bly
im-per-cep´tive
im-per´fect
im-per-fec´tion
im-pe´ri-al-ist
im-pe´ri-al-is´tic
im-pe´ri-al·ly
im-per´il
im-pe´ri-ous·ly
im-per´ish-a·ble
im-per´ma-nent
im-per´me-a·ble
im-per´son-al
im-per´son-ate

im-per-son-a´tion
im-per´son-a-tor
im-per´ti-nence
im-per´ti-nen·cy
im-per´ti-nent
im-per´ti-nent·ly
im-per-turb´a·ble
im-per´vi-ous·ly
im-pet´u-ous·ly
im-pi´e·ty
im-pinge´
im´pi-ous·ly
imp´ish·ly
im-plac·a-bil´i·ty
im-plac´a·ble
im-plac´a·bly
im-plau´si·ble
im´ple-ment
im-ple-men´ta-tion
im´pli-cate
im-pli-ca´tion
im-plic´it·ly
im-plic´i·ty
im-plied´
im-plore´
im-plor´ing
im-ply´
im-po-lite´
im-pon´der-a·ble
im-port´ *(v.)*
im´port *(n., v.)*
im-por´tance
im-por´tant·ly

im-por-ta´tion
im-port´er
im-por´tu-nate
im´por-tune´ly
im-pose´
im-pos´ing
im-po-si´tion
im-pos´si·ble
im-pos´si·bly
im´po-tence
im´po-ten·cy
im´po-tent
im-pound´ment
im-pov´er-ished
im-prac´ti-cal
im-prac-ti-cal´i·ty
im´pre-cate
im-pre-ca´tion
im-pre-cise´ly
im-pre-ci´sion
im-preg-na·bil´i·ty
im-preg´na·ble
im-preg´nate
im-preg-na´tion
im-pre-sar´i·o
im-press´ *(v.)*
im´press *(n.)*
im-pres´sion
im-pres´sion-a·ble
im-pres´sion-ist
im-pres´sive·ly
im-pri-ma´tur
im-pri´mis

im´print (n.)
im-print´ (v.)
im-pris´on
im-pris´on-ment
im-prob´a·ble
im-prop´er·ly
im-pro-pri´e·ty
im-prove´ment
im-prov´i-dent·ly
im-prov´ing
im-prov·i-sa´tion
im´pro-vise
im-pru´dent·ly
im´pu-dent·ly
im-pugn´
im´pulse
im-pul´sive·ly
im-pu´ni·ty
im-pure´
im-pute´
in-a·bil´i·ty
in-ac-ces-si·bil´i·ty
in-ac-ces´si·ble
in-ac-ces´si·bly
in-ac´cu-ra·cy
in-ac´cu-rate·ly
in-ac´tion
in-ac´tive·ly
in-ad´e-qua·cy
in-ad´e-quate·ly
in-ad-mis´si·ble
in-ad-mis´si·bly
in-ad-ver´tent·ly

in-ad-vis´a·ble
in-a´lien-a·ble
in-al´ter-a·ble
in-al´ter-a·bly
in-ane´ly
in-an´i-mate·ly
in-an´i·ty
in-ap´pli-ca·ble
in-ap-pre´cia·ble
in-ap-proach´a·ble
in-ap-pro´pri-ate
in-apt´ness
in-as-much´
in-at-ten´tive
in-au´di·ble
in-au´di·bly
in-au´gu-ral
in-au´gu-rate
in-au´gu-rat-ing
in-au-gu-ra´tion
in-aus-pi´cious·ly
in´breed-ing
in-cal´cu-la·ble
in-can-desce´
in-can-des´cence
in-can-des´cent
in-can-ta´tion
in-ca´pa·ble
in-ca-pac´i-tate
in-ca-pac-i-ta´tion
in-ca-pac´i·ty
in-car´cer-ate
in-car-cer-a´tion

in-car´nate
in-car-na´tion
in-cau´tious·ly
in-cen´di-ar·y
in´cense (n.)
in-cense´ (v.)
in-cen´tive
in-cep´tion
in-ces´sant·ly
in´cest
in-ces´tu-ous
in-ci-dent
in-ci-den´tal·ly
in-cin´er-ate
in-cin-er-a´tion
in-cin´er-a-tor
in-cip´i-ent
in-cise´
in-ci´sion
in-ci´sive
in-cite´
in-cit´er
in-cit´ing
in-clem´ent
in-cli-na´tion
in-cline´ (v., n.)
in´cline (n.)
in-clined´
in-clin´ing
in-clude´
in-clud´ed
in-clud´ing
in-clu´sion

in-clu´sive·ly
in-cog-ni´to
in-co-her´ence
in-co-her´ent·ly
in-com-bus´ti·ble
in´come
in´com-ing
in-com-mo´di-ous
in-com-mu-ni-
  ca´do
in-com´pa-ra·ble
in-com´pa-ra·bly
in-com-pat´i·ble
in-com´pe-tence
in-com´pe-ten·cy
in-com´pe-tent·ly
in-com-plete´
in-com-pli´ant
in-com-pre-hen´-
  si·ble
in-con-ceiv´a·ble
in-con-clu´sive
in-con´gru-ent·ly
in-con-gru´i·ty
in-con´gru-ous
in-con-se-quen´tial
in-con-sid´er-a·ble
in-con-sid´er-ate
in-con-sist´en·cy
in-con-sist´ent·ly
in-con-sol´a·ble
in-con-spic´u-ous
in-con-test´a·ble

in-con´ti-nence
in-con-trol´la·ble
in-con-tro-vert´-
  i·ble
in-con-ve´nience
in-con-ven´ient·ly
in-cor´po-rate
in-cor´po-rat·ed
in-cor-po-ra´tion
in-cor-po´re·al
in-cor-rect´ly
in-cor´ri-gi·ble
in-cor-rupt´i·ble
in-crease´ (v.)
in´crease (n.)
in-creas´ing·ly
in-cred´i·ble
in-cred´i·bly
in-cre-du´li·ty
in-cred´u-lous·ly
in´cre-ment
in´cre-men´tal·ly
in-crim´i-nate
in-crim-i-na´tion
in-crim´i-na-to·ry
in-crus-ta´tion
in´cu-bate
in-cu-ba´tion
in´cu-bus
in-cul´cate
in-cul-ca´tion
in-cul´pate
in-cul-pa´tion

in-cul´pa-to·ry
in-cum´ben·cy
in-cum´bent·ly
in-cur´
in-cur´a·ble
in-cur´sion
in-debt´ed-ness
in-de´cen·cy
in-de´cent
in-de-ci´pher-a·ble
in-de-ci´sion
in-de-ci´sive·ly
in-dec´o-rous·ly
in-deed´
in-de-fen´si·ble
in-de-fin´a·ble
in-def´i-nite·ly
in-del´i·ble
in-del´i·bly
in-del´i-cate·ly
in-del´i-cate-ness
in-dem-ni-fi-ca´tion
in-dem´ni-fied
in-dem´ni-fies
in-dem´ni·fy
in-dem´ni·ty
in-dent´
in-den-ta´tion
in-dent´ed
in-den´ture
in-de-pen´dence
in-de-pen´dent·ly
in-de-scrib´a·ble

in-de-struc´ti·ble
in-de-ter´mi-na·cy
in-de-ter´mi-nate
in´dex·er
in´dex·es
in´di-cate
in-di-ca´tion
in-dic´a-tive
in-dic´a-to·ry
in-di´cia
in-dict´a·ble
in-dict´er
in-dif´fer-ence
in-dif´fer-ent·ly
in´di-gence
in-dig´e-nous
in´di-gent
in-di-gest´i·ble
in-di-ges´tion
in-dig´nant·ly
in-dig-na´tion
in-di-rect´ly
in-dis-cern´i·ble
in-dis-creet´
in´dis-crete´
in-dis-cre´tion
in-dis-crim´i-nate
in-dis-pens´a·ble
in´dis-posed´
in-dis-put´a·ble
in-dis-tinct´
in-dis-tin´guish-
  a·ble

in-dite´ment
in-di-vid´u-al
in-di-vid-u-al´i·ty
in-di-vid´u-al·ly
in-di-vis´i·ble
in-doc´tri-nate
in-doc-tri-na´tion
in´do-lence
in´do-lent·ly
in-dom´i-ta·ble
in´doors´
in-du´bi-ta·ble
in-du´bi-ta·bly
in-duce´ment
in-duc´ing
in-dulge´
in-dul´gent
in-dulg´ing
in-dus´tri-al-ist
in-dus-tri-al-i·za´-
  tion
in-dus´tri-al-ize
in´dus-tries
in-dus´tri-ous·ly
in´dus-try
in-e´bri-ant
in-e´bri-ate
in-e·bri-a´tion
in-ed´i·ble
in-ef-fec´tive·ly
in-ef-fec´tu-al·ly
in-ef-fi´cient·ly
in-el´e-gant·ly

in-el´i-gi·ble
in-ept´
in-ep´ti-tude
in-e´qual´i·ty
in-eq´ui-ta·ble
in-eq´ui·ty
in-ert´
in-er´tia
in-es-cap´a·ble
in-es´ti-ma·ble
in-ev´i-ta·ble
in-ex-act´
in-ex-ac´ti-tude
in-ex-act´ly
in-ex-cus´a·ble
in-ex-haust´i·ble
in-ex´o-ra·ble
in-ex-pen´sive·ly
in-ex-pe´ri-enced
in-ex´pert·ly
in-ex´pert-ness
in-ex-plain´a·ble
in-ex-plic´a·ble
in-ex-tric´a·ble
in-ex-tric´a·bly
in-fal-li-bil´i·ty
in-fal´li·ble
in-fal´li·bly
in´fa-mous·ly
in´fa·my
in´fan·cy
in´fant
in´fan-tile

in´fan-try
in-fat´u-ate
in-fat´u-at·ed
in-fat-u-a´tion
in-fect´ant
in-fec´tion
in-fec´tious·ly
in-fer´
in´fer-ence
in-fe´ri·or
in-fe-ri-or´i·ty
in-fer´nal
in-fer´no
in-ferred´
in-fer´ring
in-fer-til´i·ty
in-fest´
in-fes-ta´tion
in´fi-del
in-fi-del´i·ty
in-fil´trate
in-fil-tra´tion
in´fi-nite·ly
in-fin-i-tes´i-mal
in-firm´
in-fir´ma·ry
in-fir´mi·ty
in-flame´
in-flam´ma·ble
in-flam-ma´tion
in-flam´ma-to·ry
in-flat´a·ble
in-flate´

in-flat´ed
in-flat´ing
in-fla´tion
in-fla´tion-ar·y
in-flec-tion
in-flex´i·ble
in-flict´
in´flu-ence
in´flu-en´tial
in-flu-en´za
in-fo-mer´cial
in-form´
in-for´mal
in-for-mal´i·ty
in-for´mant
in-for-ma´tion
in-form´a-tive
in-formed´
in-form´er
in-frac´tion
in´fra-struc-ture
in-fre´quent·ly
in-fringe´ment
in-fu´ri-ate
in-fu´ri-at-ing
in-fuse´
in-fu´sion
in-ge´nious
in-gen´ious·ly
in-ge-nu´i·ty
in-gen´u-ous
in-gest´
in-grained´

in-gra´ti-ate
in-gra´ti-at-ing·ly
in-grat´i-tude
in-gre´di-ent
in´grown
in-hab´i-tant
in-hab´it-ed
in-hal´ant
in-ha-la´tion
in-hale´
in-hal´er
in-hal´ing
in-har-mo´ni-ous
in-her´ent
in-her´it
in-her´i-tance
in-hib´it
in-hib´it-ed
in-hib´it-er
in-hi-bi´tion
in-hos-pit´a-ble
in-hu´man
in-hu-mane´
in-hu-man´i-ty
in-hu´man·ly
in-im´i-cal
in-im´i-ta·ble
in-iq´ui-tous
in-iq´ui-ty
in·i´tial-ize
in·i´tial·ly
in·i´ti-ate
in-i-ti-a´tion

in-ject′
in-jec′tion
in-ju-di′cious
in-junc′tion
in′jure
in′ju-ries
in-ju′ri-ous
in′ju·ry
in-jus′tice
in′kling
ink′well
ink′y
in′laid
in′lay
in-nate′ly
in′ner
in′ner-most
in′no-cence
in′no-cent·ly
in-noc′u-ous·ly
in-no-va′tion
in′no-va-tive
in-nu-en′do
in-nu-en′does
in-nu′mer-a·ble
in-of-fen′sive·ly
in-op′er-a·ble
in-op-por-tune′
in-or′di-nate·ly
in-or′di-nate-ness
in-or-gan′ic
in-or-gan′i-cal·ly
in′put

in′quest
in-quire′
in-quir′er
in′quir-ies
in-quir′ing
in-quir′ing·ly
in′quir·y
in-qui-si′tion
in-quis′i-tive
in′road
in-sane′ly
in-san′i-ty
in-sa′tia·ble
in-scribe′
in-scrib′er
in-scrib′ing
in-scrip′tion
in-scru′ta·ble
in′seam
in′sect
in-sec′ti-cide
in-se-cure′
in-se-cur′i-ty
in-sen′si-tive
in-sen-si-tiv′i-ty
in-sep′a-ra·ble
in-sep′a-ra·bly
in-sert′ (v.)
in′sert (n.)
in-ser′tion
in-sid′i-ous
in′sight
in′sight-ful-ness

in-sig′ni·a
in-sig-nif′i-cant·ly
in-sin-cere′
in-sin-cer′i·ty
in-sin′u-ate
in-sin′u-at-ing·ly
in-sin-u-a′tion
in-sip′id
insist′
in-sis′tence
in-sis′tent·ly
in′so-lence
in′so-lent·ly
in-sol′u·ble
in-solv′a·ble
in-sol′ven·cy
in-sol′vent
in-som′ni·ac
in-spect′
in-spec′tion
in-spec′tor
in-spi-ra′tion·al
in-spire′
in-spir′ing
in-sta-bil′i·ty
in-stall′
in-stal-la′tion
in-stalled′
in-stall′ing
in-stall′ment
in′stance
in′stant
in-stan-ta′ne·ous

in´step
in´sti-gate
in´sti-gat-ing
in´sti-ga-tor
in-stil´ (Br.)
in-still´
in-stil-la´tion
in-still´ing
in´stinct (n.)
in-stinc´tive·ly
in-stinc´tu-al·ly
in´sti-tute
in-sti-tu´tion-al
in-struct´ed
in-struc´tion-al
in-struc´tive·ly
in-struc´tor
in´stru-ment
in-stru-men´tal
in-stru-men-ta´tion
in-sub-or´di-nate
in-sub-or-di-na´-
  tion
in-sub-stan´tial
in-suf´fer-a-ble
in-suf-fi´cient
in-suf-fi´cient·ly
in´su-lar
in-su-lar´i·ty
in´su-late
in´su-la´tion
in´sult (n.)
in-sult´ (v.)

in-sult´ing·ly
in-sup-port´a·ble
in-sur´a·ble
in-sur´ance
in-sure´
in-sured´
in-sur´er
in-sur´gence
in-sur´gen·cy
in-sur´gent
in-sur´ing
in-sur-mount´a·ble
in-sur-rec´tion
in-sus-cep´ti·ble
in-tact´

in´take
in-tan´gi·ble
in´te-ger
in´te-gral
in´te-grate
in-te-gra´tion
in-teg´ri·ty
in´tel-lect
in-tel-lec´tu-al
in-tel´li-gence
in-tel´li-gent·ly
in-tel-li-gen´tsi·a
in-tem´per-ance
in-tem´per-ate
in-tend´ing
in-tense´
in-tense´ly

in-ten´si-fied
in-ten´si-fi·er
in-ten´si-fies
in-ten´si·fy
in-ten´si·ty
in-tent´
in-ten´tion-al
in-tent´ly
in-ter´
in-ter-act´
in-ter-ac´tion
in-ter-ac´tive
in-ter-cede´
in-ter-ced´ing
in-ter-cept´ (v.)
in-ter-cep´tion
in-ter-col-le´giate
in-ter-con-nect´ed
in´ter-course
in-ter-de-nom-i-
  na´tion-al
in-ter-de-part-
  men´tal
in-ter-dict´
in-ter-dic´tion
in´ter-est-ed
in´ter-est-ing
in´ter-face
in´ter-faith
in-ter-fere´
in-ter-fer´ence
in-ter-fer´ing
in´ter-im

in-te´ri·or
in-ter-ject´
in-ter-jec´tion
in´ter-leaf
in-ter-leav´ing
in´ter-lop·er
in´ter-lude
in-ter-me´di-ate
in-ter´ment
in-ter´mi-na·ble
in-ter-min´gle
in-ter-min´gling
in-ter-mis´sion
in-ter-mit´tent·ly
in-ter-mix´
in´tern
in-ter´nal
in-ter´nal-ize
in-ter-na´tion·al
in-terned´
In´ter-net
in-tern´ment
in-ter´nist
in-ter-o-cep´tor
in-ter-per´son·al
in-ter-plan´e-tar·y
in´ter-play
in-ter´po-late
in-ter-po-la´tion
in-ter´pret
in-ter-pre-ta´tion
in-ter´pret·er
in-ter´pre-tive

in-ter-ra´cial
in-ter-re-late´
in-ter-re-lat´ed
in-ter´ro-bang
in-ter´ro-gate
in-ter-ro-ga´tion
in-ter-rog´a-tive
in-ter´ro-ga-tor
in-ter-rupt´ed
in-ter-rupt´ing
in-ter-rup´tion
in-ter-rup´tive
in-ter-sec´tion
in´ter-state´
in-ter-stel´lar
in´ter-val
in-ter-vene´
in-ter-ven´tion
in´ter-view·er
in-tes´tate
in-tes´ti-nal
in-tes´tine
in´ti-ma·cy
in´ti-mate·ly
in-ti-ma´tion
in-tim´i-date
in-tim-i-da´tion
in´to
in-tol´er-a·ble
in-tol´er-ance
in-tol´er-ant
in´to-nate
in-to-na´tion

in-tone´
in-tox´i-cant
in-tox´i-cate
in-tox´i-cat-ing
in-tox-i-ca´tion
in-trac´ta·ble
in-tra-ga-lac´tic
in-tra-mu´ral·ly
in-tran´si-gence
in-tran´si-gent
in-tra-pre-neur´i·al
in-tra-state´
in-trep´id·ly
in´tri-ca·cy
in´tri-cate·ly
in-trigued´
in-tri´guing
in-tro-duce´
in-tro-duc´tion
in-tro-duc´to·ry
in-tro-spec´tion
in-tro-spec´tive
in-tro-ver´sion
in´tro-vert
in-trude´
in-trud´er
in-tru´sion
in-tru´sive
in-tu-i´tion
in-tu´i-tive
in´un-date
in-un-da´tion
in-ure´

in-vade′
in-vad′er
in-vad′ing
in-val′id *(void)*
in′va-lid *(disabled)*
in-val′i-date
in-val-i-da′tion
in-val′u-a·ble
in-var′i-a·ble
in-var′i-a·bly
in-va′sion
in-va′sive
in-vec′tive
in-vent′
in-ven′tion
in-ven′tive
in-ven′tor
in′ven-to-ries
in′ven-to·ry
in-verse′ly
in-ver′sion
in-vest′
in-ves′ti-gate
in-ves-ti-ga′tion
in-ves′ti-ga-tor
in-ves′ti-ga-to·ry
in-vest′ment
in-ves′tor
in-vet′er-ate
in-vig′o-rate
in-vig′o-rat-ing
in-vin′ci·ble
in-vi′o-la·ble

in-vis′i·ble
in-vi-ta′tion·al
in-vite′
in-vit′ing
in-vo-ca′tion
in′voice
in′voic-ing
invoke′
in-vok′ing
in-vol′un-tar·y
in-volved′
in-volve′ment
in-volv′ing
in-vul′ner-a·ble
in′ward·ly
i′o-dine
i′on
i·on-i-za′tion
i′on-ize
i·on′o-sphere
i·o′ta
i·ras′ci·ble
i·rate′ly
ir-i-des′cence
ir-i-des′cent·ly
irk′some
i′ron
i·ron′ic
i·ron′i-cal·ly
i′ron-ing
i′ron-mon-ger
i′ron-work·er
i′ro·ny *(satire)*

ir-ra′di-ant
ir-ra′di-ate
ir-ra′tion·al
ir-rec′on-cil-a·ble
ir-re-cov′er-a·ble
ir-re-deem′a·ble
ir-re-fut′a·ble
ir-reg′u-lar
ir-reg-u-lar′i·ty
ir-rel′e-vant
ir-rep′a-ra·ble
ir-re-press′i·ble
ir-re-proach′a·ble
ir-re-sist′i·ble
ir-res′o-lute·ly
ir-re-spon′si·ble
ir-re-triev′a·ble
ir-rev′er-ence
ir-rev′er-ent·ly
ir-re-vers′i·ble
ir-rev′o-ca·ble
ir′ri-ga·ble
ir′ri-gate
ir-ri-ga′tion
ir′ri-ta·ble
ir′ri-tant
ir′ri-tate
ir′ri-tat-ing
ir′ri-ta′tion
is′land·er
is′let
i′so-late
i·so-la′ting

i·so-la´tion-ist
i·so-met´ric
i´so-ton´ic
is´sue
is´su-ing
isth´mus
i·tal´ic
i·tal-i-ci-za´tion
i·tal´i-cize
itch´i-ness
itch´y
i´tem-i·za´tion
i´tem-ize
it´er-ate
it-er-a´tion
i·tin´er-ant
i·tin´er-ar·y
its *(possessive)*
it´s *(it is)*
it-self´
i´vied
i´vo·ry
i´vy

J

jab
jabbed
jab´ber
jab´bing
jack´al
jack´ass
jack´et·ed
jack´pot

jad´ed
jag´ged
jail´bird
jail´break
jail´er
ja-la-pe´ño
ja-lop´y
jal´ou-sie
jam´ming
jan´gle
jan´gling
jan´gly
jan´i-tor
jan-i-to´ri·al
jar´gon
jar´ring
jaun´diced
jaunt
jaun´ti·ly
jaun´ti-ness
jaun´ty
jav´e-lin
jaw´bone
jawed
jazz´er-cize
jazz´y
jeal´ous·ly
jeal´ou·sy
jeer´ing·ly
je-june´
jel´lied
jel´ly
jeop´ar-dize

jeop´ar·dy
jerk´y *(shaky)*
jer´ky *(meat)*
jer´sey
jest´er
jet´sam
jet´ti-son
jet´ty
jew´eled
jew´el·er
jew´el·ry
jif´fy
jig´ger
jig´gle
jig´gly
jilt´ed
jin´gle
jin´gling
jin´gly
jit´ney
jit´ter-bug
jit´ters
jit´ter·y
job´ber
job´less
jock´ey
joc´u-lar
joc-u-lar´i·ty
jog´ging
join´er
joint´ed
joint´er
joint´ly

joist	ju´di-ca-to·ry	jus-ti-fi-ca´tion
joked	ju-di´cial·ly	jus´ti-fied
jok´er	ju-di´ciar·y	jus´ti-fi·er
joke´ster	ju-di´cious·ly	jus´ti-fy
jok´ing·ly	jug´gler	ius´ti-fy-ing
jol´li·ty	jug´gling	just´ly
jol´ly	jug´u-lar	just´ness
josh´er	juice	jut´ting
josh´ing·ly	juic´er	ju´ve-nile
jos´tle	juic´i-ness	jux-ta-po-si´tion
jos´tled	juic´y	
jos´tling	ju-li·enne´	**K**
jounce	jum´bled	
jounc´ing	jum´bling	ka-lei´do-scope
jour´nal	jump´er	ka-lei´do-scop´ic
jour´nal-ism	jump´i-ness	ka´pok
jour´nal-ist	jump´ing	kar´ma
jour´nal-ize	jump´y	kay´ak
jour´ney	junc´tion	keen´ly
jo´vi-al·ly	junc´ture	keen´mess
joy´ful·ly	jun´gle	keep´er
joy´ful-ness	jun´ior	keep´ing
joy´less	jun´ket	keep´sake
joy´ous·ly	junk´ie	ken´nel
joy´ous-ness	ju´ried	ker´a-tin
joy´ride	ju´ries	ker´chief
ju´bi-lance	ju-ris-dic´tion·al	kerned
ju´bi-lant·ly	ju-ris-pru´dence	ker´nel
ju-bi-la´tion	ju´rist	ke´tone
judge´ship	ju´ror	ket´tle-drum
judg´ing	ju´ry	key´board
judg´ment	jus´tice	key´hole
judg-men´tal	jus´ti-fi-a·ble	key´note
		khak´i

kib´itz-er
kick´back
kid´ded
kid´ding
kid´nap
kid´naped
kid´nap-er
kid´nap-ing
kid´napped
kid´nap-per
kid´nap-ping
kid´ney
kill´er
kill´ing
kill´joy
kiln
ki´lo
kil´o-cy-cle
kil´o-gram
ki-lom´e-ter
kil´o-watt
kil´o-watt–hour
kilt´ed
ki-mo´no
ki-mo´nos
kin´der-gar-ten
kind´heart-ed
kin´dle
kind´li-ness
kin´dling
kind´ly
kind´ness
kin´dred

ki-net´ic
kin´folk
king´dom
king´li-ness
king´ly
king´pin
kink´y
kin´ship
ki´osk
kis´met
kiss´a·ble
kitch´en-ette´
kit´ten
kit´ten-ish
kit´ty
klep-to-ma´ni·a
klep-to-ma´ni-ac
knap´sack
knav´er·y
knead
knee´cap
knee´–deep´
knee´–high´
kneel´ing
knick´knack
knife
knight–er´rant
knight´hood
knight´ly
knit´ter
knit´ting
knives
knobbed

knob´by
knock´a·bout
knock´out
knoll
knot´hole
knot´ted
knot´ting
knot´ty
know´–how
know´ing-ly
knowl´edge
knowl´edge-a·ble
knuck´led
knuck´ling
knurl´y
koi-no-ni´a
ko´sher
kow´tow
kum´quat
ky´ack

L

la´bel
la´beled
la´bel-ing
la´bor
lab´o-ra-to-ry
la´bored
la´bor-er
la-bo´ri-ous
la-bo´ri-ous-ly
la´bour (Br.)
lab´y-rinth

lab-y-rin´thi-an	la´ger	land´locked
lab-y-rin´thine	lag´gard	land´lord
lac´er-ate	lag´ging	land´mark
lac´er-at-ing	la-goon´	land´own-er
lac-er-a´tion	la´ic	land´–poor
lace´work	lais´sez–faire	land´scape
lac´ing	la´i-ty	land´slide
lack-a-dai´si-cal	lake´side	lan´guage
lack´ey	lam-baste´	lan´guid-ly
lack´ing	la-mé´	lan´guish
lack´lus-ter	lame´ly	lan´guished
la-con´ic	lame´ness	lan´guish-ing
la-con´i-cal-ly	la-ment´	lan´guor
lac´quer	lam´en-ta-ble	lan´guor-ous
lac´tate	lam´en-ta-bly	lank´i-er
lac-ta´tion	lam-en-ta´tion	lank´y
lac´tose	la-ment´ed	lan´tern
lac´y	lam´i-na	lan´yard
lad´der	lam´i-nal	la-pel´
lad´die	lam´i-nar	lap´ping
lad´en	lam´i-nate	lapsed
lad´en-ing	lam-i-na´tion	lar´ce-nist
la´dies	lamp´black	lar´ce-nous
lad´ing	lamp´light	lar´ce-ny
la´dle	lam-poon´	lar´der
la´dle-ful	lamp´post	large´ly
la´dler	lanc´er	large´ness
la´dy	lan´dau	larg´er
la´dy-bird	land´ed	lar-gess´
la´dy-bug	land´fall	larg´est
la´dy-fin-ger	land´hold-er	lar´go
la´dy–kill-er	land´ing	lar´i-at
la´dy-like	land´la-dy	lar´va

lar´vae

lar´val

lar-yn-gi´tis

lar´ynx

las-civ´i-ous

la´ser

lash´ing

las´sie

las´si-tude

las´so

las´so-er

last´ing

last´ly

latch´et

late´ly

late´ness

la´tent-ly

lat´er

lat´er-al

lat´er-al-ly

lat´est

la´tex

lath

lathe

lath´er

lath´er-ing

lath´ing

lat´i-ces

lat´ish

lat´i-tude

la-trine´

lat´ter

lat´tice-work

laud´a·ble

lau´da-to-ry

laugh´a·ble

laugh´ing

laugh´ter

launched

launch´er

laun´der

laun´dries

laun´dry

lau´rel

la´va

lav´a-to-ry

lav´en-der

lav´ish

law´–a·bid´ing

law´break-er

law´ful

law´giv-er

law´less

law´suit

law´yer

lax´a-tive

lax´i-ty

lay´er

lay-ette´

lay´man

la´zi-er

la´zi-ly

la´zi-ness

la´zy

lead´en

lead´er-ship

leaf´less

leaf´y

league

leak´y

lean´ing

lean´ness

lean´–to

leap´frog

leap´ing

learned (detected)

learn´ed (smart)

learn´er

learn´ing

leased

lease´hold

leas´ing

leath´er

leath´er·y

leav´en

leav´ing

lech´er-ous

lech´er·y

lec´i-thin

lec´tern

lec´ture

lee´tured

lec´tur-er

lec´tur-ing

ledg´er

leer´ing

leer´ing-ly

leer´y

lee´way

left´o·ver
leg´a-cies
leg´a-cy
le´gal
le-gal´i-ty
le´gal-i·za´tion
le´gal-ize
le´gal-ly
leg´ate *(delegate)*
le-gate´ *(bequeath)*
leg´a-tee´
le-ga´tion
leg´end-ar·y
leg´er-de-main´
leg´ged
leg´gings
leg-i-bil´i-ty
leg´i-ble
le´gion
leg´is-late
leg-is-la´tion
leg´is-la-tive
leg´is-la-tor
leg´is-la-ture
le-git´i-ma-cy
le-git´i-mate
le-git´i-mize
lei´sure-ly
lem´on-ade´
lend´er
lend´ing
length´en
length´wise

length´y
le´nience
le´nien-cy
le´nient
le´nient-ly
len´til
le´o-nine
le´o-tard
lep´er
lep´re-chaun
lep´ro-sy
lep´rous
le´sion
les-see´
less´en
less´er
les´son
le´thal
le-thar´gic
le-thar´gi-cal-ly
leth´ar-gy
let´ter
let´rered
let´ter-head
let´ter–per´fect
let´ter-press
let´tuce
leu-ke´mi·a
lev´el
lev´eled
lev´el-er
lev´el-ing
lev´er-age

le-vi´a-than
lev´i-tate
lev´i-tat-ing
lev-i-ta´tion
lev´i-ty
lev´y-ing
lewd´ness
lex-i-cog´ra-pher
lex-i-cog´ra-phy
lex´i-con
li-a-bil´i-ty
li´a·ble
li´ai-son
li´ar
li-ba´tion
li´bel
li´beled
li´bel-er
li´bel-ing
li´bel-ous
lib´er-al
lib´er-al-ism
lib´er-al-ize
lib´er-al-ly
lib´er-ate
lib-er-a´tion
lib´er-a-tor
lib-er-tar´i-an
lib´er-tine
lib´er-ty
li-bi´do
li-brar´i-an
li´brar·y

li-bret´tist
li-bret´to
li´cens-a·ble
li´cense
li´censed
li´cens-ee´
li´cens-er
li´cens-ing
li-cen´tious
lic´it
lien
lieu-ten´ant
life´blood
life´boat
life´guard
life´less
life´like
life´line
life´long
life´sav-er
life´time
lift´er
lig´a-ment
li-ga´tion
lig´a-ture
light´ed
light´en
light´ened
light´en-ing
light´er
light´–fin-gered
light´heart-ed
light´house

light´ing
light´ning (adj., n.)
light´weight
like´li-hood
like´ly
lik´en
like-ness
like´wise
lik´ing
lim´ber
lim´bo
lime´ade
lime´kiln
lime´light
lim´er-ick
lime´stone
lim´it
lim-i-ta´tion
lim´it-ed
lim´it-less
lim´ou-sine
lim´pid
limp´ly
lin´e·age
lin´e·ar
line´man
lin´en
lin´er
lin´ger
lin-ge-rie´
lin´gua
lin´gual
lin´guist

lin-guis´tic
lin-guis´ti-cal-ly
lin-guis´tics
lin´i-ment
lin´ing
link´age
link´ing
li-no´le-um
lin´seed
lin´tel
li´on-ess
li´on-heart-ed
li´on-ize
lip´stick
liq´ue-fied
liq´ue-fy-ing
li-queur´
liq´uid
liq´ui-date
liq´ui-da´tion
liq´ui-da-tor
li-quid´i-ty
li´quor
lisp´ing
lis´some
lis´ten-er
list´er
list´less-ness
lit´a-ny
li´ter
lit´er-a-cy
lit´er-al
lit´er-al-ly

lit´er-ar·y

lit´er-ate

lit-e-ra´ti

lit´er-a-ture

lithe´some

lith´i-um

li-thog´ra-pher

lith´o-graph´ic

li-thog´ra-phy

lit´i-gant

lit´i-gate

lit-i-ga´tion

lit´i-ga-tor

li-ti´gious

lit´mus

li´tre (Br.)

lit´ter

lit´tle

li-tur´gi-cal

lit´ur-gy

liv´a·ble

live´li-hood

live´li-ness

live´long

live´ly

liv´er-ied

liv´er·y

live´stock

liv´id

liv´ing

lla´ma

load´er

loaf´er

loam´y

loath (adj.)

loathe (v.)

loath´ing

loath´some

loaves

lobbed

lob´bied

lob´bing

lob´by-ing

lob´by-ist

lo-bot´o-my

lo´cal

lo-cale´

lo-cal´i-ty

lo-cal-i·za´tion

lo´cal-ize

lo´cal-ly

lo´cate

lo-cat´er

lo-cat´ing

lo-ca´tion

lock´er

lock´et

lock´jaw

lock´smith

lock´stitch

lo´co

lo-co-mo´tion

lo-co-mo´tive

lo´cust

lodg´er

lodg´ing

loft´i-ly

loft´i-ness

loft´y

log´a-rithm

log´book

log´ger-head

log´ging

log´ic

log´i-cal-ly

lo-gis´tic

lo-gis´tics

log´o-type

loin´cloth

loi´ter-er

loll´ing

lol´li-pop

lone´li-ness

lone´ly

lone´some

long´er

long´est

lon-gev´i-ty

long´–haired

long´hand

long´ing

lon´gi-tude

lon-gi-tu´di-nal

long´–lived´

long´–suf´fer-ing

long´–term

long´–wind-ed

look´er

look´ing

look´out	love´sick	lu-gu´bri-ous
loop´hole	lov´ing–kind´ness	luke´warm
loose´–leaf	low´boy	lull´a-by
loose´ly	low´brow	lum-ba´go
loos´en	low´–cut´	lum´ber-jack
loot´er	low´er	lum´ber-yard
lop´sid-ed	low´er-ing	lu´men
lo-qua´cious	low´land	lu´mi-nar·y
lo-quac´i-ty	low´li-ness	lu-mi-nes´cence
lord´li-ness	low´ly	lu-mi-nes´cent
lor-gnette´	loy´al	lu´mi-nous
los´er	loy´al-ist	lum´mox
los´ing	loy´al-ly	lump´i-er
lo´tion	loy´al-ty	lump´ish
lot´ter·y	lu´bri-cant	lump´y
lo´tus	lu´bri-cate	lu´na-cy
loud´ness	lu-bri-ca´tion	lu´nar
loud´speak-er	lu´cent	lunch´eon-ette´
lounged	lu´cid	lunch´room
loung´er	lu-cid´i-ty	lunged´
loung´ing	lu´cid-ness	lung´er
louse	lu´ci-fer	lung´ing
lous´i-ness	luck´i-er	lurched
lous´y	luck´i-est	lurch´ing
lout´ish	luck´i-ly	lured
lou´ver	luck´y	lu´rid-ly
lov´a·ble	lu´cra-tive	lur´ing
love´less	lu´cre	lurk´er
love´li-er	lu´di-crous	lurk´ing
love´li-ness	lu´di-crous-ness	lus´cious
love´lorn	lug´gage	lush´ly
love´ly	lug´ger	lus´ter
lov´er	lug´ging	lust´ful

lust´i-er

lust´i-ly

lus´trous

lust´y

lux-u´ri-ance

lux-u´ri-ant

lux-u´ri-ate

lux-u´ri-at-ing

lux´u-ries

lux-u´ri-ous

lux´u-ry

ly´can-throp´ic

ly-can´thro-py

ly´ing

lymph

lym-phat´ic

lynch´ing

lyr´ic

lyr´i-cal

M

ma-ca´bre

mac-ad´am

mac-ad´am-ize

mac´er-ate

ma-chet´e

mach-i-a-vel´li-an

mach-i-na´tion

mach´i-na-tor

ma-chine´

ma-chin´er·y

ma-chin´ist

mack´i-naw

mack´in-tosh

mac´ra-me´

mac´ro-cosm

mac´ro-scop´ic

mad´am

ma-dame´

mad´cap

mad´den-ing

mad´der

mad´dest

ma-de-moi-selle´

mad´house

mad´ly

mad´man

mad´ness

ma-dras´

mad´ri-gal

mael´strom

mae´stro

mag´a-zine´

ma-gen´ta

mag´got

ma´gi

mag´ic

mag´i-cal

mag´i-cal-ly

ma-gi´cian

mag-is-te´ri-al

mag´is-trate

mag´ma

mag-na-nim´i-ty

mag-nan´i-mous

mag´nate

mag´net

mag-net´ic

mag´net-ism

mag´net-ize

mag-ne´to

mag-nif´i-cence

mag-nif´i-cent

mag-nif´i-co

mag´ni-fied

mag´ni-fi-er

mag´ni-fy

mag´ni-tude

ma-hog´a-ny

maid´en-hood

maid´en-ly

mail´a·ble

mail´bag

mail´box

mail´er

main´land

main´ly

main´stay

main-tain´

main´te-nance

ma-jes´tic

ma-jes´ti-cal

ma-jes´ti-cal-ly

maj´es-ty

ma´jor

ma-ior-do´mo

ma-jor´i-ties

ma-jor´i-ty

make´–be-lieve

mak´er
make´shift
mak´ing
mal´ad-just´ed
mal´ad-just´ment
mal´a-droit´
mal´a-dy
mal-aise´
mal´a-prop-ism
ma-lar´ia
ma-lar´i-al
mal´con-tent
mal-e-dic´tion
mal´e-fac´tor
ma-lev´o-lence
ma-lev´o-lent
mal-fea´sance
mal´formed´
mal´ice
ma-li´cious-ly
ma-lign´
ma-lig´nan-cy
ma-lig´nant
ma-lin´ger
ma-lin´ger-er
mal-le-a·bil´i-ty
mal´le·a-ble
mal´let
mal-nu-tri´tion
mal-o´dor-ous
mal´prac-tice
malt´ose
mal-treat´

mal-treat´ment
malt´y
mam´mal
mam-ma´li-an
mam´ma-ry
mam´mon
mam´moth
man´age
man´age-a·bil´i-ty
man´age-a·ble
man´age-ment
man´ag-er
man´a-ge´ri-al
man´ag-ing
man´akin
man´date
man´da-to-ry
man´do-lin´
man´–eat-er
ma-neu´ver
ma-neu´ver-a·bil´-
  i-ty
ma-neu´ver-er
man´ful-ly
man´ger
man´gi-er
nian´gi-ly
man´gi-ness
man´gle
man´gler
man´gling
man´gy
man´han-dle

man´hole
ma´nia
ma´ni-ac
ma-ni´a-cal
man´ic
man´ic–de-pres´-
  sive
man´i-cure
man´i-cur-ist
man´i-fest
man-i-fes-ta´tion
man´i-fest-ly
man-i-fes´to
man-i-fes´tos
man´i-fold
man´i-kin
ma-nil´la
ma-nip´u-late
ma-nip-u-la´tion
ma-nip´u-la-tive
ma-nip´u-la-to-ry
man´kind´
man´li-ness
man´ly
man´ne-quin
man´ner-ism
man´ner-ly
man´ni-kin
man´nish
man´or
ma-no´ri-al
man´pow-er
man´sard

man´ser-vant	mar´i-ner	mar´tyr-dom
man´sion	mar´i-o-nette´	mar´vel
man´slaugh-ter	mar´i-tal-ly	mar´veled
man´tel	mar´i-time	mar´vel-ing
man´tel-piece	mark´ed-ly	mar´vel-ous-ly
man´tle	mark´er	mas-car´a
man´tling	mar´ket	mas´cot
man´tra	mar-ket-a·bil´i-ty	mas´cu-line
man´u-al-ly	mar´ket-a·ble	mas-cu-lin´i-ty
man-u-fac´ture	mar´ket-er	ma´ser
man-u-fac´tur-er	mar´ket-ing	mash´er
man-u-fac´tur-ing	mar´ket-place	mas´och-ism
ma-nure´	marks´man-ship	mas´och-ist
man´u-script	mar´ma-lade	mas´och-is´tic
man-y	ma-roon´	ma´son
mar´a-thon	mar-quee´	ma-son´ic
ma-raud´er	mar´riage	ma´son-ry
ma-raud´ing	mar´riage-a·ble	mas´quer-ade´
mar´ble	mar´ried	mas´sa-cred
mar´bled	mar´row	mas´sa-cring
mar´ble-ize	mar´ry	mas-sage´
mar´bling	mar´shal	mas-sag´er
march´er	mar´shaled	mas-sag´ing
mar´ga-rine	mar´shal-er	mas-seur´
mar´gin-al	marsh´i-ness	mas-seuse´
mar-i-jua´na	marsh´mal-low	mas´sive
ma-rim´ba	marsh-y	mas´ter-ful
ma-ri´na	mar-su´pi-al	mas´ter-ful-ly
mar´i-nade´	mar´tial	mas´ter-piece
mar´i-nate	mar´tial-ly	mas´ter-y
mar´i-nat-ing	mar´ti-net´	mas´ti-cate
mar-i-na´tion	mar-ti´ni	mas-ti-ca´tion
ma-rine´	mar´tyr	mas-ti´tis

mas´to-don
mas´toid
mas-toid-i´tis
mat´a-dor
match´less
match´mak-er
match´mak-ing
ma-te´ri-al-ist
ma-te´ri-al-is´tic
ma-te´ri-al-ism
ma-te´ri-al-ly
ma-te-ri-el´
ma-ter´nal
ma-ter´nal-ly
ma-ter´ni-ty
math-e-mat´i-cal
math-e-ma-ti´cian
math-e-mat´ics
mat´i-nee´
mat´ing
ma´tri-arch
ma´tri-ar´chal
ma´tri-ar-chy
ma´tri-ci´dal
ma´tri-cide
ma-tric´u-late
ma-tric-u-la´tion
mat´ri-mo´ni-al
mat´ri-mo-ny
ma´trix
ma´tron
ma´tron-ly
mat´ted

mat´ter
mat´ting
mat´tress
mat´u-rate
mat-u-ra´tion
ma-ture´
ma-ture´ly
ma-ture´ness
ma-tur´i-ty
maud´lin
maul´er
mau-so-le´um
mauve
mav´er-ick
mawk´ish
max´im
max´i-mal
max´i-mize
max´i-miz-er
max´i-mum
may´be
may´hem
may´on-naise
may´or
may´or-al-ty
may´pole
maze
ma-zur´ka
mead´ow
mea´gre (Br.)
meal´time
meal´y
meal´y-mouthed

mean
me-an´der
mean´ing
mean´ing-ful
mean´ing-less
mean´ly
mean´ness
meant
mean´time
mean´while
mea´sles
mea´sly
mea´sur-a·ble
mea´sure
mea´sured
mea´sure-less
mea´sure-ment
mea´sur-er
me-chan´ic
me-chan´i-cal
me-chan´i-cal-ly
mech´a-nism
mech´a-nize
med´al
med´aled
med´al-ist
me-dal´lion
med´dle
med´dler
med´dle-some
me´dia
me´di-an
me´di-ate

me-di-a´tion

me´di-a-tor

med´ic

med´i-cal

med´i-cal-ly

me-dic´a-ment

med´i-cate

med-i-ca´tion

med´i-ca-tive

me-dic´i-nal

med´i-cine

me-di-e´val

me´di-o´cre

me-di-oc´ri-ty

med´i-tate

med-i-ta´tion

med´i-ta-tive

med´i-tat-or

me´di-um

med´ley

me-du´sa

meek´ly

meek´ness

meer´schaum

meet´ing

meg´a-cy-cle

meg´a-phone

meg´a-ton

mel´an-choly

me-lange´

meld´er

me´lee

mel´io-rate

mel-io-ra´tion

mel´io-ra-tive

mel-lif´er-ous

mel-lif´lu-ence

mel-lif´lu-ent

mel-lif´lu-ous

mel´low-ness

me-lo´de-on

me-lod´ic

me-lod´i-cal-ly

me-lo´di-ous

mel´o-dra-ma

mel´o-dra-mat´ic

mel´o-dy

melt´a·ble

melt´er

mem´ber-ship

mem´brane

mem´bra-nous

me-men´to

me-men´tos

mem´oir

mem-o-ra-bil´ia

mem´o-ra-ble

mem-o-ran´da

mem-o-ran´dum

me-mo´ri-al

me-mo´ri-al-ize

mem´o-ries

mem-o-ri-za´tion

mem´o-rize

mem´o-riz-er

mem´o-riz-ing

mem´o-ry

men´ace

men´ac-ing

men´ac-ing-ly

me-nag´er-ie

men-da´cious

men-dac´i-ty

mend´er

men´di-cant

me´nial

men-in-gi´tis

men´o-pause

men´ses

men´stru-al

men´stru-ate

men-stru-a´tion

men´tal

men-tal´i-ty

men´tal-ly

men´thol

men´thyl

men´tion-a·ble

men´tion-er

men´tor

men´u

mer´can-tile

mer´ce-nary

mer´chan-dise

mer´chan-dis-er

mer´chan-dis-ing

mer´chant

mer´cies

mer´ci-ful-ly

mer´ci-ful-ness
mer´ci-less
mer-cu´ri-al
mer´cy
mere´ly
me-ren´gue
mer´est
mer-e-tri´cious
mer-gan´ser
merge
mer´gence
merg´er
me-rid´i-an
me-ringue´
mer´it
mer´it-ed
mer-i-to´ri-ous
mer´maid
mer´man
mer´ri-ly
mer´ri-ment
mer´ri-ness
mer´ry
mer´ry-mak-ing
me´sa
mesh´work
mesh´y
mes´mer-ism
mes´mer-ize
mes´mer-iz-ing
mes-quite´
mes´sage
mes´sen-ger

mess´i-ness
mess´mate
mess´y
met´a-bol´ic
me-tab´o-lism
me-tab´o-lize
met´al
me-tal´lic
met´al-lur´gic
met´al-lur´gi-cal
met´al-lur-gist
met´al-lur-gy
met´al-work
met´al-work-ing
met·a-mor´phic
met·a-mor´pho-sis
met´a-phor
met-a-phor´i-cal
meta-phys´i-cal
met´a-phys´ics
me´te-or
me-te-or´ic
me´te-or-ite
me-te-o-rol´o-gist
me-te-o-rol´o-gy
me´ter
meth´a-done
meth´ane
meth´a-nol
meth´od
me-thod´i-cal
me-thod´i-cal-ly
meth-od-ol´o-gy

me-tic´u-lous
met´ric
met´ri-cal
met´ro-nome
me-trop´o-lis
met´ro-pol´i-tan
met´tle
mez´za-nine´
mi´crobe
mi´cro-bi-ol´o-gist
mi´cro-bi-ol´o-gy
mi´cro-cosm
mi´cro-fiche
mi´cro-film
mi-crom´e-ter
mi´cron
mi-cro-or´ga-nism
ml´cro-phone
mi´cro-scope
mi´cro-scop´ic
mi´cro-wave
mid´dle
mid´dle–aged´
mid´dle-man
mid´dle-of–the
    road´
midg´et
mid´night
mid´riff
mid´stream´
mid´sum´mer
mid´way
mid´wife

mid'wife-ry
might'i-er
might'i-ly
might'i-ness
might'y
mi'graine
mi'grant
mi'grate
mi'grat-ing
mi-gra'tion
mi'gra-to-ry
mil'dew
mild'ly
mild'ness
mile'age
mile'post
mile'stone
mi-lieu'
mil'i-tan-cy
mil'i-tant-ly
mi -i-tar'i-ly
mil'i-ta-rism
mil'i-ta-ris'tic
mil'i-tary
mi-li'tia
milk'i-ness
milk shake
milk'y
mil'le-nary
mill'er
mil'li-gram
mil'li-me-ter
mil'li-ner

mil'li-ner·y
mill'ing
mil'lion
mi'lion-aire'
mil'lionth
mill'pond
mill'stream
mim'e-o-graph
mim'er
mim'ic
mim'icked
mim'ick-er
mim'ick-ing
mim'ic-ry
mim'ing
min'a-ret'
mince'meat
minc'er
minc'ing
mind'er
mind'ful
mind'less
min'er
min'er-al
min'er-al-ize
min'er-al-og'i-cal
min-er-al'o-gist
min-er-al'o-gy
min'gle
min'gling
min'i-a-ture
min'i-a-tur-ist
min'i-cam

min'i-mal
min'i-mize
min'i-miz-er
min'i-mum
min'ing
min'is-ter
min'is-te'ri-al
min'is-try
min'now
mi'nor
mi-nor'i-ty
min'strel
mint'er
min-u-et'
mi'nus
min'us-cule
min'ute *(time)*
mi-nute' *(tiny)*
min'ute hand
min'ute-ly *(time)*
min'ute-man
mi-nute'ness *(tiny)*
mi-nu'tia
mi-nu'ti-ae
mir'a-cle
mi-rac'u-lous
mi-rac'u-lous-ly
mi-rage'
mired
mir'ing
mir'ror
mirth'ful
mirth'less

mis-ad-ven´ture
mis-al-li´ance
mis´an-thrope
mis´an-throp´ic
mis´ap-pre-hend´
mis-ap-pre-hen´-
  sion
mis-be-got´ten
mis-be-have´
mis-be-hav´ing
mis-be-hav´ior
mis-cal´cu-late
mis-cal-cu-la´tion
mis-car´riage
mis-car´ried
mis-car´ry
mis-car´ry-ing
mis-cel-la´neous
mis´cel-la-ny
mis´chief–mak´er
mis´chie-vous
mis´ci-ble
mis-con-ceive´
mis-con-cep´tion
mis-con´duct
mis´con-strue´
mis´cre-ance
mis´cre-an-cy
mis´cre-ant
mis-deed´
mis´de-mean´or
mis-di-rec´tion
mis-do´er

mi´ser
mis´er-a-ble
mis´er-a-bly
mi´ser-li-ness
mi´ser-ly
mis´ery
mis-fire´
mis´fit´
mis-for´tune
mis-giv´ing
mis-guide´
mis-guid´ed
mis-han´dle
mis´hap
mis´in-form´
mis´in-for-ma´-
  tion
mis-in-ter´pret
mis´in-ter-pre-ta´-
  tion
mis-judge´
mis-laid´
mis-lay´
mis-lead´ing
mis-man´age
mis-man´age-
  ment
mis-match´
mis-no´mer
mi-sog´a-mist
mi-sog´a-my
mi-sog´y-nist
mi-sog´y-ny

mis-place´
mis´print
mis´pro-nounce´
mis´quote´
mis´quot´ing
mis´rep-re-sent´
mis´sal
mis-shape´
mis-shap´en
mis´sile
miss´ing
mis´sion
mis´sion-ar-ies
mis´sion-ary
mis´sive
mis-spell´
mis-spelled´
mis-spell´ing
mis-spent´
mis-step´
mis-tak´able
mis-take´
mis-tak´en
mis-tak´en-ly
mis-tak´ing
mis´ter
mist´i-ness
mis-took´
mis-treat´ment
mis´tress
mist´y
mis-un-der-stand´
mis-un-der-stood´

mis-use´   mo-der´ni-ty   mold´i-ness
mi´ter   mod-ern-i·za´tion   mold´ing
mit´i-gate   mod´ern-ize   mold´y
mit´i-gat-ing   mod´ern-iz-ing   mo-lec´u-lar
mit-i -ga´tion   mod´est-ly   mol´e-cule
mit´i-ga-tive   mod´es-ty   mole´hill
mit´i-ga-to-ry   mod´i-cum   mo-lest´
mit´ten   mod´i-fi´able   mo-les-ta´tion
mix´er   mod-i-fi-ca´tion   mo-lest´er
mix´ture   mod´i-fied   mol´li-fied
mix´–up   mod´i-fi-er   mol´li-fy
mne-mon´ic   mod´i-fy-ing   mol´li-fy-ing
moan´ing   mod´ish   mol´lusk
mobbed   mod´u-lar   mol´ten
mob´bing   mod´u-late   mo´ment
mo´bile   mod-u-la´tion   mo´men-tar´i-ly
mo-bil´i-ty   mod´u-la-tor   mo´men-tar·y
mo-bi-li-za´tion   mod´ule   mo-men´tous
mo´bi-lize   mod´u-lus   mo-men´tum
mock´er   mo´gul   mon´arch
mock´er·y   mo´hair   mon´ar-chist
mock´ing   moi´e-ty   mon´ar-chy
mock´ing-ly   moi-ré´   mon´as-te´ri-al
mo-dal´i-ty   moist´en   mon´as-tery
mod´el   moist´en-er   mo-nas´tic
mod´eled   moist´ly   mo-nas´ti-cism
mod´el-ing   moist´ness   mon-e-tar´i-ly
mo´dem   mois´ture   mon´e-tar·y
mod´er-ate-ly   mois´ture-proof   mon´ey
mod´er-at-ing   mo´lar   mon´eyed
mod-er-a´tion   mo-las´ses   mon´ey-mak-er
mod´er-a-tor   mold´able   mon´ey-mak-ing
mod´ern-ist   mold´er   mon´ger

mon´grel

mon´i-ker

mon´i-tor

monk´ery

mon´key-shine

monk´ish

monks´hood

mon´o-chro-mat´-
ic

mon´o-cle

mo-nog´a-mist

mo-nog´a-mous

mo-nog´a-my

mon´o-gram

mon´o-grammed

mon´o-lith

mon´o-lith´ic

mon´o-log

mon´o-logue

mon´o-ma´nia

mon´o-nu-cle-o´sis

mo-nop´o-lis´tic

mo-nop´o-lize

mo-nop´o-ly

mon´o-rail

mon´o-syl-lab´ic

mon´o-syl´la-ble

mon´o-the-ism

mon´o-the-ist

mon´o-the-is´tic

mon´o-tone

mo-not´o-nous

mo-not´o-ny

mon-sieur´

mon-soon´

mon´ster

mon-stros´i-ty

mon´strous

mon-tage´

month´ly

mon´u-ment

mon-u-men´tal

mood´i-ly

mood´i-ness

mood´y

moon´beam

moon´less

moon´light

moon´lit

moon´shine

moon´struck

moor´age

moor´ing

moped

mop´ing

mop´pet

mop´ping

mor´al

mo-rale´

mor´al-ism

mor´al-ist

mo-ral´i-ty

mor´al-ize

mor´al-ly

mo-rass´

mor-a-to´ri-um

mor´bid

mor-bid´i-ty

mor´bid-ly

mor-bif´ic

more-o-ver

morgue

mor´i-bund

morn´ing

mo´ron

mo-ron´ic

mo-rose´

mo-rose´ly

mor´phine

mor´sel

mor´tal

mor-tal´i-ty

mor´tal-ly

mor´tar

mor´tar-board

mort´gage

mort´ga-gee´

mort´gag-ing

mor-ti´cian

mor-ti-fi-ca´tion

mor´ti-fied

mor´ti-fy

mor´ti-fy-ing

mor´tise

mor´tis-ing

mor´tu-ary

mo-sa´ic

mosque

mos-qui´to

mos-qui´toes	moun´tain-ous	muf´fler
moss´i-er	mount´ed	muf´fling
moss´i-ness	mount´er	muf´ti
moss´y	mount´ing	mug´ger
most´ly	mourn´er	mug´gi-ness
mo-tel´	mourn´ful	mug´ging
moth´er	mourn´ing	mug´gy
moth´er-land	mouse´trap	mul´ber-ry
moth´er-li-ness	mous´tache	mulch´er
moth´er-ly	mous´y	mul´ish
mo-tif´	mouth´ful	mul´ti-col´ored
mo´tile	mouth´piece	mul´ti-far´i-ous
mo-til´i-ty	mov´able	mul´ti-lat´er-al
mo-tion	move´ment	mul´ti-lay-er
mo´tion-less	mov´er	mul-ti-lev´el
mo´ti-vate	mov´ie	mul´ti-lin´gual
mo-ti-vat-ing	mov´ies	mul´ti-me´dia
mo-ti-va´tion	mov´ing	mul´ti-na´tion-al
mo-tive	mowed	mul´ti-ple
mot´ley	mow´er	mul´ti-plex
mo´tor-boat	mow´ing	mul-ti-pli-ca´tion
mo´tor-cade	mown	mul-ti-plic´i-ty
mo´tor-cy-cle	mu´ci-lage	mul´ti-plied
mo´tor-cy-clist	muck´er	mul´ti-pli-er
mo´tor-ist	muck´rake	mul´ti-ply
mo´tor-ize	muck´y	mul´ti-ply-ing
mot´tle	mud´di-ness	mul´ti-tude
mot´tled	mud´dle	mul-ti-tu´di-nous
mot´tling	mud´dled	mum´ble
mot´to	mud´dy	mum´bling
mot´toes	mud´guard	mun´dane´
moun´tain	muf´fin	mu-nic´i-pal
moun´tain-eer´	muf´fle	mu-nic-i-pal´i-ty

mu-nif´i-cence

mu-nif´i-cent

mu-ni´tion

mu´ral

mur´der-er

mur´der-ess

mur´der-ous

murk´i-er

murk´i-ly

murk´y

mur´mur

mur´mur-ing

mus´cle–bound

mus´cu-lar

mus-cu-lar´i-ty

mus´cu-la-ture

mu-se´um

mush´room

mush´y

mu´sic

mu´si-cal

mu´si-cale´

mu´si-cal-ly

mu-si´cian

mu-si-col´o-gy

mus´ing

mus´ket

mus´ket-ry

musk´y

mus´lin

muss´y

mus´ter

must´i-ness

must´y

mu´tant

mu´tate

mu´tat-ing

mu-ta´tion

mut´ed

mute´ly

mute´ness

mu´ti-late

mu-ti-la´tion

mu´ti-la-tor

mu´ti-neer´

mut´ing

mu´ti-nied

mu´ti-nous

mu´tiny

mut´ter

mut´ter-ing

mu´tu-al

mu´tu-al-ly

mu´tu-el

muz´zle

muz´zling

my-o´pia

my-op´ic

myr´i-ad

myrrh

my-self´

mys´ter-ies

mys-te´ri-ous

mys-te´ri-ous-ly

mys´tery

mys´tic

mys´ti-cal

mys´ti-cism

mys´ti-fied

mys´ti-fy

mys´ti-fy-ing

mys-tique´

myth´ic

myth´i-cal

myth´i-cal-ly

myth´i-cist

myth´i-cize

myth-o-log´i-cal

my-thol´o-gy

N

nabbed

nab´bing

na´bob

na´dir

nag´ging

na´iad

nail´er

na-ive´

na-ive-té´

na´ked

na´ked-ness

nam´by–pam´by

name´less

name´ly

nam´er

name´sake

nam´ing

na´per·y

naph´tha
nap´kin
nap´per
nap´ping
nar´cis-sism
nar´cis-sist
nar-cis´sus
nar´co-lep-sy
nar-co-lep´tic
nar-co´sis
nar-cot´ic
nar´rate
nar-ra´tion
nar´ra-tive
nar´ra-tor
nar´row
nar´row-ly
nar´row–mind´ed
nar´row-ness
na´sal
na´sal-ly
nas´cent
nas´ti-ly
nas´ti-ness
nas´ty
na´tal
na´tion
na´tion-al
na´tion-al-ism
na´tion-al-ist
na´tion-al-is´tic
na-tion-al´i-ty
na´tion-al-ize

na´tion-al-ly
na´tion-wide´
na´tive
na´tive–born´
na-tiv´i-ty
nat´ti-ly
nat´ty
nat´u-ral
nat´u-ral-ist
nat´u-ral-is´tic
nat-u-ral-i·za´tion
nat´u-ral-ize
nat´u-ral-ly
nat´u-ral-ness
na´ture
naught
naugh´ti-ly
naugh´ti-ness
naugh´ty
nau´sea
nau´se-ate
nau´se-at-ed
nau´seous
nau´ti-cal
nau´ti-cal-ly
na´val *(marine)*
na´vel *(mark)*
na´vies
nav´i-ga-ble
nav´i-gate
nav-i-ga´tion
nav´i-ga-tor
na´vy

near´by´
near´est
near´ly
near´ness
near´sight-ed
neat´ly
neat´ness
neb´u-la
neb´u-lae
neb´u-lar
neb´u-lous
nec´es-sar´i-ly
nec´es-sar·y
ne-ces´si-tate
ne-ces´si-ties
ne-ces´si-ty
neck´lace
neck´tie
nec´ro-man-cer
nec´ro-man-cy
nec´tar
need´ful
need´i-er
need´i-est
nee´dle
nee´dler
need´less
need´less-ly
nee´dle-work
need´y
ne'er´–do—well
ne-far´i-ous
ne-gate´

ne-ga´tion	nerv´y	new´ly
neg´a-tive	nest´er	new´–mown
neg´a-tive-ly	nes´tle	new´ness
neg´a-tiv-ism	nes´tling *(snuggle)*	news´boy
neg-a-tiv´i-ty	nest´ling *(bird)*	news´cast-er
ne-glect	neth´er-most	news´let-ter
ne-glect´er	net´ting	news´pa-per
ne-glect´ful	net´tle	news´print
neg-li-gee´	net´tled	news´reel
neg´li-gence	net´work	news´room
neg´li-gent	neu´ral	news´stand
neg´li-gent-ly	neu-ral´gia	news´y
neg´li-gi-ble	neu-ral´gic	ni´a-cin
ne-go´tia-ble	neu-ri´tis	nib´ble
ne-go´ti-ate	neu-rol´o-gist	nib´bling
ne-go´ti-at-ing	neu-rol´o-gy	nice´ly
ne-go-ti-a´tion	neu-rol´y-sis	nice´ness
ne-go´ti-a-tor	neu-ro´ses	nic´est
neigh´bor	neu-ro´sis	ni´ce-ty
neigh´bor-hood	neu-rot´ic	niche
neigh´bor-li-ness	neu´tral	nick´el
neigh´bor-ly	neu-tral´i-ty	nick-el-o´de-on
neigh´bour (Br.)	neu´tral-ize	nick´name
nei´ther	neu´tral-iz-er	nic´o-tine
nem´e-sis	neu´tral-ly	niece
ne´on	neu-tri´no	nif´ty
ne´o-phyte	neu´tron	nig´gle
neph´ew	nev´er	nig´gling
nep´o-tism	nev´er-the-less´	night´club
nerve´less	new´born	night´fall
ner´vous	new´com-er	night´gown
ner´vous-ly	new´el	night´ly
ner´vous-ness	new´fan´gled	night´mare

night´time
ni´hi-lism
ni´hi-list
ni´hi-lis´tic
nim´ble
nim´ble-ness
nim´bly
nim´bus
nin´com-poop
nine´fold
nine´teen´
nine´teenth
nine´ti-eth
nine´ty
nin´ny
ninth
nip´per
nip´ping
nip´ple
nip´py
ni´trate
ni´tric
ni´tride
ni´trite
ni´tro-gen
ni´trous
no-bil´i-ty
no´ble
no´ble-man
no´ble-wom-an
no´bly
no´body
noc-tur´nal

noc´turne
nod´ding
nod´u-lar
nod´ule
noise´less
noise´less-ly
nois´i-ly
nois´i-ness
nois´ing
noi´some
nois´y
no´mad
no-mad´ic
no´men-cla-ture
nom´i-nal
nom´i-nal-ly
nom´i-nal-ism
nom´i-nal-ist
nom´i-nal-ize
nom´i-nate
nom´i-nat-ed
nom-i-na´tion
nom´i-na-tive
nom´i-nee´
non·a-ge-nar´i-an
non-ag-gres´sion
non´cha-lance´
non´cha-lant´
non´cha-lant-ly
non-com-bat´ant
non-com-mis´-
  sioned
non-com-mit´tal

non-con-duc´tor
non-con-form´ist
non-con-form´i-ty
non´de-script
non-en´ti-ty
non-ex-is´tént
non´fic´tion
non-in-ter-ven´-
  tion
non-par´ti-san
non´pay´ment
non-plussed´
non-pro-duc´tive
non-prof´it
non-pro-li-fer-
  a´tion
non-sec-tar´i-an
non´sense
non-sen´si-cal
non se´qui-tur
non´stop´
noo´dle
noon´time
nor´mal
nor-mal´i-ty
nor´mal-ize
nor´mal-ly
nor´ma-tive
north´east´
north-east´er-ly
north-east´ern
north´er-ly
north´ern

north´ern-er
north´ern-most
north´ward
north´west´
north´west´er-ly
north-west´ern
nose´bleed
nose´–dive
nos-tal´gia
nos-tal´gic
nos´tril
nos´y
no´ta-ble
no´ta-bly
no´ta-ries
no´ta-rize
no´ta-ry
no-ta´tion
notched
notch´er
note´book
not´ed
note´pa-per
note´wor-thy
noth´ing
no´tice-able
no´tice-ably
no´tic-ing
no´ti-fi-ca´tion
no´ti-fied
no´ti-fi-er
no´ti-fy
no´ti-fy-ing

not´ing
no-to-ri´e-ty
no-to´ri-ous
no-to´ri-ous-ly
not-with-stand´-
   ing
nou´gat
nour´ish
nour´ish-ing
nour´ish-ment
nov´el
nov-el-ette´
nov´el-ist
nov´el-ize
no-vel´la
nov´el-ties
nov´el-ty
no-ve´na
nov´ice
no-vi´tiate
no´where
nox´ious
noz´zle
nu´ance
nu´bile
nu´cle-ar
nu´clei
nu-cle´ic
nu´cle-us
nude´ness
nudged
nudg´er
nudg´ing

nud´ism
nud´ist
nu´di-ty
nug´get
nui´sance
nul-li-fi-ca´tion
nul´li-fied
nul´li-fi-er
nul´li-fy
nul´li-fy-ing
num´ber
num´bered
num´ber-er
num´ber-less
numb´ing
numb´ly
numb´ness
nu´mer-al
nu-mer´i-cal
nu-mer´i-cal-ly
nu-mer-ol´o-gy
nu´mer-ous
nu-mis-mat´ics
nu-mis´ma-tist
num´skull
nun´nery
nup´tial
nurse´maid
nur´sery
nurs´ing
nur´ture
nur´tur-ing
nu´tri-ent

nu´tri-ment
nu-tri´tion
nu-tri´tion-al
nu-tri´tion-ist
nu-tri´tious
nu´tri-tive
nut´ti-er
nut´ti-ness
nut´ty
nuz´zle
ny´lon
nymph

O

oak´en
oar´lock
oars´man
oa´ses
oa´sis
oat´meal
ob´du-ra-cy
ob´du-rate
o·be´di-ence
o·be´di-ent
o·be´di-ent-ly
o·bei´sance
o·bei´sant
ob´e-lisk
o·bese´
o·be´si-ty
o·bey´
o·bey´ing
ob-fus´cate

ob-fus-ca´tion
o·bit´u-ar-ies
o·bit´u-ary
ob´ject *(n.)*
ob-ject´ *(v.)*
ob-ject´ing
ob-jec´tion
ob-jec´tion-able
ob-jec´tive
ob-jec´tive-ly
ob-jec´tive-ness
ob-jec-tiv´i-ty
ob´late
ob´li-gate
ob´li-gat-ing
ob-li-ga´tion
ob´li-ga-tor
o·blig´a-to-ry
o·blige´
o·blig´er
o·blig´ing
o·blig´ing-ly
o·blique´
o·blique´ly
ob-lit´er-ate
ob-lit-er-a´tion
ob-liv´i-on
ob-liv´i-ous
ob´long
ob-nox´ious
o´boe
o´bo-ist
ob-scene´

ob-scene´ly
ob-scen´i-ty
ob-scure´
ob-scure´ness
ob-scur´ing
ob-scu´ri-ty
ob-se´qui-ous
ob-se´qui-ous-ness
ob-serv´able
ob-serv´ance
ob-serv´ant
ob-ser-va´tion
ob-serv´a-to-ry
ob-serve´
ob-serv´er
ob-serv´ing
ob-sess´
ob-ses´sion
ob-ses´sive
ob-so-les´cence
ob-so-les´cent
ob-so-lete´
ob´sta-cle
ob-stet´rics
ob´sti-na-cy
ob´sti-nance
ob´sti-nate
ob´sti-nate-ly
ob-strep´er-ous
ob-struct´
ob-struct´er
ob-struc´tion
ob-struc´tion-ist

ob-struc´tive	oc-cur´rence	off´–col´or
.ob-tain´able	oc-cur´rent	of-fend´
ob-trude´	oc-cur´ring	of-fend´er
ob-trud´er	o´cean	of-fend´ing
ob-trud´ing	o·ce-an´ic	of-fense´
ob-tru´sion	o·cean-og´ra-phy	of-fen´sive
ob-tru´sive	oc´ta-gon	of-fen´sive-ness
ob-tru´sive-ly	oc-tag´o-nal	of´fer
ob-tuse´	oc´tal	of´fer-ing
ob´vi-ate	oc´tane	of-fer-to´ri-al
ob´vi-at-ing	oc´tave	of´fer-to-ry
ob-vi-a´tion	oc-tet´	of´fice
ob´vi-ous	Oc-to´ber	of´fice-hold-er
ob´vi-ous-ly	oc-to-ge-nar´i-an	of´fi-cer
ob´vi-ous-ness	oc´u-list	of-fi´cial
oc-ca´sion	odd´i-ty	of-fi´cial-ly
oc-ca´sion-al	odd´ly	of-fi´ci-ate
oc-ca´sion-al-ly	odd´ment	of-fi´cious
oc´ci-den´tal	odd´ness	of-fi´cious-ly
oc-clu´sion	od´ic	off´shoot
oc-cult´	o´di-ous	off´spring
oc-cul-ta´tion	od´ist	of´ten
oc-cult´ism	o´di-um	of´ten-times
oc´cupan-cy	odom´e-ter	o´gle
oc´cu-pant	o´dor	o´gling
oc-cu-pa´tion	o´dor-ant	o´gre
oc-cu-pa´tion-al	o·dor-if´er-ous	oil´cloth
oc´cu-pied	o´dor-less	oil´er
oc´cu-pi-er	o´dor-ous	oil´i-ness
oc´cu-py	o´dour (Br.)	oil´stone
oc´cu-py-ing	of´fal	oil´y
oc-cur´	off´beat	oint´ment
oc-curred´	off´–cen´ter	o·kay´

old´en
old–fash´ioned
old´-line´
old´ster
old´-time´
old–tim´er
o´leo
o´le-o-mar´ga-rine
ol-fac´tive
ol-fac´to-ry
ol´i-gar-chy
o·meg´a
o´men
om´i-nous
om´i-nous-ly
o·mis´sion
o·mit´
o·mit´ted
o·mit´ting
om´ni-bus
om-nip´o-tence
om-nip´o-tent
om-ni-pres´ent
om-niv´o-rous
once–o´ver
on´com-ing
one´ness
one´-piece´
on´er-ous
one-self´
one´-sid´ed
one´time
one´-way´

on´ion-skin
on´look-er
on´ly
on-o-mat-o-poe´ia
on´rush
on´set
on´slaught
on´to
o´nus
on´ward
on´yx
oozed
ooz´ing
o·pac´i-ty
o´pal
o·pal-esce´
o·pal-es´cence
o·pal-es´cent
o·paque´
o·paque´ly
o·paqu´er
o·paqu´ing
o´pen
o´pen–air´
o´pen–door´
o´pen-er
o´pen–faced
o´pen-hand´ed
o´pen-ing
o´pen-ly
o´pen–mind´ed
o´pen-ness
o´pen-work

op´er-a-ble
op´er-ate
op-er-a´tion
op-er-a´tion-al
op´er-a-tive
op´er-a-tor
op-er-et´ta
oph-thal-mol´o-
    gist
oph-thal-mol´o-gy
o´pi-ate
opin´ion
opin´ion-at-ed
o´pi-um
op-po´nent
op´por-tune´
op´por-tune´ly
op-por-tune´ness
op-por-tun´ism
op-por-tun´ist
op-por-tu´ni-ty
op-pos´a·ble
op-pose´
op-pos´ing
op´po-site
op-po-si´tion
op-press´
op-pres´sion
op-pres´sive
op-pres´sor
op-pro´bri-ate
op-pro´bri-ous
op-pro´bri-um

153

op´tic
op´ti-cal
op-ti´cian
op´tics
op´ti-mal
op´ti-mism
op´ti-mist
op´ti-mis´tic
op-ti-mis´ti-cal-ly
op´ti-mum
op´tion
op´tion-al
op-tom´e-trist
op-tom´e-try
op´u-lence
op´u-len-cy
op´u-lent
o´pus
or´a-cle
o´ral
o´ral-ly
o·rate´
o·ra´tion
or´a-tor
or-a-tor´i-cal
or-a-tor´i-cal-ly
or-a-to´rio
or´a-to-ry
or´bit
or´bit-al
or´bit-ed
or´bit-er
or´bit-ing

or´chard
or´ches-tra
or-ches´tral
or-ches-trate
or-ches-tra´tion
or-dain´
or´deal
or´der
or´dered
or´der-li-ness
or´der-ly
or´di-nal
or´di-nance
or-di-nar´i-ly
or´di-nary
or´di-nate
or-di-na´tion
ord´nance
or´gan
or´gan-dy
or-gan´ic
or-gan´i-cal-ly
or´ga-nism
or´gan-ist
or´ga-niz´a·ble
or-ga-ni-za´tion
or´ga-nize
or´ga-niz-er
or´ga-niz-ing
or´gy
o´ri-ent
o·ri-en´tal
o´ri-en-tate

o·ri-en-ta´tion
or´i-fice
or´i-gin
o·rig´i-nal
o·rig-i-nal´i-ty
o·rig´i-nal-ly
o·rig´i-nate
o·rig´i-nat-ing
o·rig-i-na´tion
o·rig´i-na-tor
or´na-ment
or´na-men´tal
or-na-men-ta´tion
or´nate´
or-nate´ness
or´nery
or-ni-thol´o-gist
or-ni-thol´o-gy
or´ni-thop-ter
or´phan
or´phan-age
or-tho-don´tia
or´tho-don´tics
or´tho-don´tist
or´tho-dox
or´tho-dox·y
or´tho-pae´dic
or´tho-pae´dist
os´cil-late
os-cil-la´tion
os-cil´lo-scope
os-si-fi-ca´tion
os´si-fied

os´si-fy
os-ten´si-ble
os-ten´si-bly
os-ten-ta´tion
os-ten-ta´tious
os-ten-ta´tious-ly
os´te o-my-e-li´tis
os´te-o-path
os´te-o-path´ic
os-te-op´a-thy
os´tra-cism
os´tra-cize
os´tra-ciz-ing
oth´er
oth´er-wise
ought
ounce
our-selves´
oust´er
out´break
out´burst
out´cast
out´class´
out´come
out´crop-ping
out´cry
out-do´
out-doors´
out´er-most
out´fit
out´fit-ter
out´go´ing
out´grew´

out´grow´
out´growth
out-ing
out-land´ish
out´law
out´let
out´line
out´look
out´mod´ed
out–of–date
out´post
out´pour-ing
out´put
out´rage
out-ra´geous
out-ra´geous-ly
out´reach
out´right
out´set
out-side´
out-sid´er
out´skirts
out´spo´ken
out-stand´ing
out-stretched´
out´ward-ly
out´wit´
o´va
o´val
o·va´tion
ov´en
o·ver-bear´ing
o·ver-came´

o´ver-cast
o´ver-coat
o·ver-come´
o´ver-draft
o´ver-drive´
o·ver-es´ti-mate
o´ver-flow
o´ver-hang´
o´ver-head
o´ver-joyed
o´ver-lap´
o·ver-lap´ping
o´ver-look´
o´ver-ly
o·ver-night´
o·ver-rate´
o·ver-rule´
o·ver-see´
o´ver-seer
o·ver-shad´ow
o´ver-sight´
o·ver-slept´
o·vert´
o·ver-tak´en
o·ver-throw´
o´ver-time
o·vert´ly
o´ver-tone
o´ver-ture
o´ver-weight
o·ver-whelm´ing
o·ver-worked´
o´ver-wrought´

o´vu-late
o·vu-la´tion
o´vule
ow´ing
own´er
own´er-ship
ox´en
ox´i-da´tion
ox´ide
ox´i-dize
ox´y-gen
ox´y-gen-ate
ox-y-gen-a´tion
o´zone

P

paced
pace´mak-er
pac´er
pa-cif´ic
pac-i-fi-ca´tion
pac´i-fied
pac´i-fi-er
pac´i-fism
pac´i-fist
pac´i-fy
pac´i-fy-ing
pac´ing
pack´age
pack´ag-er
pack´ag-ing
pack´er
pack´et

pack´ing
pack´ing-house
pad´ding
pad´dle
pad´dler
pad´dling
pad´lock
pa´gan
pa´gan-ism
pag´eant
pag´eant-ry
paged
pag´er
pag´i-nate
pag-i-na´tion
pag´ing
pa-go´da
pail´ful
pain´ful
pain´ful´ly
pain´less
pain´less-ly
pains´tak-ing
pains´tak-ing-ly
paint´brush
paint´er
paint´ing
pa-ja´ma
pal´ace
pal´at-able
pal´ate
pa-la´tial
pale´ness

pal´ette
pal´i-mo-ny
pal´in-drome
pal´ing
pal-i-sade´
pall´bear-er
pal´li-ate
pal´li·a-tive
pal´lid
pal´lor
palm´ist
palm´is-try
pal-pa-bil´i-ty
pal´pa-ble
pal´pa-bly
pal´pate
pal-pa´tion
pal´pi-tate
pal´pi-tat-ing
pa´pi-ta´tion
pal´sied
pal´sy
pal´tri-ness
pal´try
pam´per
pamph´let
pam´phle-teer
pan-a-ce´a
pan-chro-mat´ic
pan-de-mo´ni-um
pan´el
pan´eled
pan´el-ing

pan´el-ist

pan´ic

pan´icked

pan´ick-ing

pan´icky

pan´ic–strick-en

pan´o-ply

pan-o-ram´a

pan-o-ram´ic

pant´ing

pan´to-mime

pan´to-mimist

pan´tries

pan´try

pa´pa-cy

pa´pal

pa´per-back

pa´per-board

pa´per-hang-er

pa´per-weight

par´a-ble

par´a-chute

pa-rade´

pa-rad´er

pa-rad´ing

par´a-digm

par´a-dise

par´a-dox

par´a-gon

par´a-graph

par´al-lax

par´al-lel

par´al-leled

par´a-lyse (Br.)

pa-ral´y-sis

par´a-lyt´ic

par´a-lyze

par´a-lyz-ing

par´a-mount

par´a·mour

par-a-noi´a

par´a-noid

par´a-ple´gic

par´a-site

par´a-sit´ic

par´a-sol

par´boil

par´cel

par´celed

par´cel-ing

parch´ment

par´don

par´don-able

par´don-er

pared

par´ent-age

pa-ren´tal

pa-ren´the-ses

pa-ren´the-sis

pa-ren´the-size

par´en-thet´ic

par´en-thet´i-cal

par´ing

par´ish

pa-rish´ion-er

par´i-ty

park´way

par´lance

par´lay (a bet)

par´ley (a talk)

par´lia-ment

par-lia-men´ta-ry

par´lor

pa-ro´chial

par´o-dy

par´o-dy-ing

pa-role´

pa-roled´

pa-rol-ee´

pa-rol´ing

par-quet´

par´ried

par´ry

par´ry-ing

parse

par-si-mo´nious

par´si-mo-ny

pars´ing

par´son

par´son-age

par-take´

par-tak´en

par-tak´er

part´ed

par´tial

par-ti·al´i-ty

par´tial-ly

par-tic´i-pant

par-tic´i-pate

par-tic-i-pa´tion
par-tic´u-lar
par-tic´u-lar-ly
par´ties
part´ing
par´ti-san
par-ti´tion
par-ti´tion-er
par-ti´tion-ing
part´ly
part´ner
part´ner-ship
par-took´
part´–time´
par´ty
pass´able
pass´ably
pas´sage
pas´sage-way
pass´book
pas-sé´
pas´sen-ger
pass´er
pass´er-by
pass´ing
pas´sion
pas´sion-ate
pas´sion-ate-ly
pas´sive
pas´sive-ly
pas´sive-ness
pas´siv-ism
pas´siv-ist

pass´port
pass´word
paste´board
past´ed
pas-tel´
past´er
pas-teur-i-za´tion
pas´teur-ize
pas´time
past´ing
pas´tor
pas´to-ral
pas-to-rale´
pas´try
pas´ture
patch´er
patch´i-ness
patch´ing
patch´work
patch´y
pat´ent
pat´ent-able
pat´ent-ly
pa-ter´nal
pa-ter´nal-ism
pa-ter´nal-is´tic
pa-ter´nal-ly
pa-ter´ni-ty
pa-thet´ic
pa-thet´i-cal-ly
pa-thol´o-gist
pa-thol´o-gy
pa´thos

path´way
pa´tience
pa´tient
pa´tient-ly
pat´io
pa-tis´se-rie
pa´tois
pa´tri-arch
pa´tri-ar´chal
pa´tri-archy
pa-tri´cian
pa´tri-ot
pa´tri-ot´ic
pa´tri-ot´i-cal-ly
pa´tri-ot-ism
pa-trol´
pa-trolled´
pa-trol´ler
pa-trol´ling
pa´tron
pa´tron-age
pa´tron-ize
pa´tron-iz-ing
pat´ter
pat´tern
pat´terned
pat´tern-mak-er
pat´ting
pat´ty
pau´ci-ty
paunch´i-ness
paunch´y
pau´per

pau´per-ism
paus´ing
pave´ment
pav´er
pa-vil´ion
pav´ing
pawn´bro-ker
pawn´shop
pay´able
pay´day
pay-ee´
pay´er
pay´ing
pay´ment
pay-o´la
pay´roll
peace´able
peace´ably
peace´ful
peace´ful-ly
peace´ful-ness
peace´mak-er
peace´time
peach´y
peaked *(crested)*
peak´ed *(sickly)*
peas´ant
peas´ant-ry
peb´ble
peb´bled
peb´bling
peb´bly
pec´cant

peck´ing
pec´u-late
pec´u-lat-ing
pec-u-la´tion
pe-cu´liar
pe-cu-li·ar´i-ty
pe-cu´ni·ar·y
ped´a-gog´ic
ped´a-gogue
ped´a-gogy
ped´al
ped´aled
pe-dan´tic
ped´ant-ry
ped´dle
ped´dler
ped´dling
ped´es-tal
pe-des´tri-an
pe-di-a-tri´cian
pe-di-at´rics
ped´i-gree
peel´er
peel´ing
peep´er
peep´hole
peer´age
peer´less
pee´vish
pee´vish-ness
peign-oir´
pel-la´gra
pel´let

pel´vic
pel´vis
pe´nal
pe´nal-ize
pe´nal-iz-ing
pen´al-ties
pen´al-ty
pen´ance
pench´ant
pen´cil
pen´ciled
pen´cil-ing
pend´ing
pen´du-lous
pen´du-lum
pen´e-tra-ble
pen´e-trate
pen´e-trat-ing
pen-e-tra´tion
pen-i-cil´lin
pe-nin´su-la
pe-nin´su-lar
pen´i-tence
pen´i-tent
pen-i-ten´tia-ry
pen´i-tent-ly
pen´man-ship
pen´nant
pen´nies
pen´ni-less
pen´ning
pen´ny
pe-nol´o-gist

pe-nol´o-gy
pen´sion
pen´sion-er
pen´sive
pen´sive-ly
pen´ta-gon
pent´house
pent´–up´
pe´on
peo´ple
pep´per·y
pep´py
pep´sin
pep´tic
per-cale´
per-ceiv´a·ble
per-ceiv´a·bly
per-ceive´
per-cent´
per-cent´age
per-cent´ile
per-cep´ti-ble
per-cep´ti-bly
per-cep´tion
per-cep´tive
per´co-late
per´co-la´tion
per´co-la-tor
per-cus´sion
per-cus´sive
pe-remp´tive
pe-remp´to-ri-ly
pe-remp´to-ry

pe-ren´nial
per´fect (adj.)
per-fect´ (v.)
per-fect´er
per-fec´tion
per´fect-ly
per-fec´tor
per-fid´i-ous
per-fid´i-ous-ly
per-fid´i-ous-ness
per´fi-dy
per´fo-rate
per´fo-rat-ed
per´fo-ra´tion
per´fo-ra-tor
per-form´
per-form´ance
per-form´er
per´fume
per-fum´er
per-fum´er·y
per-func´to-ry
per-haps´
per´il
per´il-ous
per´il-ous-ly
pe-rim´e-ter
pe´ri-od
pe-ri-od´ic
pe-ri-od´i-cal
pe-ri-od´i-cal-ly
per·i-pa-tet´ic
pe-riph´er-al

pe-riph´er-al-ly
pe-riph´er·y
per´i-phrase
per´i-scope
per´ish
per´ish-a·ble
per´jure
per´jur-er
per´jur-ing
per-ju´ri-ous
per´jur·y
perk´i-ness
perk´y
per´ma-nence
per´ma-nen-cy
per´ma-nent
per´ma-nent-ly
per´me-a·ble
per´me-ate
per-mis´si-ble
per-mis´sion
per-mis´sive
per-mit´ (v., n.)
per´mit (n.)
per-mit´ted
per-mit´ting
per-mu-ta´tion
per-ni´cious
per-ox´ide
per-pen-dic´u-lar
per´pe-trate
per´pe-tra-tor
per-pet´u-al

per-pet´u-ate
per-pe-tu´it·y
per-plex´
per-plexed´
per-plex´ing
per´qui-site
per´se-cute
per-se-cu´tion
per´se-cu-tor
per-se-ver´ance
per´se-vere´
per´se-ver´ing
per´si-flage
per-sist´
per-sist´ence
per-sist´ent
per-sist´ent-ly
per-snick´e-ty
per´son
per´son-al
per´son-al´i-ty
per´son-al-ize
per´son-al-ly
per´son-i-fi-ca´-
    tion
per-son´i-fy
per-son´i-fy-ing
per´son-nel´
per-spec´tive
per-spi-ca´cious
per-spi-cac´i-ty
per-spi-cu´ity
per-spic´u-ous

per-spi-ra´tion
per-spire´
per-spir´ing
per-suad´a·ble
per-suade´
per-suad´er
per-suad´ing
per-sua´si·ble
per-sua´sion
per-sua´sive
per-sua´sive-ly
per-tain´
per´ti-nence
per´ti-nent
per-turb´
per-turb´a·ble
pe-rus´al
pe-ruse´
pe-rus´er
pe-rus´ing
per-vade´
per-vad´ing
per-va´sive
per-va´sive-ly
per-verse´
per-verse´ly
per-verse´ness
per-ver´sion
per-ver´sity
per-vert´ *(v.)*
per´vert *(n.)*
per-vert´ed
per´vi-ous

pes´ky
pes´si-mism
pes´si-mist
pes-si-mis´tic
pes-si-mis´ti-cal-ly
pes´ter
pes´tered
pes´ti-lence
pes´tle
pe-tite´
pe-ti´tion
pe-ti´tion-er
pet´ri-fied
pet´ri-fy
pet´ti-ly
pet´ti-ness
pet´ty
pet´u-lance
pet´u-lant
pew´ter
pha´lanx
phal´lic
phal´lus
phan´tasm
phan´tom
phar´aoh
phar´ma-ceu´ti-
    cal
phar´ma-ceu´tics
phar´ma-cist
phar´ma-col´o-gy
phar´ma-co-pe´ia
phar´ma-cy

phase
phas´er
phe´no-bar´bi-tal
phi´al
phi-lan´der
phi-lan´der-er
phil´an-throp´ic
phi-lan´thro-pist
phi-lan´thro-py
phil´a-tel´ic
phi-lat´e-list
phil´har-mon´ic
phi-los´o-pher
phil´o-soph´i-cal
phi-los´o-phize
phi-los´o-phy
phil´ter
phle-bi´tis
phlegm
pho´bia
pho´bic
pho-net´ic
pho-net´i-cal-ly
phon´ic
pho´no-graph
pho´ny
phos´phate
phos´phor
phos-pho-resce´
phos-pho-res´cent
pho´to
pho´to-gen´ic
pho´to-graph

pho-tog´ra-pher
pho´to-graph´ic
pho-tog´ra-phy
pho´ton
pho´to-stat
pho-to-syn´the-sis
phras´al
phrase
phras´ing
phre-nol´o-gist
phre-nol´o-gy
phy´lum
phys´i-cal
phys´i-cal-ly
phy-si´cian
phys´i-cist
phys´ics
phy-sique´
pi-an´ist
pi-a´no *(softly)*
pi-an´o
   (instrument)
pi-an´o-forte
pic´a-resque´
pic´co-lo
pic´co-lo-ist
pick´ax
pick´er
pick´et
pick´et-er
pick´et-ing
pick´ing
pick´le

pick´led
pick´ling
pick´pock-et
pic´nic
pic´nicked
pic´nick-er
pic´nick-ing
pic-to´ri-al
pic´ture
pic-tur-esque´
pic´tur-ing
pieced
piece´meal
piece´work
piec´ing
pie´crust
pierced
pierc´er
pierc´ing
pi´e-tism
pi´e-ty
pif´fle
pi´geon
pi´geon-hole
pi´geon–toed
pig´head-ed
pig´ment
pig-men-ta´tion
pig´pen
pig´skin
pik´er
pi-las´ter
pil´fer

pil´fer-age	pi´ra-cy	pix´y
pil´grim-age	pi´rate	piz-ze-ri´a
pil´ing	pir´ou-ette´	plac´a-ble
pil´lage	pir´ou-ett´ed	plac´ard
pil´lag-er	pir´ou-ett´ing	pla´cate
pil´low	pis´ca-to´ri-al	pla´cat-er
pil´low-case	pis´ca-to-ry	pla´cat-ing
pil´low-slip	pis´tol	pla-ce´bo
pi´lot	pis´ton	place´–kick
pim´ple	pitch´er	place´ment
pim´pled	pitch´ing	plac´er
pim´ply	pit´e-ous	plac´id
pin´a-fore	pit´e-ous-ly	plac´id-ly
pince´–nez´	pit´fall	plac´ing
pin´cers	pith´i-ness	pla´gia-rist
pinch´–hit	pith´y	pla´gia-rize
pin´hole	pit´i-a·ble	pla´gia-riz-ing
pin´na-cle	pit´ied	pla´gia-ry
pin´ning	pit´i-er	plague
pin´point	pit´ies	plagu´ed
pin´up	pit´i-ful	plagu´ing
pin´y	pit´i-ful-ly	plaid
pi´o-neer´	pit´i-less	plain´ly
pi´o-neered´	pit´tance	plain´ness
pi´ous	pit´ted	plain´tiff
pi´ous-ly	pit´ter–pat´ter	plain´tive
pipe´line	pit´ting	plain´tive-ly
pip´er	pit´y	plait
pip´ing	pit´y-ing	plan´et
pi´quan-cy	piv´ot	plan-e-tar´i-um
pi´quant	piv´ot-al	plan´e-tar·y
pique	piv´ot-er	plank´ing
piqued	pix´ie	plank´ton

planned
plan´ner
plan´ning
plan´tain
plan-ta´tion
plant´er
plant´ing
plaque
plas´ma
plas´ter
plas´tered
plas´ter-er
plas´ter-ing
plas´tic
pla-teau´
plat´ed
plate´ful
plat´en
plat´form
plat´ing
plat´i-num
plat´i-tude
pla-ton´ic
pla-toon´
plat´ter
plau´dit
plau´si·ble
plau´sive
play´bill
play´boy
play´er
play´ful
play´ful-ly

play´ful-ness
play´go-er
play´ground
play´house
play´ing card
play´mate
play´–off (n.)
play´thing
plaz´a
plea
plead´er
plead´ing
plead´ing-ly
pleas´ant
pleas´ant-ly
pleas´ant-ness
pleas´ant-ry
pleas´ing
plea´sur-a·ble
plea´sure
pleat
pleat´ed
ple-be´ian
pleb´i-scite
plec´trum
pledged
pledg´er
pledg´ing
ple´na-ry
plen´te-ous
plen´ti-ful
plen´ti-ful-ly
plen´ty

pleu´ri-sy
pli´a·ble
pli´an-cy
pli´ant
plied
pli´ers
plight
plod´ded
plod´der
plod´ding
plot´ter
plot´ting
plow
plow´er
plow´–hand
plow´ing
plow´share
pluck´i-er
pluck´y
plu´mage
plumb
plumb´er
plumb´ing
plum´met
plump´er
plump´ness
plun´der
plun´der-er
plun´der-ous
plung´er
plung´ing
plu´ral
plu-ral´i-ty

plu-toc´ra-cy
ply´ing
pneu-mat´ic
pneu-mo´nia
poach´er
pock´et
pock´et-book
pock´et-ful
po-di´a-trist
po-di´a-try
po´di-um
po´em
po´e-sy
po´et
po-et´ic
po-et´i-cal
po´et-ry
po-grom´
poi´gnan-cy
poi´gnant
point´ed
point´ed-ly
point´er
poin´til-lism
point´less
poised
pois´ing
poi´son
poi´son-er
poi´son-ous
pok´er
pok´ing
pok´y

po´lar
po-lar´i-ty
po-lar-i-za´tion
po´lar-ize
po´lar-iz-er
po´lar-iz-ing
po-lice´
po-lic´ing
pol´i-cy
pol´ish
pol´ish-er
po-lite´
po-lite´ly
po-lite´ness
pol´i-tic
po-lit´i-cal
po-lit´i-cal-ly
pol-i-ti´cian
po-lit´i-cize
pol´ka
pol´len
pol´len-ize
pol´li-nate
pol´li-nat-ing
po´li-na´tion
poll´ster
pol-lu´tant
pol-lute´
pol-lut´er
pol-lut´ing
pol-lu´tion
pol´o-naise´
poly-chro-mat´ic

pol´y-chrome
pol´y-es-ter
poly-eth´yl-ene
po-lyg´a-mist
po-lyg´a-mous
po-lyg´a-my
pol´y-graph
pol´y-mer
pol´y-no´mi-al
pol´yp
pol´y-syl-lab´ic
pol´y-the-ism
pol´y-the-ist
pol´y-the-is´tic
poly-vi´nyl
pom´mel
pom´meled
pom´pa-dour
pom-pos´i-ty
pomp´ous
pon´cho
pon´der
pon´der-a·ble
pon´der-ous
po´nies
pon´tiff
pon-tif´i-cate
pon-tif´i-ca-tor
pon-toon´
po´ny
poo´dle
poor´ly
pop´gun

pop´lar
pop´lin
pop´over
pop´pies
pop´ping
pop´py
pop´py-cock
pop´u-lace
pop´u-lar
pop-u-lar´i-ty
pop-u-lar-i·za´tion
pop´u-lar-ize
pop´u-lar-ly
pop´u-late
pop-u-la´tion
pop´u-lous
por´ce-lain
por-nog´ra-pher
por-no-graph´ic
por-nog´ra-phy
po-ros´i-ty
po´rous
por´ridge
por´ta-ble
por´tal
por-tend´
por´ter
port-fo´lio
port´hole
por´ti-co
por´ti-coes
por´tion
port´li-er

port´li-ness
port´ly
por´trait
por´trai-ture
por-tray´
posed
pos´er
pos´ing
po-si´tion
po-si´tion-er
pos´i-tive
pos´i-tive-ly
pos´i-tiv-ism
pos´i-tiv-is´tic
pos´i-tron
pos´se
pos-sess´
pos-sessed´
pos-sess´es
pos-ses´sion
pos-ses´sive
pos-ses´sive-ly
pos-ses´sive-ness
pos-ses´sor
pos-si-bil´i-ty
pos´si-ble
pos´si-bly
post´age
post´al
post´card
post´date´
post´er
pos-te´ri-or

pos-ter´i-ty
post´hu-mous
post´hu-mous-ly
post -hyp-not´ic
post´mark
post´mas-ter
post´mis-tress
post´–mor´tem
post´paid´
post-pone´
post-pone´ment
post´script
pos´tu-late
pos´tu-lat-ing
pos´ture
pos´tur-ing
po´ta-ble
pot´bel-lied
pot´bel-ly
pot´boil-er
po´ten-cy
po´tent
po-ten´tial
po-ten-ti-al´i-ty
po-ten´tial-ly
po´tent-ly
pot´hole
po´tion
pot´luck´
pot-pour-ri´
pot´shot
pot´ted
pot´ter

pot´ter·y
poul´tice
poul´try
pounc´ing
pound´age
pound´er
pound´–fool´ish
poured
pour´er
pour´ing
pout´er
pout´ing
pout´ing-ly
pout´y
pov´er-ty
pov´er-ty–strick´-
  en
pow´der
pow´dered
pow´der·y
pow´er
pow´ered
pow´er-ful
pow´er-ful-ly
pow´er-house
pow´er-less
pow´wow
prac´ti-cal
prac-ti-cal´i-ty
prac´ti-cal-ly
prac´tice
prac´ticed
prac´tic-er

prac´tic-ing
prac-ti´tion-er
prag-mat´ic
prag-mat´i-cal-ly
prag´ma-tism
prag´ma-tist
prai´rie
praise´wor-thy
prais´ing
pranced
pranc´er
pranc´ing
prank´ster
prat´tle
prat´tler
prayed
prayer (plea)
pray´er (asker)
prayer´ful
preached
preach´er
preach´ing
preach´ment
preach´y
pre´am-ble
pre´ar-range´
pre-car´i-ous
pre-cau´tion
pre-cau´tion-ar·y
pre-cau´tious
pre-cede´
prec´e-dence
prec´e-dent

pre-ced´ing
pre´cept
pre-ces´sion
pre´cinct
pre´cious
prec´i-pice
pre-cip´i-tate
pre-cip´i-tate-ly
pre-cip-i-ta´tion
pre-cip´i-tous
pre-cip´i-tous-ly
pre-cise´
pre-cise´ly
pre-cise´ness
pre-ci´sion
pre-clude´
pre-clud´ing
pre-clu´sion
pre-co´cious
pre-coc´i-ty
pre´con-ceive´
pre-con-cep´tion
pre-cur´sor
pre-cur´so-ry
pred´a-tor
pred´a-to-ry
pred´e-ces-sor
pre-des-ti-na´tion
pre-des´tine
pre-de-ter´mine
pre-dic´a-ment
pre-dict´
pre-dict´a·ble

pre-dic´tion
pre-dic´tor
pred´i-lec´tion
pre´dis-pose´
pre-dis-pos´ing
pre-dis-po-si´tion
pre-dom´i-nant
pre-dom´i-nate
pre-em´i-nence
pre-em´i-nent
pre-em´i-nent-ly
pre-empt´
pre-emp´tion
pre-emp´tive
pre-emp´to-ry
preened
pre-fab´ri-cate
pref´ace
pref´ac-ing
pref´a-to-ry
pre-fer´
pref´er-a·ble
pref´er-a·bly
pref´er-ence
pref´er-en´tial
pre-ferred´
pre-fer´ring
pre´fix
preg´na-ble
preg´nan-cy
preg´nant
pre-hen´sile
pre-his-tor´ic

prej´u-dice
prej-u-di´cial
prel´ate
pre-lim´i-nar·y
prel´ude
pre-ma-ture´
pre-ma-ture´ly
pre-med´i-tate
pre-med-i-ta´tion
pre-med´i-ta-tive
pre-med´i-ta-tor
pre-mier´
pre-miere´
prem´ise
pre´mi-um
pre-mo-ni´tion
pre-oc-cu-pa´tion
pre-oc´cu-pied
pre-oc´cu-py
pre-or-dain´
pre-paid´
prep-a-ra´tion
pre-par´a-tive
pre-par´a-to-ry
pre-pare´
pre-pared´
pre-par´ed-ness
pre-par´er
pre-pay´ment
pre-pon´der-ance
pre-pos´ter-ous
pre-pos´ter-ous-ly
pre-req´ui-site

pre-rog´a-tive
pre´school´
pre´scient
pre-scribe´
pre-scrip´tion
pres´ence
pres´ent *(now, gift)*
pre-sent´ *(give)*
pre-sent´able
pre-sen-ta´tion
pre-sent´er
pres´ent-ly
pres-er-va´tion
pre-serv´a-tive
pre-serve´
pre-serv´er
pre-side´
pres´i-den-cy
pres´i-dent
pres´i-den´tial
pre-sid´er
pre-sid´ing
press´er
press´ing
press´man
pres´sure
pres´sur-ize
pres-ti-dig-i-ta´-
  tion
pres-tige´
pres-tig´i-ous
pre-sum´a·ble
pre-sum´a·bly

pre-sume´
pre-sumed´
pre-sum´er
pre-sump´tion
pre-sump´tive
pre-sump´tu-ous
pre-sup-pose´
pre-tend´
pre-tend´ed
pre-tend´er
pre´tense
pre-ten´tious
pre´text
pret´ti-ly
pret´ti-ness
pret´ty
pret´zel
pre-vail´
pre-vail´ing
prev´a-lence
prev´a-lent
pre-var´i-cate
pre-vent´
pre-vent´a·ble
pre-vent´a·tive
pre-ven´tion
pre-ven´tive
pre´view
pre´vi-ous
pre´vi-ous-ly
price´less
pric´ing
prick´le

prick´ly
priest´hood
priest´ly
prig´gish
pri´ma-cy
pri´mal
pri-mar´i-ly
pri´mar·y
pri-me´val
prim´i-tive
prim´ness
pri-mor´di-al
prince-ly
prin´cess
prin´ci-pal
prin-ci-pal´i-ty
prin´ci-pal-ly
prin´ci-ple
print´er
print´ing
pri´or
pri-or´i·tize
pri-or´i-ty
prism
pris´on-er
pris´sy
pris´tine
pri´va-cy
pri´vate
pri´vate-ly
pri-va´tion
pri´vat-ize
priv´i-lege

priv´i-leged
prob-a-bil´i-ty
prob´a·ble
prob´a·bly
pro´bate
pro-ba´tion
pro-ba´tion-al
pro-ba´tion-ar·y
prob´ing
prob´lem
prob´lem-at´ic
prob´lem-at´i-cal
pro-ce´dur-al
pro-ce´dure
pro-ceed´
pro-ceed´ing
proc´ess
proc´ess-ing
pro-ces´sion
pro-ces´sion-al
pro-claim´
proc-la-ma´tion
pro-cliv´i-ty
pro-cras´ti-nate
proc-tol´o-gy
proc´tor
pro-cure´
pro-cured´
pro-cure´ment
pro-cur´er
pro-cur´ing
prod´ding
prod´i-gal

pro-di´gious
prod´i-gy
pro-duce´ *(make)*
prod´uce *(product)*
pro-duc´ing
prod´uct
pro-duc´tion
pro-duc´tive
pro-duc-tiv´i-ty
pro-fane´
pro-fane´ly
pro-fan´er
pro-fan´ing
pro-fan´i-ty
pro-fess´
pro-fessed´
pro-fes´sion
pro-fes´sion-al
pro-fes´sion-al-ly
pro-fes´sor
pro´fes-so´ri-al
prof´fer
pro-fi´cien-cy
pro-fi´cient
pro´file
prof´it
prof´it-able
prof´it-ably
prof´it-less
prof´li-ga-cy
prof´li-gate
pro-found´
pro-found´ly

pro-fuse´
pro-fuse´ly
pro-fu´sion
prog´e-ny
prog-no´sis
prog-nos´ti-cate
prog-nos´ti-ca-tor
pro´gram
pro´gramed
pro´gram-er
pro´gram-ing
pro´grammed
pro´gram-mer
pro´gram-ming
prog´ress *(n.)*
pro-gress´ *(v.)*
pro-gres´sion
pro-gres´sive
pro-gres´sive-ly
pro-hib´it
pro-hi-bi´tion
pro-hi-bi´tion-ist
pro-hib´i-tive
proj´ect *(n.)*
pro-ject´ *(v.)*
pro-ject´ed
pro-jec´tile
pro-jec´tion
pro-lif´er-ate
pro-lif´ic
pro´log
pro´logue
pro-long´

pro-longed´
prom´e-nade´
prom´i-nence
prom´i-nent
prom´i-nent-ly
prom-is-cu´i-ty
pro-mis´cu-ous
prom´ise
prom´is-er
prom´is-ing
prom´is-so-ry
prom´on-to-ry
pro-mote´
pro-mot´er
pro-mot´ing
pro-mo´tion
pro-mo´tion-al
prompt
prompt´er
prompt´ly
prompt´ness
prom´ul-gate
prom-ul-ga´tion
pro´noun
pro-nounce´
pro-nounce´able
pro-nounced´
pro-nounce´ment
pro-nounc´ing
pro-nun-ci-a´tion
proof´read-er
prop-a-gan´da
prop´a-gate

prop-a-ga´tion
prop´a-ga-tive
pro-pelled´
pro-pel´ler
pro-pel´ling
pro-pen´si-ty
prop´er
prop´er-ly
prop´er-ties
prop´er-ty
proph´e-cies
proph´e-cy
  (prediction)
proph´e-sied
proph´e-si-er
proph´e-sy
  (predict)
proph´et
pro-phet´ic
pro-phet´i-cal
pro´phy-lac´tic
pro-pi´ti-ate
pro-pi´tious
pro-po´nent
pro-por´tion
pro-por´tion-al
pro-por´tion-ate
pro-por´tioned
pro-pos´al
pro-pose´
pro-pos´er
pro-pos´ing
prop-o-si´tion

pro-pri´e-tar·y
pro-pri´e-tor
pro-pri´e-ty
pro-pul´sion
pro-ra´ta
pro-rate´
pro-sa´ic
pro-scribe´
prose
pros´e-cute
pros-e-cu´tion
pros´e-cu-tor
pros´e-cu-to-ry
pros´e-lyte
pros´e-ly-tize
pros´pect
pro-spec´tive
pro-spec´tive-ly
pro-spec´tus
pros´per
pros-per´i-ty
pros´per-ous
pros´per-ous-ly
pros´the-sis
pros-thet´ic
pros´trate
pros´trat-ing
pros-tra´tion
pro-tect´
pro-tect´ing
pro-tect´ing-ly
pro-tec´tion
pro-tec´tive

pro-tec´tive-ly
pro-tec´tor
pro´té-gé´
pro´té-gée´
pro´tein
pro´test (n.)
pro-test´ (v.)
prot-es-ta´tion
pro-test´er
pro-test´ing
pro´to-col
pro´ton
pro-tract´ed
pro-trude´
pro-tru´sion
proud´ly
prov´a·ble
proved
prov´en
prov´en-der
prov´erb
pro-ver´bi·al
pro-vide´
pro-vid´ed
prov´i-dence
prov´i-dent
prov´i-den´tial
pro-vid´er
pro-vid´ing
pro-vin´cial
prov´ing
pro-vi´sion
prov-o-ca´tion

pro-voke´
pro-vok´ing
prow´ess
prowl´er
prox´ies
prox´y
prude
pru´dence
pru´dent
prud´er·y
prud´ish
prun´er
prun´ing
pru´ri-ence
pru´ri-ent
pried
pry´ing
psalm´ist
psal´ter
pseu´do
pso-ri´a-sis
pso-ro´sis
psy´che
psy-chi-at´ric
psy-chi´a-trist
psy-chi´a-try
psy´chic
psy-cho-anal´y-sis
psy-cho-an´a-lyze
psy´cho-log´i-cal
psy-chol´o-gist
psy-chol´o-gy
psy´cho-path´ic

psy-cho´sis
psy-chot´ic
pto-maine´
pu´ber-ty
pu-bes´cence
pu-bes´cent
pub´lic
pub-li-ca´tion
pub´li-cist
pub-lic´i-ty
pub´li-cize
pub´lic-ly
pub´lic–spir´it-ed
pub´lish
pub´lish-er
puck´er
puck´ered
puck´ish
pud´dle
pud´dling
pudg´i-ness
pudg´y
puff´i-ness
puff´y
pu´gi-lism
pu´gi-list
pug-na´cious
pug-na´cious-ly
pul´chri-tude
pul´ley
pull´ing
pul´mo-nary
pulp´i-ness

pul´pit
pulp´y
pul-sa´tion
pu´ver-i-za´tion
pul´ver-ize
pum´mel
punc´tu-al
punc-tu-al´i-ty
punc´tu-ate
punc-tu-a´tion
punc´ture
punc´tured
punc´tur-ing
pun´dit
pun´gen-cy
pun´gent
pu´ni-ness
pun´ish
pun´ish-a·ble
pun´ish-ment
pu´ni-tive
punned
pun´ning
pun´ster
pu´ny
pu´pil
pup´pet
pup´pe-teer´
pup´py
pur´chase
pur´chased
pur´chas-er
pur´chas-ing

172

pure´ly
pur´ga-to-ry
purge
purg´er
purg´ing
pu-ri-fi-ca´tion
pu´ri-fi-er
pu´ri-fy
pur´ist
pu-ri-tan´i-cal
pu´ri-ty
pur-loin´
pur-port´
pur´pose
pur´pose-ful
pur´pose-ly
pur-su´ant
pur-sue´
pur-sued´
pur-su´er
pur-su´ing
pur-suit´
push´er
push´ing
push´over
pu´sil-lan´i-mous
puz´zle
puz´zle-ment
puz´zler
puz´zling
pyr´a-mid

Q

quack´ery
quack´ish
quack´ish-ly
quack´ish-ness
quad
quad´ded
quad´ran-gle
quad-ran´gu-lar
quad´rant
quad-ra-phon´ic
quad-ra-phon´ics
qua-draph´o-ny
qua-drat´ic
qua-dren´ni-al
qua-dren´ni-al-ly
qua-dren´ni-um
quad´ric
quad-ri-cen-
  ten´ni-al
quad´ri-ceps
quad-ri-cip´i-tal
quad´ri-lat´er-al
quad´ri-lat´er-al-
  ly
quad´ri-lin´gual
qua-drille´
qua-dril´lion
qua-dril´lionth
quad-ri-phon´ic
quad-ri-phon´ics
quad´ru-ped
quad´ru-pe-dal

quad-ru´ple
quad-ru´ple-ness
quad-ru´ply
quad-rup´let
quad´ru-plex
qua-dru´pli-cate
quad-ru´pling
quads
quaff
quaffed
quag´gy
quag´mire
quag´mir-y
qua´hog
quail
quaint
quaint´ly
quaint´ness
quake
quaked
quake´proof
quak´i-ly
quak´i-ness
quak´ing
quak´ing-ly
quak´y
qua´le
qual-i-fi-ca´tion
qual´i-fi-ca-to-ry
qual´i-fied
qual´i-fied-ly
qual´i-fied-ness
qual´i-fi-er

qual´i-fy
qual´i-fy-ing
qual´i-fy-ing-ly
qual´i-ta-tive
qual´i-ta-tive-ly
qual´i-ty
qualm
qualm´ish
qualm´ish-ly
qualm´ish-ness
quan´da-ry
quan´tic
quan´ti-fi-a-ble
quan´ti-fi-a-bly
quan-ti-fi-ca´tion
quan´ti-fi-er
quan´ti-fy
quan´tile
quan-tim´e-ter
quan´ti-tate
quan´ti-ta-tive
quan´ti-ta-tive-ly
quan´ti-ta-tive-
　ness
quan´ti-ty
quan-ti-za´tion
quan´tum
quar´an-tin-a-ble
quar´an-tine
quar´an-tin-er
quark
quar´rel
quar´reled

quar´rel-ing
quar´rel-ing-ly
quar´rel-some
quar´rel-some-ly
quar´rel-some-
　ness
quar´ri-er
quar´ry
quart
quar´tan
quar´ter
quar´ter-age
quar´ter-back
quar´ter-deck
quar´tered
quar-ter-fi´nal
quar´ter–hour´
quar´ter-ing
quar´ter-ly
quar´ter-mas-ter
quar´tern
quar´ter-staff
quar-tet´
quar´tic
quar´tile
quar´to
quar´tos
quarts
quartz
quartz-if´er-ous
quartz´ite
quartz-it´ic
quartz´ose

qua´sar
quash
qua´si
qua-si-crys´tal
qua-si–ju-di´cial
qua-si-par´ti-cle
quas´sia
qua´train
qua´tre
qua´ver
qua´vered
qua´ver-er
qua´ver-ing
qua´ver-ing-ly
qua´ver-y
quay
quay´age
quea´si-ly
quea´si-ness
quea´sy
queen´dom
queen´hood
queen´like
queen´li-ness
queen´ly
queen´–size
queer´ly
queer´ness
quell
quelled
quell´er
quench
quench´a·ble

quenched
quench´er
quench´less
que-nelle´
que´ried
que´rist
quer´u-lous
quer´u-lous-ly
quer´u-lous-ness
que´ri-er
que´ry
que´ry-ing
que´ry-ing-ly
que-sa-dil´la
quest
quest´er
quest´ing-ly
ques´tion
ques-tion-a-bil´i-
ty
ques´tion-a-ble
ques´tion-a-ble-
ness
ques´tion-a-bly
ques´tion-ar-y
ques´tion-er
ques´tion-ing
ques´tion-ing-ly
ques´tion-less
ques´tion-less-ly
ques´tion-naire´
quet-zal´
queue

queu´ing
quib´ble
quib´bled
quib´bler
quib´bling
quiche
quick
quick´en
quick´en-er
quick´en-ing
quick´–freeze´
quick´ie
quick´lime
quick´ly
quick´ness
quick´sand
quick´sand-y
quick´–set´ting
quick´sil-ver
quick´sil-ver-y
quick´step
quick´–tem´pered
quick´–wit´ted
quick´–wit´ted-ly
quick´–wit´ted-
ness
quid
quid´di-ty
quid´nunc
qui-es´cence
qui-es´cen-cy
qui-es´cent
qui-es´cent-ly

qui´et
qui´et-ism
qui´et-ist
qui-et-is´tic
qui´et-ly
qui´et-ness
qui´e-tude
qui-e´tus
quill
quilt
quilt´ed
quilt´ing
quince
qui-nel´la
qui´nine
qui-nin´ic
quin´sy
quin´tain
quin´tal
quin´tant
quin-tes´sence
quin-tes-sen´tial
quin-tes-sen´tial-
ly
quin-tet´
quint-tile
quin-til´lion
quin-til´lionth
quin-tu´ple
quin-tup´let
quip
quipped
quip´ping

quip´ster
quirk
quirk´i-ly
quirk´i-ness
quirk´y
quirt
quit
quit´claim
quite
quit´tance
quits
quit´ted
quit´ter
quit´ting
quit´tor
quiv´er
quiv´ered
quiv´er-er
quiv´er-ing
quiv´er-ing-ly
quiv´er-y
quix-ot´ic
quix-ot´i-cal-ly
quix´o-tism
quiz
quiz´mas-ter
quizzed
quiz´zi-cal
quiz-zi-cal´i-ty
quiz´zi-cal-ly
quiz´zing
quoin
quoit

quon´dam
quo´rum
quo´ta
quot-a-bil´i-ty
quot´a-ble
quot´a-bly
quo-ta´tion
quote
quot´ed
quot´er
quoth
quo-tid´i-an
quo´tient
quot´ing

R

rab´bet
rab´bet-ed
rab´bi
rab´bin-ate
rab-bin´ic
rab-bin´i-cal
rab´bin-ism
rab´bit
rab´bit-ry
rab´ble
rab´ble-ment
rab´bler
rab´ble–rous-er
rab´ble–rous-ing
rab´id
ra-bid´i-ty
rab´id-ly

rab´id-ness
ra´bies
rac-coon´
race
race´course
race´horse
rac´er
race´track
race´way
ra´cial
ra´cial-ism
ra´cial-ly
rac´i-ly
rac´ing
rac´ism
rac´ist
rack
rack´er
rack´et
rack´e-teer´
rack´ety
rack´ing-ly
rack´–rent
rac´i-ly
rac´i-ness
ra´con
rac´on-teur
rac´quet
rac´y
rad
ra´dar
ra´dar-scope
ra´di-al

ra´di-al-ly
ra´di-an
ra´di-ance
ra´di-an-cy
ra´di-ant
ra´di-ant-ly
ra´di-ate
ra-di-a´tion
ra-di-a´tion-al
ra´di-a-tive
ra´di-a-tor
rad´i-cal
rad´i-cal-ism
rad-i-cal-i-za´tion
rad´i-cal-ize
rad´i-cal-ly
ra´di·i
ra´di·o
ra-di·o-ac´tive
ra-di·o-ac´tive-ly
ra-di·o-ac-tiv´i-ty
ra-di·o-broad-cast
ra-di·o-car´bon
ra-di·o-cast
ra´dio-gram
ra´dio-graph
ra-di·og´ra-pher
ra-di·o-graph´ic
ra-di·o-graph´i-
   cal-ly
ra-di·og´ra-phy
ra´di·o-i´so-tope
ra-di·o-lo-ca´tion

ra-di·o-log´i-cal
ra-di-ol´o-gist
ra-di-ol´o-gy
ra-di·o-lu´cent
ra-di-om´e-ter
ra-di-o·paque´
ra´di·o-phone
ra-di·o-scop´ic
ra-di·o-scop´i-cal
ra-di-os´co-py
ra-di·o-sen´si-tive
ra-di·o-sen-si-
   tiv´i-ty
ra´di·o-tel´e-gram
ra´di·o-tel´e-
   graph
ra-di·o-te-leg´ra-
   phy
ra-di·o-tel´e-
   phone
ra´di·o-te-leph´o-
   ny
ra-di·o-ther´a-pist
ra-di·o-ther´a-py
ra´di-um
ra´di-us
ra´don
raf´fia
raff´ish
raff´ish-ly
raff´ish-ness
raf´fle
raf´fled

raf´fling
raft
raf´ter *(timber)*
raft´er *(boatman)*
rafts´man
rag
rag´a-muf-fin
rag´ged
rag´ged-ly
rag´ged-ness
rag´ged-y
rag´ing
rag´gle–tag´gle
rag´man
ra-gout´
rag´pick-er
rag´time
raid
raid´er
rail
rail´er
rail´head
rail´ing
rail´lery
rail´road
rail´road-ing
rail´–split-ter
rail´way
rai´ment
rain´bow
rain´coat
rain´drop
rain´fall

rain´i-er
rain´mak-er
rain´mak-ing
rain´proof
rain´squall
rain´storm
rain´wa´ter
rain´wear
rain´y
raise
raised
rais´er
rai´sin
rais´ing
rai-son´
rake
raked
rake´–off
rak´er
rak´ing
rak´ish
rak´ish-ly
rak´ish-ness
ral´lied
ral´ly
ram
ram´ble
ram´bler
ram´bling
ram´bling-ly
ram´bling-ness
ram-bunc´tious
ram-bunc´tious-ly

ram-bunc´tious-
   ness
ram´e-kin
ra´men
ram-i-fi-ca´tion
ram´i-fied
ram´i-form
ram´i-fy
ram´i-fy-ing
ram´jet
rammed
ram´ming
ramp
ram´page
ram-pa´geous
ram-pa´geous-ly
ram-pa´geous-
   ness
ram´pag-er
ram´pag-ing
ramp´an-cy
ram´pant
ram´pant-ly
ram´part
ram´rod
ram´shack-le
ram´shack-le-ness
ranch
ranch´er
ran-che´ro
ranch´man
ran´cid
ran-cid´i-ty

ran´cid-ly
ran´cid-ness
ran´cor
ran´cor-ous
ran´cor-ous-ly
ran´cor-ous-ness
rand´i-ness
ran´dom
ran´dom–ac´cess
ran-dom-i-za´tion
ran´dom-ize
ran´dom-iz-er
ran´dom-ly
ran´dom-ness
rand´y
range
ranged
rang´er
rang´i-ness
rang´ing
rang´y
rank
rank´er
rank´ing
rank´ish
ran´kle
ran´kled
ran´kling
ran´kling-ly
rank´ly
rank´ness
ran´sack
ran´som

ran´som-er
rant
rant´er
rant´ing
rant´ing-ly
ra-pa´cious
ra-pa´cious-ly
ra-pa´cious-ness
ra-pac´i-ty
rape
rap´id
rap´id–fire
ra-pid´i-ty
rap´id-ly
ra´pier
rap´ine
rap´ist
rapped
rap-pel´
rap´per
rap´ping
rap-port´
rap-proche-ment´
rap-scal´lion
rapt
rapt´ly
rapt´ness
rap-to´ri-al
rap´ture
rap´tur-ous
rap´tur-ous-ly
rap´tur-ous-ness
rare

rare´bit
rar´e-fied
rar´e-fy
rare´ly
rare´ness
rar´ing
rar´i-ty
ras´cal
ras-cal´i-ty
ras´cal-ly
rash
rash´er
rash´like
rash´ly
rash´ness
rasp
rasp´ber-ry
rasp´er
rasp´i-ness
rasp´ing
rasp´ing-ly
rasp´ing-ness
rasp´ish
rasp´y
ras´ter
rat´a-ble
rat´a-bly
ra-ta-touille´
ratch´et
rate
rat´er
rath´er
raths´kel-ler

rat-i-fi-ca´tion
rat´i-fied
rat´i-fy
rat´i-fy-ing
rat´ing
ra´tio
ra´tion
ra´tio-nal
ra´tion-al-ly
ra´tion-al-ness
ra´tio-nale´
ra´tio-nal-ism
ra´tio-nal-ist
ra-tio-nal-is´tic
ra-tio-nal´i-ty
ra-tio-nal-i·za´tion
ra´tio-nal-ize
ra´tio-nal-ly
rat´ite
rat´line
rat-tan´
rat´tle
rat´tle-brained
rat´tler
rat´tle-trap
rat´tling
rat´tly
rat´ty
rau´cous
rau´cous-ly
rau´cous-ness
raunch
raun´chi-ly

179

raun´chi-ness	reach´a-ble	read´y–mix
raun´chy	reach´er	read´y–to–wear´
rav´age	re-act´	re-af-firm´
rav´age-ment	re-ac´tance	re-a´gent
rav´ag-er	re-ac´tant	re´al-ism
rav´ag-ing	re-ac´tion	re´al-ist
rave	re-ac´tion-al	re´al-is´tic
rav´el	re-ac´tion-ar-y	re-al-is´ti-cal-ly
rav´eled	re-ac´ti-vate	re-al´i-ty
rav´el-er	re-ac-ti-va´tion	re´al-iza´tion
rav´el-ment	re-ac´tive	re´al-ize
rav´el-ing	re-ac´tive-ly	re´al–life
rav´en-ous	re-ac´tive-ness	re´al-ly
rav´en-ous-ly	re-ac´tor	realm
rav´en-ous-ness	read	re´al-ness
ra-vine´	read-a-bil´i-ty	re-al´po-li-tik
rav´ing	read´a-ble	re´al-tor
rav´ing-ly	read´a-ble-ness	re´al-ty
rav-i-o´li	read´a-bly	ream´er
rav´ish	re-ad-dress´	re-an´i-mate
rav´ish-er	read´er	re-an-i-ma´tion
rav´ish-ing	read´er-ship	reap
rav´ish-ing-ly	read´i-ly	reap´er
raw´boned´	read´i-ness	re-ap-pear´
raw´hide	read´ing	re-ap-pear´ance
raw´ly	re-ad-just´	re-ap-point´
raw´ness	re-ad-just´a-ble	re-ap-por´tion
ray	re-ad-just´er	re-ap-por´tion-
ray´on	re-ad-just´ment	ment
raze	read´–on´ly	rear
ra´zor	read´out	rear´–end´
ra´zor-back	read´y	re-arm´
.raz´zle–daz-zle	read´y–made	re-ar´ma-ment

rear´most
re-ar-range´
re-ar-range´ment
re-ar-rang´ing
rear´ward
rea´son
rea´son-a-ble
rea´son-a-ble-ness
rea´son-a-bly
rea´son-er
rea´son-ing
re-as-sem´ble
re-as-sert´
re-as-sume´
re-as-sur´ance
re´as-sure´
re-as-sur´ing
re-as-sur´ing-ly
re-awak´en
re´bar
re´bate
re´bat-er
reb´el (n., adj.)
re-bel´ (v.)
re-belled´
re-bel´ling
re-bel´lion
re-bel´lious
re-bel´lious-ly
re-bel´lious-ness
re´birth´
re´born´
re-bound´

re-broad´cast
re-buff´
re-build´
re-built´
re-buke´
re-buk´ing
re´bus
re-but´
re-but´ta-ble
re-but´tal
re-but´ted
re-but´ter
re-but´ting
re-cal´ci-tran-cy
re-cal´ci-trance
re-cal´ci-trant
re-call´ (v., n.)
re´call (n.)
re-call´a-ble
re-cant´
re´cap
re-cap-i-tal-i-za´-
    tion
re-cap´i-tal-ize
re-ca-pit´u-late
re-ca-pit-u-la´tion
re-ca-pit´u-la-tive
re-ca-pit´u-la-to-
    ry
re-cap´pa-ble
re´capped´
re´cap´ping
re-cap´ture

re-cast´
re-cede´
re-ced´ed
re-ced´er
re-ced´ing
re-ceipt´
re-ceiv´a-ble
re-ceive´
re-ceived´
re-ceiv´er
re-ceiv´er-ship
re-ceiv´ing
re´cent
re´cent-ly
re´cent-ness
re-cep´ta-cle
re-cep´tion
re-cep´tion-ist
re-cep´tive
re-cep´tive-ly
re-cep´tive-ness
re-cep-tiv´i-ty
re-cep´tor
re´cess
re´cess´er
re-ces´sion
re-ces´sion-al
re-ces´sion-ar-y
re-ces´sive
re-ces´sive-ly
re-ces´sive-ness
re-charge´
re-charge´a-ble

re-charge´er
re-cid´i-vism
re-cid´i-vist
re-cid-i-vis´tic
re-cid´i-vous
rec´i-pe
re-cip´i-ence
re-cip´i-ent
re-cip´ro-cal
re-cip-ro-cal´i-ty
re-cip´ro-cal-ly
re-cip´ro-cal-ness
re-cip´ro-cate
re-cip-ro-ca´tion
re-cip´ro-ca-tive
re-cip´ro-ca-tor
re-cip´ro-ca-to-ry
rec-i-proc´i-ty
re-ci´sion
re-cit´a-ble
re-cit´al
rec-i-ta´tion
rec´i-ta-tive´
re-cite´
re-cit´er
re-cit´ing
reck´less
reck´less-ly
reck´less-ness
reck´on
reck´on-a-ble
reck´on-er
reck´on-ing

re-claim
re-claim´able
rec-la-ma´tion
re-clas-si-fi-ca´-
    tion
re-clas´si-fy
re-clin´able
re-cline´
re-clin´er
re-clin´ing
re-clos´a-ble
rec´luse
re-clu´sive
rec-og-ni´tion
re-cog´ni-tive
re-cog´ni-to·ry
rec´og-niz-a-ble
rec´og-niz-a-bly
re-cog´ni-zance
rec´og-nize
rec´og-niz-er
re-coil´ *(react)*
re-coil´ *(to wind)*
re-coil´ing-ly
re-coil´less
rec-ol-lect´ *(recall)*
re–col-lect´
    (amass)
rec-ol-lect´ed
rec-ol-lect´ed-ly
rec-ol-lect´ed-ness
rec-ol-lec´tion
re´com-bine´

re-com-mence´
rec-om-mend´
rec-om-mend´a-
    ble
rec-om-men-da´-
    tion
rec-om-mend´er
re-com-mit´
re-com-mit´tal
re-com-mit´ment
rec´om-pen-sa·ble
rec´om-pense
rec´om-pens-er
rec´om-pens-ing
re-con´
re-con´cen-trate
rec-on-cil-a-bil´i-
    ty
rec´on-cil-a-ble
rec´on-cil-a-ble-
    ness
rec´on-cil-a-bly
rec´on-cile
rec´on-cile-ment
rec´on-cil-er
rec-on-cil-i-a´tion
rec´on-cil´ia-to-ry
rec´on-cil-ing
rec´on-dite
rec´on-dite-ly
rec´on-dite-ness
re-con-di´tion
re-con´nais-sance

re-con-noi´ter
re-con-sid´er
re-con-sid´er-a´-
  tion
re-con´sti-tute
re-con´sti-tut-
  a·ble
re-con´sti-tut-i·ble
re-con-sti-tu´tion
re-con-struct´
re-con-struct´er
re-con-struct´i-ble
re-con-struc´tion
re-con-struc´tion-
  al
re-con-struc´tor
re-cord´ *(v.)*
rec´ord *(n., adj.)*
re-cord´able
re-cord´er
rec´ord–hold-er
re-cord´ing
re-count´
re-coup´
re-coup´a-ble
re-coup´ment
re´course
re-cov´er
re-cov´er-a·ble
re-cov´ery
rec´re-ance
rec´re-an·cy
rec´re-ant

rec´re-ant-ly
rec´re-ate *(to play)*
re–cre-ate´ *(to do
  over)*
rec-re-a´tion
rec-re-a´tion-al
re–cre-a´tive
rec´re-a-tive
re-crim´i-nate
re-crim´i-nat-ing
re-crim-i-na´tion
re-crim´i-na-tive
re-crim´i-na-tor
re-crim´i-na-to-ry
re-cru-desce´
re-cru-des´cence
re-cru-des´cent
re-cruit´
re-cruit´a-ble
re-cruit´er
re-cruit´ment
rec´tal-ly
rec´tan-gle
rec-tan´gu-lar
rec-tan-gu-lar´i-ty
rec´ti-fi-a·ble
rec-ti-fi-ca´tion
rec´ti-fied
rec´ti-fi-er
rec´ti-fy
rec´ti-tude
rec´to
rec´tor

rec´tor-ate
rec-to´ri-al
rec´to-ry
re-cum´bence
re-cum´ben-cy
re-cum´bent
re-cum´bent-ly
re-cu´per-ate
re-cu-per-a´tion
re-cu´per-a-tive
re-cur´
re-curred´
re-cur´rence
re-cur´rent
re-cur´rent-ly
re-cur´ring
re-cuse´
re-cy´cla·ble
re-cy´cle
re-dact´
re-dac´tion
re-dac´tor
red´–blood´ed
red´cap
red´den
red´dish
red´dish-ness
re-dec´o-rate
re-dec-o-ra´tion
re-deem´
re-deem´a-ble
re-deem´er
re-demp´ti-ble

re-demp´tion
re-demp´tion-al
re-demp´tive
re-demp´tor
re-demp´to-ry
re-de-ploy´
re-de-ploy´ment
red´-faced
red´-hand´ed
red´head
red´head-ed
red´-hot´
re-di-rect´
re-dis-cov´er
re-dis-cov´er·y
re-dis-trib´ute
re-dis-tri-bu´tion
re-dis´trict
red´-let´ter
red´ness
re-do´
red´o-lence
red´o-len-cy
red´o-lent
red´o-lent-ly
re-dou´ble
re-dou´bling
re-doubt´
re-doubt´a-ble
red´-pen´cil
re-draw´
re-dress´
re-dress´able

re-dress´er
re-duce´
re-duc´er
re-duc-i-bil´i-ty
re-duc´i-ble
re-duc´i-bly
re-duc´ing
re-duc´tion
re-duc´tion-al
re-duc´tion-ist
re-duc-tion-is´tic
re-duc´tive
re-duc´tive-ly
re-dun´dan-cy
re-dun´dant
re-dun´dant-ly
re-du´pli-cate
re-du-pli-ca´tion
re-du´pli-ca-tive
reed´i-ness
reed´ing
re-ed´u-cate
re-ed´u-ca-tive
reed´y
reef
reek
reel´a-ble
re-elect´
re-elec´tion
reel´er
reel´-to-reel´
re-em-bark´
re-en-act´

re-en-force´
re-en-force´ment
re-en-gage´
re´en-list´
re-en´ter
re-en´trant
re-en´try
re-es-tab´lish
re-es-tab´lish-
   ment
re-ex-am-i-na´tion
re-ex-am´ine
re-fas´ten
re-fer´
ref´er-ee´
ref´er-ence
ref-er-en´dum
ref´er-ent
ref-er-en´tial
re-fer´ral
re-ferred´
re-fer´ring
re´fill *(n.)*
re-fill´ *(v.)*
re-fill´a-ble
re-fi-nance´
re-fine´
re-fined´
re-fine-ment
re-fin´er
re-fin´ery
re-fin´ing
re-fin´ish

re-fit´
re-flect´
re-flec´tance
re-flect´i·ble
re-flec´tion
re-flec´tion-al
re-flec´tive
re-flec´tive-ly
re-flec´tive-ness
re-flec-tiv´i·ty
re-flec´tor
re´flex
re-flex´ive
re-flex´ive·ly
re-flex´ive-ness
re-flex-iv´i·ty
re-flex-ol´o-gist
re-flex-ol´o-gy
ref´lu-ent
re´flux
re-for-est-a´tion
re-form´ *(amend)*
re–form *(remold)*
re-form´a-ble
ref-or-ma´tion
 (improvement)
re–for-ma´tion
 (new mold)
re-for´ma-to-ry
re-formed´
re-form´er
re-form´ism
re-form´ist

re-for´mu-late
re-for-mu-la´tion
re-fract´
re-frac´tion
re-frac´tion-al
re-frac´tive
re-frac´tive·ly
re-frac´tive-ness
re-frac´tor
re-frac´to-ri-ness
re-frac´to-ry
re-frain´
re-fran-gi-bil´i·ty
re-fran´gi-ble
re-fran´gi-ble-ness
re-fresh´
re-fresh´ing
re-fresh´ing-ly
re-fresh´ment
re-frig´er-ant
re-frig´er-ate
re-frig´er-at-ing
re-frig-er-a´tion
re-frig´er-a-tor
re-fu´el
ref´uge
ref´u-gee
re-ful´gence
re-ful´gen-cy
re-ful´gent
re-ful´gent-ly
re´fund *(n.)*
re-fund´ *(v.)*

re-fund´a-ble
re-fur´bish
re-fur´bish-ment
re-fur´nish
re-fus´a-ble
re-fus´al
re-fuse´ *(decline)*
ref´use *(trash)*
re–fuse´ *(join)*
re-fus´ing
re-fut´able
re-fut´ably
re-fute´
re-fut´er
re-fut´ing
re-gain´
re-gain´a-ble
re´gal
re-gale´
re-gale´ment
re-ga´lia
re-gal´ing
re´gal-ly
re´gal-ness
re-gard´
re-gard´ful
re-gard´ful-ly
re-gard´ing
re-gard´less
re-gard´less-ly
re´gen-cy
re-gen´er-a-ble
re-gen´er-a-cy

re-gen´er-ate
re-gen-er-a´tion
re-gen´er-a-tive
re-gen´er-a-tive-ly
re-gen´er-a-tor
re´gent
reg´gae
re-gime´
reg´i-men
reg´i-ment
reg´i-men´tal
reg´i-men´tal-ly
reg-i-men´ta-ry
reg-i-men-ta´tion
re´gion
re´gion-al
re´gion-al-ism
re-gion-al-is´tic
re´gion-al-ize
re´gion-al-ly
reg´is-ter
reg´is-tered
reg´is-tra-ble
reg´is-trant
reg´is-trar
reg´is-trate
reg-is-tra´tion
reg´is-try
re-gress´
re-gres´sion
re-gres´sive
re-gres´sive-ly
re-gres´sor

re-gret´
re-gret´ful
re-gret´ful-ly
re-gret´ful-ness
re-gret´ta-ble
re-gret´ta-ble-ness
re-gret´ta-bly
re-gret´ted
re-gret´ter
re-gret´ting
re-group´
reg´u-lar
reg-u-lar´i-ty
reg-u-lar-i-za´tion
reg´u-lar-ize
reg´u-lar-ly
reg´u-lat-able
reg´u-late
reg-u-la´tion
reg´u-la-tive
reg´u-la-tive-ly
reg´u-la-tor
reg´u-la-to-ry
re-gur´gi-tate
re-gur-gi-ta´tion
re´hab
re-ha-bil´i-tant
re-ha-bil´i-tate
re-ha-bi´i-ta´tion
re-ha-bil´i-ta-tive
re-ha-bil´i-ta-tor
re´hash´
re-hear´

re-hear´ing
re-hears´a·ble
re-hears´al
re-hearse´
re-hears´er
re-hears´ing
re-heat´
re-house´
re-hy´drate
re-hy-dra´tion
re-i-fi-ca´tion
re´i-fy
reign
re-im-burs´able
re-im-burse´
re-im-burse´ment
re-im-port´
re-im-por-ta´tion
re-in-car´nate
re-in-car-na´tion
re-in-dus-tri-al-i-
  za´tion
re-in-dus´tri-al-ize
re-in-force´
re-in-forced´
re-in-force´ment
reins
re-in-sert´
re-in-stall´
re-in-stal-la´tion
re-in-state´
re-in-state´ment
re-in-sur´ance

re-in-sure′
re-in′te-grate
re-in-te-gra′tion
re-in-vent′
re-in-vest′
re-in-vig′o-rate
re-is′su-a-ble
re-is′sue
re-it′er-a-ble
re-it′er-ate
re-it-er-a′tion
re-it′er-a-tive
re-it′er-a-tive-ly
re-ject′ *(v.)*
re′ject *(n.)*
re-ject′able
re-ject′er
re-jec′tion
re-jec′tive
re-jec′tor
re-joice′
re-joic′ing
re-joic′ing-ly
re-join′
re-join′der
re-ju′ve-nate
re-ju-ve-na′tion
re-ju′ve-na-tive
re-ju′ve-na-tor
re-ju-ve-nes′cence
re-kin′dle
re-lapse′
re-lapsed′

re-laps′ing
re-lat′a-ble
re-late′
re-lat′ed
re-lat′ed-ness
re-lat′er
re-lat′ing
re-la′tion
re-la′tion-al
re-la′tion-ship
rel′a-tive
rel′a-tive-ly
rel′a-tive-ness
rel′a-tiv-ism
rel′a-tiv-ist
rel-a-tiv-is′tic
rel-a-tiv′i-ty
re-la′tor
re-lax′
re-lax′ant
re-lax-a′tion
re-laxed′
re′lay *(send on)*
re–lay′ *(lay again)*
re′layed
re-lease′ *(liberate)*
re′–lease′ *(rent anew)*
re-leased′
re-leas′er
re-leas′ing
rel′e-gate
rel′e-gat-ed

rel-e-ga′tion
re-lent′
re-lent′ing
re-lent′ing-ly
re-lent′less
re-lent′less-ly
re-lent′less-ness
rel′e-vance
rel′e-van·cy
rel′e-vant
rel′e-vant·ly
re-li-a-bil′i·ty
re-li′a-ble
re-li′a-ble-ness
re-li′a-bly
re-li′ance
re-li′ant
re-li′ant·ly
rel′ic
re-lied′
re-lief′
re-liev′a·ble
re-lieve′
re-lieved′
re-liev′er
re-liev′ing
re-li′gion
re-li′gion-ism
re-li′gion-ist
re-li-gi-ose′
re-li-gi-os′i-ty
re-li′gious
re-li′gious-ly

re-li´gious-ness
re-lin´quish
re-lin´quish-er
re-lin´quish-ment
rel´ish-ing
re-live´
re-load´
re-lo´cat-a·ble
re-lo´cate
re-lo-ca´tion
re-lu´cent
re-luc´tance
re-luc´tant
re-luc´tant·ly
rel-uc-tiv´i·ty
re-lume´
re-ly´
re-ly´ing
re-made´
re-main´
re-main´der
re-main´ing
re-make´
re-mand´
re-mand´ment
re-mark´
re-mark´a·ble
re-mark´a·ble-
  ness
re-mark´a·bly
re-mar´riage
re-mar´ry
re´match

re-me´di-a-ble
re-me´di-a-ble-
  ness
re-me´di-a-bly
re-me´di-al
re-me´di-al-ly
re-me-di-a´tion
rem´e-died
rem´e-dies
rem´e-dy
re-mem´ber
re-mem´ber-a·ble
re-mem´brance
re-mem´branc-er
re-mind´
re-mind´er
rem-i-nisce´
rem-i-nis´cence
rem-i-nis´cent
rem-i-nis´cent-ly
rem-i-nis´cer
rem-i-nis´cing
re-miss´
re-miss-i-bil´i-ty
re-miss´i-ble
re-miss´i-ble-ness
re-mis´sion
re-mis´sive
re-mit´
re-mit´ta·ble
re-mit´tal
re-mit´tance
re-mit´ted

re-mit´tence
re-mit´ten-cy
re-mit´tent
re-mit´tent-ly
re-mit´ter
re-mit´ting
re-mix´
rem´nant
re-mod´el
re-mod´eled
re-mon-e-ti-za´-
  tion
re-mon´e-tize
re-mon´strance
re-mon´strant
re-mon´strate
re-mon´strat-ing-
  ly
re-mon-stra´tion
re-mon´stra-tive
re-mon´stra-tive-
  ly
re-mon´stra-tor
re-morse´
re-morse´ful
re-morse´ful-ly
re-morse´ful-ness
re-morse´less
re-morse´less-ly
re-morse´less-ness
re-mote´
re-mote´ly
re-mote´ness

re-mot´est
ré-mou-lade´
re-mount´
re-mov´a-ble
re-mov´a-ble-ness
re-mov´a-bly
re-mov´al
re-move´
re-moved´
re-mov´ed-ly
re-mov´ed-ness
re-mov´er
re-mov´ing
re-mu´da
re-mu-ner-a-bil´i-ty
re-mu´ner-a-ble
re-mu´ner-a-bly
re-mu´ner-ate
re-mu-ner-a´tion
re-mu´ner-a-tive
re-mu´ner-a-tive-ly
re-mu´ner-a-tive-ness
re-mu´ner-a-tor
ren´ais-sance´
re-name´
rend
ren´der
ren´der-a-ble
ren´dez-vous
ren-di´tion

ren´e-gade
re-nege´
re-neg´er
re-neg´ing
re-ne-go´ti-ate
re-ne-go-ti-a´tion
re-new´
re-new-a-bil´i-ty
re-new´a-ble
re-new´al
re-newed´
ren´net
ren´nin
re-nom´i-nate
re-nom-i-na´tion
re-nounce´
re-nounce´a-ble
re-nounce´ment
re-nounc´ing
ren´o-vat-a-ble
ren´o-vate
ren´o-vat-ing
ren-o-va´tion
ren´o-va-tor
re-nown´
re-nowned´
rent´a-ble
rent´–a–car
rent´al
rent´er
rent´–free´
rent´ing
re-nun-ci-a´tion

re-nun´ci-a-tive
re-nun´ci-a-to·ry
re-oc´cu-py
re-o´pen
re-or-ga-ni-za´-tion
re-or´ga-nize
re-pack´age
re-paid´
re-paint´
re-pair´
re-pair-a-bil´i-ty
re-pair´a·ble
re-pair´er
re-pair´man
rep´a-ra·ble
rep´a-ra·bly
rep-a-ra´tion
re-par´a-tive
re-par´a-to·ry
re-par-ti´tion
re-past´
re-pa´tri-ate
re-pa-tri-a´tion
re-pay´
re-pay´a·ble
re-pay´ing
re-pay´ment
re-peal´
re-peal´a·ble
re-peal´er
re-peat´
re-peat-a-bil´i-ty

re-peat´a·ble
re-peat´ed
re-peat´ed-ly
re-peat´er
re-pel´
re-pelled´
re-pel´lence
re-pel´len·cy
re-pel´lent
re-pel´lent·ly
re-pel´ling
re-pent´
re-pent´ance
re-pent´ant
re-pent´ant-ly
re-pent´ing-ly
re-peo´ple
re-per-cus´sion
re-per-cus´sive
rep´er-toire
rep-er-to´ri-al
rep´er-to-ry
rep-e-ti´tion
rep´e-ti´tious
rep-e-ti´tious-ly
rep´e-ti´tious-ness
re-pet´i-tive
re-pet´i-tive-ly
re-pet´i-tive-ness
re-phrase´
re-place´
re-place´able
re-place´ment

re-plac´ing
re-plant´
re´play (n.)
re-play´ (v.)
re-plen´ish
re-plen´ish-er
re-plen´ish-ment
re-plete´
re-plete´ness
re-ple´tion
rep´li-ca
rep´li-cate
rep-li-ca´tion
rep´li-ca-tive
re-plied´
re-ply´
re-ply´ing
re´po
re-port´
re-port´a·ble
re-port´age
re-port´ed·ly
re-port´er
rep-or-to´ri-al
rep-or-to´ri-al-ly
re-pose´
re-pos´er
re-pose´ful
re-pose´ful-ly
re-pose´ful-ness
re-pos´ing
re-pos´it
re-po-si´tion

re-pos´i-to·ry
re-pos-sess´
re-pos-sess´a·ble
re-pos-ses´sion
rep-re-hend´
rep-re-hend´a·ble
rep-re-hend´er
rep-re-hen-si-bil´-
    i·ty
rep-re-hen´si·ble
rep-re-hen´si·ble-
    ness
rep-re-hen´si·bly
rep-re-hen´sion
rep-re-sent´
rep-re-sent-a-bil´-
    i·ty
rep-re-sent´a·ble
rep-re-sen-ta´tion
rep-re-sen-ta´tion-
    al
rep-re-sen-ta´tion-
    al-ism
rep-re-sent´a-tive
rep-re-sent´a-tive-
    ly
rep-re-sent´a-tive-
    ness
rep-re-sent´er
re-press´
re-pressed´
re-press´er
re-press´i·ble

re-pres´sion
re-pres´sive
re-pres´sive-ly
re-pres´sive-ness
re-pres´sor
re-prieve´
rep´ri-mand
rep´ri-mand-er
rep´ri-mand-ing-
  ly
re-print´ *(v.)*
re´print *(n.)*
re-pri´sal
re-prise´
re-proach´
re-proach´a·ble
re-proach´a·ble-
  ness
re-proach´a·bly
re-proach´ful
re-proach´ful-ly
re-proach´ful-ness
re-proach´ing
re-proach´ing-ly
rep´ro-bate
rep-ro-ba´tion
re´pro-duce´
re´pro-duc´er
re-pro-duc´i·ble
re-pro-duc-i-bil´-
  i·ty
re´pro-duc´ing
re-pro-duc´tion

re-pro-duc´tive
re-pro-duc´tive-ly
re-pro-duc´tive-
  ness
re-proof´
re-prov´a·ble
re-prov´a·ble-ness
re-prov´al
re-prove´
re-prov´ing
re-prov´ing-ly
rep´tile
rep-til´i·an
re-pub´lic
re-pub´li-can
re-pub´li-can-ism
re-pub-li-can-i-
  za´tion
re-pub´li-can-ize
re-pub-li-ca´tion
re-pub´lish
re-pu´di-ate
re-pu-di-a´tion
re-pu´di-a-tive
re-pu´di-a-tor
re-pu´di-a-to·ry
re-pugn´
re-pug´nance
re-pug´nan-cy
re-pug´nant
re-pug´nant-ly
re-pulse´
re-puls´ing

re-pul´sion
re-pul´sive
re-pul´sive-ly
re-pul´sive-ness
re-pur´chase
rep-u-ta-bil´i·ty
rep´u-ta-ble
rep´u-ta·ble-ness
rep´u-ta·bly
rep-u-ta´tion
re-pute´
re-put´ed
re-put´ed-ly
re-put´ing
re-quest´
re-quest´er
req´ui-em
re-quir´a·ble
re-quire´
re-quire´ment
re-quir´er
re-quir´ing
req´ui-site
req´ui-site-ly
req´ui-site-ness
req-ui-si´tion
req-ui-si´tion-ar·y
req-ui-si´tion-er
re-quit´a·ble
re-quit´al
re-quite´
re-quit´ed
re-quite´ment

re-quit´ing
re-read´
re´-re-cord´
re-re-lease´
re-run´
re-sal´a·ble
re´sale
re-scale´
re-sched´ule
re-scind´
re-scind´a·ble
re-scind´ment
re-scis´si·ble
re-scis´sion
re-scis´so·ry
re´script
res´cu-a·ble
res´cue
rea´cued
res´cu-er
res´cu-ing
re-search´
re-search´a·ble
re-search´er
re-search´ist
re-seat´
re-sect´
re-sect-a-bil´i·ty
re-sect´a·ble
re-sec´tion
re-sell´
re-sem´blance
re-sem´blant

re-sem´ble
re-sem´bler
re-sem´bling
re-sem´bling-ly
re-sent´
re-sent´ful
re-sent´ful-ly
re-sent´ful-ness
re-sent´ing-ly
re-sent´ment
re-serv´a·ble
res-er-va´tion
re-serve´
re-served
re-serv´ed-ly
re-serv´ed-ness
re-serv´ist
res´er-voir
re-set´
re-set´ting
re-set´tle-ment
re-ship´
re-ship´ment
re-side´
res´i-dence
res´i-den-cy
res´i-dent
res´i-den´tial
res-i-den´ti-ar·y
re-sid´ing
re-sid´u-al
re-sid´u-al-ly
re-sid´u-ar·y

res´i-due
re-sid´u-um
re-sign´
res-ig-na´tion
re-signed´
re-sign´ed-ly
re-sign´ed-ness
re-sil´ience
re-sil´ien-cy
re-sil´ient
re-sil´ient-ly
res´in
res´in-ous
re-sist´
re-sist´ance
re-sist´ant
re-sist´ant-ly
re-sist´er
re-sist-i·bil´i·ty
re-sist´i·ble
re-sist´i-ble-ness
re-sist´i·bly
re-sist´ing-ly
re-sis´tive
re-sis´tive-ly
re-sis´tive-ness
re-sis-tiv´i·ty
re-sis´tor
re-sold´
re-sole´
re-sol-u-bil´i·ty
re-sol´u·ble
re-sol´u·ble-ness

res´o-lute
res´o-lute-ly
res´o-lute-ness
res-o-lu´tion
re-solv´a·ble
re-solve´
re-solved´
re-solv´ed-ly
re-solv´ed-ness
re-solv´er
re-solv´ing
res´o-nance
res´o-nant
res´o-nant-ly
res´o-nate
res-o-na´tion
res´o-na-tor
re-sorb´
re-sorb´ent
re-sorp´tive
re-sort´
re-sound´
re-sound´ed
re-sound´ing
re-sound´ing-ly
re´source
re-source´ful
re-source´ful-ly
re-source´ful-ness
re-spect´
re-spect-a·bil´i·ty
re-spect´a·ble
re-spect´a·ble-ness

re-spect´a·bly
re-spect´er
re-spect´ful
re-spect´ful-ly
re-spect´ful-ness
re-spect´ing
re-spec´tive
re-spec´tive-ness
re-spell´
res´pi-ra·ble
res-pi-ra´tion
res-pi-ra´tion-al
res´pi-ra-tor
res´pi-ra-to·ry
re-spire´
re-spir´ing
res´pite
re-splen´dence
re-splen´den·cy
re-splen´dent
re-splen´dent-ly
re-spond´
re-spon´dence
re-spon´den-cy
re-spon´dent
re-spond´er
re-sponse´
re-spon-si-bil´i·ty
re-spon´si·ble
re-spon´si-ble-ness
re-spon´si·bly
re-spon´sive
re-spon´sive·ly

re-spon´sive-ness
re-spon-siv´i·ty
re-spon´sor
re-spon´so·ry
re·state´
res´tau-rant
res´tau-ra-teur´
rest´ful
rest´ful-ly
rest´ful-ness
rest´ing
res´ti-tute
res-ti-tu´tion
res´tive
res´tive-ly
res´tive-ness
rest´less
rest´less-ly
rest´less-ness
re´stock´
re-stor´a·ble
re-stor´a·ble-ness
re-stor´al
res-to-ra´tion
re-stor´a·tive
re-store´
re-stor´er
re-stor´ing
re-strain´
re-strain´a·ble
re-strained´
re-straint´
re-strict´

re-strict´ed
re-stric´tion
re-stric´tive
re-stric´tive-ly
re-stric´tive-ness
re-strike´
re-struc´ture
re-sult´
re-sult´ant
re-sum´a·ble
re-sume´ *(go on)*
ré´su-mé´
  (summary)
re-sum´ing
re-sump´tion
re-sur´face
re-surge´
re-sur´gence
re-sur´gent
res-ur-rect´
res-ur-rec´tion
res-ur-rec´tion-al
res-ur-rec´tion-ist
res-ur-rec´tor
re-sus´ci-ta·ble
re-sus´ci-tate
re-sus-ci-ta´tion
re-sus´ci-ta-tive
re-sus´ci-ta-tor
re´tail
re´tail-er
re-tain´
re-tain´a·ble

re-tain´er
re-tain´ing
re-take´
re-tal´i-ate
re-tal-i-a´tion
re-tal´i-a-tive
re-tal´i-a-tor
re-tal´i-a-to·ry
re-tard´
re-tard´ant
re-tar-da´tion
re-tard´ed
retch
re-tell´
re-ten´tion
re-ten´tive
re-ten´tive-ly
re-ten´tive-ness
re-ten-tiv´i-ty
re-ten´tor
re-think´
ret´i-cence
ret´i-cen-cy
ret´i-cent
ret´i-cent-ly
ret´i-na
ret´i-nal
ret-i-ni´tis
ret´i-nue
re-tire´
re-tired´
re-tir´ee´
re-tire´ment

re-tir´ing
re-tir´ing-ly
re-told´
re-tool´
re-tort´
re-touch´
re-trace´
re-trace´a·ble
re-trac´ing
re-tract´
re-tract-a·bil´i-ty
re-tract´a·ble
re-trac´tile
re-trac´tion
re-trac´tive
re-trac´tive-ly
re-trac´tive-ness
re-trac´tor
re´tread´
re-treat´
re-trench´
re-trench´ment
ret-ri-bu´tion
re-trib´u-tive
re-trib´u-tive-ly
re-trib´u-to-ry
re-triev-a-bil´i-ty
re-triev´a·ble
re-triev´al
re-trieve´
re-triev´er
re-triev´ing
ret-ro-ac´tive

ret-ro-ac´tive-ly
ret-ro-ac-tiv´i-ty
ret´ro-fit
ret´ro-grade
ret´ro-gress
ret-ro-gres´sion
ret-ro-gres´sive
ret-ro-gres´sive-ly
ret´ro-rock-et
ret´ro-spect
ret-ro-spec´tion
ret-ro-spec´tive
ret-ro-spec´tive-ly
re-turn´
re-turn´a·ble
re-turn´ee´
re-un´ion
re-u-nit´a·ble
re-u-nite´
re-u-nit´ing
re-used´
re-val´u-ate
re-val-u-a´tion
re-val´ue
re-vamp´
re-vamp´er
re-vamp´ment
re-veal´
re-veal´a·ble
re-veal´ing
re-veal´ing-ly
re-veal´ment
re-veg´e-tate

re-veg-e-ta´tion
rev´eil-le
rev´el
rev-e-la´tion
rev-e-la´tion-al
re-vel´a-to-ry
rev´eled
rev´el-er
rev´el-ing
rev´el-ment
rev´el-ry
re-venge´
re-venge´ful
re-venge´ful-ly
re-venge´ful-ness
re-veng´er
re-veng´ing
re-veng´ing-ly
rev´e-nue
re-ver´ber-ant
re-ver´ber-ant-ly
re-ver´ber-ate
re-ver-ber-a´tion
re-ver´ber-a-tive
re-ver´ber-a-tor
re-ver´ber-a-to-ry
re-vere´
rev´er-ence
rev´er-end
rev´er-ent
rev´er-en´tial
rev´er-ent-ly
rev´er-ie

re-ver´ing
re-ver´sal
re-verse´
re-verse´ly
re-vers´er
re-vers-i-bil´i-ty
re-vers´i·ble
re-vers´i·ble-ness
re-vers´i·bly
re-vers´ing
re-ver´sion
re-ver´sion-al
re-ver´sion-ar·y
re-vert´
re-vert´er
re-vert-i-bil´i-ty
re-vert´i·ble
re-vert´ment
re-view´
re-view´a·ble
re-view´er
re-vile´
re-vile´ment
re-vil´er
re-vil´ing
re-vil´ing-ly
re-vin´di-cate
re-vis´a·ble
re-vis´al
re-vise´
re-vised´
re-vis´er
re-vi´sion

re-vi´sion-al
re-vi´sion-ar-y
re-vi´sion-ism
re-vi´sion-ist
re-vis´it
re-vis-i-ta´tion
re-vis´er
re-vi´so-ry
re-vi-tal-i-za´tion
re-vi´tal-ize
re-viv-a-bil´i-ty
re-viv´a·ble
re-viv´a·bly
re-viv´al
re-viv´al-ism
re-viv´al-ist
re-viv-al-is´tic
re-vive´
re-viv´i-fy
re-viv´ing
rev-o-ca-bil´i-ty
rev´o-ca·ble
rev´o-ca·ble-ness
rev´o-ca·bly
rev-o-ca´tion
rev´o-ca-tive
rev´o-ca-to·ry
re-voice´
re-vok´a·ble
re-voke´
re-vok´er
re-vok´ing
re-volt´

re-volt´ing
re-volt´ing-ly
rev-o-lu´tion
rev´o-lu´tion-ar·y
rev-o-lu´tion-ist
rev-o-lu´tion-ize
re-volv´a·ble
re-volv´a·bly
re-volve´
re-volv´er
re-volv´ing
re-volv´ing–door´
re-vue´
re-vul´sion
re-vul´sion-ar·y
re-vul´sive
re-ward´
re-ward´a·ble
re-ward´ing
re-ward´ing-ly
re-wind´
re-wind´er
re-wir´a·ble
re-wire´
re-word´
re-write´ *(v.)*
re´write *(n.)*
re-zone´
rhap-sod´ic
rhap-sod´i-cal
rhap-sod´i-cal-ly
rhap´so-dize
rhap´so-diz-ing

rhap´so-dy
rhe´o-stat
rhet´o-ric
rhe-tor´i-cal
rhe-tor´i-cal-ly
rhe-tor´i-cal-ness
rhet-o-ri´cian
rheu-mat´ic
rheu´ma-tism
rhine´stone
rhi-ni´tis
rhi´no
rhi-noc´er-os
rhi-nol´o-gist
rhi-nol´o-gy
rhi´no-plas-ty
rhom´boid
rhom´bus
rhu´barb
rhyme
rhyme´ster
rhym´ing
rhythm
rhyth´mic
rhyth´mi-cal
rhyth´mi-cal-ly
rhyth´mics
rhyth´mist
rib´ald
rib´ald-ly
rib´al-dry
rib´and
ribbed

rib´bing
rib´bon
rib´boned
rib´bon-y
ri-bo-fla´vin
ri-bo-nu´cle-ase
ri´bo-nu-cle´ic
ri´bo-some
riç´er
rich´en
rich´es
rich´ly
rich´ness
rick
rick´et-i-ness
rick´ets
rick-ett´si-al
rick´et·y
rick´ey
ric´o-chet
ric´o-cheted
ri-cot´ta
rid´dance
rid´den
rid´der
rid´ding
rid´dle
rid´dled
ride´a·ble
rid´er
rid´er-less
rid´er-ship
ridge

ridge´pole
ridg´ing
ridg´y
rid´i-cule
ri-dic´u-lous
ri-dic´u-lous-ly
ri-dic´u-lous-ness
rid´ing
rife´ly
rife´ness
riff
rif´fle
rif´fling
riff´raff
ri´fle
ri´fle-man
ri´fle-ry
ri´fling
rig-a-to´ni
rigged
rig´ger
rig´ging
right´–an´gled
righ´teous
righ´teous-ly
righ´teous-ness
right´ful
right´ful-ly
right´ful-ness
right´–hand-ed
right´–hand-ed-ly
right´–hand-ed-
  ness

right´–hand-er
right´ist
right´ly
right´–mind-ed
right´ness
right´–of–way
right´–think´ing
right´–to–die´
right´–to–life´
right´–to–work´
right´ward
rig´id
ri-gid´i-ty
rig´id-ly
rig´id-ness
rig´ma-role
rig´or
rig´or-ism
rig´or-ist
rig-or-is´tic
rig´or-ous
rig´or-ous-ly
rig´or-ous-ness
rig´our (Br.)
rime
rim´fire
rim´less
rimmed
rim´ming
rim´y
rind
ring
ringed

ring´er
ring´ing
ring´ing-ly
ring´lead-er
ring´let
ring´mas-ter
ring´–necked
ring´side
ring´–tailed
ring´toss
rink´y–dink
rins´a·ble
rinse
rinsed
rins´er
rins´ing
ri´ot
ri´ot-er
ri´ot-ous
ri´ot-ous-ly
ri´ot-ous-ness
ripe´ly
rip´en
ripe´ness
rip´off
ripped
rip´per
rip´ping
rip´ple
rip´pled
rip´plet
rip´pling
rip´pling-ly

rip´ply
rip´–roar-ing
rip´saw
rip´snort´er
rise
ris´en
ris´er
ris´i·ble
ris´ing
risk
risk´i-ly
risk´i-ness
risk´less
risk´y
ri-sot´to
ris-qué´
rite
rit´u-al
rit´u-al-ism
rit´u-al-ist
rit´u-al-is´tic
rit´u-al-is´ti-cal-ly
rit´u-al-ize
rit-u-al-i-za´tion
rit´u-al-ly
ritz´i-ness
ritz´y
ri´val
ri´valed
ri´valing
ri´val-ly
ri´val-rous
ri´val-ry

rive
riv´en
riv´er
riv´er-bank
riv´er-bed
riv´er-boat
riv´er-side
riv´et
riv´et-er
riv´et-ing
riv´u-let
road´bed
road´block
road´house
road´ie
road´run-ner
road´side
road´ster
road´way
road´work
roam´er
roar´ing
roar´ing-ly
roast´a·ble
roast´ed
roast´er
rob
robbed
rob´ber
rob´ber·y
rob´bing
robe
rob´in

198

rob´ing
ro´bot
ro-bot´ics
ro´bot-ize
ro-bust´
ro-bus´tious
ro-bus´tious-ly
ro-bust´ly
ro-bust´ness
rock´–bot´tom
rock´er
rock´et
rock´e-teer´
rock´et-er
rock´et-ry
rock´ing
rock´ing-ly
rock´y
ro-co´co
ro´dent
ro´de·o
roe
roent´gen
roent-gen-og´ra-
 phy
roent-gen-ol´o·gy
rogue
rogu´er·y
rogu´ish
rogu´ish-ly
rogu´ish-ness
roil
rois´ter

rois´ter-er
rois´ter-ous
rois´ter-ous-ly
role´–play-ing
roll´a-way
roll´back
rolled
roll´er
rol´lick
rol´lick-ing
rol´lick-ing-ly
rol´lick-some
roll´ing
roll´mops
roll´–on
ro´ly–po´ly
ro-maine´
ro-mance´
ro-manc´er
ro-manc´ing
ro-man´tic
ro-man´ti-cal-ly
ro-man´ti-cism
ro-man´ti-cist
ro-man-ti-ci-za´-
 tion
ro-man´ti-cize
romp´er
romp´ing-ly
romp´ish
ron´do
roof´er
roof´ing

roof´less
roof´line
roof´top
rook´er·y
rook´ie
room´er
room-ette´
room´ful
room´ie
room´i-ly
room´i-ness
room´mate
room´y
roost´er
root´age
root´ed
root´ed-ness
root´er
root´less
root´less-ness
root´let
root´stock
root´y
rope
roped
rope´dance
rope´danc-er
rope´danc-ing
rope´mak-er
rope´mak-ing
rop´er
rop´i-ness
rop´y

ro´sa-ry
rose´bud
rose´bush
rose´–col-ored
rose´mar·y
ro-se´o-la
ro-sette´
rose´wood
ros´in
ros´i-ness
ros´ter
ros´trum
ros´y
ro´ta-ry
ro´tat-a·ble
ro´tate
ro-ta´tion
ro-ta´tion-al
ro´ta-tive
ro´ta-tive-ly
ro´ta-tor
rote
ro-tis´ser-ie
ro´to-gra-vure´
ro´to-till-er
rot´ten-ly
rot´ten-ness
rot´ter
rot´ting
ro-tund´
ro-tun´da
ro-tun´di-ty
ro-tund´ly

ro-tund´ness
rou·é´
rouge
rouged
rough
rough´age
rough´–and–
  read´y
rough´–and–
  tum´ble
rough´en
rough´en-er
rough´er
rough´house
rough´ish
rough´ly
rough´neck
rough´ness
rough´shod
roug´ing
rou-lade´
rou-lette´
round´a·bout
round´ed
round´ed-ly
round´ed-ness
round´er
round´house
round´ish
round´ly
round´ness
round´–shoul-
  dered

round´up *(n.)*
rouse
roused
rous´er
rous´ing
roust´a·bout
rout
route
rout´ed
rout´er
rou-tine´
rou-tine´ly
rou-tine´ness
rou-tin´ize
rout´ing
roux
rove
rov´er
rov´ing
row´boat
row´dies
row´di-ly
row´di-ness
row´dy
row´dy-ish
row´dy-ism
row´er
roy´al
roy´al-ist
roy´al-ly
roy´al-ty
rubbed
rub´ber

rub´ber-ize
rub´ber-neck
rub´ber-y
rub´bing
rub´bish
rub´bish-y
rub´ble
rub´bly
rub´down
rube
ru-be´o-la
ru´bric
ru´bri-cal
ru´bri-cate
ru-bri-ca´tion
ru´bri-ca-tor
ru´by
ruck´sack
ruck´us
rud´der
rud´di-ness
rud´dy
rude
rude´ly
rude´ness
rud´est
ru´di-ment
ru-di-men-ta´ri-ly
ru-di-men´ta-ri-
  ness
ru-di-men´ta-ry
rue´ful
rue´ful-ly

rue´ful-ness
ru-fes´cence
ru-fes´cent
ruff
ruffed
ruf´fi-an
ruf´fi-an-ly
ruf´fi-an-ism
ruf´fle
ruf´fled
ruf´fler
ruf´fling
rug
rug´ged
rug´ged-ly
rug´ged-ness
ru´in
ru´in-a·ble
ru´in-ate
ru-in-a´tion
ru´ined
ru´in-ing
ru´in-ous
ru´in-ous-ly
ru´in-ous-ness
rul´a·ble
rule
ruled
rul´er
rul´er-ship
rul´ing
rum
ru-ma´ki

rum´ble
rum´bler
rum´bling
rum´bling-ly
rum´bly
ru´mi-nant
ru´mi-nate
ru-mi-na´tion
ru´mi-na-tive
ru´mi-na-tive-ly
ru´mi-na-tor
rum´mage
rum´mag-er
rum´mag-ing
rum´my
ru´mor
ru´mor-mon-ger
rump
rump´er
rum´ple
rum´pled
rum´pling
rum´ply
rum´pus
rum´run-ner
run´a·bout
run´a·round
run´a·way
run´dle
run´–down´
rung
run´–in
run´ner

run´ner–up´
run´ning
run´ny
run´off
run´–of–the–mill´
runt
run´–through
runt´ish
runt´y
run´way
rup´tur-a·ble
rup´ture
rup´tured
rup´tur-ing
ru´ral
ru´ral-ism
ru´ral-ist
ru´ral-ite
ru-ral-i-za´tion
ru´ral-ize
ru´ral-ly
ru´ral-ness
rush´ing
rus´set
rust
rus´tic
rus´ti-cal-ly
rus´ti-cate
rus-ti-ca´tion
rus´ti-ca-tor
rus-tic´i·ty
rust´i-ness
rus´tle

rus´tler
rust-tling
rust´proof
rust´y
ru´ta-ba´ga
ruth´ful
ruth´ful-ly
ruth´ful-ness
ruth´less
ruth´less-ly
ruth´less-ness
rut´ted
rut´tish
rut´tish-ly
rut´tish-ness
rut´ty

S

sab-bat´i-cal
sa´ber
sa´ber–rat-tling
sa´ber-tooth
sa´ber–toothed
sa´ble
sa·bot´
sab´o-tage
sab´o-teur´
sac´cha-rate
sac´cha-ride
sac´cha-rin
  (swetener)
sac´cha-rine
  (sweet)

sa-chet´
sack´cloth
sack´ful
sack´ing
sac´ra-ment
sac-ra-men´tal
sac-ra-men´tal-
  ism
sac-ra-men´tal-ist
sac-ra-men´tal-ly
sa´cred
sa´cred-ly
sa´cred-ness
sac´ri-fice
sac´ri-fice-a·ble
sac´ri-fi´cial
sac´ri-fic-ing
sac´ri-lege
sac´ri-le´gious
sac´ri-le´gious-ly
sac´ri-le´gious-
  ness
sac´ris-ty
sac´ro-il´i·ac
sac´ro-sanct
sac´ro-sanc´ti-ty
sac´ro-sanct-ness
sad
sad´den
sad´den-ing
sad´der
sad´dle
sad´dle-bag

sad´dler
sad´dler·y
sad´dle-sore
sad´dle-tree
sa´dism
sa´dist
sa-dis´tic
sa-dis´ti-cal-ly
sad´ly
sad´ness
sa-fa´ri
safe–con´duct
safe´crack-er
safe´–de-pos-it
safe´guard
safe´keep-ing
safe´ly
saf´est
safe´ty
saf´fron
sa´ga
sa-ga´cious
sa-ga´cious-ly
sa-ga´cious-ness
sa-gac´i-ty
sage´ly
sage´ness
sagged
sag´ger
sag´ging
sag´gy
sail´boat
sail´cloth

sailed
sail´er
sail´fish
sail´ing
sail´or
sail´or-ing
sail´plane
saint´ed
saint´hood
saint´li-ness
saint´ly
sa´ke *(wine)*
sa-laam´
sal-a·bil´i-ty
sal´a·ble
sal´a·bly
sa-la´cious
sa-la´cious-ly
sa-la´cious-ness
sa-lac´i-ty
sal´ad
sal´a-man-der
sa-la´mi
sal´a-ried
sal´a-ry
sales´clerk
sales´peo-ple
sales´per-son
sa´lience
sa´li-ent
sal-i-na´tion
sa´line
sa-lin´i-ty

sa-li´va
sal´i-var·y
sal´i-vate
sal-i-va´tion
sal´lied
sal´low
sal´ly
sal´ly-ing
sal-mo-nel´la
sa-lon´
sa-loon´
sal´sa
sal´si-fy
salt´box
salt´cel-lar
salt´ed
salt´er
salt´i-er
salt´i-ly
sal-tim-boc´ca
sal-tine´
salt´i-ness
salt´ish
salt´ish-ness
salt´less
salt´ness
salt´shak-er
salt´wa-ter
salt´y
sa-lu´bri-ous
sa-lu´bri-ous-ly
sa-lu´bri-ous-ness
sa-lu´bri-ty

sal-u-tar´i·ly
sal´u-tar-i-ness
sal´u-tar·y
sal-u-ta´tion
sal-u-ta´tion-al
sa-lu´ta-to·ry
sa-lute´
sa-lut´ing
sal´va·ble
sal´vage
sal´vage-a·ble
sal´vag-er
sal-va´tion
sal-va´tion-al
salve
salved
sal´ver
sal´vo
same´ness
sam´o-var
sam´pan
sam´ple
sam´pler
sam´pling
sa´mu-rai
san´a-tive
san-a-to´ri-um
san´a-to·ry
sanc´ti-fi-a-ble
sanc-ti-fi-ca´tion
sanc´ti-fied
sanc´ti-fi-er
sanc´ti-fy

sanc´ti-fy-ing
sanc-ti-mo´ni-ous
sanc-ti-mo´ni-ous-
  ly
sanc-ti-mo´ni-ous-
  ness
sanc´ti-mo-ny
sanc´tion
sanc´tion-a·ble
sanc´tion-er
sanc´ti-ty
sanc´tu-ar·y
sanc´tum
sanc´tus
sand
san´dal
san´daled
san´dal-wood
sand´bag
sand´bank
sand´blast
sand´box
sand´er
sand´i-er
sand´i-ness
sand´lot
sand´man
sand´pa-per
sand´stone
sand´storm
sand´wich
sand´y
sane

san-er
sane´ly
sane´ness
san´for-ize
san-grí´a
san´guine
san´guine-ly
san´guine-ness
san-guin´e-ous
san-guin´e-ous-
  ness
san-i-tar´i-an
san´i-tar-i-ly
san´i-tar-i-ness
san´i-tar´i·um
san´i-tar·y
san-i-ta´tion
san-i-ti-za´tion
san´i-tize
san´i-tiz-er
san´i-ty
sap´id
sa-pid´i-ty
sap´id-ness
sap´i-ence
sa´pi-ens
sap´i-ent
sap´i-ent-ly
sap´ling
sa´por
sap´o-rif´ic
sap´per
sap´phire

sap´ping
sap´py
sap-sa´go
sap´suck-er
sar´casm
sar-cas´tic
sar-cas´ti-cal-ly
sar-co´ma
sar-coph´a-gi
sar-coph´a-gus
sar-dine´
sar-don´ic
sar-don´i-cal-ly
sar-don´i-cism
sa´ri
sa-rong´
sar-sa-pa-ril´la
sar-to´ri-al
sar-to´ri-al-ly
sash
sa-shay´
sa-shi´mi
sas´sa-fras
sas´sy
sa-tan´ic
sa-tan´i-cal
sa-tan´i-cal-ly
satch´el
sat´ed
sa-teen´
sat´el-lite
sa-tia-bil´i·ty
sa´tia-ble

sa´tia-bly
sa´ti-ate
sa-ti-a´tion
sa-ti´e·ty
sat´in
sat´in·y
sat´ire
sa-tir´ic
sa-tir´i-cal
sa-tir´i-cal-ly
sat´i-rist
sat´i-riz-a·ble
sat-i-ri-za´tion
sat´i-rize
sat´i-riz-er
sat´i-riz-ing
sat-is-fac´tion
sat-is-fac´to-ri-ly
sat-is-fac´to-ri-
    ness
sat´is-fac´to-ry
sat´is-fied
sat´is-fi-er
sat´is-fy
sat´is-fy-ing
sat´is-fy-ing-ly
sa-to´ri
sa´trap
sa´tra-py
sat´u-ra·ble
sat´u-rant
sat´u-rate
sat´u-rat-ed

sat´u-rat-er
sat´u-rat-ing
sat-u-ra´tion
sat´u-ra-tor
sat-ur-na´lia
sa´tyr
sauced
sauce´pan
sau´cer
sau´ci-ly
sau´ci-ness
sau´cy
sau´er-bra-ten
sau´er-kraut
sau´na
saun´ter
saun´ter-ing
sau´sage
sau-té´
sau-téed´
sau-té´ing
sau-terne´
sav´able
sav´age
sav´age-ly
sav´age-ness
sav´age-ry
sa-van´na
sa-vant´
saved
sav´er
sav´ing
sav´ior

sa´vor
sa´vor-ous
sa´vory
sa´vour (Br.)
sav´vi-ness
sav´vy
saw´buck
saw´dust
sawed´–off´
saw´horse
saw´mill
saw´tooth
saw´–toothed
saw´yer
sax´o-phone
sax´o-phon-ist
say´a-ble
say´ing
say´–so
scab´bard
scabbed
scab´bi-ly
scab´bi-ness
scab´bing
sca´bi-ous
scab´ble
scab´bler
scab´by
sca´bies
scab´rous-ly
scaf´fold
scaf´fold-ing
scag

scal´a-ble
scal´a-wag
scald´ed
scald´er
scale
scaled
scale´down
scal´er
scal´ing
scal´lion
scal´lop
scal´loped
sca-lop-pi´ni
scalp
scal´pel
scalp´er
scal´y
scam
scamp
scam´per
scam´pi
scamp´ish
scan´dal
scan´dal-ize
scan´dal-monger
scan´dal-ous
scan´dal-ous-ly
scan´dal-ous-ness
scanned
scan´ner
scan´ning
scant´i-ly
scant´i-ness

scant´ling
scant´ly
scant´ness
scant´y
scape´goat
scarce
scarce´ly
scarce´ness
scar´city
scare´crow
scared
scarf
scar´i-ly
scar´ing
scar´let
scarred
scar´ring
scary
scathe
scath´ing
scat´ter
scat´ter-brain
scat´tered
scat´ter-er
scat´ter-ing
scat´ter-shot
scav´enge
scav´eng-er
scav´eng-ing
sce-nar´io
scene
sce´ner·y
sce´nic

sce´ni-cal
scent´ed
scep´ter
scep´tic
scep´ti-cal
scep´ti-cism
sched´ule
sched´uled
sched´ul-ing
sche-mat´ic
sche-mat´i-cal-ly
scheme
schem´er
schem´ing
schem´ing-ly
schism
schiz´oid
schiz-o-phre´ni-a
schiz-o-phren´ic
schlep
schlock
schmaltz
schmaltz´y
schmear
schmooze
schmuck
schnook
schol´ar
schol´ar-li-ness
schol´ar-ly
schol´ar-ship
scho-las´tic
scho-las´ti-cal-ly

school´book
school´boy
school´child
school´girl
school´house
school´ing
school´marm
school´mas-ter
school´mate
school´room
school´teach-er
school´work
school´yard
schoo´ner
schuss
sci-at´ic
sci-at´i-ca
sci´ence
sci-en-tif´ic
sci-en-tif´i-cal-ly
sci´en-tism
sci´en-tist
scim´i-tar
scin-til´la
scin´til-late
scin´til-lat-ing
scin-til-la´tion
scin´til-la-tor
sci´on
scis´sors
scle-ro´sis
scoff´er
scoff´ing-ly

scoff´law
scold´er
scold´ing
scold´ing-ly
sco-li-o´sis
sconce
scone
scoop´er
scoop´ful
scoot´er
scope
scorch´er
scorch´ing
score´board
score´card
scored
score´keep-er
scor´ing
scorn´er
scorn´ful
scorn´ful-ly
scorn´ful-ness
scor´pi-on
scot´–free´
scoun´drel
scour
scourge
scourg´er
scourg´ing
scour´ings
scout
scout´ing
scowl´er

scowl´ing-ly
scrab´ble
scrab´bler
scrab´bling
scrab´bly
scrag´gi-ly
scrag´gi-ness
scrag´gly
scrag´gy
scram´ble
scram´bler
scram´bling
scrap´book
scrape
scraped
scrap´er
scrap´ing
scrapped
scrap´per
scrap´pi-ly
scrap´pi-ness
scrap´ping
scrap´ple
scrap´py
scratch´board
scratch´er
scratch´i-ly
scratch´i-ness
scratch´proof
scratch´y
scrawl´er
scrawl´y
scrawn´i-ness

scrawn´y
screak
screak´y
scream
scream´er
scream´ing
screech
screech´y
screed
screen´a-ble
screen´er
screen´ing
screen´play
screen´writ-er
screw´ball
screw´driv-er
screw´up
screw´y
scrib´ble
scrib´bler
scrib´bling
scribe
scrib´er
scrim´mage
scrim´mag-er
scrimp
scrimp´i-ly
scrimp´i-ness
scrimp´y
scrim´shaw
scrip
script´er
scrip´tur-al

scrip´tur-al-ly
scrip´ture
script´writ-er
script´writ-ing
scriv´en-er
scrof´u-lous
scrof´u-lous-ly
scrof´u-lous-ness
scroll
scroll´work
scro´tum
scrounge
scroung´er
scroung´ing
scrub´ba-ble
scrub´ber
scrub´bi-ness
scrub´bing
scrub´by
scruff´y
scrump´tious
scrump´tious-ly
scrump´tious-ness
scrunch
scru´ple
scru-pu-los´i-ty
scru´pu-lous
scru´pu-lous-ly
scru´pu-lous-ness
scru-ta-bil´i-ty
scru´ta-ble
scru-ti-ni-za´tion
scru´ti-nize

scru´ti-niz-er
scru´ti-niz-ing-ly
scru´ti-ny
scu´ba–dive
scud´ded
scuff
scuf´fle
scuf´fling
scuf´fling-ly
scull
scul´ler·y
sculpt
sculp´tor
sculp´tur-al
sculp´tur-al-ly
sculp´ture
sculp´tured
scum
scum´ble
scum´bled
scum´my
scurf
scurf´y
scur-ril´i-ty
scur´ril-ous
scur´ril-ous-ly
scur´ril-ous-ness
scur´ried
scur´ry
scur´ry-ing
scur´vy
scut
scutch´eon

scut´tle
scut´tle-butt
scut´tling
scuzz´y
scythe
scyth´ing
sea´bed
sea´bird
sea´borne
sea´coast
sea´far-er
sea´far-ing
sea´floor
sea´food
sea´go-ing
seal´able
seal´ant
sealed´–beam
seal´er
sea´lift
seal´ing
seal´skin
sea´man
sea´man-like
sea´man-ship
sea´men
seam´i-ness
seam´less
seam´less-ly
seam´less-ness
seam´ster
seam´stress
seam´y

sé´ance
sea´plane
sea´port
search´a-ble
search´er
search´ing
search´ing-ly
search´light
sea´scape
sea´shell
sea´shore
sea´sick
sea´sick-ness
sea´side
sea´son
sea´son-a-ble
sea´son-a-bly
sea´son-al
sea´son-al-ly
sea´son-ing
seat´ed
seat´er
seat´ing
seat´mate
seat´–of–the–
    pants´
sea´wall
sea´ward
sea´way
sea´weed
sea´wor-thi-ness
sea´wor-thy
se-ba´ceous

se´bum
se´cant
se-cede´
se-ced´ed
se-ced´er
se-ced´ing
se-ces´sion
se-ces´sion-al
se-ces´sion-ism
se-ces´sion-ist
se-clude´
se-clud´ed
se-clud´ed-ness
se-clud´ing
se-clu´sion
se-clu´sive
se-clu´sive-ly
se-clu´sive-ness
sec´ond
sec´ond-ar-i-ly
sec´ond-ar-i-ness
sec´ond-ar-y
sec´ond-er
sec´ond–guess´
sec´ond-hand´
sec´ond-ly
sec´ond–rate´
se´cre-cy
se´cret
sec´re-tar´i-al
sec-re-tar´i-at
sec´re-tary
se-crete´

se-cret´ed
se-cre´tion
se-cre´tion-ar-y
se´cre-tive
se´cre-tive-ly
se´cre-tive-ness
se´cret-ly
se´cret-ness
sect
sec-tar´i-an
sec-tar´i-an-ism
sec´tion-al
sec´tion-al-ism
sec´tion-al-ist
sec´tion-al-ly
sec-tion-al-i-za´-
  tion
sec´tion-al-ize
sec´tor
sec-to´ri-al
sec´u-lar
sec´u-lar-ism
sec´u-lar-ist
sec-u-lar´i-ty
sec-u-lar-i·za´tion
sec´u-lar-ize
sec´u-lar-ly
se-cur´a·ble
se-cure´
se-cure´ly
se-cure´ness
se-cur´ity
se-dan´

se-date´
se-date´ly
se-date´ness
se-da´tion
sed´a-tive
sed´en-tar´i-ly
sed´en-tar´i-ness
sed´en-tar·y
sed´i-ment
sed´i-men´tal
sed´i-men-tar´i-ly
sed´i-men´ta-ry
sed-i-men-ta´tion
sed-i-men-tol´o-gy
sed-i-men-to-log´-
  ic
sed-i-men-to-log´i-
  cal
sed-i-men-tol´o-
  gist
se-di´tion
se-di´tious
se-di´tious-ly
se-di´tious-ness
se-duce´
se-duc´er
se-duc´i-ble
se-duc´ing
se-duc´tion
se-duc´tive
se-duc´tive-ly
se-duc´tive-ness
se-duc´tress

se-du′li-ty
sed′u-lous
sed′u-lous-ly
sed′u-lous-ness
seed′bed
seed′cake
seed′case
seed′er
seed′i-ness
seed′ing
seed′less
seed′ling
seed′pod
seed′y
see′ing
seek′er
seem′ing
seem′ing-ly
seem′li-ness
seem′ly
seep′age
seer′suck-er
see′saw
seethe
seeth′ing
seeth′ing-ly
see′–through
seg′ment
seg-men′tal
seg-men′tal-ly
seg′men-tar-y
seg-men-ta′tion
seg′re-ga·ble

seg′re-gate
seg′re-gat-ed
seg-re-ga′tion
seg-re-ga′tion-ist
se′gue
sei-gneur′
seine
seis′mic
seis′mi-cal-ly
seis-mic′i-ty
seis′mism
seis′mo-gram
seis′mo-graph
seis-mog′ra-pher
seis-mo-graph′ic
seis-mog′ra-phy
seis-mo-log′ic
seis-mo-log′i-cal
seis-mol′o-gist
seis-mol′o-gy
seis-mom′e-ter
seis-mom′et-ry
seiz′a·ble
seize
seiz′er
seiz′ing
sei′zure
sel′dom
se-lect′
se-lec′tion
se-lec′tive
se-lec′tive-ly
se-lec′tive-ness

se-lec-tiv′i-ty
se-lect′man
se-lec′tor
self′–a-base′ment
self′–ab-sorbed′
self′–ab-sorp′tion
self′–act′ing
self′–ap-point′ed
self′–as-sur′ance
self′–as-sured′
self′–cen′tered
self′–cen′tered-
  ness
self′–com-posed′
self′–con-fessed′
self–con′fi-dence
self–con′fi-dent
self–con′fi-dent-ly
self–con-grat′u-la-
  to·ry
self–con′scious
self–con′scious-ly
self–con′scious-
  ness
self–con-tained′
self–con-tra-dic′-
  ting
self–con-tra-dic′-
  tion
self–con-tra-dic′-
  tor-y
self–con-trol′
self–con-trol′led

self–de-ceit´
self–de-cep´tion
self–de-fense´
self–de-lud´ed
self–de-lu´sion
self–de-ni´al
self–de-ny´ing
self´–de-struct´
self´–de-struc´tion
self´–de-struc´tive
self–de-ter-mi-na´-
　tion
self–de-vo´tion
self–dis´ci-pline
self–dis´ci-plined
self´–doubt´
self´–doubt´ing
self´–ef-face´ment
self´–ef-fac´ing
self´–em-ployed´
self–es-teem´
self–ev´i-dent
self–ev´i-dent·ly
self´–ex-plan´a-
　to·ry
self´–ex-pres´sion
self–ful-fill´ing
self–ful-fill´ment
self–gov´erned
self–gov´ern-ing
self–gov´ern-ment
self´–grat-i-fi-ca´-
　tion

self–help´
self´–hyp-no´sis
self´–im´age
self–im-por´tance
self–im-por´tant
self–im-por´tant·ly
self–im-posed´
self´–im-prove´-
　ment
self´–in-crim´-
　i·nat-ing
self´–in-crim-in-
　a´tion
self´–in-duced´
self´–in-dul´gence
self´–in-dul´gent
self–in´ter-est
self´ish
self´ish-ly
self´ish-ness
self–know´ledge
self´less
self´less-ly
self´less-ness
self´–lim´it-ing
self–liq´ui-dat-ing
self–load´er
self–load´ing
self–love´
self–made´
self–mail´er
self´–per-pet´u-at-
　ing

self–pit´y
self–por´trait
self–pos-sessed´
self–pres-er-va´-
　tion
self´–pro-pelled´
self´–pro-pul´sion
self–pro-tec´tion
self–re-gard´
self–reg´ulating
self–re-li´ance
self–re-li´ant
self–re-spect´
self–re-spect´ing
self´–re-straint´
self–right´eous
self–right´eous·ly
self–right´eous-
　ness
self–sac´ri-fice
self–sac´ri-fic-ing
self´same
self–sat´is-fied
self´–serv´ing
self´–start-er
self´–start-ing
self–suf-fi´cien-cy
self–suf-fi´cient
self–sup-port´ing
self´–taught´
self´–will´
self´–wind´ing
self´–worth´

sell´a·ble
sell´er
sell´ing
sell´–off
sell´out
selt´zer
sel´vage
selves
se-man´tic
se-man´ti-cal´ly
se-man´tics
sem´a-phore
sem-a-phor´ic
sem´blance
se-mes´ter
sem-i-ab´stract
sem-i-ab-strac´-
  tion
sem-i-an´nu-al
sem-i-an´nu-al-ly
sem-i-ar´id
sem-i-au-to-mat´ic
sem-i-au-ton´o-
  mous
sem´i-cir-cle
sem-i-cir´cu-lar
sem-i-clas´si-cal
sem´i-co-lon
sem´i-con-duc-tor
sem-i-con´scious
sem-i-con´scious-
  ness
sem-i-dark´ness

sem´i-de-tached´
sem´i-fi-nal
sem-i-fi´nal-ist
sem-i-for´mal
sem´i-gloss
sem-i-lit´er-a-cy
sem-i-lit´er-ate
sem´i-month´ly
sem´i-nal
sem´i-nal-ly
sem´i-nar
sem-i-nar´i-an
sem´i-nary
sem-i-of-fi´cial
sem-i-per´me-
  a·ble
sem´i-pre´cious
sem-i-pri´vate
sem-i-pro-fes´-
  sion-al
sem-i-pro-fes´-
  sion-al-ly
sem-i-pub´lic
sem-i-skilled´
sem-i-soft´
sem-i-sol´id
sem-i-sweet´
sem-i-week´ly
sem-i-year´ly
sem-o-li´na
sen´ate
sen´a-tor
sen-a-to´ri-al

send´a-ble
send´er
send´ing
send´–off
se´nile
se-nil´i-ty
sen´ior
se-nior´i-ty
sen´na
se-ñor´
se-ño´ra
se-ño-ri´ta
sen´sate
sen-sa´tion
sen-sa´tion-al
sen-sa´tion-al-ism
sen-sa´tion-al-ist
sen-sa-tion-al-is´-
  tic
sen-sa´tion-al-ize
sen-sa´tion-al-ly
sensed
sense´less
sense´less-ly
sense´less-ness
sen-si-bil´i-ty
sen´si-ble
sen´si-ble-ness
sen´si-bly
sens´ing
sen´si-tive
sen´si-tive-ly
sen´si-tive-ness

sen-si-tiv´i·ty
sen-si-ti·za´tion
sen´si-tize
sen´si-tiz-er
sen´sor
sen-so´ri-al
sen´so-ry
sen´su-al
sen´su-al-ism
sen´su-al-ist
sen-su-al-is´tic
sen-su-al-i-za´tion
sen´su-al-ize
sen-su-al´i-ty
sen´su-al-ly
sen´su-ous
sen´su-ous-ly
sen´su-ous-ness
sen´tence
sen-ten´tial
sen-ten´tial-ly
sen´tience
sen´tient
sen´tient-ly
sen´ti-ment
sen-ti-men´tal
sen-ti-men´tal-ism
sen-ti-men´tal-ist
sen-ti-men-tal´i-ty
sen-ti-men-tal-i-
  za´tion
sen-ti-men´tal-ize
sen-ti-men´tal-ly

sen´ti-nel
sen´try
sep-a-ra-bil´i-ty
sep´a-ra·ble
sep´a-ra·bly
sep´a-rate
sep´a-rate-ly
sep´a-rate-ness
sep-a-ra´tion
sep´a-rat-ism
sep´a-rat-ist
sep´a-ra-tive
sep´a-ra-tor
se´pia
sep´sis
sep-ten´ni-al
sep-ten´ni-al-ly
sep-tet´
sep´tic
sep-ti-ce´mia
sep-tic´i-ty
sep-til´lion
sep´tu´age-nar´i-
  an
sep´tu-ple
sep´ul-cher
se-pul´chral
se-pul´chral-ly
se-qua´cious
se-qua´cious-ly
se-quac´i-ty
se´quel
se´quence

se´quenc-er
se´quenc-ing
se´quent
se-quen´tial
se-quen-ti-al´i-ty
se-quen´tial-ly
se-ques´ter
se-ques´tered
se´quin
se´quined
se-quoi´a
se-ra´glio
se-ra´pe
ser´a-phim
ser´e-nade´
ser´e-nad´er
ser´e-nad´ing
ser-en-dip´i-tous
ser-en-dip´i-tous-
  ly
ser-en-dip´i-ty
se-rene´
se-rene´ly
se-rene´ness
se-ren´i-ty
serf´dom
serge
ser´geant
se´ri-al
se´ri-al-ism
se´ri-al-ist
se´ri-al-ize
se´ri-al-ly

se´ri-ate
se´ri-ate-ly
se´ries
ser´if
se-ri-o-com´ic
se´ri-ous
se´ri-ous-ly
se´ri-ous–mind´ed
se´ri-ous–mind´-
  ed-ly
se´ri-ous–mind´-
  ed-ness
se´ri-ous-ness
ser´mon
ser-mon´ic
ser-mon´i-cal
ser´mon-ize
ser´mon-less
se´rous-ness
ser´pent
ser´pen-tine
ser´rate
ser´rat-ed
ser-ra´tion
ser´ried
ser´ried-ly
se´rum
serv´a-ble
ser´vant
served
serv´er
serv´ice
serv-ice-a-bil´i-ty

serv´ice-a·ble
serv´ice-a·ble-ness
serv´ice-a·bly
ser-vi-ette´
ser´vile
ser´vile-ly
ser´vile-ness
ser-vil´i-ty
serv´ing
ser´vi-tor
ser´vi-tude
ses´a-me
ses´qui-cen-ten´ni-
  al
ses´sion
ses´tet
set´back
set´off
set´screw
set-tee´
set´ter
set´ting
set´tle
set´tle-a-ble
set´tle-ment
set´tler
set´tling
set´–to
set´up
sev´en
sev´en-fold
sev´en-teen´
sev´en-teenth´

sev´enth
sev´en-ti-eth
sev´en-ty
sev´en-ty–six´
sev´er
sev-er-a-bil´i-ty
sev´er-a-ble
sev´er-al
sev´er-al-ly
sev´er-al-ty
sev´er-ance
se-vere´
sev´ered
se-vere´ly
se-vere´ness
se-ver´i-ty
sew´a-ble
sew´age
sew´er
sew´er-age
sew´ing
sex-a-ge-nar´i-an
sex-ag´e-nary
sex´i-ly
sex´i-ness
sex´ism
sex´ist
sex´less
sex-ol´o-gist
sex-ol´o-gy
sex´tant
sex-tet´
sex-til´lion

sex´ton
sex-tup´let
sex´u-al
sex-u-al´i-ty
sex´u-al-ly
sex´y
shab´bi-ly
shab´bi-ness
shab´by
shack´le
shack´led
shack´ling
shade
shad´ed
shad´i-er
shad´i-ly
shad´i-ness
shad´ing
shad´ow
shad´ow-box
shad´ow-i-ness
shad´ow-ing
shad´ow·y
shad´y
shaft
shag´gi-ly
shag´gi-ness
shag´gy
shak´a·ble
shake´down
shak´en
shak´er
shake´–up

shak´i-ly
shak´ing
shak´y
shal-lot´
shal´low-ly
shal´low-ness
sha´man
sham´ble
shame
shamed
shame´faced
shame´ful
shame´ful-ly
shame´ful-ness
shame´less
shame´less-ly
shame´less-ness
sham´ing
shammed
sham´mer
sham´ming
sham-poo´
sham-pooed´
sham´rock
shan´dy
shan´dy-gaff
shank
shan´ty
shan´ty-town
shap´a-ble
shape
shaped
shape´less

shape´less-ly
shape´less-ness
shape´li-ness
shape´ly
shap´er
shape´–up
shap´ing
shar´able
shard
share
share´crop-per
share´hold-er
shar´er
share´ware
shar´ing
shark´skin
sharp´–eared´
sharp´–edged´
sharp´en
sharp´en-er
sharp´en-ing
sharp´er
sharp´–eyed´
sharp´ly
sharp´ness
sharp´shoot-er
sharp´shoot-ing
sharp´–sight-ed
sharp´–tongued
sharp´–wit´ted
shat´ter
shat´tered
shat´ter-er

shat´ter-proof

shaved

shave´ling

shave´tail

shav´en

shav´er

shav´ing

shawl

sheaf

shear

shear´er

shear´ing

sheath

sheathe

sheathed

sheath´ing

sheave

shed´der

she´–dev-il

shed´ding

sheen

sheep´cote

sheep dog

sheep´fold

sheep´herd-er

sheep´ish

sheep´ish-ly

sheep´ish-ness

sheep´shank

sheep´shear-ing

sheep´skin

sheep´walk

sheer

sheer´ness

sheet´ing

sheik´dom

shelf

shel-lac´

shel-lacked´

she´lack´ing

shelled

shell´er

shell´fish

shell´–shocked

shel´ter

shel´tered

shel´ter-ing

shel´ter-less

shelves

shelv´ing

she-nan´i-gan

shep´herd

shep´herd-ess

sher´bet

sher´iff

sher´ry

shi-at´su

shib´bo-leth

shield

shift´er

shift´i-er

shift´i-ly

shift´i-ness

shift´ing

shift´less

shift´less-ly

shift´less-ness

shift´y

shil´ling

shil´ly–shal-ly

shim´mer

shim´mer-ing-ly

shim´mery

shim´ming

shim´my

shin´bone

shin´dig

shine

shin´er

shin´gle

shin´gled

shin´i-er

shin´i-ly

shin´ing

shin´i-ness

shin´ing

shin´ny

shin´plas-ter

shin´y

ship´board

ship´build-er

ship´build-ing

ship´fit-ter

ship´load

ship´mate

ship´ment

ship´own-er

shipped

ship´per

ship´ping

ship´shape

ship´wreck

ship´wright

ship´yard

shire

shirk´er

shirr

shirred

shirr´ing

shirt´ing

shirt´mak-er

shirt´mak-ing

shirt´sleeve

shirt´tail

shirt´waist

shiv´ery

shoal

shoat

shock

shock´a-ble

shock´er

shock´ing

shock´ing-ly

shock´proof

shock´--re-sist´ant

shod´di-ly

shod´di-ness

shod´dy

shoe´horn

shoe´ing

shoe´lace

shoe´mak-er

shoe pol´ish

shoe´shine

shoe´string

sho´gun

shoo´--in

shoot´er

shoot´ing

shoot´out

shop´keep-er

shop´keep-ing

shop´lift

shop´lift-er

shopped

shop´per

shop´ping

shop´talk

shop´worn

shore´line

shor´ing

short´age

short´bread

short´cake

short´change

short´com-ing

short´cut

short´en

short´en-er

short´en-ing

short´fall

short´haired

short´hand´ed

short´--haul

short´--lived´

short´ly

short´ness

short´--range´

short´sight-ed

short´sight-ed-ly

short´sight-ed-
 ness

short´stop

short´--tem´pered

short´wave´

short´--wind´ed

short´y

shot´gun

should

shoul´der

shoul´dered

shout´ed

shout´er

shove

shoved

shov´el

shov´eled

shov´el-er

shov´el-ful

shov´el-ing

shov´er

shov´ing

show´boat

show´case

show´down

showed

show´er

show´i-ness

show´ing	shrub´ber-y	sick´en-ing-ly
show´man	shrub´by	sick´ie
show´man-ship	shrug	sick´le
shown	shrugged	sick´led
show´–off	shrug´ging	sick´li-er
show´room	shrunk´en	sick´li-ness
show´–stop-per	shtick	sick´ly
show´y	shuck´ing	sick´ness
shrap´nel	shud´der	sick´room
shred´der	shuf´fle	side´bar
shred´ding	shuf´fle-board	side´board
shrew	shuf´fled	side´burns
shrewd´ly	shut´fling	side´car
shrewd´ness	shunned	sid´ed
shrew´ish	shun´ning	side´kick
shrieked	shun´pike	side´line
shriek´ing	shunt´ing	si-de´re-al
shrill	shut´down *(n.)*	side´sad-dle
shril´ly	shut´eye	side´show
shrill´ness	shut´–in	side´split-ter
shril´ly	shut´off	side´split-ting
shrimp´er	shut´out	side´swipe
shrine	shut´ter	side´track
shrined	shut´ting	side´walk
shrin´er	shut´tle	side´wall
shrink´a·ble	shut´tle-cock	side´ways
shrink´age	shy´ly	side´wind-er
shrink´–wrap	shy´ness	si´dle
shrive	shy´ster	si´dled
shriv´el	sib´ling	si´dling
shriv´eled	sick´bed	siege
shriv´el-ing	sick´en	si-es´ta
shroud´ed	sick´en-ing	sieve

sift´er
sift´ings
sigh´ing
sight´ed
sight´er
sight´less
sight´less-ly
sight´less-ness
sight´ly
sight´–read
sight´–read-er
sight´see
sight´see-ing
sight´seer
sig´ma
sig´moid
sign
sig´nal
sig´naled
sig´nal-ing
sig-nal-i-za´tion
sig´nal-ize
sig´nal-ly
sig´nal-man
sig´na-to-ry
sig´na-ture
sign´board
sig´net
sig-nif´i-cance
sig-nif´i-cant
sig-nif´i-cant-ly
sig-ni-fi-ca´tion
sig-nif´i-ca-tive

sig-nif´i-ca-tive-
  ness
sig´ni-fi-a·ble
sig´ni-fied
sig´ni-fier
sig´ni-fy
sig´ni-fy-ing
sign´post
si´lence
si´lenc-er
si´lenc-ing
si´lent
si´lent-ly
sil-hou-ette´
sil-hou-et´ted
sil´i-con
silk´en
silk´i-er
silk´i-ly
silk´i-ness
silk´screen
silk´worm
silk´y
sil´li-ly
sil´li-ness
sil´ly
si´lo
si´los
silt´y
sil´van
sil´ver
sil´ver–plat´ed
sil´ver-smith

sil´ver–tongued´
sil´ver-ware
sil´very
sim´i-lar
sim-i-lar´i-ty
sim´i-lar-ly
sim´i-le
si-mil´i-tude
sim´mer
sim-pat´i-co
sim´per
sim´pered
sim´per-er
sim´per-ing
sim´per-ing-ly
sim´ple
sim´ple–mind´ed
sim´ple–mind´ed-
  ly
sim´ple–mind´ed-
  ness
sim´ple-ness
sim´pler
sim´plest
sim´ple-ton
sim´plex
sim-plic´i-ty
sim-pli-fi-ca´tion
sim´pli-fied
sim´pli-fi-er
sim´pli-fy
sim´pli-fy-ing
sim-plis´tic

sim-plis′ti-cal-ly

sim′ply

sim′u-late

sim′u-lat-ing

sim-u-la′tion

sim′u-la-tive

sim′u-la-tor

si′mul-cast

si-mul-ta-ne′i-ty

si-mul-ta′ne-ous

si-mul-ta′ne-ous-
ly

si-mul-ta′ne-ous-
ness

since

sin-cere′

sin-cere′ly

sin-cere′ness

sin-cer′est

sin-cer′i-ty

sin′e-cure

sin′e-cur-ist

sin′ew

sin′ew-y

sin′ful

sin′ful-ly

sin′ful-ness

sing′a·ble

singe

singed

singe′ing

sing′er

sing′ing

sin′gle

sin′gle–act′ing

sin′gle–ac′tion

sin′gle–breast′ed

sin′gle–dig′it

sin′gle–hand′ed

sin′gle–hand′ed-ly

sin′gle–knit

sin′gle–mind′ed

sin′gle–mind′ed-
ness

sin′gle-ness

sin′gle–phase

sin′gle–space′

sin′gling

sin′gly

sing′song

sin′gu-lar

sin-gu-lar′i-ty

sin′gu-lar-ize

sin′gu-lar-ly

sin′is-ter

sin′is-ter-ly

sin′is-ter-ness

sin′is-tral

sin′is-tral-ly

sink′a·ble

sink′age

sink′er

sink′hole

sink′ing

sin′less

sinned

sin′ner

sin′ning

sin′u-ate

sin′u-ate-ly

sin-u-a′tion

sin-u-os′i-ty

sin′u-ous

sin′u-ous-ly

sin′u-ous-ness

si′nus

si-nus-i′tis

si′phon

sipped

sip′per

sip′ping

sired

si′ren

sir′ing

sir′loin

sis′si-ness

sis′sy

sis′sy-ish

sis′ter

sis′ter-hood

sis′ter–in–law

sis′ter-li-ness

sis′ter-ly

si-tar′

si-tar′ist

sit′com

sit′–in

sit′ter

sit′ting

sit´u-ate	skel´e-tal	skim´mer
sit´u-at-ed	skel´e-tal-ly	skim´ming
sit-u-a´tion	skel´e-ton	skimp´i-est
sit-u-a´tion-al	skel´e-ton-ize	skimp´i-ly
sit-u-a´tion-al-ly	skep´tic	skimp´i-ness
sit´–up	skep´ti-cal	skimp´ing
six´fold	skep´ti-cal-ly	skimp´ing-ly
six´–foot´	skep´ti-cism	skimp´y
six´–pack	sketch	skin–deep´
six´pence	sketch´book	skin´–dive
six´–shoot-er	sketched	skin´flint
six´teen´	sketch´i-est	skin´ful
six´teenth´	sketch´i-ly	skin´head
sixth	sketch´i-ness	skin´less
six´ti-eth	sketch´y	skinned
six´ty	skew´er	skin´ner
six´ty–nine´	skew´ness	skin´ni-est
siz´a-ble	skid´ded	skin´ni-ness
siz´a-ble-ness	skid´der	skin´ning
siz´a-bly	skid´ding	skin´ny
sized	skid´dy	skin´ny–dip
siz´ing	skid´proof	skin´tight´
siz´zle	skied	skip´pa-ble
siz´zled	skies	skip´per
siz´zling	skiff	skip´ping
siz´zling-ly	ski´ing	skip´ping-ly
skate´board	skilled	skir´mish
skat´ed	skil´let	skir´mish-er
skat´er	skill´ful	skirt´ing
skat´ing	skill´ful-ly	skit´ter
ske-dad´dle	skill´ful-ness	skit´ter-y
skeet	skim	skit´tish
skein	skimmed	skit´tish-ly

skit´tish-ness
skit´tles
skive
skiv´er
skoal
skul´dug´ger-y
skulk´er
skulk´ing
skull´cap
sky´–blue´
sky´box
sky´cap
sky´dive
sky´div-er
sky´div-ing
sky´–high
sky´hook
sky´jack
sky´lark
sky´light
sky´line
sky´rock-et
sky´scrap-er
sky´writ-ing
slack´en
slack´ened
slack´er
slack´ness
slacks
slag´gy
slain
slake
slaked

slak´ing
sla´lom
slam´–bang´
slammed
slam´mer
slam´ming
slan´der
slan´der-er
slan´der-ing-ly
slan´der-ous
slan´der-ous-ly
slang´i-ness
slang´y
slant´ing
slant´ing-ly
slant´wise
slap´dash
slap´hap-py
slap´jack
slapped
slap´ping
slap´stick
slash´er
slash´ing
slat´–back
slate
slat´ed
slat´ing
slat´ted
slat´tern
slat´tern-li-ness
slat´tern-ly
slat´ting

slat´y
slaugh´ter
slaugh´ter-er
slaugh´ter-house
slaugh´ter-ous
slave
slav´ery
slav´ish
slav´ish-ly
slav´ish-ness
slay´er
slay´ing
sleaze
slea´zi-er
slea´zi-ly
slea´zi-ness
slea´zy
sled´der
sled´ding
sledge
sledge´ham-mer
sleek´ly
sleek´ness
sleep
sleep´er
sleep´i-ly
sleep´i-ness
sleep´ing
sleep´less
sleep´less-ly
sleep´less-ness
sleep´walk-er
sleep´walk-ing

sleep´wear
sleep´y
sleep´y-head
sleet
sleet´y
sleeve´less
sleigh´ing
sleight
slen´der
slen´der-ize
slen´der-ness
slept
sleuth
slew
slice´a-ble
sliced
slic´er
slic´ing
slick
slick´er
slick´ly
slick´ness
slid´able
slide
slid´er
slid´ing
slight
slight´ing
slight´ing-ly
slight´ly
slight´ness
slime
slim´i-er

slim´i-ly
slim´i-ness
slim´ly
slim´ness
slim´y
sling´–back
sling´er
sling´shot
slink´i-ly
slink´i-ness
slink´ing
slink´y
slip´case
slip´cov-er
slip´knot
slip´–on
slip´page
slipped
slip´per
slip´per-i-ness
slip´pery
slip´ping
slip´shod
slip´stream
slip´–up
slip´way
slith´er
slith´ery
slit´ting
sliv´er
sliv´o-vitz
slob´ber
slob´ber-ing

sloe´berry
sloe´–eyed
slo´gan
slo-gan-eer´
slog´ging
sloped
slop´ing
slopped
slop´pi-ly
slop´pi-ness
slop´ping
slop´py
sloshed
slosh´y
slot
sloth
sloth´ful
sloth´ful-ly
sloth´ful-ness
slot´ted
slouch
slouch´i-ly
slouch´i-ness
slouch´ing
slouch´y
slough
slough´y
slov´en
slov´en-li-ness
slov´en-ly
slow´down
slow´–foot´ed
slow´–foot´ed-ness

slow´ly
slow´ness
slow´poke
slow´–release
slow´–wit´ted
slow´–wit´ted-ly
slow´–wit´ted-ness
sludge
sludg´er
sludg´y
slug´fest
slug´gard
slug´gard-li-ness
slug´gard-ly
slug´ger
slug´gish
slug´gish-ly
slug´gish-ness
sluice´way
sluic´ing
slum´ber
slum´ber-ous
slum´ber-ous-ly
slum´ber-ous-ness
slum´lord
slum´ming
slum´my
slump
slurp
slurred
slur´ring
slur´ry
slush´i-ness

slush´y
slut´tish
slut´tish-ly
slut´tish-ness
sly´ly
sly´ness
smack´er
smack´ing
smack´ing-ly
small´–claims´
small´ish
small´–mind´ed
small´–mind´ed-ly
small´–mind´ed-
  ness
small´ness
small´pox
small´–time´
smarm´i-ness
smarm´y
smart´en
smart´ly
smart´ness
smart´y
smart´y–pants
smashed
smash´er
smash´ing
smash´ing-ly
smash´up
smat´ter-ing
smear
smeared

smear´i-ness
smear´y
smell´er
smell´i-ness
smell´ing
smell´y
smelt´er
smid´gen
smiled
smil´ing
smil´ing-ly
smirk´er
smirk´ing
smirk´ing-ly
smith-er-eens´
smith´y
smit´ten
smock
smock´ing
smog´gy
smok´able
smoke´house
smoke´less
smok´er
smoke´stack
smok´i-er
smok´ing
smok´i-ness
smok´y
smol´der
smol´dered
smol´der-ing
smooch

smooth´bore
smooth´en
smooth´ie
smooth´ly
smooth´ness
smooth´–tongued
smor´gas-bord
smoth´er
smoth´ered
smoth´er-y
smudge
smudg´er
smudg´i-ly
smudg´i-ness
smudg´ing
smudg´y
smug
smug´gle
smug´gler
smug´ly
smug´ness
smut
smut´ti-ly
smut´ti-ness
smut´ty
sna´fu´
snag
snagged
snag´ging
snag´gle-tooth
snag´gle-toothed
snail´like
snake´bite

snake´skin
snak´i-ly
snak´i-ness
snak´y
snap´per
snap´pi-ly
snap´pi-ness
snap´pish
snap´pish-ly
snap´pish-ness
snap´py
snap´shot
snared
snar´ing
snarled
snarl´ing
snarl´ing-ly
snarl´ish
snatch´er
snatch´y
snaz´zy
sneaked
sneak´er
sneak´i-ly
sneak´i-ness
sneak´ing
sneak´y
sneer´ing
sneer´ing-ly
sneezed
sneeze´guard
sneez´er
sneez´ing

snick´er
snick´er-ing
snide´ness
sniff´er
sniff´ing
snif´fle
snif´fler
snif´fly
snif´ter
snig´ger
snipe
snip´er
snip´ing
snipped
snip´pet
snip´pi-er
snip´pi-ly
snip´pi-ness
snip´ping
snip´py
snit
snitch
sniv´el
sniv´el-er
sniv´el-ing
snob´ber-y
snob´bish
snob´by
snook´er
snoop´er
snoop´y
snoot´i-ly
snoot´i-ness

snoot´y
snooze
snored
snor´er
snor´ing
snor´kel-er
snort´er
snort´ing
snout
snow´ball
snow´bank
snow´bird
snow´–blind
snow´bound
snow´drift
snow´fall
snow´flake
snow´i-er
snow´i-ly
snow´i-ness
snow´man
snow´mo-bile
snow´pea
snow´plow
snow´shoe
snow´slide
snow´storm
snow´suit
snow´tire
snow´y
snub
snubbed
snub´ber

snub´bing
snub´–nosed
snuff´box
snuff´er
snuf´fle
snuf´fled
snuf´fler
snuf´fly
snug´ger-y
snug´gle
snug´gled
snug´gling
snug´ly
snug´ness
soak´ing
soap´box
soap´i-er
soap´i-ly
soap´i-ness
soap op´era
soap´stone
soap´suds
soap´y
soar´ing
soar´ing-ly
so´a-ve
sob´bing
so´ber
so´ber-ly
so´ber–mind´ed
so´ber-ness
so´ber-sides
so-bri´e-ty

so´bri-quet
so´–called´
soc´cer
so-cia-bil´i-ty
so´cia-ble
so´cia-ble-ness
so´cia-bly
so´cial
so´cial-ism
so´cial-ist
so-cial-is´tic
so´cial-ite
so-ci-al´i-ty
so-cial-i-za´tion
so´cial-ize
so´cial-iz-er
so´cial-ly
so´cial–mind´ed
so´cial-ness
so-ci´e-tal
so-ci´e-tal-ly
so-ci´e-ty
so-ci-o-ec-o-
    nom´ic
so-ci-o-ec-o-
    nom´i-cal-ly
so´ci-o-log´ic
so´ci-o-log´i-cal
so´ci-o-log´i-cal-ly
so-ci-ol´o-gist
so-ci-ol´o-gy
so´ci-o-path
so-ci-o-path´ic

sock´et	sog´gi-ly	sol-em-ni-za´tion
so´da	sog´gi-ness	sol´em-nize
sod´bust-er	sog´gy	sol´emn-ly
sod´den	soil´age	sol´emn-ness
sod´den-ly	soiled	so´le-noid
sod´den-ness	soil´ure	sole´plate
sod´ding	soi-rée´	so-lic´it
so´di-um	so´journ	so-lic-i-ta´tion
sod´om-ite	so´journ-er	so-lic´i-tor
sod´omy	sol´ace	so-lic´i-tous
so´fa	sol´aced	so-lic´i-tous-ly
sof´fit	sol´ac-er	so-lic´i-tous-ness
soft´–boiled´	sol´ac-ing	so-lic´i-tude
soft´bound	so´lar	sol´id
soft´–core	so-lar´i-um	so´i-dar´i-ty
soft´–cov-er	so-lar-iza´tion	so-lid-i-fi-ca´tion
soft´en	so´lar-ize	so-lid´i-fied
soft´en-er	sol´der	so-lid´i-fi-er
soft´en-ing	sol´der-a-ble	so-lid´i-fy
soft´head	sol´dered	so-lid´i-ty
soft´head´ed	sol´der-er	sol´id–look-ing
soft´head´ed-ness	sol´dier	sol´id-ly
soft´heart-ed	sol´dier-li-ness	sol´id-ness
soft´heart-ed-ly	sol´dier-ly	sol´id–state´
soft´heart-ed-ness	sold´–out´	so-lil´o-quist
soft´ly	sol´e-cism	so-lil´o-quize
soft´ness	sol´e-cist	so-lil´o-quy
soft´–shell	sol´e-cis´tic	sol´ip-sism
soft´–shoe	soled	sol´ip-sist
soft´–soap	sole´ly	sol-ip-sis´tic
soft´–spo´ken	sol´emn	sol´i-taire
soft´ware	so-lem´ni-fy	sol´i-tar-i-ly
soft´y	so-lem´ni-ty	sol´i-tar-i-ness

sol´i-tar-y

sol´i-tude

sol-i-tu-di-nar´i-
an

so´lo

so´lo-ist

sol´stice

sol-sti´tial

sol-u-bil´i-ty

sol´u-ble

sol´u-ble-ness

sol´u-bly

sol´ute

so-lu´tion

solv-a-bil´i-ty

solv´a·ble

solve

solved

sol´ven-cy

sol´vent

solv´ing

so-mat´ic

so-mat´i-cal-ly

so´ma-to-gen´ic

so-ma-tol´o-gy

som´ber-ly

som´ber-ness

som-bre´ro

some´body

some´day

some´how

some´one

some´place

som´er-sault

some´thing

some´time

some´times

some´way

some´what

some´where

som-me-lier´

som-nam´bu-lant

som-nam´bu-late

som-nam-bu-
la´tion

som-nam´bu-lism

som-nam´bu-list

som-nam´bu-
lis´tic

som-ni-fa´cient

som-nif´er-ous

som-nif´ic

som-nil´o-quist

som-nil´o-quy

som´no-lence

som´no-lent

som´no-lent-ly

so´nance

so´nant

so´nar

so-na´ta

song´bird

song´book

song´fest

song´ster

song´stress

song´writ-er

son´ic

son´–in–law

son´net

son´ne-teer´

son´ny

son´o-gram

so-nom´e-ter

so-nor´i-ty

so-no´rous

so-no´rous-ly

so-no´rous-ness

soon´er

soon´est

soothe

soothed

sooth´er

sooth´ing

sooth´ing-ly

sooth´say

sooth´say-er

sooth´say-ing

soot´i-ly

soot´i-ness

soot´y

soph´ism

soph´ist

soph´is-ter

so-phis´tic

so-phis´ti-cal-ly

so-phis´ti-cate

so-phis´ti-cat-ed

so-phis-ti-ca´tion

soph´is-try
soph´o-more
soph-o-mor´ic
soph-o-mor´i-cal-
  ly
so´por
sop-o-rif´er-ous
sop-o-rif´ic
sop´ping
sop´py
so-pra´no
sorb-a·bil´i-ty
sorb´a·ble
sor´be-fa´cient
sor´bet
sor´cer-er
sor´cer-ess
sor´cer-ous
sor´cery
sor´did
sor´did-ly
sor´did-ness
sore´head
sore´head-ed-ness
sore´ly
sore´ness
sor´ghum
so-ror´i-ty
sorp´tion
sorp´tive
sor´rel
sor´ri-ly
sor´ri-ness

sor´row-ful
sor´row-ful-ly
sor´row-ful-ness
sor´ry
sort
sort´a-ble
sort´ed
sor´ter
sor´tie
sort´ing
sot´ted
sot´tish
sot´tish-ly
sot´tish-ness
souf-flé´
sought´-af-ter
soul´ful
soul´ful-ly
soul´ful-ness
soul´less
soul´less-ly
soul´less-ness
soul´-search-ing
sound´a·ble
sound´a-like
sound´board
sound´er
sound´ing
sound´less
sound´less-ly
sound´less-ness
sound´ly
sound´ness

sound´proof
sound´proof-ing
sound´track
soup-çon´
soup´i-er
soup´spoon
soup´y
sour´ball
source´book
source´ful
source´ful-ness
source language
source´less
sour´dough
sour´ish
sour´ly
sour´ness
sour´puss
sou´sa-phone
souse
soused
south´bound
south-east´
south-east´er
south-east´er-ly
south-east´ern
south´er-ly
south´ern
south´ern-er
south´ern-ly
south´ern-most
south´land
south´ward

230

south-west′
south-west′er
south-west′er-ly
south-west′ern
sou-ve-nir′
souv-la′ki
sov′er-eign
sov′er-eign-ty
so′vi-et
soy′a
soy′bean
space′–age
space′borne
space′craft
spaced′–out
space′flight
space′less
space′man
space′port
space′ship
space′shot
space′suit
space′walk
spac′ey
spa′cial
spac′ing
spa′cious
spa′cious-ly
spa′cious-ness
spack′le
spade
spad′ed
spade′ful

spade′work
spad′er
spad′ing
spa-ghet′ti
span
span′dex
span′gle
span′gled
span′gly
span′iel
spank′er
spank′ing
spanned
span′ner
span′ning
spare′a-ble
spared
spare′ly
spare′ness
spare′rib
spar′ing
spar′ing-ly
spar′ing-ness
spark′i-ly
spark′ish
spar′kle
spar′kler
spark′let
spark′like
spar′kling
spar′kling-ly
spar′kly
spark′y

sparred
spar′ring
spar′row
sparse′ly
sparse′ness
spar′si-ty
spasm
spas-mod′ic
spas-mod′i-cal-ly
spas′tic
spas′ti-cal-ly
spate
spa′tial
spa-ti-al′i-ty
spat′ter
spat′ter-ing
spat′ting
spat′u-la
spat′u-late
spawn
spawned
spawn′er
speak′able
speak′easy
speak′er
speak′er-phone
speak′ing
spear′fish
spear′head
spear′mint
spec
spe′cial-ism
spe′cial-ist

spe-ci-al´i-ty
spe-cial-i·za´tion
spe´cial-ize
spe´cial-ly
spe´cial-ty
spe´cie *(money)*
spe´cies *(class)*
spec´i-fi-a·ble
spe-cif´ic
spe-cif´i-cal-ly
spec-i-fi-ca´tion
spec-i-fic´i-ty
spec´i-fied
spec´i-fi-er
spec´i-fy
spec´i-fy-ing
spec´i-men
spe´cious
spe´cious-ly
spe´cious-ness
speck´le
speck´led
speck´ling
specs
spec´ta-cle
spec´ta-cled
spec-tac´u-lar
spec-tac´u-lar-ly
spec´tate
spec´ta-tor
spec´ter
spec´tral
spec-tral´i-ty

spec´tral-ly
spec´tral-ness
spec´tro-gram
spec´tro-graph
spec-tro-graph´ic
spec-trol´o-gy
spec´tro-scope
spec-tro-scop´ic
spec´trum
spec´u-late
spec´u-lat-ing
spec-u-la´tion
spec´u-la-tive
spec´u-la-tive-ly
spec´u-la-tive-ly
spec´u-la-tive-ness
spec´u-la-tor
speech´i-fi-er
speech´i-fy
speech´less
speech´less-ly
speech´less-ness
speed´boat
speed´boat-ing
speed´er
speed´i-ly
speed´i-ness
speed´ing
speed-om´e-ter
speed´–read
speed´ster
speed´–up
speed´way

speed´writ-ing
speed´y
spe´le-ol´o-gist
spe-le-o-log´i-cal
spe-le-ol´o-gist
spe-le-ol´o-gy
spell´bind-er
spell´bind-ing-ly
spell´bound
spell´er
spell´ing
spe-lunk´er
spe-lunk´ing
spend´a-ble
spend´er
spend´ing
spend´thrift
spent
sperm
sphere
spher´i-cal
spher´i-cal-ly
sphe´roid
sphinx
spiced
spic´i-ly
spic´i-ness
spic´ing
spic´y
spi´der
spi´dery
spiel´er
spiff´i-ly

spiff´i-ness
spiff´y
spig´ot
spiked
spik´i-ly
spik´i-ness
spik´ing
spik´y
spill´a-ble
spill´age
spilled
spill´er
spill´ing
spill´–o-ver
spill´proof
spill´way
spin
spin´ach
spi´nal
spin´dle
spin´dling
spin´dly
spin´–dry´
spine´less
spine´less-ly
spine´less-ness
spin´et
spin´ner
spin´ning
spin´–off
spin´ster
spin´ster-ish
spin´y

spi´ral
spi´raled
spi´ral-ing
spi´ral-ly
spire
spir´it
spir´it-ed
spir´it-ed-ly
spir´it-ed-ness
spir´it-ism
spir´it-less
spir´it-less-ly
spir´it-less-ness
spi-ri-to´so
spir´i-tu-al
spir´i-tu-al-ism
spir´i-tu-al-ist
spir-i-tu-al-is´tic
spir-i-tu-al´i-ty
spir´i-tu-al-ize
spir´i-tu-al-ly
spit´ball
spite´ful
spite´ful-ly
spite´ful-ness
spit´ing
spit´ting
spit´tle
splash´down
splash guard
splash´i-ly
splash´i-ness
splash´ing

splash´y
splat´ter
splay
splen´dent-ly
splen´did
splen´did-ly
splen´did-ness
splen-dif´er-ous
splen-dif´er-ous-ly
splen-dif´er-ous-
  ness
splen´dor
splen´dor-ous
splen´drous
spliced
splic´er
splic´ing
splint
splin´ter
splin´tered
split´–lev´el
split´ting
split´–up
splotch´y
splurge
splurged
spoil´age
spoiled
spoil´er
spoil´ing
spoil´sport
spoke
spo´ken

233

spokes´per-son
sponge
sponged
spong´er
spon´gi-ness
spong´ing
spong´y
spon´sor
spon´sor-ship
spon-ta-ne´i-ty
spon-ta´ne-ous
spon-ta´ne-ous-ly
spon-ta´ne-ous-
  ness
spook´i-ness
spook´ish
spook´y
spool´er
spoon´–feed
spoon´ful
spoon´y
spo-rad´ic
spo-rad´i-cal-ly
sport´fish-ing
sport´i-ly
sport´i-ness
sport´ing
sport´ing-ly
spor´tive
spor´tive-ly
spor´tive-ness
sports´cast-er
sports´cast-ing

sports´man
sports´man-like
sports´man-ship
sports´wear
sports´woman
sports´writ-er
sports´writ-ing
sport´y
spot´less
spot´less-ly
spot´less-ness
spot´light
spot´ted
spot´ter
spot´ti-er
spot´ti-ness
spot´ting
spot´ty
spot´–weld
spous´al
spouse
spout´er
sprained
sprang
sprawl´er
sprawl´ing
sprayed
spray´er
spread´er
spread´ing
spright´ful
spright´ful-ly
spright´li-ness

spright´ly
spring´board
spring´er
spring´i-ly
spring´i-ness
spring´ing
spring´–load´ed
spring´time
spring´y
sprin´kle
sprin´kler
sprin´kling
sprint´er
spritz´er
sprock´et
spruced
spruc´ing
spruce´ly
spry´ly
spry´ness
spu-mo´ni
spunk
spunk´i-ly
spunk´i-ness
spunk´y
spu´ri-ous
spu´ri-ous-ness
spurn´ing
spurred
spur´ring
spurt´ed
sput´ter
sput´ter-ing

spy'ing
squab'ble
squab'bled
squab'bler
squab'bling
squad'ron
squal'id
squal'id-ly
squal'id-ness
squall
squal'or
squan'der
squan'dered
squan'der-er
squan'der-ing
square
squared
square'ly
squar'ing
squar'ish
squash'i-ness
squash'ing
squash'y
squat'ly
squat'ness
squat'ted
squat'ter
squat'ting
squat'ty
squawked
squawk'er
squawk'y
squeak'er

squeak'i-ly
squeak'i-ness
squeak'ing
squeak'y
squeak'y–clean'
squeal'er
squeal'ing
squea'mish
squeam'ish-ly
squeam'ish-ness
squee'gee
squeez'a-ble
squeez'a-bly
squeeze'box
squeezed
squeez'er
squeez'ing
squelch
squelched
squelch'er
squig'gle
squig'gly
squint'ed
squint'er
squint'ing
squint'y
squirm
squirm'er
squirm'ing
squirm'y
squirt'ed
squirt'ing
squish'y

stabbed
stab'bing
sta-bil'i-ty
sta-bi-li-za'tion
sta'bi-lize
sta'bi-liz-er
sta'ble
sta'bled
sta'ble-ness
sta'bly
sta'bling
stack'a-ble
stacked
stack'er
sta'di-um
staffed
staff'er
stage'coach
stage'hand
stag'er
stage'struck
stage'y
stag'ger
stag'ger-ing
stag'i-ness
stag'ing
stag'nance
stag'nant
stag'nant-ly
stag'nate
stag'nat-ing
stag-na'tion
stag'y

stain´a-ble
stain´er
stain´ing
stain´less
stair´case
stair´way
stair´well
stake´out
stak´ing
stalac´tite
stalag´mite
stale´mate
stale´ness
stalked
stalk´er
stalk´ing
stal´wart
stam´i-na
stam´mer
stam´mer-er
stam´mer-ing
stamped
stam-pede´
stamp´er
stance
stand´a-lone
stan´dard–bear-er
stan-dard-i-za´-
  tion
stan´dard-ize
stand´ing
stand´off´ish
stand´out

sta´ple
sta´pled
sta´pler
sta´pling
star´board
starch´i-ness
starch´y
star´–crossed
star´dom
stared
star´er
star´gaze
star´gaz-er
star´gaz-ing
star´ing
stark´ly
stark´ness
star´less
star´let
star´light
starred
star´ri-ness
star´ring
star´ry
star´ry–eyed
star´–shaped
star´ship
star´–stud-ded
start´er
star´tle
star´tling
star´tling-ly
start´–up

star-va´tion
starve
starved
starve´ling
starv´er
starv´ing
stat´ed
state´hood
state´li-ness
state´ly
state´ment
state´room
states´man
states´man-like
state´wide
stat´ic
sta´tion
sta´tion-ary
sta´tio-ner
sta´tio-nery
sta´tion-mas-ter
sta-tis´tic
sta-tis´ti-cal
sta-tis´ti-cal-ly
stat-is-ti´cian
sta-tis´tics
stat´u-ary
stat´ue
stat-u-esque´
stat´u-ette´
stat´ure
sta´tus
stat´ute

stat´u-to-ry
staunch´ly
staunch´ness
stay´ing
stead´fast
stead´fast-ly
stead´fast-ness
stead´i-ly
stead´i-ness
stead´y
stealth´ful
stealth´ful-ly
stealth´i-ly
stealth´i-ness
stealth´y
steam´bath
steam´boat
steam´er
steam´i-ness
steam´roll-er
steam´ship
steam´y
steel´i-ness
steel´work-er
steel´y
steep´en
steep´er
stee´ple
stee´ple-chase
stee´pled
stee´ple-jack
stee´ple-less
steep´ly

steep´ness
steer´age
steer´ing
stein
stel´lar
stemmed
stem´ming
stem´ware
sten´cil
sten´ciled
sten´cil-ing
sten´o
ste-nog´ra-pher
sten´o-graph´ic
sten-to´ri-an
step´broth-er
step´child
step´daugh-ter
step´fa-ther
step´lad-der
step´moth-er
step´par-ent
stepped´–up´
step´per
step´ping
step´sis-ter
ster-e-o-phon´ic
ster´e-o-type
ster-e-o-typ´i-cal
ster´ile
ster´ile-ness
ste-ril´i-ty
ster-i-li-za´tion

ster´i-lize
ster´i-liz-er
stern´ly
stern´most
stern´ness
ster´oid
steth´o-scope
ste´ve-dore
stew´ard
stew´ard-ess
stew´ard-ship
stick´ball
stick´er
stick´i-er
stick´i-ness
stick´ing
stick´–in–the–
  mud
stick´ler
stick´pin
stick´y
stiff´en
stiff´en-er
stiff´en-ing
stiff´ly
stiff´–necked´
stiff´ness
sti´fle
sti´fling
sti´fling-ly
stig´ma
stig´ma-tize
sti-let´to

237

still´born
still´ness
stilt´ed
stim´u-lant
stim´u-late
stim-u-la´tion
stim´u-la-tor
stim´u-li
stim´u-lus
sting´er
stin´gi-er
stin´gi-ly
stin´gi-ness
sting´ing
stin´gy
stink´er
stink´ing
stink´y
stint´ing
sti´pend
stip´ple
stip´pled
stip´pling
stip´u-la-ble
stip´u-late
stip´u-lat-ing
stip-u-la´tion
stip´u-la-tor
stip´u-la-to-ry
stir´–fry
stirred
stir´ring
stitch´er

stitch´ing
stock-ade´
stock´bro-ker
stock´hold-er
stock´ing
stock´pile
stock´room
stock´y
stodg´i-ness
stodg´y
sto´gie
sto´gy
sto´ic
sto´i-cal
sto´i-cism
stoke
stoked
stok´er
stok´ing
stole
sto´len
stol´id
stol´id-ly
stom´ach
stom´ach-ache
stone´–broke
stone china
stone crush´er
stone´cut-ter
stone´–deaf
ston´i-ly
ston´i-ness
ston´ing

ston´y
stop´gap
stop´light
stop´–off
stop´o-ver
stopped
stop´per
stop´ping
stop´watch
stor´age
stored
store´front
store´house
store´keep-er
store´room
sto´ried
stor´ing
storm´i-ly
storm´i-ness
storm´proof
storm´y
sto´ry-board
sto´ry-book
sto´ry-tell-er
stout´–heart´ed
stout´–heart´ed-ly
stout´–heart´ed-
  ness
stout´ish
stout´ly
stout´ness
stove´pipe
stow´age

strad´dle
strad´dler
strad´dling
strag´gle
strag´gler
strag´gling
strag´gly
straight´–ahead
straight´away
straight´en-er
straight´–faced
straight-for´ward
straight´ness
straight´–out´
strained
strain´er
strait´jacket
strait´–laced
strange´ly
strange´ness
strang´er
stran´gle
stran´gler
stran´gling
stran´gu-late
stran-gu-la´tion
strap´less
strapped
strap´ping
stra´ta
stra-te´gic
stra-te´gi-cal
stra-te´gi-cal-ly

strat´e-gist
strat´e-gy
strat-i-fi-ca´tion
strat´i-fied
strat´i-form
strat´i-fy
strat´i-fy-ing
strat´o-sphere
straw´ber-ry
stray´er
stray´ing
streak´i-ness
streak´y
stream
stream´bed
stream´er
stream´ing
stream´let
stream´lined
street´car
street´light
street´–smart
strength´en
strength´en-er
strength´en-ing
stren´u-ous
stren´u-ous-ly
stren´u-ous-ness
stressed´–out´
stress´ful
stress´ful-ly
stress´less
stretch´a-ble

stretch´er
stretch´er–bear-er
stretch´i-ness
strewn
stri´ate
stri´at´ed
stri-a´tion
strick´en
strict´ly
strict´ness
stric´ture
stride
stri´dence
stri´den-cy
stri´dent
stri´dent-ly
strid´er
strid´ing
strike´break-er
strike´break-ing
strike´out
strik´er
strik´ing
strik´ing-ly
strin´gen-cy
strin´gent
strin´gent-ly
string´er
string´i-ness
string´ing
string´y
striped
strip´er

strip´ing	strut´ting	stu-pen´dous-ly
strip´ling	stub´ble	stu´pid
stripped	stub´born-ly	stu-pid´i-ty
stripped´–down´	stub´born-ness	stu´pid-ly
strip´per	stuc´co	stu´pid-ness
strip´ping	stuck´–up	stu´por
strive	stu´dent	stur´di-ness
striv´en	stud´ied	stur´dy
striv´ing	stu´dio	stur´geon
stroke	stu´di-ous	stut´ter
stroked	stu´di-ous-ly	stut´ter-er
strok´er	stu´di-ous-ness	stut´ter-ing
strok´ing	stud´y	style
stroll´er	stud´y-ing	styled
strong	stuffed	style´less
strong´box	stuff´i-ly	styl´ing
strong´hold	stuff´i-ness	styl´ish
strong´–mind´ed	stuff´ing	styl´ish-ly
strong´–willed´	stuff´y	styl´ish-ness
struc´tur-al	stul´ti-fied	styl´ist
struc´tur-al-ize	stul´ti-fy	styl´ize
struc´tur-al-ly	stul´ti-fy-ing	sty´lus
struc´ture	stum´ble	sty´mie
strug´gle	stum´bler	sty´mied
strug´gled	stum´bling	suave´ly
strug´gler	stunned	suave´ness
strug´gling	stun´ning	suav´i-ty
strum´mer	stun´ning-ly	sub´com-mit-tee
strum´ming	stunt´ed	sub-con´scious
strum´pet	stu´pe-fied	sub-con´scious-ly
strung´–out´	stu´pe-fy	sub-con´scious-
strut´ted	stu´pe-fy-ing	ness
strut´ter	stu-pen´dous	sub-con´tract

sub´con-trac-tor
sub´cul-ture
sub´di-vide
sub´di-vid-er
sub´di-vid-ing
sub´di-vi-sion
sub-due´
sub-dued´
sub-du´er
sub-du´ing
sub´ject *(n., adj.)*
sub-ject´ *(v.)*
sub-jec´tion
sub-jec´tive
sub-jec´tive-ly
sub-jec´tive-ness
sub-jec-tiv´i-ty
sub´ju-gate
sub´ju-gat-ing
sub-ju-ga´tion
sub´lease´
sub´let´
sub´let´ting
sub-lime´
sub-lime´ly
sub-lim´in-al
sub-lim´in-al-ly
sub´ma-rine
sub-ma-rin´er
sub-merge´
sub-merged´
sub-merse´
sub-mersed´

sub-mers´i-ble
sub-mer´sion
sub-min´i-a-ture
sub-mis´sion
sub-mis´sive
sub-mis´sive-ly
sub-mis´sive-ness
sub-mit´ted
sub-mit´ter
sub-mit´ting
sub-or´di-nate
sub-or´di-nate-ly
sub-or-di-na´tion
sub-poe´na
sub-poe´naed
sub´rou-tine
sub-scribe´
sub-scrib´er
sub-scrib´ing
sub-script
sub´sec´tion
sub´se-quent
sub´se-quent-ly
sub-ser´vi-ence
sub-ser´vi-ent
sub-ser´vi-ent-ly
sub-side´
sub-sid´ence
sub-sid´i-ar-y
sub-sid´ing
sub´si-dize
sub´si-dy
sub-sist´

sub-sist´ence
sub-sist´ent
sub´stance
sub-stand´ard
sub-stan´tial
sub-stan´tial-ly
sub-stan´ti-ate
sub-stan-ti-a´tion
sub´stan-tive
sub´sta-tion
sub´sti-tute
sub´sti-tut-ed
sub´sti-tut-ing
sub-sti-tu´tion
sub´strate
sub´ter-fuge
sub-ter-ra´ne-an
sub-ter-ra´ne-ous
sub´ti-tle
sub´tle
sub´tle-ness
sub´tle-ty
sub´tly
sub´to-tal
sub-tract´
sub-trac´tion
sub-trac´tive
sub-trop´ics
sub´urb
sub-ur´ban
sub-ur´ban-ite
sub-ur´bi-a
sub-ver´sive

sub-vert′
sub′way
sub–ze′ro
suc-cess′ful
suc-cess′ful-ly
suc-ces′sion
suc-ces′sive-ly
suc-ces′sor
suc-cinct′
suc-cinct′ly
suc-cinct′ness
suc′cor
suc′co-ry
suc′cu-lence
suc′cu-lent
suc-cumb′
suck′er
suck′le
suck′ling
suc′tion
sud′den-ly
sud′den-ness
suds-y
sued
suede
su′et
suf′fer
suf′fer-ance
suf′fer-er
suf′fer-ing
suf-fice′
suf-ficed′
suf-fi′cien-cy

suf-fi′cient
suf-fi′cient-ly
suf-fic′ing
suf′fix
suf′fo-cate
suf′fo-cat-ing
suf-fo-ca′tion
suf′frage
suf′frag-ette′
suf′frag-ist
suf-fuse′
suf-fus′ing
suf-fu′sion
suf-fu′sive
sug′ar-free
sug′ar-i-ness
sug′ar-less
sug′ar-plum
sug′ar-y
sug-gest′
sug-gest′i-ble
sug-gest′i-bly
sug-ges′tion
sug-ges′tive
sug-ges′tive-ly
su′i-ci′dal
su′i-cide
suit′a-ble
suit′a-bly
suit′case
suite
suit′ing
suit′or

sul′fate
sul′fide
sul′fite
sul′fur
sul-fu′ric
sul′fu-rous
sulk′i-ly
sulk′i-ness
sulk′y
sul′len-ly
sul′len-ness
sul′lied
sul′ly
sul′tri-er
sul′tri-ness
sul′try
sum′mable
sum-mar′i-ly
sum′ma-rize
sum′ma-ry
sum-ma′tion
sum′mer
sum′mer-house
sum′mer-sault
sum′mer-time
sum′mery
sum′ming-up
sum′mit
sum′mon
sum′moned
sum′mon-er
sum′mon-ing
sum′mons

sump´tu-ous
sump´tu-ous-ly
sump´tu-ous-ness
sun´beam
sun´burn
sun´burned
sun´dae
sun´der
sun´di-al
sun´down
sun´dried
sun´dry
sun´glass-es
sunk´en
sun´lamp
sun´light
sun´lit
sun´ni-er
sun´ning
sun´ny
sun´rise
sun´room
sun´screen
sun´set
sun´shine
sun´stroke
sun´tan
su´per
su-per-
   abun´dance
su-per-abun´dant
su-perb´
su-perb´ly

su-per-cil´i-ous
su´per-com-put-er
su-per-con-duc´-
   tor
su-per-e-go
su-per-fi´cial
su-per-fi-ci-al´i-ty
su-per-fi´cial-ly
su-per´flu-ous
su-per´flu-ous-ly
su´per-he-ro
su´per-high-way
su-per-hu´man
su-per-hu´man-ly
su´per-im-pose´
su-per-in-tend´
su-per-in-tend´ent
su-pe´ri-or
su-pe-ri-or´i-ty
su-per´la-tive
su-per´la-tive-ly
su´per-mar-ket
su-per-nat´u-ral
su-per-no´va
su´per-nu´mer-
   ary
su-per-sede´
su´per-sed´ing
su-per-son´ic
su´per-star
su-per-sti´tion
su-per-sti´tious
su-per-sti´tious-ly

su´per-struc-ture
su´per-vise
su´per-vis-ing
su´per-vi´sion
su´per-vi-sor
su´per-vi´so-ry
sup´per
sup´per-time
sup-plant´
sup-plant´er
sup´ple
sup´ple-ment
sup-ple-men´tal
sup-ple-men´tal-ly
sup´ple-men´tary
sup´ple-ness
sup´pli-cant
sup´pli-cate
sup´pli-cat-ing
sup-pli-ca´tion
sup-plied´
sup-pli´er
sup-ply´
sup-ply´ing
sup-port´a-ble
sup-port´er
sup-port´ing
sup-port´ive
sup-pos´a-bly
sup-pose´
sup-posed´
sup-pos-ed´ly
sup-pos´ing

sup-po-si´tion
sup-pos´i-to-ry
sup-press´
sup-pres´sant
sup-pres´sion
sup-pres´sor
su-prem´a-cy
su-preme´
su-preme´ly
sur-cease´
sur´charge
sure´fire´
sure´foot-ed
sure´ly
sur´e-ty
sur´face
sur´faced
sur´fac-er
sur´fac-ing
surf´board
sur´feit
surf´er
surf´ing
surge
sur´geon
sur´gery
sur´gi-cal
sur´gi-cal-ly
surg´ing
sur´li-ness
sur´ly
sur-mise´
sur-mis´ing

sur-mount´
sur-mount´a-ble
sur-mount´ed
sur´name
sur-pass´
sur-pass´ing
sur´plice
sur´plus
sur-pris´able
sur-prise´
sur-prised´
sur-pris´ing
sur-pris´ing-ly
sur-re´al
sur-re´al-ist
sur-ren´der
sur-ren´der-er
sur-rep-ti´tious
sur-rep-ti´tious-ly
sur´rey
sur´ro-gate
sur-round´ed
sur-round´ing
sur´tax
sur-veil´lance
sur-vey´ *(v.)*
sur´vey *(n.)*
sur-vey´ing
sur-vey´or
sur-viv´a-ble
sur-viv´al
sur-viv´al-ist
sur-vive´

sur-vi´vor
sus-cep-ti-bil´i-ty
sus-cep´ti-ble
sus-cep´tive
sus´pect *(n.)*
sus-pect´ *(v.)*
sus-pend´ed
sus-pend´er
sus-pend´i-ble
sus-pense´
sus-pense´ful
sus-pen´sion
sus-pi´cion
sus-pi´cious
sus-pi´cious-ly
sus-pi´cious-ness
sus-tain´
sus-tain´a-ble
sus-tained´
sus-tain´ing
sus´te-nance
su´ture
su´tur-ing
svelte
swabbed
swab´ber
swab´bing
swad´dle
swad´dled
swad´dling
swag´ger
swag´ger-ing
swag´ger-ing-ly

swal´low
swal´low-er
swamp
swamp´i-ness
swamp´land
swamp´y
swank´i-ness
swank´y
swarmed
swarm´ing
swarth´i-ness
swarth´y
swash´buck-ler
swash´buck-ling
swathe
swat´ter
sway´back
sway´backed
sway´ing
swear´ing
sweat´band
sweat´i-ness
sweat´pants
sweat´shirt
sweat´shop
sweat´y
sweep´er
sweep´ing
sweep´stakes
sweet´–and–sour´
sweet´bread
sweet´en
sweet´en-er

sweet´en-ing
sweet´heart
sweet´ie
sweet´ish
sweet´ly
sweet´meats
sweet´ness
sweet´shop
swelled
swell´ing
swel´ter
swel´ter-ing
swept´back
swerved
swerv´ing
swift´ly
swift´–foot´ed
swift´ness
swim´mer
swim´ming
swin´dle
swin´dler
swin´dling
swing´er
swing´ing
swiped
swip´ing
swirl´ing
swirl´y
switch´board
switch´er
switch´man
switch´yard

swiv´el
swiv´eled
swiv´el-ing
swiz´zle
swol´len
swoon´ing
sword´fish
sword´play
swords´man
syc´o-phant
sy-co´sis
syl-lab´ic
syl-lab-i-ca´tion
syl-lab´i-fy
syl´la-ble
syl´la-bub
sylph´like
syl´van
sym-bi´o-sis
sym-bi-ot´ic
sym´bol
sym-bol´ic
sym-bol´i-cal-ly
sym´bol-ism
sym´bol-ize
sym-met´ri-cal
sym´me-try
sym-pa-thet´ic
sym´pa-thize
sym´pa-thiz-er
sym´pa-thiz-ing
sym´pa-thy
sym-phon´ic

sym-phon´i-cal-ly
sym´pho-ny
sym-po´si-um
symp´tom
symp-to-mat´ic
syn´a-gogue
syn´chro-nize
syn´chro-niz-ing
syn´co-pate
syn´co-pat-ed
syn´co-pat-ing
syn-co-pa´tion
syn´di-cate
syn´di-cat-ing
syn-di-ca´tion
syn´di-ca-tor
syn´drome
syn´er-gy
syn´od
syn´o-nym
syn-on´y-mous
syn-on´y-mous-ly
syn-op´sis
syn´tax
syn´the-sis
syn´the-size
syn´the-siz-er
syn´the-siz-ing
syn-thet´ic
syn-thet´i-cal-ly
sy´phon
sy-ringe´
syr´up

syr´up-y
sys´tem
sys-tem-at´ic
sys-tem-at´i-cal-ly
sys´tem-a-tize
sys-tem´ic
sys-tol´ic

T

tabbed
tab´bing
tab´by
tab´er-na-cle
ta´ble
tab´leau
tab´leaux
ta´ble-cloth
ta´ble-ful
ta´ble–hop
ta´ble-land
tab´let
ta´ble-top
ta´ble-ware
ta´bling
tab´loid
ta-boo´
tab´u-lar
tab´u-late
tab´u-lat-ing
tab-u-la´tion
ta-chom´e-ter
tac´it
tac´it-ly

tac´i-turn
tac-i-tur´ni-ty
tac´i-turn-ly
tack´i-ness
tack´le
tack´ler
tack´less
tack´ling
tack´y
tact´ful
tact´ful-ly
tact´ful-ness
tac´tic
tac´ti-cal
tac´ti-cal-ly
tac-ti´cian
tac´tics
tac´tile
tac-til´i-ty
tact´less
tact´less-ly
tad´pole
taf´fe-ta
taf´fy
tag´a-long
tagged
tag´ging
tail´board
tailed
tail´gate
tail´ing
tail´less
tail´light

tai´lor	tam´able	tank´ful
tai´lored	tam´bou-rine´	tanned
tai´lor-ing	tam´a-ble	tan´ner
tai´lor–made´	tame´a-ble	tan´nery
tail´pipe	tamed	tan´nic
tail´spin	tame´ly	tan´nin
tail´wind	tame´ness	tan´ning
taint	tam´er	tan´nish
take´a-way	tam´ing	tan´ta-lize
tak´en	tamp	tan´ta-liz-er
take´out	tam´per	tan´ta-liz-ing-ly
take´o-ver	tan´dem	tant´amount
tak´er	tan´ge-lo	tan´trum
tak´ing	tan´gent	taped
talc	tan-gen´tial	tape´line
tal´cum	tan-gen´tial-ly	ta´per
tale´bear-er	tan´ger-ine´	tap´er
tal´ent-ed	tan-gi-bil´i-ty	ta´per-ing
tale´tell-er	tan´gi-ble	ta´per-ing-ly
tale´tell-ing	tan´gi-ble-ness	tap´es-tried
tal´is-man	tan´gi-bly	tap´es-try
talk´a-thon	tang´i-ness	tape´worm
talk´a-tive	tan´gle	tap-i-o´ca
talk´a-tive-ly	tan´gled	tapped
talk´a-tive-ness	tan´gle-ment	tap´per
talk´er	tan´gler	tap´ping
talk´i-ness	tan´gling	tap´room
talk´ing-to	tan´gly	tap´root
tal´lied	tan´go	tar-an-tel´la
tall´ness	tan´goed	ta-ran´tu-la
tal´low	tang´y	tar´di-ly
tal´ly	tan´kard	tar´di-ness
ta´lus	tank´er	tar´dy

tar´get	taste´less-ness	taw´ni-ness
tar´get-a-ble	taste´mak-er	tawn´y
tar´iff	tast´er	tax-a-bil´i-ty
tar-na´tion	tast´i-ness	tax´a-ble
tar´nish	tast´ing	tax´a-ble-ness
tar´nish-able	tast´y	tax-a´tion
ta´rot	tat´ter	tax´–ex-empt´
tar´pa-per	tat´tered	tax´–free
tar-pau´lin	tat´ter-sall	tax´i
tar´pon	tat´ting	tax´i-cab
tar´ra-gon	tat´tle	tax´i-der-mist
tarred	tat´tler	tax´i-der-my
tar´ried	tat´tle-tale	tax´ied
tar´ring	tat-too´	tax´ing
tar´ry	tat-too´er	tax´pay-er
tar´ry-ing	taught	tax´pay-ing
tar´sus	taunt´er	tea´cake
tar´tan	taunt´ing	teach´a-ble
tar´tar	taunt´ing-ly	teach´a-bly
tart´ish	taupe	teach´er
tart´ly	taut´en	teach´–in
tart´ness	taut´ly	teach´ing
tart´y	taut´ness	tea´cup
task´mas-ter	tau-to-log´ic	tea´cup-ful
tas´sel	tau-to-log´i-cal	tea´house
tas´seled	tau-to-log´i-cal-ly	tea´ket-tle
tas´sel-ing	tau-tol´o-gy	team´mate
taste	tav´ern	team´ster
taste´ful	ta-ver´na	team´work
taste´ful-ly	taw´dri-ly	tea´pot
taste´ful-ness	taw´dri-ness	tear´a-ble
taste´less	taw´dry	tear´a-way
taste´less-ly	tawn´i-er	tear´drop

tear´ful
tear´ful-ly
tear´ful-ness
tear´i-ly
tear´i-ness
tear´ing
tear´ing-ly
tear´jerk-er
tear´less
tea´room
tear´–stained
tear´y
teas´a-ble
teased
teas´er
teas´ing
teas´ing-ly
tea´spoon
tea´spoon-ful
tea´time
tech
tech´ie
tech´ni-cal
tech-ni-cal´i-ty
tech´ni-cal-ly
tech-ni´cian
tech´nics
tech-nique´
tech´no-crat
tech-nol´o-gy
tech´y
tec-ton´ic
tec-ton´i-cal-ly

tec-ton´ics
ted´dy
te´di-ous
te´di-ous-ly
te´di-ous-ness
te´di-um
teem´ing
teen´age
teen´–ag´er
teen´sy
teen´y-bop-per
tee´ny–wee´ny
tee´ter-board
teethe
teethed
teeth´ing
tee-to´tal
tee´to-tal-er
teg´u-ment
teg-u-men´tal
tel´e-cast
tel´e-cast-er
tel-e-com-mu´ni-
　cate
tel-e-com-mu-ni-
　ca´tions
tel´e-com-mut-ing
tel´e-con-fer-ence
tel´e-gram
tel´e-graph
te-leg´ra-pher
tel-e-graph´ic
te-leg´ra-phy

tel-e-ki-ne´sis
tel-e-ki-net´ic
tel´e-mar-ket-er
tel´e-mar-ket-ing
te-lem´e-try
tel-e-path´ic
tel-e-path´i-cal-ly
te-lep´a-thy
tel´e-phone
tel-e-phon´ic
tel´e-pho´to
tel´e-port
tel-e-por-ta´tion
tel´e-scope
tel´e-scop´ic
tel´e-scop´i-cal-ly
tel´e-thon
tel´e-vise
tel´e-vi-sion
tel´ex
tell´a-ble
tell´er
tell´ing
tell´ing-ly
tell´tale
te-mer´i-ty
tem´peh
tem´per
tem´per-a
tem´per-a-ment
tem´per-a-men´tal
tem´per-a-men´-
　tal-ly

tem´per-ance
tem´per-ate
tem´per-ate-ly
tem´per-ate-ness
tem´per-a-ture
tem´pered
tem´per-er
tem´pest
tem-pes´tu-ous
tem-pes´tu-ous-ly
tem-pes´tu-ous-
  ness
tem´plar
tem´plate
tem´ple
tem´plet
tem´po
tem´po-ral
tem´po-ral-ly
tem´po-rar´i-ly
tem´po-rar-i-ness
tem´po-rar-y
tem´po-rize
tempt´a-ble
temp-ta´tion
tempt´er
tempt´ing
tempt´ing-ly
tempt´ing-ness
tempt´ress
tem-pu´ra
ten´a-ble
ten´a-ble-ness

ten´a-bly
te-na´cious
te-na´cious-ly
te-na´cious-ness
te-nac´i-ty
ten´an-cy
ten´ant
tend´en-cy
ten-den´tious
ten-den´tious-ly
ten-den´tious-ness
tend´er
ten´der
ten-der-a-bil´i-ty
ten´der-a-ble
ten´der-foot
ten´der-heart-ed
ten´der-ize
ten´der-iz-er
ten´der-loin
ten´der-ly
ten´der-ness
ten-di-ni´tis
ten´don
ten´dril
ten´e-ment
ten´et
ten´fold
ten´nis
ten´on
ten´or
ten´pins
tense

tense´ly
tense´ness
ten´si-ble
ten´sile
ten´sile-ly
ten´sile-ness
ten´sion
ten´sion-less
ten´sor
ten´–speed
ten´–spot
ten´ta-cle
ten´ta-cled
tent´age
ten´ta-tive
ten´ta-tive-ly
ten´ta-tive-ness
tent´ed
tent´er
ten´ter-hook
tent´mak-er
ten´u-ous
ten´u-ous-ly
ten´u-ous-ness
ten´ure
tep´id
tep´id-ly
tep´id-ness
te-qui´la
ter-i-ya´ki
term´er
ter´mi-na-ble
ter´mi-na-bly

ter´mi-nal
ter´mi-nal-ly
ter´mi-nate
ter-mi-na´tion
ter´mi-na-tive
ter´mi-na-tive-ly
ter´mi-na-tor
ter-mi-nol´o-gy
ter´mi-nus
ter´mite
ter´ra
ter´race
ter´ra-cot´ta
ter-rain´
ter´ra-pin
ter-raz´zo
ter´ri-ble
ter´ri-ble-ness
ter´ri-bly
ter´ri-er
ter-rif´ic
ter-rif´i-cal-ly
ter´ri-fied
ter´ri-fy
ter´ri-fy-ing-ly
ter-rine´
ter-ri-to´ri-al
ter-ri-to´ri-al-ize
ter-ri-to´ri-al-ly
ter´ri-to-ry
ter´ror
ter´ror-ism
ter´ror-ist

ter´ror-ize
ter´ror-iz-er
ter´ry-cloth
terse´ly
terse´ness
ter´ti-ar-y
test´a-ble
tes´ta-ment
tes´tate
test´–drive
test´er
tes´ti-fi-er
tes´ti-fy
tes´ti-ly
tes-ti-mo´ni-al
tes´ti-mo-ny
tes´ti-ness
tes-tos´ter-one
test´–tube
tes´ty
tet´a-nus
tet´a-ny
tête–à–tête
teth´er
teth´ered
te´trarch
text´book
tex´tile
tex´tu-al
tex´ture
thank´ful
thank´ful-ly
thank´ful-ness

thank´less
thanks´giv´ing
thank´–you
that
thatch
thatch´er
the´a-ter
the´a-ter-go-er
the´a-ter–in–the–
　round´
the´a-tre (Br.)
the-at´ri-cal
the-at-ri-cal´i-ty
the-at´ri-cal-ly
the-at´rics
their
the-mat´ic
the-mat´i-cal-ly
theme
them-selves´
thence´forth
the-oc´ra-cy
the-o-crat´ic
the-o-crat´i-cal
the-o-lo´gian
the-o-log´i-cal
the-ol´o-gize
the-ol´o-giz-er
the-ol´o-gy
the´o-rem
the-o-ret´i-cal
the-o-ret´ics
the´o-rist

the´o-rize	thick´et	thir´teenth´
the´o-ry	thick´–head-ed	thir´ti-eth
the-os´o-phy	thick´ish	thir´ty
ther´a-peu´tic	thick´ness	this´tle
ther´a-peu´ti-cal-ly	thick´set´	thith´er
	thick´–skinned´	thong
ther´a-pist	thief	tho´rax
ther´a-py	thieve	thorn´bush
there´abouts	thiev´ery	thorn´i-ly
there´af´ter	thieves	thorn´i-ness
there´by´	thiev´ing	thorn´less
there´fore´	thiev´ish	thorn´like
there-in´	thiev´ish-ly	thorn´y
there-in-af´ter	thiev´ish-ness	thor´ough
there-of´	thigh´bone	thor´ough-bred
there-to´	thim´ble	thor´ough-fare
there-to-fore´	thim´ble-ful	thor´ough-go-ing
there´upon´	think´a-ble	thor´ough-ly
there-with´	think´a-bly	thor´ough-ness
ther´mal	think´er	thought´ful
ther´mo-cou-ple	think´ing	thought´ful-ly
ther-mo-dy-nam´-ics	thin´ly	thought´ful-ness
	thin´ner	thought´less
ther-mog´ra-phy	thin´ness	thought´less-ly
ther-mom´e-ter	thin´–skinned´	thought´less-ness
ther´mo-nu´cle-ar	third´–class	thought´–out´
ther´mo-stat	third´–degree´	thou´sand
ther´mo-stat´ic	third´ly	thou´sandth
the-sau´rus	third´–rate´	thrash´er
the´sis	thirst´i-ly	thrash´ing
thi-am´ine	thirst´i-ness	thread´bare
thick´en	thirst´y	thread´er
thick´en-ing	thir´teen´	thread´worm

thread´y
threat´en
threat´en-ing
threat´en-ing-ly
three´–cor´nered
three´–di-men´-
  sion-al
three´fold
three´–leg´ged
three´pence
three´pen-ny
three´–phase
three´–piece´
three´–ply´
three´–quar´ter
three´–ring
three´some
three´–speed
three´–wheel´er
thresh´er
thresh´ing
thresh´old
threw
thrice
thrift´i-er
thrift´i-ly
thrift´i-ness
thrift´shop
thrift´y
thrill´er
thrill´ing
thrill´ing-ly
thrive

thriv´ing
throat´i-ly
throat´i-ness
throat´y
throb´bing
throb´bing-ly
throe
throm-bo´sis
throne
throng
throt´tle
throt´tled
through-out´
throw´a-way
throw´back
thrust´er
thrust´ing
thru´way
thug´ger-y
thug´gish
thumb´hole
thumb´nail
thumb´print
thumb´screw
thumbs´–down
thumbs´–up
thumb´tack
thump´er
thump´ing
thun´der
thun´der-a-tion
thun´der-bolt
thun´der-clap

thun´der-cloud
thun´der-head
thun´der-ing
thun´der-ing-ly
thun´der-ous
thun´der-ous-ly
thun´der-show-er
thun´der-storm
thun´der-struck
thus´ly
thwart
thyme
thy´roid
thy-roid-ec´to-my
ti-ar´a
tick´er
tick´et
tick´et-er
tick´ing
tick´le
tick´ler
tick´lish
tick´lish-ly
tick´lish-ness
tid´al
tid´bit
tide´land
tide´wa-ter
ti´di-ly
ti´di-ness
ti´dings
ti´dy
tie´back

253

tie′break-er
tie′–dye
tie′–dye-ing
tie′pin
tiered
tight′en
tight′en-er
tight′en-ing
tight′–fist′ed
tight′–fist′ed-ness
tight′–knit′
tight′–lipped
tight′ly
tight′ness
tight′rope
tight′wad
ti′gress
tiled
til′ing
till′age
till′er
tilt′a-ble
tilt′er
tim′ber
tim′bered
tim′ber-land
tim′ber-line
tim′bre
time′card
time′–con-sum′-
  ing
time′–hon′ored
time′keep-er

time′less
time′less-ly
time′less-ness
time′li-er
time′li-ness
time′ly
time′–out
time′piece
tim′er
time′sav-ing
time′–share
time′ta-ble
time′–test-ed
time′worn
tim′id
ti-mid′i-ty
tim′id-ly
tim′id-ness
tim′ing
tim′o-rous
tim′o-rous-ly
tim′o-rous-ness
tinc′ture
tin′der-box
tin′foil
tinge′ing
tin′gle
tin′gled
tin′gler
tin′gly
tin′gling
ti′ni-er
ti′ni-ness

tin′ker
tin′ker-er
tin′ner
tin′ni-er
tin′ni-ly
tin′ni-ness
tin′ny
tin′sel
tin′seled
tin′sel-ly
tin′smith
tint′er
tin′type
tin′work
ti′ny
tip′off
tip′per
tip′ping
tip′ple
tip′si-ly
tip′si-ness
tip′ster
tip′sy
tip′toe
tip′–top
ti′rade
tired
tired′ly
tire′less
tire′less-ly
tire′less-ness
tire′some
tire′some-ly

tir´ing
tis´sue
ti´tan
ti-tan´ic
ti-ta´ni-um
tithe
tith´er
tith´ing
tit´il-late
tit´il-lat-ing
tit-il-la´tion
tit´il-la-tive
ti´tle
ti´tled
ti´tle-hold-er
tit´ter
tit´ter-ing
tit´u-lar
toad´ish
toad´stool
toad´y
to´–and–fro´
toast´er
toast´mas-ter
toast´mis-tress
toast´i-ness
toast´y
to-bac´co
to-bac´co-nist
to-bog´gan-er
to-bog´gan-ing
to-bog´gan-ist
to-day´

tod´dle
tod´dler
tod´dy
to-do´
toe´hold
toe´nail
toe´–to-toe´
tof´fee
to´fu
to´ga
to´gaed
to-geth´er
to-geth´er-ness
tog´ger-y
tog´gle
toil´er
toi´let
toi´let-ry
toi-lette´
toil´some
toil´some-ly
toil´some-ness
to´ken
to´ken-ism
tol´er-a-ble
tol´er-a-ble-ness
tol´er-a-bly
tol´er-ance
tol´er-ant
tol´er-ant-ly
tol´er-ate
tol-er-a´tion
toll´booth

toll´–free´
toll´gate
toll´house
to-ma-til´lo
to-ma´to
tom´boy
tomb´stone
tom´cat
tom-fool´er-y
to-mor´row
ton´al
to-nal´i-ty
tone´–deaf
tone´less
ton´er
tongs
tongue
tongue´–tied
ton´ic
to-night
ton´nage
ton-neau´
ton´sil
ton-sil-lec´to-my
ton-sil-li´tis
ton-so´ri-al
ton´y
tool´box
tool´mak-er
tool´mak-ing
tool´room
tool´shed
tooth´ache

tooth´brush
tooth´less
tooth´paste
tooth´some
tooth´y
top´coat
top´flight´
top´–heavy
top´ic
top´i-cal-ly
top´less
top´most
top´–notch´
to-pog´ra-pher
top-o-graph´ic
to-pog´ra-phy
top´per
top´ping
top´ple
top´pling
top´–se´cret
top´soil
torch´bear-er
torch´light
tor-ment´ *(v.)*
tor´ment *(n.)*
tor-ment´ing-ly
tor-men´tor
tor-na´do
tor-na´does
tor-pe´do
tor-pe´does
tor´pid

tor-pid´i-ty
tor´pid-ly
tor´por
tor´por-if´ic
torque
tor´rent
tor-ren´tial
tor´rid
tor´sion
tor´sion-al
tor´so
tor´toise
tor´toise-shell
tor´tu-ous
tor´ture
tor´tur-er
tor´tur-ous-ly
toss´ing
toss´pot
to´tal
to´taled
to´tal-ing
to´tal-ism
to-tal´i-tar´i-an
to-tal´i-ty
to´tal-ize
to´tal-ly
to´tem
tot´ing
tot´ter
tot´ter-ing
touch´a-ble
touch´down

tou-ché´
touched
touch´i-ness
touch´ing
touch´stone
touch´–type
touch´–typ´ist
touch´–up
touch´y
tough´en
tough´en-er
tough´ie
tough´ly
tough´–mind´ed
tough´ness
tou-pee´
tour´ism
tour´ist
tour´ist-y
tour´na-ment
tour´ney
tour´ni-quet
tou´sle
tou´sled
tow´a-ble
tow´age
to´ward
tow´el
tow-el-ette´
tow´el-ing
tow´er
tow´er-ing
tow´line

town´house
towns´folk
town´ship
towns´peo-ple
tow´rope
tox´ic
tox´i-cant
tox-ic´i-ty
tox-i-col´o-gist
tox-i-col´o-gy
tox´in
trace´a-ble
trace´a-bly
trac´er
tra´chea
tra´che-al
trac´ing
track´a-ble
track´er
track´ing
track´less
tract
trac-ta-bil´i-ty
trac´ta-ble
trac´ta-ble-ness
trac´ta-bly
trac´tion
trac´tor
trade´mark
trade´–off
trad´er
trad´ing
tra-di´tion

tra-di´tion-al
tra-di´tion-al-ism
tra-di´tion-al-ist
tra-di´tion-al-ly
tra-duce´
tra-duce´ment
tra-duc´er
tra-duc´ing-ly
traf´fic
traf´ficked
traf´fick-er
traf´fick-ing
tra-ge´di-an
trag´e-dy
trag´ic
trag´i-cal-ly
trag-i-com´e-dy
trail´blaz-er
trail´er
train´a-ble
train-ee´
train´er
train´ing
train´load
trai´tor
trai´tor-ous
trai´tor-ous-ly
trai´tor-ous-ness
tra-jec´to-ry
tramp´er
tram´ple
tram´pler
tram´pling

tram´po-line´
tram´way
trance´like
tran´quil
tran´quil-ize
tran´quil-iz-er
tran-quil´li-ty
tran´quil-ly
tran´quil-ness
trans-act´
trans-ac´tion
tran-scend´
tran-scen´den-cy
tran-scen´dent
tran-scen-den´tal
trans-con-ti-nen´-
    tal
tran-scribe´
tran-scrib´er
tran´script
tran-scrip´tion
trans´fer *(n., v.)*
trans-fer´ *(v.)*
trans-fer´a-ble
trans-fer´al
trans-fer´ence
trans-ferred´
trans-fer´ring
trans-fig-u-ra´tion
trans-fig´ure
trans-fix´
trans-form´
trans-for-ma´tion

trans-form´er
trans-fuse´
trans-fu´sion
trans-gress´
trans-gres´sion
trans-gres´sor
tran´sience
tran´sien-cy
tran´sient
tran´sient-ly
tran-sis´tor
tran-sis´tor-ize
tran´sit
tran-si´tion
tran-si´tion-al
tran-si´tion-al-ly
tran-si-to´ri-ly
tran´si-to-ri-ness
tran´si-to-ry
trans-lat´a-ble
trans-late´
trans-la´tion
trans-la´tion-al
trans-la´tive
trans-la´tor
trans-lit-er-a´tion
trans-lu´cence
trans-lu´cen-cy
trans-lu´cent
trans-lu´cent-ly
trans-mi´grate
trana-mi-gra´tion
trans-mis´si-ble

trans-mis´sion
trans-mit´
trans-mit´ta·ble
trans-mit´tal
trans-mit´ter
trans-mog´ri-fy
trans-oce-an´ic
tran´som
trans-par´en-cy
trans-par´ent
trans-par´ent-ly
trans-par´ent-ness
tran-spire´
trans-plant´
trans-plant´er
tran-spon´der
trans-port´ (v.)
trans´port (n.)
trans-port´a-ble
trans-por-ta´tion
trans-pose´
trans-po-si´tion
trans-ship´ment
tran-sub-stan´ti-
   ate
trans-verse´
tra-peze´
trap´per
trap´pings
trash´i-ness
trash´man
trash´y
trat-to-ri´a

trau´ma
trau-mat´ic
trau-mat´i-cal-ly
trau´ma-tism
trau´ma-tize
travail´
trav´el
trav´eled
trav´el-er
trav´el-ing
trav´el-ogue
tra-vers´able
trav´erse
tra-verse´
trav´es-ty
trawl´er
treach´er-ous
treach´er-ous-ly
treach´er-ous-ness
treach´ery
trea´cle
tread´ing
trea´dle
tread´mill
trea´son
trea´son-a-ble
trea´son-ous
trea´son-ous-ly
trea´sure
trea´sur-er
trea´sur·y
treat´a-ble
trea´ties

trea′tise
treat′ment
trea′ty
tre′ble
tree′less
tree′lined
tree′top
trek′king
trel′lis
trel′lis-work
trem′ble
trem′bler
trem′bling
trem′bling-ly
trem′bly
tre-men′dous
tre-men′dous-ly
tre-men′dous-ness
trem′e-tol
trem′or
trem′u-lous
trem′u-lous-ly
trem′u-lous-ness
tren′chant
trench′er-man
trend′i-ness
trend′set-ter
trend′y
tres′pass-er
tressed
tres′tle
tri′ad
tri′al

tri′an-gle
tri-an′gu-lar
tri-an′gu-late
tri-an-gu-la′tion
tri-ath′lon
trib′al
trib′al-ism
trib′al-ly
tribes′man
tri-bu′nal
trib′u-tar-y
trib′ute
trich-i-no′sis
tri′chro-mat′ic
tri-chro′ma-tism
tri′–cit′y
trick′er-y
trick′i-ly
trick′i-ness
trick′le
trick′ster
trick′y
tri′cy-cle
tried′–and–true′
tri-en′nial
tri-en′nial-ly
tri′fle
tri′fler
tri′fling
tri′fling-ly
tri-fo′cal
trig′ger
trig-o-nom′e-try

tri-lat′er-al
tri-lat′er-al-ly
tri-lin′gual
tri-lin′gual-ly
tril′lion
tril′lionth
tril′o-gy
tri-mes′ter
trim′ly
trim′mer
trim′ming
trin′ket
tri′o
tri′ple
tri′ple–deck′er
tri′ple–space
trip′let
trip′li-cate
tri′pod
trip′ping-ly
trip′tych
trip′wire
tri-sect′
tri-sec′tion
tris-kai-dek-a-
  pho′bi-a
tris-kai-dek-a-
  pho′bic
tri′state
trite′ly
trite′ness
tri′umph
tri-um′phal

259

tri-um´phant
tri-um´phant-ly
tri-um´vi-rate
triv´et
triv´ia
triv´i-al
triv-i-al´i-ty
triv´i-al-ize
triv´i-al-ly
tri-week´ly
tro´che
trod´den
trog´lo-dyte
troi´ka
troll´er
trol´ley
trol´lop
trom-bone´
trom-bon´ist
tromp
troop´er
troop´ship
tro´phy
trop´ic
trop´i-cal
trop´i-cal-ly
trot´ter
trot´ting
trou´ba-dour
trou´ble
trou´bled
trou´ble-mak-er
trou´ble-mak-ing

trou´ble-shoot
trou´ble-shoot-er
trou´ble-some
trough
trounce
troupe
troup´er
trou´sers
trous´seau
trow´el
trow´eled
tru´an-cy
tru´ant-ly
truck´driv-er
truck´er
truck´le
truck´ling
truck´load
truc´u-lence
truc´u-lent
trudge
trudg´ing
true´heart´ed
true´–life´
truf´fle
tru´ism
tru´ly
trumped´–up´
trum´pery
trum´pet
trum´pet-er
trun´cate
trun´cat-ed

trun-ca´tion
trun´cheon
trun´dle
trunk´ful
truss´ing
trust´bust-er
trust´bust-ing
trust-ee´
trust-ee´ship
trust´ful
trust´ful-ness
trust´i-ness
trust´ing
trust´wor-thi-ness
trust´wor-thy
trust´y
truth´ful-ly
truth´ful-ness
try´ing
try´ing-ly
tryst
tsu-nam´i
tub´by
tube´less
tu´ber
tu´ber-ous
tub´ing
tu´bu-lar
tuft´ed
tuft´ing
tug´–of–war´
tu-i´tion
tu´lip

tum´ble-down	tur´moil	twinge
tum´bler	turn´a-bout	twin´ing
tum´bling	turn´a-round	twin´kle
tum´my	turn´coat	twin´kling
tu´mor	turn´ing	twist´a-ble
tu´mour (Br.)	tur´nip	twist´er
tu´mult	turn´off	twitch´er
tu-mul´tu-ous	turn´on	twitch´ing
tu-mul´tu-ous-ly	turn´pike	twitch´y
tun´dra	turn´stile	twit´ter-ing
tune´ful	turn´ta-ble	twit´ter-y
tune´less	tur´pen-tine	two´–faced
tun´er	tur´pi-tude	two´fer
tune´–up	tur´quoise	two´–fist´ed
tu´nic	tur´ret	two´–seat´er
tun´ing	tur´ret-ed	two´–sid´ed
tun´nel	tur´tle	two´some
tun´neled	tus´sle	two´–step
tun´nel-er	tu´te-lage	two´–tone
tun´nel-ing	tu´tor	ty-coon´
tur´ban	tu´tored	ty´ing
tur´bine	tu-to´ri-al	tyke
tur´bo-charg-er	tux-e´do	tym´pan
tur´bot	twad´dle	tym´pa-nist
tur´bu-lence	twang´y	type´cast
tur´bu-lent	tweez´ers	type´set
tu-reen´	twelfth	type´writ-er
tur´gid	twelve	type´writ-ten
tur-gid´i-ty	twen´ti-eth	ty´phoid
tur´gid-ly	twen´ty	ty-phoon´
tur´gid-ness	twice´–told´	ty´phus
tur´key	twi´light	typ´i-cal-ly
tur´mer-ic	twine	typ-i-fi-ca´tion

typ´i-fy
typ´ist
ty´po
ty-pog´ra-pher
ty-po-graph´ic
ty-po-graph´i-cal
ty-pog´ra-phy
ty-pol´o-gist
ty-pol´o-gy
ty-ran´ni-cal
tyr´an-nize
tyr´an-nous
tyr´an-nous-ly
tyr´an-ny
ty´rant
ty´ro

U

ubiq´ui-tous
ubiq´ui-tous-ly
ubiq´ui-tous-ness
ubi´qui-ty
ud´der
ug´li-ness
ug´ly
uku-le´le
ul´cer
ul´cer-ate
ul-cer-a´tion
ul´cer-a-tive
ul´cer-ous
ul-te´ri-or
ul´ti-ma

ul´ti-ma-cy
ul´ti-mate
ul´ti-mate-ly
ul-ti-ma´tum
ul´tra
ul-tra-clean´
ul-tra-con-serv´a-
   tive
ul-tra-fine´
ul-tra-light´
ul´tra-ma-rine´
ul-tra-mod´ern
ul-tra-pure´
ul-tra-pu´ri-ty
ul-tra-son´ic
ul-tra-son´i-cal-ly
ul-tra-son´ics
ul-tra-sound´
ul-tra-vi´o-let
um´ber
um-bil´i-cal
um-bil´i-cal-ly
um´brage
um-bra´geous
um-bra´geous-ly
um´bral
um´laut
um´pire
un-abat´ed
un-a´ble
un-abridged´
un-ac-cept´a-ble
un-ac-cent´ed

un-ac-com´pa-
   nied
un-ac-count´a-ble
un-ac-count´a-ble-
   ness
un-ac-count´a-bly
un-ac-cus´tomed
un-ac-quaint´ed
un-adorned´
un-adul´ter-at-ed
un-ad-vised´
un-ad-vis´ed-ly
un-ad-vis´ed-ness
un-af-fect´ed
un-af-fect´ed-ly
un-af-fect´ed-ness
un-afraid´
un-aid´ed
un-al´ter-a-ble
un-al´ter-a-ble-
   ness
un-al´ter-a-bly
un-al´tered
un-am-bi´tious
un-am-biv´a-lent
una-nim´i-ty
u-nan´i-mous
u-nan´i-mous-ly
u-nan´i-mous-ness
un-an-nounced´
un-an´swer-a-ble
un-an´swer-a-bly
un-ap-peal´a-ble

un-ap-peal´a·bly

un-ap-proach´-
 a·ble

un-ap-proach´-
 a·ble-ness

un-ap-proach´-
 a·bly

un-ap-pro´pri-at-
 ed

un-apt´

un-apt´ly

un-apt´ness

un-arm´

un-armed´

un-a-shamed´

un-a-sham´ed-ly

un-a-sham´ed-
 ness

un-asked´

un-as-sail´a·ble

un-as-sail´a·ble-
 ness

un-as-sail´a·bly

un-as-sist´ed

un-as-sum´ing

un-at-tached´

un-at-tain´able

un-at-tend´ed

un-at-trac´tive

un-au´tho-rized

un-a-vail´ing

un-a-vail´ing-ly

un-avoid´a·ble

un-avoid´a·bly

un-a-ware´

un-a-ware´ly

un-a-ware´ness

un-a-wares´

un-bal´ance

un-bal´anced

un-barred´

un-bear´a·ble

un-bear´a·ble-ness

un-bear´a·bly

un-beat´a·ble

un-beat´a·bly

un-beat´en

un-be-com´ing

un-be-com´ing-ly

un-be-com´ing-
 ness

un-be-got´ten

un-be-known´

un-be-lief´

un-be-liev´a·ble

un-be-liev´a·bly

un-be-liev´er

un-be-liev´ing

un-bend´

un-bend´a·ble

un-bend´ing

un-bend´ing-ly

un-bent´

un-bi´ased

un-bi´ased-ly

un-bid´den

un-bind´

un-blam´able

un-bleached´

un-blem´ished

un-blink´ing

un-blink´ing-ly

un-block´

un-blush´ing

un-blush´ing-ly

un-blush´ing-ness

un-bolt´

un-bolt´ed

un-born´

un-bos´om

un-bound´

un-bound´ed

un-bound´ed-ly

un-bound´ed-ness

un-bowed´

un-brace´

un-braid´

un-brand´ed

un-break´able

un-bri´dle

un-bri´dled

un-bro´ken

un-bro´ken-ly

un-bro´ken-ness

un-buck´le

un-budge´a·ble

un-budge´a·ble-
 ness

un-budge´a·bly

un-bun´dle
un-bun´dled
un-bur´den
un-but´ton
un-but´toned
un-cage´
un-caged´
un-called—for
un-can´ni-ly
un-can´ni-ness
un-can´ny
un-cap´
un-cared´–for
un-ceas´ing
un-ceas´ing-ly
un-ceas´ing-ness
un-cer-e-mo´ni-ous
un-cer-e-mo´ni-ous-ly
un-cer-e-mo´ni-ous-ness
un-cer´tain
un-cer´tain-ly
un-cer´tain-ness
un-cer´tain-ty
un-chain´
un-chained´
un-chal´lenged
un-change´able
un-changed´
un-charged´
un-char´i-ta·ble

un-char´i-ta·ble-ness
un-char´i-ta·bly
un-chart´ed
un-char´tered
un-chaste´
un-checked´
un-chris´tian
un-chris´tian-ly
un´ci-al
un´ci-form
un-cir´cum-cised
un-civ´il
un-civ´il-ized
un-civ´il-ly
un-civ´il-ness
un-clad´
un-clasp´
un-clasped´
un-clas´si-fied
un´cle
un-clean´
un-clean´li-ness
un-clean´ly
un-clean´ness
un-cloak´
un-clog´
un-closed´
un-clothe´
un-cloud´ed
un-coil´
un-com´fort-a·ble
un-com´fort-a·bly

un-com-mer´cial
un-com-mit´ted
un-com´mon
un-com´mon-ly
un-com´mon-ness
un-com-mu´ni-ca-tive
un-com-plain´ing
un-com´pro-mis-ing
un-com´pro-mis-ing-ly
un-con-cern´
un-con-cerned´
un-con-cern´ed-ly
un-con-cern´ed-ness
un-con-di´tion-al
un-con-di´tion-al-ly
un-con-di´tioned
un-con-di´tioned-ness
un-con-form-a·bil´i-ty
un-con-form´a·ble
un-con-form´a·bly
un-con-form´i-ty
un-con-nec´ted
un-con-nect´ed-ly
un-con-nect´ed-ness
un-con´quered

un-con´scion-a·ble
un-con´scion-a·ble-ness
un-con´scion-a·bly
un-con´scious
un-con´scious-ly
un-con´scious-ness
un-con-sti-tu´tion-al
un-con-sti-tu´tion-al´i-ty
un-con-sti-tu´tion-al-ly
un-con-trol´la·ble
un-con-trolled´
un-con-struct´ed
un-con-ven´tion-al
un-con-ven´tion-al-ist
un-con-ven-tion-al´i-ty
un-con-ven´tion-al-ly
un-cork´
un-cor-rupt´ed
un-count´ed
un-cou´ple
un-couth´
un-couth´ly
un-couth´ness
un-cov´er
un-cov´ered

un-crit´i-cal
un-crit´i-cal-ly
un-cross´
unc´tion
unc´tu-ous
unc´tu-ous-ly
unc´tu-ous-ness
un-cul´ti-vat-ed
un-cul´tured
un-cured´
un-curl´
un-cut´
un-damped´
un-daunt´ed
un-daunt´ed-ly
un-daunt´ed-ness
un-de-ceiv´a·ble
un-de-ceive´
un-de-ceiv´er
un-de-cid´ed
un-de-cid´ed-y
un-de-cid´ed-ness
un-de-feat´ed
un-de-filed´
un-de-fined´
un-dem-o-crat´ic
un-de-mon´stra-ble
un-de-mon´stra-tive
un-de-mon´stra-tive-ly
un-de-ni´a·ble

un-de-ni´a·ble-ness
un-de-ni´a·bly
un´der
un-der-a-chieve´
un-der-a-chieve´ment
un-der-a-chiev´er
un-der-act´
un-der-ac´tive
un-der-age´
un´der-age
un´der-arm
un´der-bel-ly
un-der-bid´
un´der-bid-der
un´der-bite
un´der-bod-y
un´der-brush
un-der-cap-i-tal-i-za´tion
un-der-cap´i-tal-ize
un´der-car-riage
un-der-charge´
un´der-class
un-der-class´man
un´der-clothes
un´der-cloth´ing
un´der-coat
un´der-coat-ing
un-der-com´pen-sate

un-der-cov´er
un´der-croft
un´der-cur-rent
un´der-cut
un-der-de-vel´op
un-der-de-vel´oped
un-der-de-vel´op-ment
un´der-dog
un´der-done
un-der-em´pha-size
un-der-em-ployed´
un-der-em-ploy´ment
un-der-es´ti-mate
un-der-es-ti-ma´tion
un-der-ex-pose´
un-der-ex-po´sure
un-der-feed´
un´der-foot´
un´der-fur
un´der-gar-ment
un-der-gird´
un´der-glaze
un-der-go´
un´der-gone´
un´der-grad
un-der-grad´u-ate
un´der-ground

un´der-growth
un´der-hand
un´der-hand-ed
un´der-hand-ed-ly
un´der-hand-ed-ness
un-der-in-sure´
un-der-in-sured´
un-der-lay´
un-der-lie´
un´der-line
un´der-lin-er
un´der-ling
un´der-ly-ing
un-der-mine´
un´der-most
un-der-neath´
un-der-nour´ished
un-der-nour´ish-ment
un´der-paid´
un´der-pants
un´der-pass
un-der-pay´
un-der-pay´ment
un-der-pin´
un´der-pin-ning
un-der-price´
un´der-priv´i-leged
un-der-pro-duc´tion
un-der-rate´

un-der-re-port´
un-der-run´
un´der-score
un´der-sea
un-der-seas´
un´der-sec´re-tary
un-der-sell´
un´der-shirt
un-der-shoot´
un´der-side
un´der-sign
un´der-signed
un´der-size
un´der-sized
un´der-skirt
un-der-staffed´
un-der-stand´
un-der-stand´a·ble
un-der-stand´a·bly
un-der-stand´ing
un-der-stand´ing-ly
un-der-state´
un-der-stat´ed
un-der-stat´ed-ness
un´der-state-ment
un-der-stood´
un-der-strength´
un´der-study
un´der-sur-face
un´der-take

un´der-tak-er
un´der-tak´ing
un´der–the–
    coun´ter
un´der–the–ta´ble
un´der-things
un´der-tone
un´der-took´
un´der-tow
un´der-trick
un-der-val-u-a´-
    tion
un-der-val´ue
un´der-wa´ter
un´der-way
un´der-wear
un´der-weight
un´der-world
un-der-work´
un´der-write
un´der-writ-er
un´der-writ´ten
un-de-served´
un-de-sign´ing
un-de-sir-a-bil´i-
    ty
un-de-sir´a-ble
un-de-sir´a-ble-
    ness
un-de-sir´a-bly
un-de-vel´oped
un´dies
un-di-rect´ed

un-dis´ci-plined
un-dis-cov´ered
un-dis-mayed´
un-dis-posed´
un-dis-put´ed
un-dis-tin´guished
un-dis-turbed´
un-di-ver´si-fied
un-di-vid´ed
un-do´
un-dock´
un-do´ing
un-done´
un-doubt´ed
un-doubt´ed-ly
un-dress´
un-dressed´
un-due´
un´du-lant
un´du-late
un´du-lat-ed
un-du-la´tion
un´du-la-tor
un´du-la-to-ry
un-du´ly
un-dy´ing
un-earned´
un-earth´
un-earth´li-ness
un-earth´ly
un-eas´i-ly
un-eas´i-ness
un-eas´y

un-ed´u-cat-ed
un-em-ploy´a-ble
un-em-ployed´
un´em-ploy´ment
un-end´ing
un-en-dur´a-ble
un-e´qual
un-e´qual-ly
un-e´qual-ness
un-e´qualed
un-e-quiv´o-cal
un-e-quiv´o-cal-ly
un-e-quiv´o-cal-
    ness
un-err´ing
un-err´ing-ly
un-err´ing-ness
un-es-sen´tial
un-es-sen´tial-ly
un-e´ven
un-e´ven-ly
un-e´ven-ness
un-e-vent´ful
un-e-vent´ful-ly
un-e-vent´ful-ness
un-ex-cep´tion-
    a-ble
un-ex-cep´tion-
    a-ble-ness
un-ex-cep´tion-
    a-bly
un-ex-cep´tion-al
un-ex-pect´ed

un-ex-pect´ed-ly
un-ex-pect´ed-
  ness
un-ex-plained´
un-ex-plored´
un-ex-pres´sive
un-ex-pres´sive-
  ness
un-ex´pur-gat-ed
un-fail´ing
un-fail´ing-ly
un-fail´ing-ness
un-fair´
un-fair´ly
un-fair´ness
un-faith´ful
un-faith´ful-ly
un-faith´ful-ness
un-fa-mil´iar
un-fa-mil-i-ar´i-ty
un-fa-mil´iar-ly
un-fas´ten
un-fath´om-a-ble
un-fa´vor-a·ble
un-fa´vor-a·ble-
  ness
un-fa´vor-a·bly
un-feel´ing
un-feel´ing-ly
un-feel´ing-ness
un-feigned´
un-feign´ed-ly
un-fet´ter

un-fet´tered
un-fin´ished
un-fit´
un-fit´ting
un-flag´ging
un-flap-pa-bil´i-ty
un-flap´pa-ble
un-flap´pa-bly
un-fledged´
un-flinch´ing
un-flinch´ing-ly
un-fo´cused
un-fold´
un-fold´a-ble
un-fore-seen´
un-for-get´ta-ble
un-for-get´ta-ble-
  ness
un-for-get´ta-bly
un-for-giv´a·ble
un-for-giv´ing
un-for-giv´ing-
  ness
un-formed´
un-for´tu-nate
un-for´tu-nate-ly
un-for´tu-nate-
  ness
un-found´ed
un-found´ed-ly
un-found´ed-ness
un-freeze´
un-friend´li-ness

un-friend´ly
un-frock´
un-fruit´ful
un-fruit´ful-ly
un-fruit´ful-ness
un´ful-filled´
un-fund´ed
un-furl´
un-fur´nished
un-gain´li-ness
un-gain´ly
un-gen´er-ous
un-gen´er-ous-ly
un-gird´
un-girt´
un-glue´
un-glued´
un-god´li-ness
un-god´ly
un-gov-ern-a·bil´i-
  ty
un-gov´ern-a·ble
un-gov´ern-a·ble-
  ness
un-gov´ern-a·bly
un-gra´cious
un-gra´cious-ly
un-gra´cious-ness
un-gram-mat´i-cal
un-gram-mat-i-
  cal´i-ty
un-grate´ful
un-grate´ful-ly

un-grate´ful-ness
un-ground´ed
un-grudg´ing
un-grudg´ing-ly
un-guard´ed
un-guard´ed-ly
un-guard´ed-ness
un´guent
un´gu-late
un-ham´pered
un-hand´
un-hand´y
un-hap´pi-ly
un-hap´pi-ness
un-hap´py
un-harmed´
un-har´ness
un-health´ful
un-health´i-ly
un-health´i-ness
un-health´y
un-heard´
un-heard´–of
un-hes´i-tat-ing
un-hes´i-tat-ing-ly
un-heed´ed
un-heed´ing
un-hes´i-tat-ing-ly
un-hinge´
un-ho´ly
un-hook´
unhoped´–for
un-horse´

un-hur´ried
un-hur´ried-ly
un-hur´ried-ness
un-hurt´
u´ni-corn
u´ni-cy-cle
un-iden´ti-fied
u´ni-fi-a-ble
u-ni-fi-ca´tion
u´ni-fied
u´ni-form
uni-form´i-ty
u´ni-form-ly
u´ni-form-ness
u´ni-fy
u´ni-fy-ing
u-ni-lat´er-al
u-ni-lat´er-al-ly
un-imag´i-na-tive
un-im-paired´
un-im-peach-a-
   bil´i-ty
un-im-peach´a·ble
un-im-peach´-
   a·ble-ness
un-im-peach´a·bly
un-im-por´tance
un-im-por´tant
un-im-proved´
un-in-cor´po-rat-
   ed
un-in-formed´
un-in-hab´it-ed

un-in-hib´it-ed
un-in-i´ti-at-ed
un-in´jured
un-in-spired´
un-in-tel´li-gent
un-in-tel´li-gent-ly
un-in-tel-lì-gi-bil´-
   i-ty
un-in-tel´li-gi-ble-
   ness
un-in-tel´li-gi-bly
un-in-ten´tion-al
un-in-ten´tion-al-
   ly
un-in´ter-est-ed
un-in´ter-est-ed-ly
un-in´ter-est-ed-
   ness
un-in-ter-rupt´ed
un-in-vit´ed
un´ion
un´ion-ist
un-ion-i-za´tion
un´ion-ize
u-ni-po´lar
u-nique´
u-nique´ly
u-nique´ness
u´ni-sex
u´ni-son
u´nit
u´ni-tary
u-nite´

u-nit´ed
u-nit´ing
u´nit-ize
u´nit-iz-er
u´ni-ty
u-ni-ver´sal
u-ni-ver´sal-ism
uni-ver-sal´i-ty
u-ni-ver-sal-i-za´-
  tion
u-ni-ver´sal-ize
u-ni-ver´sal-ly
u-ni-ver´sal-ness
u´ni-verse
u-ni-ver´si-ty
un-just´
un-jus´ti-fi-able
un-just´ly
un-just´ness
un-kempt´
un-kempt´ly
un-kempt´ness
un-kind´
un-kind´li-ness
un-kind´ly
un-kind´ness
un-know´a·ble
un-know´ing
un-know´ing-ly
un-known´
un-lace´
un-law´ful
un-law´ful-ly

un-law´ful-ness
un-lead´ed
un-learn´
un-learned´
un-learn´ed-ly
un-leash´
un-leav´ened
un-less´
un-let´tered
un-li´censed
un-like´
un-like´li-hood
un-like´ly
un-like´ness
un-lim´ber
un-lim´it-ed
un-link´
un-liq´ui-dat-ed
un-list´ed
un-live´
un-load´
un-lock´
un-looked´–for
un-loose´
un-loos´en
un-luck´i-ly
un-luck´i-ness
un-luck´y
un-made´
un-make´
un-man´
un-man´age-a·ble
un-man´li-ness

un-man´ly
un-manned´
un-man´nered
un-man´nered-ly
un-man´ner-li-
  ness
un-man´ner-ly
un-mar´ried
un-mask´
un-masked´
un-mean´ing
un-mean´ing-ly
un-meas´ur-a·ble
un-meas´ur-a·bly
un-meas´ured
un-meas´ured-ly
un-mel´lowed
un-mend´a·ble
un-men´tion-a·ble
un-men´tion-
  a·ble-ness
un-mer´ci-ful
un-mer´ci-ful-ly
un-mer´ci-ful-ness
un-mind´ful
un-mind´ful-ly
un-mind´ful-ness
un-mis-tak´a·ble
un-mit´i-gat-ed
un-mit´i-gat-ed-ly
un-mixed´
un-mix´ed-ly
un-moor´

un-mor´al
un-mo-ral´i-ty
un-mor´al-ly
un-mort´gaged
un-moved´
un-mov´ing
un-muz´zle
un-named´
un-nat´u-ral
un-nat´u-ral-ly
un-nat´u-ral-ness
un-nec-es-sar´i-ly
un-nec-es-sar´i-ness
un-nec´es-sar-y
un-nerve´
un-no´ticed
un-num´bered
un-ob-served´
un-ob-tru´sive
un-oc´cu-pied
un-of-fi´cial
un-o´pened
un-or´ga-nized
un-orig´i-nal
un-or´tho-dox
un-os´ten-ta´tious
un-pack´
un-paged´
un-paid´
un-pal-at-at-a-bil´i-ty
un-pal´at-a-ble

un-pal´at-a-bly
un-par´al-leled
un-par´don-a-ble
un-par-lia-men´-ta-ry
un-per´fo-rat-ed
un-per-turbed´
un-pile´
un-pin´
un-pleas´ant
un-pleas´ant-ly
un-pleas´ant-ness
un-plug´
un-plumbed´
un-pop´u-lar
un-pop-u-lar´i-ty
un-pop´u-lar-ly
un-prac´ti-cal
un-prac-ti-cal´i-ty
un-prac´ti-cal-ly
un-prac´ticed
un-prec´e-dent-ed
un-prec´e-dent-ed-ly
un-pre-dict-a-bil´-i-ty
un-pre-dict´a-ble
un-pre-dict´a-ble-ness
un-pre-dict´a-bly
un-prej´u-diced
un-pre-med´i-tat-ed

un-pre-pared´
un-pre-ten´tious
un-prin´ci-pled
un-print´a-ble
un-print´a-bly
un-proc´essed
un-pro-duc´tive
un-pro-fes´sion-al
un-pro-fes´sion-al-ly
un-prof-it-a-bil´i-ty
un-prof´it-a-ble
un-prof´it-a-ble-ness
un-prof´it-a-bly
un-prom´is-ing
un-prom´is-ing-ly
un-pro-pi´tious
un-pro-tect´ed
un-pro-voked´
un-pub´lished
un-pun´ished
un-qual´i-fi-a-ble
un-qual´i-fied
un-qual´i-fied-ly
un-quench´able
un-ques´tion-a-ble
un-ques´tion-a-bly
un-ques´tioned
un-qui´et
un-qui´et-ly
un-qui´et-ness

271

un-quote´
un-rav´el
un-rav´el-er
un-read´
un-read-a·bil´i-ty
un-read´a·ble
un-read´a·ble-ness
un-read´a·bly
un-read´y
un-re´al
un-re-al´i-ty
un-re´al-iz-a·ble
un-re´al-ized
un-re´al-ly
un-rea´son
un-rea´son-a·ble
un-rea´son-a·ble-
  ness
un-rea´son-a·bly
un-rea´son-ing
un-rea´son-ing-ly
un-rec´og-niz-able
un-re-con-struct´-
  ed
un-reel´
un-re-flect´ing
un-re-flect´ing-ly
un-re-flec´tive
un-re-flec´tive-ly
un-re-gen´er-a-cy
un-re-gen´er-ate
un-re-gen´er-ate-
  ly

un-re-lent´ing
un-re-lent´ing-ly
un-re-lent´ing-
  ness
un-re-li´able
un-re-li´gious
un-re-mit´ting
un-re-mit´ting-ly
un-re-quit´ed
un-re-serve´
un-re-served´
un-re-serv´ed-ly
un-re-serv´ed-ness
un-rest´
un-re-strained´
un-re-straint´
un-re-strict´ed
un-righ´teous
un-righ´teous-ly
un-righ´teous-ness
un-ripe´
un-ripe´ly
un-ripe´ness
un-ri´valed
un-roll´
un-root´
un-ruf´fled
un-ru´li-ness
un-ru´ly
un-sad´dle
un-safe´
un-said´
un-sal´able

un-san´i-tar·y
un-sat-is-fac´to-ri-
  ly
un-sat-is-fac´to-ri-
  ness
un-sat-is-fac´to-ry
un-sat´is-fied
un-sa´vor-i-ly
un-sa´vor-i-ness
un-sa´vor·y
un-scathed´
un-schol´ar-ly
un-schooled´
un-sci-en-tif´ic
un-sci-en-tif´i-cal-
  ly
un-scram´ble
un-screw´
un-script´ed
un-scru´pu-lous
un-scru´pu-lous-ly
un-scru´pu-lous-
  ness
un-seal´
un-sealed´
un-sea´son-a·ble
un-sea´son-a·ble-
  ness
un-sea´son-a·bly
un-sea´soned
un-seat´
un-seem´li-ness
un-seem´ly

un-seen´
un-self´ish
un-self´ish-ly
un-self´ish-ness
un-set´tle
un-set´tled
un-shack´le
un-shak´a·ble
un-shak´en
un-shaped´
un-shap´en
un-shav´en
un-sheathe´
un-shell´
un-shod´
un-sight´ly
un-signed´
un-skilled´
un-skill´ful
un-skill´ful-ly
un-snap´
un-snarl´
un-so´cia-ble
un-so´cia-ble-ness
un-so´cia-bly
un-so-lic´it-ed
un-so-lic´i-tous
un-so-phis´ti-cat-
    ed
un-so-phis´ti-cat-
    ed-ly
un-so-phis´ti-cat-
    ed-ness

un-so-phis-ti-ca´-
    tion
un-sound´
un-sound´ly
un-sound´ness
un-spar´ing
un-spar´ing-ly
un-spar´ing-ness
un-speak´a·ble
un-speak´a·ble-
    ness
un-speak´a·bly
un-spe´cial-ized
un-spec´u-la-tive
un-spoiled´
un-spo´ken
un-spot´ted
un-sta´ble
un-sta´ble-ness
un-sta´bly
un-stained´
un-stead´i-ly
un-stead´i-ness
un-stead´y
un-stick´
un-stop´
un-stop´pa-ble
un-stop´pa-bly
un-strap´
un-stressed´
un-string´
un-struc´tured
un-strung´

un-stuck´
un-stud´ied
un-sub-stan´tial
un-sub-stan-ti-
    al´i-ty
un-sub-stan´tial-ly
un-suc-cess´ful
un-suit´a·ble
un-suit´ed
un-sul´lied
un-sung´
un-sup-port´ed
un-sur-passed´
un-sus-pect´ed
un-sus-pect´ed-ly
un-sym-pa-thet´ic
un-taint´ed
un-tam´a·ble
un-tamed´
un-tan´gle
un-tar´nished
un-taught´
un-teach´
un-ten-a-bil´i-ty
un-ten´a·ble
un-ten´a·ble-ness
un-think´
un-think´a·ble
un-think´a·bly
un-think´ing
un-think´ing-ly
un-ti´di-ly
un-ti´di-ness

un-ti´dy
un-tie´
un-til´
un-time´li-ness
un-time´ly
un-tir´ing
un-ti´tled
un´to
un-told´
un-touch-a-bil´i-ty
un-touch´a-ble
un-touched´
un-to´ward
un-trained´
un-tram´meled
un´trans-lat´a-ble
un-trav´eled
un-tra-vers´a-ble
un-tried´
un-trou´bled
un-true´
tin-truth´
un-truth´ful
un-truth´ful-ly
un-truth´ful-ness
un-tu´tored
un-used´
un-u´su-al
un-u´su-al-ly
un-ut´ter-a-ble
un-ut´ter-a-bly
un-var´nished
un-var´y-ing

un-veil´
un-veil´ing
un-ven´ti-lat-ed
un-ver´i-fied
un-vir´tu-ous-ly
un-voiced´
un-want´ed
un-war´i-ly
un-war´i-ness
un-war´rant-ed
un-war´y
un-washed´
un-wa´ver-ing
un-wel´come
un-well´
un-wept´
un-whole´some
un-whole´some-ly
un-whole´some-
   ness
un-wield´i-ness
un-wield´y
un-will´ing
un-will´ing-ly
un-will´ing-ness
un-wind´
un-wise´
un-wise´ly
un-wished´-for
un-wit´ting
un-work´able
un-world´ly
un-wor´thi-ly

un-wor´thi-ness
un-wor´thy
un-wrap´
un-writ´ten
un-yield´ing
un-yoke´
un-zip´
up´-and-com´ing
up´-and-down´
up´beat
up´braid´
up´bring-ing
up´com-ing
up´date
up´draft
up´end´
up´-front´
up´grade
up-heav´al
up-held´
up-hill´
up-hold´
up-hold´er
up-hol´ster
up-hol´ster-er
up-hol´ster-y
up´lift´ (n.)
up´lift´ (v.)
up´load
up´most
up-on´
up´per
up´per-class´man

up´per-cut
up´per-most
up´pish
up´pish-ly
up´pish-ness
up´pi-ty
up-raise´
up-rear´
up´right
up´right-ly
up´right-ness
up´ris-ing
up´roar
up-roar´i-ous
up-roar´i-ous-ly
up-roar´i-ous-ness
up´root
up´set *(n.)*
up-set´ *(v., adj.)*
up´shot
up´stage´
up´stairs´
up-stand´ing
up´start
up´stream´
up´stroke
up-surge´
up´swept
up´sy–dai´sy
up´thrust
up´tight´
up´—to—date´
up´town´

ura´ni-um
ur´ban
ur-bane´
ur-bane´ly
ur-bane´ness
ur´ban-ize
ur´chin
urge
ur´gen-cy
ur´gent-ly
urg´ing
u´ri-nary
u-rol´o-gist
u-rol´o-gy
us´a-ble
us´a-ble-ness
us´a-bly
us´age
use´a·ble
used
use´ful
use´ful-ly
use´ful-ness
use´less
use´less-ness
us´er
us´er–friend´ly
ush´er
u´su-al-ly
u´su-al-ness
u-surp´
u-sur-pa´tion
u-surp´er

u´su-ry
uten´sil
u´ter-ine
u´tile
u-til-i-tar´i-an
u-til-i-tar´i-an-ism
u-til´i-ty
u´ti-liz-a-ble
u´ti-li-za´tion
u´ti-lize
u´ti-liz-er
ut´most
u-to´pi-an
ut´ter-a-ble
ut´ter-ance
ut´ter-er
ut´ter-most

V

va´can-cy
va´cant
va´cant-ly
va´cant-ness
va´cat-a-ble
va´cate
va´cat-ing
va-ca´tion-er
va-ca´tion-land
vac´ci-nate
vac-ci-na´tion
vac-cine´
vac´il-lant
vac´il-late

vac´il-lat-ing
vac-il-la´tion
vac´il-la-tor
vac´il-la-to-ry
va-cu´i-ty
vac´u-ous
vac´u-ous-ly
vac´u-ous-ness
vac´u-um
vac´uum–packed
vag´a-bond
va´gary
va´gran-cy
va´grant
va´grant-ly
vague
vague´ly
vague-ness
vain-glo´ri-ous
vain-glo´ri-ous-ly
vain-glo´ri-ous-
 ness
vain´glo-ry
vain´ly
vain´ness
val´ance
val-e-dic´tion
val-e-dic-to´ri-an
val´e-dic´to-ry
va´lence
val´en-tine
val´et
val´iance

val´ian-cy
val´iant
val´iant-ly
val´id
val´i-date
val-i-da´tion
va-lid´i-ty
val´id-ly
val´id-ness
va-lise´
val´ley
val´or
va´o-ri-za´tion
val´or-ous
val´or-ous-ly
val´our (Br.)
val´u-a·ble
val´u-a·ble-ness
val´u-a·bly
val´u-ate
val-u-a´tion
val-u-a´tion-al
val´u-a-tor
val´ue
val´ue–add´ed
val´ued
val´ue-less
val´u-ing
valve
val´vu-lar
val´vu-late
val´vule
val-vu-li´tis

va-moose´
vamp´er
vam´pire
vam-pir´ic
vam´pir-ish
vam´pir-ism
vamp´ish
van´dal
van´dal-ism
van-dal-is´tic
van´dal-ize
van-dyke´
vane
van´guard
van´guard-ism
van´guard-ist
va-nil´la
va-nil´lin
van´ish-er
van´ish-ing
van´i-ty
van´quish
van´quish-a·ble
van´quish-er
van´quish-ment
van´tage
vap´id
va-pid´i-ty
vap´id-ly
vap´id-ness
va´por
va-por-es´cence
va´por-if´ic

va´por-ish
va´por-ish-ness
va´por-iz-a·ble
va-por-i·za´tion
va´por-ize
va´por-iz-er
va´por-ous
va´por-ous-ly
va´por-ous-ness
va´por-ware
var-i-a·bil´i-ty
var´i-a·ble
var´i-a·ble-ness
var´i-a·ble–rate´
var´i-a·bly
var´i-ance
var´i-ant
var-i-a´tion
var-i-a´tion-al
var´i-col-ored
var´i-cose
var-i-cos´i-ty
var´ied
var´ied-ness
var´i-e-gate
var´i-e-gat-ed
var-i-e-ga´tion
var´i-e-ga-tor
va-ri´e-tal
va-ri´e-ty
var´i-ous
var´i-ous-ly
var´i-ous-ness

var´nish
var´nish-er
var´si-ty
var´y
var´y-ing-ly
vas´cu-lar
vase
va-sec´to-my
vast´ly
vast´ness
vaude´ville
vaude-vil´lian
vault´ing
vaunt
vaunt´ing
vaunt´ing-ly
vec´tor
veer
veer´ing
ve´gan
veg´e-ta·ble
veg-e-tar´i-an
veg-e-tar´i-an-ism
veg´e-tate
veg-e-ta´tion
veg´e-ta-tive
veg´e-ta-tive-ly
veg´gie
ve´he-mence
ve´he-ment
ve´he-ment-ly
ve´hi-cle
ve-hic´u-lar

veiled
veil´ing
veined
veldt
vel´lum
ve-loc´i-ty
ve-lour´
ve-lou-té´
vel´vet
vel´vet·y
ve´nal
ve-nal´i-ty
ve´nal-ly
vend´er
ven-det´ta
vend´i·ble
vend´i·bly
ven´dor
ve-neer´
ve-neer´ing
ven´er-a·ble
ven´er-a·ble-ness
ven´er-a·bly
ven´er-ate
ven-er-a´tion
ven´er-a-tor
ven´geance
venge´ful
venge´ful-ly
venge´ful-ness
ve´ni-al
ve´ni-al´i-ty
ve´ni-al-ly

ven´i-son
ven´om
ven´om-ous
ven´om-ous-ly
ve´nous
ve´nous-ly
ve´nous-ness
ven´ti-late
ven-ti-la´tion
ven´ti-la-tor
ven-tril´o-quism
ven-tril´o-quist
ven´ture
ven´tur-er
ven´ture-some
ven´tur-ing
ven´tur-ous
ven´tur-ous-ly
ven´tur-ous-ness
ven´ue
ve-ra´cious
ve-ra´cious-ly
ve-ra´cious-ness
ve-rac´i-ty
ve-ran´da
ver´bal *(adj.)*
verb´al *(n.)*
ver´bal-ist
ver´bal-i-za´tion
ver´bal-ize
ver´bal-iz-er
ver´bal-ly
ver-ba´tim

ver´bi-age
verb´i-fy
ver-bose´
ver-bose´ly
ver-bose´ness
ver-bos´i-ty
ver´dan-cy
ver´dant
ver´dant-ly
ver´dict
verge
verg´ing
ver´i-fi-a·ble
ver-i-fi-ca´tion
ver´i-fied
ver´i-fy
ver-i-si-mil´i-tude
ver´i-ta-ble
ver´i-ta-bly
ver´i-ty
ver-mi-cel´li
ver-mil´ion
ver´min
ver-mouth´
ver-nac´u-lar
ver-nac´u-lar-ism
ver-nac´u-lar-ly
ver´nal
ver´nal-ly
ver´sant
ver´sa-tile
ver´sa-tile-ly
ver-sa-til´i-ty

versed
ver-si-fi-ca´tion
ver´si-fied
ver´si-fi-er
ver´si-fy
ver´sion
ver´so
ver´sus
ver´te-bra
ver´te-brae
ver´te-bral
ver´te-brate
ver´ti-cal
ver´ti-cal-ly
ver´ti-go
verve
ver´y
ves´per
ves´sel
vest´ed
ves´tige
ves-tig´ial
ves-tig´ial-ly
vest´ing
ves´ti-ture
vest´ment
vest´–pock-et
ves´try
ves´try-man
vet´er-an
vet-er-i-nar´i-an
vet´er-i-nar·y
ve´to

ve´toed
ve´to-er
ve´toes
ve´to-ing
vex-a´tion
vex-a´tious
vex-a´tious-ly
vex´ed
vex´ed-ly
vi-a·bil´i-ty
vi´a-ble
vi´a-duct
vi´al
vi´and
vi´bran-cy
vi´brant
vi´brant-ly
vi´bra-phone
vi´bra-phon-ist
vi´brate
vi´brat-ing
vi-bra´tion
vi-bra´tion-al
vi-bra´to
vi´bra-tor
vi´bra-to-ry
vic´ar
vic´ar-age
vi-car´i-ous
vi-car´i-ous-ly
vi-car´i-ous-ness
vice—con´sul
vice—pres´i-dent

vice´roy
vi-chys-soise´
vi-cin´i-ty
vi´cious
vi´cious-ly
vi´cious-ness
vi-cis´si-tude
vi-cis-si-tu´di-nar-
 y
vi-cis-si-tu´di-
 nous
vic´tim
vic-tim-i-za´tion
vic´tim-ize
vic´tim-iz-er
vic-to´ri-ous
vic´to-ry
vict´ual
vict´ualed
vict´ual-er
vid´e-o-cas-sette
vid´e-o-con-fer-
 ence
vid´e-o-disc
vid´e-o-re-cord-er
vid´e-o-tape
vid´e-o-tap-er
view´a·ble
view´er
view´er-ship
view´find-er
view´ing
view´point

view´y
vig´il
vig´i-lance
vig´i-lant
vig´i-lant-ly
vig-i-lan´te
vig-i-lan´tism
vi-gnette´
vig´or
vig´or-ous
vig´or-ous-ness
vig´our (Br.)
vile
vile´ly
vile´ness
vil-i-fi-ca´tion
vil´i-fi-er
vil´i-fy
vil´i-fy-ing
vil´la
vil´lage
vil´lag-er
vil´lain
vil´lain-ess
vil´lain-ous
vil´lain-y
vin-ai-grette´
vin-ci-bil´i-ty
vin´ci-ble
vin´di-ca-ble
vin´di-cate
vin-di-ca´tion
vin´di-ca-tive

vin´di-ca-tor
vin-dic´tive
vin-dic´tive-ly
vin-dic´tive-ness
vin´e-gar
vin´e-gar-y
vin´er·y
vine´yard
vin´tage
vint´ner
vi´nyl
vi-o´la
vi-o-la-bil´i-ty
vi´ol-a·ble
vi´ol-a·ble-ness
vi´ol-a·bly
vi´o-late
vi-o-la´tion
vi´o-la-tor
vi´o-lence
vi´o-lent-ly
vi´o-let
vi-o-lin´
vi-o-lin´ist
vi´per
vi´per-ish
vi´per-ous
vi´per-ous-ly
vi´ral
vir´gin
vir´gin-al
vir-gin´i-ty
vir´ile

vir´il-ism
vi-ril´i-ty
vi-rol´o-gist
vi-rol´o-gy
vir´tu-al
vir-tu-al´i-ty
vir´tu-al-ly
vir´tue
vir´tue-less
vir-tu-os´i-ty
vir-tu-o´so
vir´tu-ous-ly
vir´tu-ous-ness
vir´u-lence
vir´u-lent-ly
vi´rus
vis´age
vis´cose
vis-cos´i-ty
vis´cous
vis´cous-ly
vis´cous-ness
vis-i·bil´i-ty
vis´i·ble
vis´i·ble-ness
vis´i·bly
vi´sion
vi´sion-al
vi´sion-ar-i-ness
vi´sion-ar·y
vi´sioned
vi´sion-less
vis´it

vis´i-tant
vis-it-a´tion
vis´i-tor
vi´sor
vis´ta
vi´su-al
vis´u-al-ist
vis-u-al´i-ty
vis´u-al-iz-a·ble
vis-u-al-i-za´tion
vis´u-al-ize
vis´u-al-iz-er
vis´u-al-ly
vi´tal
vi-tal´i-ty
vi-tal-i-za´tion
vi´tal-ize
vi´tal-ly
vi´tal-ness
vi´ta-min
vi-ta-min´ic
vi´ti-ate
vi´ti-at-ed
vi-ti-a´tion
vi´ti-a-tor
vit´re-ous
vit´re-ous-ly
vit´re-ous-ness
vi-tres´cence
vi-tres´cent
vit´ric
vit´ri-fi-a·ble
vit-ri-fi-ca´tion

vit´ri-fy
vit´ri-ol
vit´ri-ol´ic
vi-tu´per-ate
vi-tu-per-a´tion
vi-tu´per-a-tive
vi-tu´per-a-tor
vi-va´cious
vi-va´cious-ly
vi-va´cious-ness
vi-vac´i-ty
viv´id
viv´id-ly
viv´id-ness
viv-i-fi-ca´tion
viv´i-fied
viv´i-fy
viv´i-sect
viv-i-sec´tion
viv-i-sec´tion-al
viv-i-sec´tion-ist
vix´en
vix´en-ish
vix´en-ly
vi-zier´
vo-cab´u-lar·y
vo´cal
vo´cal-ist
vo-cal-i-za´tion
vo´cal-ize
vo´cal-iz-er
vo´cal-ly
vo´cal-ness

vo-ca´tion
vo-ca´tion-al
vo-ca´tion-al-ism
vo-ca´tion-al-ist
vo-ca´tion-al-ly
voc´a-tive
voc´a-tive-ly
vo-cif´er-ant
vo-cif´er-ate
vo-cif-er-a´tion
vo-cif´er-a-tor
vo-cif´er-ous
vo-cif´er-ous-ly
vo-cif´er-ous-ness
vod´ka
vogue
vogu´ish
vogu´ish-ness
voice
voiced
voic´ed-ness
voice´ful
voice´ful-ness
voice´less
voice´less-ly
voice´-o-ver
voice´print
voic´ing
void´a·ble
void´ance
void´ed
void´ness
vol´a-tile

vol´a-tile-ness
vo-a-til´i-ty
vol´a-til-iz-a·ble
vo-a-til-i-za´tion
vol-can´ic
vol-can´i-cal-ly
vol-ca´no
vol-ca´noes
vol-can-ol´o-gist
vol-can-ol´o-gy
vo-li´tion
vo-li´tion-al
vo-li´tion-al-ly
vo-li´tion-ar·y
vol´i-tive
vol´ley
vol´ley-ball
volt´age
vo´u-bil´i-ty
vol´u-ble
vol´u-ble-ness
vol´u-bly
vol´ume
vo-lu-mi-nos´i-ty
vo-lu´mi-nous
vo-lu´mi-nous-ly
vo-lu´mi-nous-
  ness
vol´un-tar´i-ly
vol´un-ta-rism
vol´un-tar-y
vol-un-tar´i-ly
vol-un-teer´

vol´un-teered
vo-lup´tu-ar·y
vo-lup´tu-ous
vo-lup´tu-ous-ly
vo-lup´tu-ous-ness
vom´it
voo´doo
vo-ra´cious-ly
vo-ra´cious-ness
vo-rac´i-ty
vor´tex
vor´ti-ces
vot´a-ble
vote
vot´er
vot´ing
vo´tive
vo´tive-ly
vouch´er
vouch-safe´
vow
vow´el
voy´age
voy´ag-er
voy´a-geur´
vo-yeur´
vo-yeur´ism
voy-eur-is´tic
voy-eur-is´ti-cal-ly
vul-can-i·za´tion
vul´can-ize
vul´can-iz-er
vul´gar

vul-gar´i-an
vul´gar-ism
vu´gar´i-ty
vul´gar-ly
vul´gar-ness
vul-ner-a·bil´i-ty
vul´ner-a·ble
vul´ner-a·ble-ness
vul´ner-a·bly
vul´ture
vul´tur-ous
vy´ing

W

wack´i-ly
wack´i-ness
wack´o
wack´y
wad´ding
wad´dle
wad´dled
wad´dler
wad´dling
wad´dling-ly
wad´dly
wade
wad´er
wad´ing
wa´fer
waf´fle
waf´fler
waf´fling
waf´fly

waft
waft´er
wage´less
wa´ger
wag´es
wag´ger-y
wag´gish
wag´gish-ness
wag´gle
wag´gling
wag´gly
wag´ing
wag´on
wag´on-er
wag´on-load
wail´ing
wain´scot-ing
waist´band
waist´coat
waist´ed
waist´line
wait´er
wait´ing
wait´list
wait´per-son
wait´ress
waive
waiv´er
wake´ful
wake´ful-ness
wak´en
wak´en-er
wak´en-ing

wake´–up
walk´a·ble
walk´a-bout
walk´a-thon
walk´a-way
walk´er
walk´ie—talk´ie
walk´–in
walk´ing
walk´–on
walk´way
wall´board
wall´cov-er-ing
walled
wal´let
wall´flow-er
wal´lop
wal´lop-er
wal´lop-ing
wal´low
wall´paper
wall´–to–wall´
wal´nut
wal´rus
waltz´er
wan´der
wan´der-er
wan´der-ing
wan´der-ing-ly
wan´der-lust
wane´y
wan´gle
wan´gled

wan´gler
wan´gling
wan´ing
wan´ly
wan´na-be
wan´ness
want´ing
wan´ton
wan´ton-ly
wan´ton-ness
war´ble
war´bled
war´bler
war´bling
war´den
ward´er
ward´robe
ward´room
ware´house
war´fare
war´–horse
war´i-ly
war´i-ness
war´like
war´lord
warm´–blood´ed
warmed´–o´ver
warm´er
warm´heart-ed
warm´heart-ed-ly
warm´heart-ed-
   ness
warm´ish

warm´ly
war´mon-ger
warm´ness
warm´up
warn´er
warn´ing
warn´ing-ly
warp´age
war´path
warp´ing
war´rant
war´rant-a-ble
war´rant-ee´
war´rant-er
war´ran-tor´
war´ran-ty
war´ri-or
war´time
war´y
wash´a-ble
wash´–and–wear´
wash´ba-sin
wash´board
wash´bowl
wash´cloth
wash´day
washed´–out´
washed´–up´
wash´er
wash´er-wom-an
wash´ing
wash´room
wash´stand

wash´tub
wash´up
wash´y
wasp´i-ly
wasp´i-ness
wasp´ish
wasp´ish-ly
wasp´ish-ness
wasp´y
was´sail
was´sail-er
wast´age
waste´bas-ket
wast´ed
waste´ful
waste´ful-ly
waste´ful-ness
waste´land
wast´er
wast´ing
was´trel
watch´band
watch cap
watch´case
watch´dog
watch´er
watch´ful
watch´ful-ly
watch´ful-ness
watch´mak-er
watch´mak-ing
watch´tow-er
watch´word

wa´ter-bed
wa´ter-borne
wa´ter bug
wa´ter-col-or
wa´ter-course
wa´ter-craft
wa´tered
wa´ter-er
wa´ter-fall
wa´ter-fowl
wa´ter-front
wa´ter-i-ness
wa´ter-less
wa´ter-less-ly
wa´ter-less-ness
wa´ter-line
wa´ter-locked
wa´ter-logged
wa´ter-mark
wa´ter-mel-on
wa´ter-pick
wa´ter-pow-er
wa´ter-proof
wa´ter-proof-ing
wa´ter–re-pel-lent
wa´ter–ski
wa´ter-sport
wa´ter-spout
wa´ter-tight
wa´ter-way
wa´ter-wheel
wa´ter-works
wa´ter-y

watt´age
wave´length
wav´er *(hailer)*
wa´ver *(vacillate)*
wa´ver-er
wa´ver-ing
wav´i-ness
wav´ing
wav´y
wax´en
wax´i-ness
wax´ing
wax´works
wax´y
way´bill
way´far-er
way´far-ing
way´laid
way´lay
way´lay-er
way´–out´
way´ward
way´ward-ness
wa-zir´
weak´en
weak´ened
weak´en-er
weak´ling
weak´–kneed´
weak´ly
weak´–mind´ed
weak´–mind´ed-ly
weak´ness

wealth´i-er
wealth´i-ness
wealth´y
wean´ling
weap´on
weap´on-ry
wear-a·bil´i-ty
wear´a·ble
wear´er
wea´ri-ful
wea´ri-ful-ly
wea´ri-ful-ness
wea´ri-less
wea´ri-less-ly
wea´ri-ly
wea´ri-ness
wear´ing
wea´ri-some
wea´ry
wea´ry-ing
wea´seled
wea´sel-ly
weath´er
weath´er—beat-en
weath´er-cock
weath´ered
weath´er-ing
weath´er-ize
weath´er-proof
weath´er-strip-
  ping
weave
weav´er

weav´ing
web
webbed
web´bing
web´site
wed´ded
wed´ding
wedged
wedge—shaped
wedg´ing
wedg´y
wed´lock
weed´er
weed´i-ness
weed´kill-er
weed´y
week´day
week´end-er
week´ly
week´night
weep´er
weep´i-ness
weep´ing
weep´y
wee´vil
weigh
weight
weight´ed
weight´i-ly
weight´i-ness
weight´less
weight´less-ness
weight´lift-er

weight´lift-ing
weight´y
weird´ly
weird´ness
wel´come
wel´com-er
weld´a-ble
weld´er
wel´fare
well´–ad-vised´
well´–ap-point´ed
well—bal´anced
well—be-haved´
well´–be´ing
well´–belov´ed
well´born
well´bred´
well´–defined´
well´–fed´
well´–found´ed
well´–groomed´
well´–ground´ed
well´–han´dled
well´–heeled´
well´–in-formed´
well´–inten´tioned
well´–known´
well´–made´
well´–man´nered
well´–mean´ing
well´–off´
well´–read´
well´–round´ed

well'spring
well'–thought'–of
well'–timed'
well'—to—do'
well'—trained'
well'–wish-er
well'–worn'
wend'ing
west'er
west'er-ly
west'ern
west'ern-er
west'ern-ism
west'ern-most
west'ward
weth'er
wet'land
wet'ness
wet'ting
whacked
whal'er
whal'ing
what-ev'er
what'not
what-so-ev'er
whee'dle
whee'dled
whee'dler
wheel'bar-row
wheel'base
wheel'chair
wheel'er–deal'er
wheel'house

wheel'wright
wheeze
wheez'y
when-ev'er
when'so-ev'er
where'a-bouts
where'as'
where'by'
where'fore'
where'of'
where'so-ev'er
where'up-on'
wher-ev'er
where'with-al
wheth'er
whet'stone
which-ev'er
whim'per
whim'pered
whim'per-ing
whim'si-cal
whim'si-cal-ly
whim'sy
whined
whin'ing
whin'nied
whin'ny
whip'cord
whip'lash
whip'ping
whip'poor-will
whip'saw
whirl'pool

whirl'wind
whirl'y-bird
whir'ring
whisk'er
whisk'ered
whisk'er-y
whis'key
whis'ky
whis'per
whis'pered
whis'per-er
whis'per-ing
whis'per-y
whis'tle
whis'tle–blow-er
whis'tle–blow-ing
whis'tler
whis'tling
white'cap
white'—hot'
whit'en-ing
white'–tie
white'wall
white'wash
whith'er
whit'ish
whit'tle
whit'tled
whit'tler
whit'tling
who-ev'er
whole'–grain
whole'heart-ed-ly

whole´ness
whole´sale
whole´sal-er
whole´some
whole´some-ly
whole´some-ness
whol´ly
whom-so-ev´er
whoop´ee
whop´per
whorl
who-so-ev´er
wick´ed
wick´ed-ly
wick´ed-ness
wick´er
wick´er-work
wick´et
wick´ing
wide´–an´gle
wide´–awake´
wide´bod·y
wide´–eyed
wide´ly
wid´en
wide´–o´pen
wide´–rang´ing
wide´–screen´
wide´spread´
wid´get
wid´ow
wid´ow-er
width

wield
wield´er
wield´y
wie´ner-wurst
wife´less
wife´li-ness
wife´ly
wig´gle
wig´gler
wig´gling
wig´gly
wig´let
wild´–and–wool´ly
wild´cat
wil´der-ness
wild´fire
wild´life
wild´ly
wild´ness
willed
will´ful
will´ful-ly
will´ful-ness
will´ing
will´ing-ly
will´ing-ness
will´—o'—the—
    wisp
wil´low-y
will´pow-er
wil´y
wimp´y
win

wince
winch
winc´ing
wind´age
wind´bag
wind´blown
wind´–borne
wind´break-er
wind´burn
wind´ed
wind´fall
wind´i-er
wind´i-ness
wind´ing
wind´ing-ness
wind´jam-mer
wind´lass
wind´less
wind´mill
win´dow
win´dow-less
win´dow-pane
win´dow–shop
win´dow–shop-er
win´dow—shop-
    ping
win´dow-sill
wind´pipe
wind´proof
wind´shield
wind´storm
wind´surf-er
wind´surf-ing

wind´–swept	wire´tap	with-hold´ing
wind´ward	wire´tap-per	with-in´
wind´y	wir´ing	with-out´
wine´glass	wir´y	with-stand´
wine´mak-ing	wis´dom	with-stand´ing
win´er-y	wise´a-cre	wit´less
wine´tast-ing	wise´crack	wit´less-ly
winged	wise´ly	wit´less-ness
wing´less	wis´est	wit´ness
wing´span	wish´bone	wit´ness–box
wing´spread	wish´ful	wit´ness-er
wing´tip	wish´ful-ly	wit´ted
wink´er	wish´ful-ness	wit´ti-cism
wink´ing	wish´y—wash·y	wit´ti-ly
win´na-ble	wisp´i-ness	wit´ti-ness
win´ner	wisp´y	wit´ting
win´ning	wist´ful	wit´ting-ly
win´ning-ly	wist´ful-ly	wit´ty
win´nings	wist´ful-ness	wiz´ard
win´now-er	witch´craft	wiz´ard-ry
win´some-ly	witch´y	wiz´ened
win´some-ness	with-al´	wob´ble
win´ter-green	with-draw´	wob´bler
win´ter-ish	with-draw´al	wob´bli-ness
win´ter-ize	with-drawn´	wob´bly
win´ter-time	with-drew´	woe´be-gone
win´try	with´er	woe´ful
wipe´out	with´ered	woe´ful-ly
wip´er	with´er-ing	woe´ful-ness
wip´ing	with´er-ing-ly	wom´an-hood
wired	with-held´	wom´an-ish
wire´less	with-hold´	wom´an-ize
wir´er	with-hold´er	wom´an-iz-er

wom´an-kind
wom´an-ly
wom´en
wom´en-folk
won´der
won´dered
won´der-er
won´der-ful
won´der-ful-ly
won´der-ful-ness
won´der-land
won´der-ment
won´der—work-er
won´drous
won´drous-ly
won´drous-ness
wont *(habit)*
won't *(will not)*
wood´block
wood´carv-ing
wood´craft
wood´cut
wood´cut-ter
wood´ed
wood´en
wood´en-ly
wood´en-ness
wood´grain
wood´i-er
wood´i-ness
wood´land
wood´pile
wood´shed

woods´y
wood´wind
wood´work
wood´work-er
wood´work-ing
wood´y
woo´er
wool´en
wool´li-ness
wool´ly
wooz´i-ly
wooz´i-ness
wooz´y
word
word´i-ly
word´i-ness
word´ing
word´less
word´less-ly
word´play
word´y
work
work´a·ble
work´a-day
work-a-hol´ic
work´bas-ket
work´bench
work´book
work´day
worked
worked´–up´
work´er
work´flow

work´horse
work´ing
work´man-ship
work´place
work´room
work´shop
work´ta-ble
work´week
world´beat-er
world´–class´
world´li-ness
world´ly–mind´ed
world´ly—wise
world´–shak-ing
world´–wea-ry
world´wide´
worm´—eat-en
worm´y
worn´—out´
wor´ried
wor´ried-ly
wor´ri-some
wor´ri-some-ly
wor´ry
wor´ry-ing
worse
wors´en
wor´ship
wor´shiped
wor´ship-er
wor´ship-ful
wor´ship-ing
worst´–case´

worth
wor´thi-ly
wor´thi-ness
worth´less
worth´less-ly
worth´less-ness
worth´while´
wor´thy
would´-be
wound´ed
wo´ven
wraith´like
wran´gle
wran´gler
wran´gling
wrap´a-round
wrap´per
wrap´ping
wrap´-up
wrath´ful
wrath´ful-ly
wrath´ful-ness
wreck´age
wreck´er
wreck´ing
wrench
wrest
wres´tle
wres´tler
wres´tling
wretch
wretch´ed
wretch´ed-ly

wretch´ed-ness
wrig´gle
wrig´gler
wrig´gly
wring´er
wring´ing
wrin´kle
wrin´kled
wrin´kling
wrin´kly
wrist´band
wrist´watch
write´-in
writ´er
writhe
writhed
writh´er
writh´ing
writh´ing-ly
writ´ing
writ´ten
wrong´do-er
wrong´do-ing
wrong´ful
wrong´ful-ly
wrong´ful-ness
wrong´head´ed
wrong´ly
wrong´ness
wroth
wrought
wrought´-up´
wry´ly

wry´ness

X

xen´o-phile
xen-o-phil´i-a
X—ray *(v.)*
xy´lo-graph
xy-log´ra-pher
xy-lo-graph´ic
xy-lo-graph´i-cal
xy-log´ra-phy
xy´lo-phone
xy´lo-phon-ist

Y

yacht
yacht´ing
yachts´man
yam´mer
yam´mer-er
yam´mer-ing-ly
yap´per
yap´ping
yap´ping-ly
yard´age
yard´stick
yawn´er
yawn´ing
year´book
year´-end´
year´ling
year´long
year´ly

yearn´ing
yearn´ing-ly
year´–round´
yeast´i-ness
yeast·y
yel´low
yel´low-ish
yel´low·y
yelp´er
yeo´man
yes´–man
yes´ter-day
yes´ter-year
yield´a-ble
yield´er
yield´ing
yo´del
yo´del-er
yo´del-ing
yo´ga
yo´gi
yo´gurt
yo´kel
yon´der
young´ish
young´ster
your-self´
youth´ful
youth´ful-ly
youth´ful-ness
yuck´y
yule
yum´my

yup´pie

Z

za´ni-ly
za´ni-ness
za´ny
zeal´ot
zeal´ot-ry
zeal´ous
zeal´ous-ly
zeal´ous-ness
ze´bra
ze´nith
zeph´yr
ze´ro
ze´roes
ze´ros
zest´ful
zest´ful-ly
zest´ful-ness
zest´y
zig´zag
zig´zag-ging
zing´er
zing´y
zin´ni-a
zip´per
zip´py
zith´er
zo´di-ac
zo-di´a-cal
zom´bie
zon´al

zon´al-ly
zo´na-ry
zoned
zon´ing
zo-o-graph´ic
zo-o-graph´i-cal
zo-og´ra-phy
zoo´keep-er
zo-o-log´i-cal
zo-o-log´i-cal-ly
zo-ol´o-gist
zo-ol´o-gy

CAPITALIZATION

There are no rules that cover every situation for capitalization, but with knowledge of certain principles and consideration of the purpose to be served, it is possible to attain a considerable degree of uniformity.

Proper names
Proper names are capitalized.

    Rome
    Brussels
    John Macadam
    the Macadam family
    Italy
    Anglo–Saxon

Derivatives of proper names
Derivatives of proper names are usually capitalized.

    Roman *(of Rome)*
    Washingtonian
    New Yorker
    Italian

Derivatives of proper names that have acquired independent common meaning or that are no longer identified with the source name are not capitalized. Generally, this depends on general and long–accepted usage.

    roman *(a type style, but **Times Roman**, a particular typeface is a proper name and should be capitalized)*
    macadam *(crushed rock)*
    italicize
    watt *(electric unit)*
    venetian blinds
    plaster of paris
    pasteurize

Common nouns and adjectives in proper names

A common noun or adjective forming an essential part of a proper name is capitalized; the common noun used alone as a substitute for the name of a place or thing is not capitalized.

Massachusetts Avenue	the avenue
Washington Monument	the monument
Statue of Liberty	the statue
Hoover Dam	the dam
Boston Light	the light
Modoc National Forest	the national forest
Panama Canal	the canal
Soldiers' Home of Ohio	the soldiers' home
Johnson House *(hotel)*	Johnson house *(residence)*
Crow Reservation	the reservation
Cape of Good Hope	the cape
Jersey City	the city
also Washington City, *but* city of Washington	
Cook County	the county
Great Lakes	the lakes
Lake of the Woods	the lake
North Platte River	the river
Charles the First	Charles I
Seventeenth Census	the 1960 census

If a common noun or adjective forming an essential part of a name becomes separated from the rest of the name by an intervening common noun or adjective, the entire expression is no longer a proper noun and is therefore not capitalized.

Eastern States	eastern farming States
Western States	western farming States

Short forms of proper names

A common noun used alone as a well-known short form of a specific proper name is usually capitalized.

> the **Capitol** *(at Washington),* **but State capitol** *(building)*
> the **Channel** *(English Channel)*
> the **District** *(District of Columbia)*

The plural form of a common noun

The plural form of a common noun that is normally capitalized as part of a proper name is also capitalized.

> **Seventh and I Streets**
> **Lakes Erie and Ontario**
> **Potomac and James Rivers**
> **State and Treasury Departments**
> **British and French Governments**
> **Presidents Washington and Adams**

Common noun as part of a reference

A common noun used with a date, number, or letter, merely to denote time or sequence, or for the purpose of reference does not usually form a proper name and is therefore not capitalized. There are, however, exceptions depending on common practice and usage, especially when the reference comes to characterize a specific item or set of items

> **act of 1928** *or* **Act of 1928**
> **amendment 5** *or* **Amendment 5**
> **article 1** *or* **Article 1**   **book I** *or* **Book I**
> **chapter 11** *or* **Chapter 11**   **column 2**
> **exhibit D**   **figure 7**
> **interstate 95,** *but usually* **Interstate 95 or Route 66**
> **page 2**   **paragraph 4**
> **part I**   **plate IV**
> **room A722**   **rule 8** *or* **Rule 8**

Common noun as part of a reference (cont.)

    schedule K *or* **Schedule K**   **section 3**
    spring 1926 *or* **Spring 1926**   **table 4**
    title IV *or* **Title IV**
    treaty of 1919 *or* **Treaty of 1919**
    volume X   **war of 1914,** *but* **War of 1812**

Definite article in proper place names

To achieve greater distinction or to adhere to the common form, the word *the* (or its equivalent in a foreign language) used as a part of an official name or title is capitalized. When such name or title is used adjectively, *the* is not capitalized.

    British Consul v. The Mermaid *(title of legal case)*
    The Dalles *(OR);* **The Weirs** *(NH); but* **the Dalles**
      region; the Weirs' streets
    The Hague; *but* **the Second Hague Conference**
    El Salvador, Las Cruces, L'Esterel
    The Netherlands, *but* **the Congo, the Sudan**

In common practice, *the* is not capitalized in references to periodicals, vessels, airships, trains, firm names, etc.

    the *Times*   **the** *Mermaid*
    the Federal Express   **the** *Atlantic Monthly*
    the *Los Angeles Times*   **the** *Washington Post*

Particles in names of persons

In foreign names such particles as *d' da, de, della, den, du, van,* and *von* are generally capitalized unless preceded by a forename or title. Individual usage, if ascertainable, should be followed.

    Da Ponte, Cardinal da Ponte
    Du Pont, E.I. du Pont de Nemours & Co.
    Van Rensselaer, Stephen van Rensselaer
    Von Braun, Wernher von Braun

but d'Orbigny, Alcide d'Orbigny
    de la Madrid, Miguel de la Madrid

In anglicized names such particles are usually capitalized, even if preceded by a forename or title, but individual usage, if ascertainable, should be followed.

    Reginald De Koven
    Thomas De Quincey
    Henry van Dyke *(his usage)*
    Samuel F. Du Pont

If copy is not clear as to the form of such a name (for example, *La Forge* or *Laforge*), the two-word form should be used.

    De Kalb County *(AL, GA, IL, IN),*
    but **DeKalb County** *(TN)*

In names set in capitals, *de, von,* etc., are also capitalized.

Names of organized bodies

The full names of organized bodies and their shortened names are capitalized; other substitutes most often regarded as common nouns are capitalized only in certain specified instances to indicate preeminence or distinction.

National governmental units:

U.S. Congress: **98th Congress, the Congress, Congress, the Senate, the House, Committee of the Whole, the Committee;** *but* **committee** *(nonspecific)*

Department of Agriculture: **the Department, Division of Publications, the Division,** *similarly* **all departmental units;** *but* **legislative, executive, and judicial departments**

Bureau of the Census: **the Census Bureau, the Bureau;** *but* **the agency**

Interstate Commerce Commission: **the Commission**

Government Printing Office: **the Printing Office, the Office**

American Embassy, British Embassy: **the Embassy;** *but* **the consulate, the consulate general**

Treasury of the United States: **General Treasury, National Treasury, Public Treasury, the Treasury, Treasury notes**

Department of Defense: **Military Establishment, Armed Forces, All–Volunteer Forces;** *but* **armed services**

Other: **French Ministry of Foreign Affairs, the Ministry; French Army, British Navy**

International organizations:

United Nations: **the Council, the Assembly, the Secretariat**

Hague Peace Conference of 1907: **the Hague Conference, the Peace Conference, the Conference**

Common–noun substitutes:

Virginia Assembly: **the assembly, the senate, the house of delegates**

California State Highway Commission: **Highway Commission of California, the highway commission**

Montgomery County Board of Health: **the Board of Health, Montgomery County, the board of health, the board**

Common Council of the City of Pittsburgh: **the common council, the council**

Buffalo Consumers' League: **the consumers' league, the league**

Republican Party: **the party**

Southern Railroad Co.: **the Southern Railroad, Southern Co., Southern Road, the railroad company, the company**

Riggs National Bank: **the Riggs Bank, the bank**

Yale School of Law: **Yale University School of Law; School of Law, Yale University; school of law**

Organized Bodies

The names of members and adherents of organized bodies are capitalized to distinguish them from the same words used merely in a descriptive sense.

a Representative (U.S. Congress)

a Socialist   a Democrat

an Odd Fellow   an Elk

a Communist   a Liberal

a Boy Scout   a Shriner

Names of countries, domains, etc.

The official designations of countries, national domains, and their principal administrative divisions are capitalized only if used as part of proper names, as proper names, or as proper adjectives.

United States: **the Republic, the Nation, the Union, the Government;** *also* **Federal, Federal Government;** *but* **republic** *(when not referring specifically to one entity),* **republican** *(in general sense),* **a nation devoted to peace**

New York State: **the State, a State** *(definite political subdivision of first rank),* **State of Veracruz, Balkan States, six States of Australia, State rights;** *but* **state** *(referring to a federal government, the body politic),* **foreign states, church and state, statehood, state's evidence**

Territory (Canada): **Yukon, Northwest Territories, the Territory(ies), Territorial;** *but* **territory of American Samoa, Guam, Virgin Islands**

Dominion of Canada: **the Dominion;** *but* **dominion** *(in general sense)*

Ontario Province, Province of Ontario: **the Province, Provincial;** *but* **province, provincial** *(in general sense)*

Crown Colony of Hong Kong, Cyprus: **the colony, crown colony**

The similar designations *commonwealth confederation (federal), government, nation (national), powers, republic,* etc., are capitalized only if used as part of proper names, as proper names, or as proper adjectives.

British Commonwealth, Commonwealth of Virginia: **the Commonwealth;** *but* **a commonwealth government**

Swiss Confederation: **the Confederation, the Federal Council, the Federal Government;** *but* **confederation**

French Government: **the Government, French and Italian Governments, Soviet Government, the Governments;** *but* **government** *(in general sense)*, **the Churchill government, European governments**

Cherokee Nation: **the nation;** *but* **Greek nation, American nations**

National Government *(of any specific nation);* **but national customs**

Allied Powers, Allies *(in World Wars I and II);* **but our allies, weaker allies, Central Powers** *(in World War I);* **but the powers, European powers**

Republic of South Africa: **the Republic,** *but* **republic** *(in general sense)*

Names of regions, localities, and geographic features

A descriptive term used to denote a definite region, locality, or geographic feature is a proper name and is therefore capitalized; also for temporary distinction a coined name of a region is capitalized.

the North Atlantic States	**the Gulf States**
the Central States	**the Pacific Coast States**
the Lake States	**East North Central States**
Eastern North Central States	
Far Western States	**Eastern United States**
the West	**the Midwest**
the Middle West	**Far West**

Names of regions, localities, etc. (cont.)
   the **Eastern Shore** (*Chesapeake Bay*)
   the **Badlands** (*SD and NE*)
   the **Continental Divide** (*Rocky Mountains*)
   Deep South   **Midsouth**
   the **Occident**   the **Orient**
   the **Far East**   **Far Eastern**   the **East**
   Middle East   **Middle Eastern Mideast**
   the **Promised Land**   the **Continent** (*continental Europe*)
   the **Western Hemisphere**
   the **North Pole**   the **North and South Poles**
   the **Temperate Zone** the **Torrid Zone**
   the **East Side, Lower East Side** (*sections of a city*)
   Western Europe (*political entity*)
     but **lower 48** (*States*), the **Northeast corridor**

A descriptive term used to denote mere direction or position is not a proper name and is therefore not capitalized.
   north   **south**   **east**   **west**
   northerly   **northern**   **northward**
   eastern   **oriental**   **occidental**
   east Pennsylvania   **southern California**
   northern Virginia
   west Florida *but* **West Florida** (*1763–1819*)
   eastern region   **western region**
   north–central region   **east coast**
   eastern seaboard   **central Europe**
   south Germany   **southern France**

Names of calendar divisions
The names of divisions are capitalized.
   January, February, March, etc.
   Monday, Tuesday, Wednesday, etc.
     but **spring, summer, autumn, fall, winter**

Names of historic events, etc.

The names of holidays, ecclesiastic feast and fast days, and historic events are capitalized.

Battle of Bunker Hill	**Christian Era**	
Middle Ages. *but* **20th century**		
Feast of the Passover	**the Passover**	
Fourth of July	**the Fourth**	
Reformation	**Renaissance**	**Veterans Day**
War of 1812, World War I, *but* **war of 1914, Korean war**		

Trade names

Trade names, variety names, and names of market grades and brands are capitalized. Common nouns following such names are not capitalized.

Foamite, Plexiglas, Snow Crop (*trade names*)
Choice lamb, Yellow Stained cotton (*market grade*)
Red Radiance rose (*variety*)

Scientific names

The name of a phylum, class, order, family, or genus is capitalized; the name of a species is not capitalized, even though derived from a proper name.

Arthropoda (*phylum*)	**Crustacea** (*class*)
Hypoparia (*order*)	**Agnostidae** (*family*)
Agnostus (*genus*) **Agnostus canadensis; Aconitum wilsoni; Epigaea repens** (*genus and species*)	

In scientific descriptions coined terms derived from proper names are not capitalized.

aviculoid   **menodontine**

Capitalize the names of the celestial bodies **Sun** and **Moon**, as well as the planets **Earth, Mercury, Venus, Mars, Jupiter, Saturn, Uranus, Neptune,** and **Pluto.** Lowercase the word *moon* in such expressions as **"the moons of Jupiter."**

Fanciful appellations

A fanciful appellation used with or for a proper name is capitalized.

Big Four	Hub *(Boston)*	New Frontier
Dust Bowl	Keystone State	
Prohibition	Great Society	New Deal
Great Depression	Holocaust	Third World

Personification

A vivid personification is capitalized.

The **Chair** recognized the gentleman from New York.

For **Nature** wields her scepter mercilessly.

All are architects of **Fate**,

Working in these walls of **Time**.

Religious terms

Words denoting the Deity except *who, whose,* and *whom;* names for the Bible and other sacred writings and their parts; and names of confessions of faith and of religious bodies and their adherents and words specifically denoting Satan are all capitalized.

Heavenly Father, the Almighty, Lord, Thee, Thou, He, Him; *but* himself, God's fatherhood

Mass, red Mass, Communion

Divine Father; *but* divine providence, divine guidance, divine service

Son of Man, Jesus' sonship, the Messiah; *but* a messiah, messiahship, messianic, messianize, christology, christological

Bible, Holy Scriptures, Scriptures, Word, Koran; *also* Biblical, Scriptural, Koranic

New Testament, Ten Commandments

Gospel (memoir of Christ); *but* gospel truth

Apostles' Creed, Augsburg Confession

Episcopal Church, an Episcopalian, Catholicism, a
  Protestant
Christian; *also* Christendom, Christianity, Christianize
Black Friars, Brother(s); King's Daughters, Daughter(s);
  Ursuline Sisters, Sister(s)
Satan, His Satanic Majesty, Father of Lies, the Devil;
  but a devil, the devils, devil's advocate

Titles of persons

Civil, religious, military, and professional titles, as well as
those of nobility, immediately preceding a name are capitalized.

President Lincoln	King George
Ambassador Gibson	Lieutenant Fowler
Chairman Smith	Dr. Bellinger
Nurse Cavell	Professor Leverett

Vice-Presidential candidate White
  but baseball player Jones, maintenance man Smith

To indicate preeminence or distinction in certain specified
instances, a common-noun title immediately following the
name of a person or used alone as a substitute for it is capitalized.

Title of a head or assistant head of state:

George Washington, President of the United States:
  the President, the President-elect, the Executive, the
  Commander in Chief, former President Truman;
  similarly the Vice President, the Vice-President-elect
Charles Robb, Governor of Virginia: the Governor of
  Virginia, the Governor; *similarly* the Lieutenant Governor; *but* secretary of state of Idaho, attorney general
  of Maine

Title of a head or assistant head of a National governmental unit:

Secretary of State: the Secretary; *similarly* the Acting Secretary, the Under Secretary, the Director; the Chief or Assistant Chief; the Chief Clerk; etc.

Titles of the military:

General of the Army   Supreme Allied Commander Chairman, Joint Chiefs of Staff; *but* the commanding general; general *(military title standing alone)*

Titles of members of diplomatic corps:

the American Ambassador   the British Ambassador
the Ambassador   the Senior Ambassador
His Excellency   the Envoy
the Minister   the Chargé d'Affaires
the Chargé   Ambassador at Large
Minister Without Portfolio
    but the consul general; the consul; the attaché; etc.

Title of a ruler or prince:

Elizabeth II, Queen of England: the Queen, the Crown, Her Most Gracious Majesty, Her Majesty;
    similarly the Emperor, the Sultan, etc.

Charles, Prince of Wales: His Royal Highness

In formal lists of delegates and representatives of governments, all titles and descriptive designations immediately following the names should be capitalized if any one is capitalized.

A title in the second person is capitalized.

Your Excellency   Your Highness
Your Honor   Mr. Chairman
Madam Chairman   Mr. Secretary
    but not salutation:
        my dear General   my dear sir

Titles of publications, documents, acts, laws, etc.

In the English titles of periodicals, series of publications, annual reports, historic documents, and works of art, the first word and all important words are capitalized.

Atlantic Charter, Balfour Declaration;
   but **British white paper**
Reader's Digest; *but* **Newsweek magazine**
**Uniform Code of Military Justice, House Resolution
   45, Presidential Proclamation No. 24, Executive Order
   No. 24, Royal Decree No. 24, Public Law 89–1;**
   but **Senate bill 416; House bill 61**
Declaration of Independence; the Declaration
Constitution (of th e United States or other country);
   but **New York State constitution: first amendment,
   12th amendment (see rule 12.10).**
Kellogg Pact, North Atlantic Pact, Treaty of Versailles;
   but **treaty of peace, treaty of 1919**
The Blue Boy, Excalibur, Whistler's Mother (*paintings*)

All principal words are capitalized in titles of addresses, articles, books, captions, chapter and part headings, editorials, essays, headings, headlines, motion pictures and plays (including television and radio programs), papers, short poems, reports, songs, subheadings, subjects, and themes.

In the short or popular titles of acts (Federal, State, or foreign) the first word and all important words are capitalized.

Revenue Act   **Walsh–Healey Act**
Freedom of Information Act;
   but **the act, Harrison narcotic law, Harrison narcotic
   bill, interstate commerce law, sunset law**

Capitalization of the titles of books, etc., written in a foreign language should conform to custom in that language.

CAPITALIZATION

First words

The first word of a sentence, of a direct quotation, or of a line of poetry, is capitalized.

> He asked, "And where are you going?"
> Lives of great men all remind us
> We can make our lives sublime.

The first word of a fragmentary quotation is not capitalized.

> He objected to "the phraseology, not to the ideas."

Headlines

Generally, centered heads are set in capitals, and sideheads are set in lowercase with only the first word and proper names capitalized, In heads making two lines, wordbreaks should be avoided.

In heads set in caps, a small-cap *c* or *ac* is usually used in such names as *McLean* or *MacLeod*; otherwise a lowercase *c* or *ac* is used.

In such names as *LeRoy, DeHostis, LaFollette,* etc. (one-word forms only), set in caps, the second letter of the particle is made a small cap, if available; otherwise lowercase is used.

In matter set in caps and small caps or caps and lowercase, capitalize all principal words, including parts of compounds which would be capitalized standing alone. The articles *a, an,* and *the*; the prepositions *at, by, for, in, of, on, to,* and *up*; the conjunctions *and, as, but, if, or,* and *nor*; and the second element of a compound numeral are not capitalized.

> World en Route to All-Out War
> Man Hit With 2-Inch Pipe
> Yankees May Be Winners in Zig-Zag Race
> Ex-Senator Is To Be Admitted
> Building on Twenty-first Street
> One Hundred and Twenty-three Years

If a normally lowercased short word is used in juxtaposition with a capitalized word of like significance, it should also be capitalized.

Buildings In and Near Minneapolis

In a heading set in caps and lowercase or in caps and small caps, a normally lowercased last word, if it is the only lowercased word in the heading, should also be capitalized.

All Returns Are In

The first element of an infinitive is capitalized.

Controls To Be Applied; *but* **Aid Sent to Disaster Area**

In matter set in caps and small caps, such abbreviations as *etc., et al.,* and *p.m.* are set in small caps; in matter set in caps and lowercase, these abbreviations are set in lowercase.

PLANES, GUNS, SHIPS, ETC.
James Bros. et al. *(no comma)*
In re the 8 p.m. Meeting
Planes, Guns, Ships, etc.

Accents in cap lines are usually omitted even if the same words carry accents in text.

Addresses, salutations, and signatures
The first word and all principal words in addresses, salutations, and signatures are capitalized.

Interjections
The interjection *O* is always capitalized; within a sentence, other interjections are not capitalized.

Sail on, O Ship of State!
For lo! the days are hastening on.
But, oh, how fortunate!

Capitalization Examples

Academy: **Air Force Academy**
    Coast Guard Academy
    National Academy of Sciences
    Naval Academy *but* **service academies**

Act (Federal, State, or foreign), popular title:
    Appropriation Act   **Flood Control Act**
    Lend–Lease Act; *but* **lend–lease materials, etc.**
    Revenue Act   **River and Harbor Act**
    Tariff Act   **Trademark Act**
    Walsh–Healey Act; *but* **Walsh–Healey law (or bill)**

ACTION *(independent Federal agency)*

Adjutant General, the

Administration: Farmers Home Administration
    Food and Drug Administration
    Veterans' Administration
    but **Adams administration; administration bill, etc.**

Administrative Law Judge Davis;
    but **Judge Davis, an administrative law judge**

Ages: **Age of Discovery**   **Dark Ages**
    Elizabethan Age   **Golden Age** *(of Pericles)*
    Middle Ages
    but **atomic age, Cambrian age, ice age, space age, etc.**

Agreement:
    General Agreement on Tariffs and Trade (GATT)
    International Wheat Agreement, the wheat agreement
    but **the Geneva agreement, the Potsdam agreement,**
    Paris peace agreement

Airport: **La Guardia Airport, National Airport, the airport**

Alliance for Progress, Alliance for Progress program

alliances and coalitions: **Atlantic alliance**
   European Economic Community
   North Atlantic Treaty Organization

Ambassador: **British Ambassador, the Ambassador, the Senior Ambassador, Ambassador at Large**

amendment: **Social Security Amendments of 1954, 1954 amendments, the social security amendments**

American: **American Legion**
   American National Red Cross, the Red Cross

Amtrak *(National Railroad Passenger Corporation)*

Ancient Free and Accepted Masons, a Mason, a Freemason

Arab States, Arabic numerals

Archives: **National Archives, the Archives, Archivist of the United States, the Archivist**

Arctic: **Arctic Circle**   **Arctic Current**
   Arctic Ocean   **Arctic zone**
   arctic clothing   **arctic conditions**

Area: **Cape Hatteras Recreational Area, White Pass Recreation Area, etc.**
   but **free trade area, Metropolitan Washington area, bay area**

Articles of Confederation *(U.S.)*

Association:
   American Association for the Advancement of Science
   Federal National Mortgage Association (Fannie Mae)
   Young Women's Christian Association

Atlantic: **Atlantic Charter**   **Atlantic coast**
   Atlantic Coast States   **mid–Atlantic**
   Atlantic time, standard time *but* **transatlantic**

Authority: Port of New York Authority, the port authority
    Tennessee Valley Authority

Awards: Academy Award, Distinguished Service Award,
    Merit Award, Mother of the Year Award, etc.

Bank: Export–Import Bank of Washington,
    Export–Import Bank   Farm Loan Bank of Dallas
    Dallas Farm Loan Bank   farm loan bank
    farm loan bank at Dallas
    Federal Reserve Bank of New York
    Richmond Federal Reserve Bank;
      but Reserve bank at Richmond
    Federal Reserve bank,   Reserve bank
      but blood bank, soil bank

bay: San Francisco Bay area, the bay area

belt: Bible Belt   Corn Belt   Cotton Belt
        Dairy Belt   Sun Belt   Wheat Belt
    but money belt

Bible, Biblical, Scriptures, etc.

Bill of Rights *(historic document); but* GI bill of rights

board: Civil Aeronautics Board
    Federal Reserve Board
    Board of Health of Montgomery County, Montgomery
    County Board of Health, the board of health

bond: Government bond   savings bond
      series EE bond   Treasury bond

borough: Borough of the Bronx, the borough

Bowl: Dust Bowl, Rose Bowl, the bowl

Boy Scouts *(organization)*, a Boy Scout, a Scout, Scouting

Brother(s) *(adherent of religious order)*

Calendar, if part of name, else calendar

Capital, Capital City, National Capital *(Washington, DC)*;
but the capital (State)

Capitol Building *(with State name)*, the capitol:
Halls of Congress   Capitol Hill; the Hill
Capitol rotunda   Senate wing

caucus: **Republican caucus**;
but **Black Caucus** *(incorporated name)*

center: **Agricultural Research Center**
Kennedy Center for the Performing Arts, the Kennedy
Center   **Lincoln Center**

Central America

Central States

central time

century: **first century, 20th century, etc.**

chairman: **Chairman of the Board of Directors** *(Federal)*;
but **chairman of the board of directors** *(non–Federal)*

chamber: **Chamber of Commerce of Ada, Ada Chamber of**
Commerce, the chamber of commerce

the Chamber *(Senate or House)*

Chargé d'Affaires, British, etc.; the Chargé d'Affaires;
the Chargé

cheese: **bleu cheese, Camembert cheese, Cheddar or ched-**
dar cheese, cottage cheese, cream cheese, Parmesan
cheese, provolone cheese, Roquefort cheese

Chief of Staff

Chief Judge, if referring to Federal unit

Christian, Christian name, Christendom, Christianity,
Christianize, *but* christen

church calendar: **Christmas**   **Easter**
   Lent   **Pentecost**   **Whitsuntide**

city: **East Side**   **French Quarter** *(New Orleans)*
   Latin Quarter *(Paris)*   **North End**
   the Loop *(Chicago)*   **City Hub** *(Boston)*
   Twin Cities   **Windy City** *(Chicago)*
   New York City; *but* **city of New York**

coast: **Atlantic, east, gulf, west**

code: **Federal Criminal Code**
   Internal Revenue Code   **Tax Code**
   Penal Code   **Criminal Code**
   Television Code   **Uniform Code of Military Justice**
   ZIP Code (copyrighted)
   but **civil code, flag code, Morse code**

college: **Cornell College**   **College of Bishops**
   but **electoral college**

college degrees: **bachelor of arts, master's degree, etc.**

commission: **Commission of Fine Arts**
                Commission on Civil Rights

commissioner:
   Commissioner of Immigration and Naturalization
   Commissioner of Patents
    but **a U.S. commissioner**

committee: **Appropriations Committee**
   Subcommittee on Appropriations
   Democratic National Committee, Democratic national committeeman, Republican National Committee, Republican national committeeman, the national committee, the committee
   but **Baker committee, ad hoc committee**

Common Cause

Common Market *(European Economic Community)*

Commonwealth of Australia, Virginia, etc.; British Commonwealth, the Commonwealth

community: **European Economic Community, the Community;** *but* **the Atlantic community**

comptroller: **Comptroller of the Currency**

confederate: **Confederate** *(of the American Confederacy)*
Confederate Army   **Confederate Government**
Confederate soldier   **Confederate States**

congress: **National Congress of Parents and Teachers**
national legislature: **Congress, the Congress, Congress of the United States, Congress of Bolivia, First Congress, Second Congress, 11th Congress**

Congressional: **Congressional Directory**
First Congressional District, the First District, the congressional district
Congressional Medal of Honor
but **congressional action, congressional committee**

constitution: Capitalized with the name of a country or standing alone when referring to a specific constitution; **New York State Constitution; the Constitution**

consul: **British consul, consul general, British consul general, consulate, British consulate**

Consumer Price Index *(official title)*
but **a consumers' price index** *(descriptive)*

continent: **American Continent, the continent**
but **the Continent** *(continental Europe)*

continental: **Continental Army, Continental Congress, Continental Divide, Continental Shelf,**

a continental shelf, continental Europe, continental
United States

Corn Belt

corporation: **Federal Deposit Insurance Corporation**
Rand Corporation, Union Carbide Corporation,
the corporation

corps: **Adjutant General's Corps**
    Job Corps   **Marine Corps**
Corps of Engineers, Army Engineers, the Engineers;
  but **Army engineer, the corps**
Peace Corps, Peace Corpsman, the corpsman
Reserve Officers' Training Corps *(ROTC)*
Youth Corps
but **diplomatic corps, corpsman, hospital corpsman**

Cotton Belt

council: **Boston City Council, the council**
Her Majesty's Privy Council; the Privy Council;
the Council

county: **Prince Georges County, county of Prince Georges,**
the county

court (of law): **Circuit Court of the United States for the**
Tenth Circuit, Circuit Court for the Tenth Circuit, the
circuit court, the court, the tenth circuit
Court of Appeals for the State of North Carolina, the
court of appeals, the court

Crown, if referring to a ruler; but crown colony, lands, etc.

current: **Arctic Current**   **Humboldt Current**
    Japan Current **customhouse** **customs official**

Dairy Belt

Dark Ages

decorations, medals, etc., awarded by any national government: the medal, the cross, the ribbon
  Commendation Ribbon, Congressional Medal of Honor, Distinguished Service Cross, Good Conduct Medal, Legion of Merit, Medal of Freedom, Medal of Honor, Purple Heart, Silver Star Medal; *also* Carnegie Medal, Olympic Gold Medal; *but* gold medal

department: Department of Agriculture
  Yale University Department of Economics, the department of economics, the department

Diet (Japanese legislative body)

disease: acquired immune deficiency syndrome *(AIDS)*
  German measles   Parkinson's

Dixie, Dixiecrat

Dust Bowl

Elizabethan Age

Emancipation Proclamation

Eurodollar

exchange: New York Stock Exchange, the stock exchange, the exchange

farm: Johnson Farm; *but* Johnson's farm

Father of his Country *(Washington)*

Federal *(sovereign power)*

Federal Government *(of any national government)*
  but a federal form of government

First Family *(Presidential)*

First Lady *(wife of President)*

flags: Old Glory, Stars and Stripes, Tricolor *(French)*, Union Jack *(British)*

CAPITALIZATION

Foreign Office: Minister of Foreign Affairs, the Minister
  Ministry of Foreign Affairs, the Ministry

forest: Angeles National Forest, Black Forest;
  but State and National forests

Girl Scouts *(organization):* a Girl Scout, a Scout, Scouting

G-man

Golden Rule

Gospel, if referring to the first four books of the
  New Testament; *but* gospel truth

great: Great Depression   Great Divide
         Great White Way (New York City)
         great circle (navigation)

gross national product *(GNP)*

High School *(if part of name);* Western High School,
  the high school

Holy Scriptures; Holy Writ *(Bible)*

Hospital, if part of a name; else the hospital, hospital
  corpsman

international: International Court of Justice, the Court
  international banks   international dateline
  international boundary   international law

Interstate 95, I-95, the interstate

Irish potato

Ivory Coast

Jersey cattle

Job Corps

judge: chief judge, circuit judge, district judge; *but* Judge
  Bryan

lake: Lake Erie, Lake of the Woods, Salt Lake; the lake

317

line: **DEW** *(Distant Early Warning)* **line**   **State line**

Metropolitan New York; *but* **New York metropolitan area**

Middle Ages

Middle Atlantic States

mint: **Philadelphia Mint, the mint**

Monument: **Bunker Hill Monument**
          Washington Monument   **the monument**

Mr. Chairman; Mr. Secretary; etc.

national: **National Archives   National Forest**
    Yellowstone National Park, Yellowstone Park,
    the national park, the park
    national anthem   national customs
    national spirit   national defense

numbers: capitalized if spelled out as part of a name
    Air Force One *(Presidential plane)*   **Charles the First**

office: **Executive Office   Foreign Office**
    Office of Management and Budget   Patent Office
    but **New York regional office, the regional office**

Pope; *but* **papal, patriarch, pontiff, primate**

prize: **Nobel Prize   Pulitzer Prize**

project: **Project Vanguard;** *but* **Vanguard project**
    Project Head Start

Quad Cities

the Reformation

Sabbath; Sabbath Day

Sermon on the Mount

Third World

ZIP Code *(Postal)*